Research Methods in the
Social Sciences

RESEARCH METHODS IN THE SOCIAL SCIENCES

THOMAS HERZOG

Grand Valley State University

HarperCollins*CollegePublishers*

To my ladies,
Chris and Catherine,
and to my parents,
Mr. and Mrs. Dayton Herzog.

Senior Editor: Catherine Woods
Project Coordinator and Text Design: Electronic Publishing Services Inc.
Cover Designer: Mary McDonnell
Electronic Production Manager: Mike Kemper
Manufacturing Manager: Helene G. Landers
Printer and Binder: R.R. Donnelley & Sons Company
Cover Printer: New England Book Components, Inc.

Research Methods in the Social Sciences

Library of Congress Cataloging-in-Publication Data

Herzog, Thomas R.
　　　Research methods and data analysis in the social sciences/Thomas Herzog.
　　　　　p.　cm.
　　　Includes bibliographical references and index.
　　　ISBN 0-673-99106-7
　　　1. Social sciences—Methodology.　2. Social sciences—Statistical
　　methods.　I.　Title.
　　H61.H457　1996
　　300'. 72—dc20　　　　　　　　　　　　　　　　　　　　　95-40976
　　　　　　　　　　　　　　　　　　　　　　　　　　　　　　　CIP

97 98 9 8 7 6 5 4 3

Brief Contents

Contents

CHAPTER 15

RESEARCH METHODS AND CRITICAL THINKING 281

Preface

The purpose of this book is to introduce the basic methods and principles of scientific research as practiced in the social sciences The essence of the scientific approach is the attempt to understand natural phenomena by making generalizations based on empirical data. The generalizations of most interest to the scientist are those involving relationships between variables (a rough synonym for phenomena), because scientists can understand fully a variable only by exploring its relationships with other variables. These seem like innocent statements, but they have strong implications for the topics I chose to emphasize, and for the way I organized the material. Two such implications should be made explicit to students and instructors.

The first is that the core concepts of relationships between variables and generalization by means of statistical inference are introduced early and stressed repeatedly throughout this book. I focus on the three basic research methods of observation, survey, and experiment, and show how generalizations about relationships are made from "typical" data for each method. This approach has two concrete consequences. First, I make strong simplifying assumptions about what kind of data are typical for each method. These assumptions are made explicit in the first chapter on measurement (Chapter 5), and they form the framework of the book. Of course, it is important for students to be warned about the many types of data that are possible with each research method, and I do so. That aside, I believe the simplifying assumptions are justified and desirable for teaching purposes. They allow me to present a complete data analysis along with each research method, something I feel is important for reinforcing a student's understanding of the core concepts of relationship and statistical generalization. The second concrete consequence of my approach is that statistical-inference procedures are covered within the text along with each research method, rather than relegated to an appendix. This, too, comes from my belief that generalization via statistical inference is a core concept that ought to be thoroughly explored within the body of the text.

A second implication of the book's focus on core concepts is that it sacrifices breadth of coverage for depth. This book is not an encyclopedia of specific methods or topics. Perhaps the best thing an introductory research methods course can do for students is to provide them with a thorough understanding of the core concepts in research, and that is plenty enough to hope for in one course. Thus, there are no separate chapters on library research or program evaluation research. Many such worthy topics could have been explored in detail, but I chose to concentrate on the core concepts of research. On the other hand, in the spirit of providing some feel for the variety of activities and topics relevant to research, I have included brief coverage of both of the above topics, and many other noncentral topics within appropriate chapters.

Any good rule has exceptions, and so I have included two chapters on non-core topics. They are the chapters on ethics and critical thinking. The topic of research ethics is simply too important for brief coverage. Even if students never actually do research, they may someday have input into decisions about ethical issues in research, and they need to begin thinking about such issues and struggling with them along with researchers and the rest of society. As for critical thinking, the implications of statistical inference for improving informal reasoning about generalizations are so important that they are explicitly discussed in several chapters, and then given a summary chapter of their own at the end of the book. The relevance of research methods to critical thinking is so great that the introductory research methods course can be seen as a key component of any general education curriculum in higher education.

This book also has several features aimed at achieving user friendliness. To generate student interest, many chapters begin with a description of an actual research project. That project is used throughout the chapter to illustrate key concepts and topics. To maintain attention and provide a self-check on comprehension, questions for students to answer are embedded within the text of most chapters. The answer or possible answers are provided at the end of the chapters. Each chapter concludes with a comprehensive summary. As for writing style, I tried to maintain a middle course between the use of excessive jargon and "talking down" to students. I also tried to avoid sexist language, mostly by using plural pronouns—a tactic I recommend to novice writers of research reports. When singular pronouns were required and gender was indeterminate, I picked on both genders equally.

TO STUDENTS

If your instructor gives you the "full treatment" (see the next section), then you will be thoroughly exploring the statistical analysis of data for each basic research method. What background do you need? This book assumes no statistical background on your part. However, if you try to read it without a prior statistics course, you will probably find it rough going because statistical concepts are difficult. Thus, a prior course in statistics is warmly recommended, though not absolutely necessary. This book is best used as a review of statistical concepts and, more importantly, an integration of research methods and statistics.

This book contains many simple numerical examples and exercises (the latter in the form of embedded questions). Their primary purpose is not to teach you how to do data analysis by hand, but to reinforce your conceptual understanding of principles and procedures by means of numerical illustrations. Your instructor may want you to do some hand calculations on summary data from class projects. If so, you will find the numerical examples helpful. However, their major purpose is to illustrate concepts and principles of analysis and methodology.

TO INSTRUCTORS

There is some flexibility in the way this book can be used. The overall approach is a methods-analysis integration that covers major topics in this order: basic concepts (Chapters 1 to 2), observation methods (Chapters 3 to 4), measurement (Chapters 5 to 6), survey research (Chapters 7 to 8), and the experiment (Chapters 9 to 12). Your freedom comes primarily in how much you cover and in where you place unconstrained topics. As to the latter, the ethics chapter (Chapter 14) is self-contained, and thus may be assigned early or late in the semester. The critical-thinking chapter (Chapter 15) contains no new material, although the discussion of errors in reasoning about relationships is considerably more detailed than in Chapter 2. Hence, the chapter may be omitted if you do not want to explore the relation between research methods and critical thinking. However, the chapter does provide a nice course review, and you may want to include it for that purpose.

On the issue of how much to cover, Figure P.1 may be helpful. It illustrates four possibilities for depth of coverage. The full-treatment option is for instructors who want to cover everything. The second option is a compromise approach for instructors who want to cover the basics of data analysis, but avoid advanced or esoteric topics. The asterisks indicate chapters in which sections may be omitted. In Chapters 4, 11, and 12, the "In-Depth" sections may be omitted; and in Chapter 8, the section on "Advanced Correlation Methods" may be omitted. After gaining

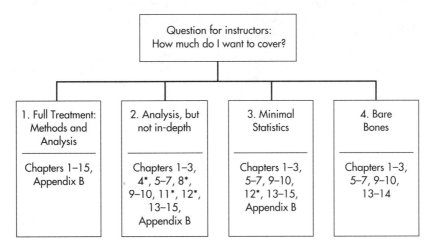

Figure P.1
Some options for how to use this book.

some experience with the compromise approach, instructors may find additional sections in some of the chapters that they can do without. The third option is for instructors who want to avoid statistics as much as possible, and still teach a respectable methods course. The fourth option is for those who want to avoid all complex or nonessential topics.

TO ALL READERS

I welcome and encourage feedback from all readers. Please send your comments either to the publisher or directly to me at: Department of Psychology Grand Valley State University Allendale, MI 49401. I'm sure you will find this text useful, and I welcome your suggestions for improvement.

ACKNOWLEDGMENTS

I would like to thank Grand Valley State University for providing sabbatical leave support that enabled me to write the first draft of this book. I also would like to thank my editor, Catherine Woods, and all the other people at HarperCollins who have helped make this a better book than it would have been without their efforts. Finally, I would like to thank the following reviewers for their input in developing this book: Mary Anne Baker, Indiana University Southeast; L. E. Banderet, Northeastern University; F. Samuel Bauer, Christopher Newport University; D. K. Beale, Cerritos College; Roger Blackman, Simon Fraser University; Curt Burgess, University of California, Riverside; J. Lynn Caldwell, Troy State University at Dothan; Rich Carlson, Pennsylvania State University; Marc Carter, University of South Florida; Hank Cetola, Adrian College; Delbert Ellsworth, Elizabethtown College; Myra Heinrich, Mesa State College; Stephen J. Lepore, Carnegie Mellon University; Linda Mealey, College of St. Benedict; Gwen Murdock, Missouri Southern State College; Blaine Peden, University of Wisconsin, Eau Claire; Joseph H. Porter, University of San Francisco; James Schirillo, Virginia Commonwealth University; Robert Stern, Pennsylvania State University; and Michael Strube, Washington University.

Thomas Herzog

The Scientific Method

1

Several years ago a small group of researchers tried to understand why people found some pictures of nature to be more aesthetically pleasing than others. At the time theories of aesthetics centered on the concept of *complexity*, defined roughly as "how much is going on" in the stimulus, or how much information it contains. Accordingly, the researchers obtained ratings for both *liking* and *complexity* for pictures of nature. They found that they had only a weak relationship. Puzzled, they did what any good scientist would do—they "eyeballed" the most- and least-liked pictures to see if they could find any features that distinguished between them. With this approach, it became clear that the most-liked pictures contained features such as a pathway bending out of sight or a brightly lit area partially hidden by vegetation in the foreground. These features were absent in the least-liked pictures. Generally, the most-liked pictures contained features that provided partial information about what might lie ahead. The researchers named this quality *mystery*. In subsequent studies, *mystery* proved to be far-and-away the strongest predictor of *liking* for natural environments (R. Kaplan & S. Kaplan, 1989; S. Kaplan & R. Kaplan, 1982).

The story of mystery illustrates both the challenge and the excitement of research in the social sciences. The researchers faced a challenging puzzle: strong differences in liking for natural settings that could not be explained by existing theories. By immersing themselves in their results and searching carefully for helpful clues, the researchers were not unlike detectives trying to crack a difficult case. Gradually, they began to sense a pattern in the results, just as a detective might sense that the clues in a case could fit together in a brand new way. The researchers were on the brink of a discovery, a breakthrough, a new way of understanding something that did not make sense before. They were on the brink of a new theory with clear implications for further investigation. The excitement and satisfaction of replacing confusion with understanding and of verifying that understanding is something that all researcher-detectives seek. For them, it is the ultimate high.

By studying scientific research methods, you can share in the excitement and satisfaction just described. When you design your first research study, carry it out, and finally see the pattern of results emerge, you will appreciate how involving and exciting this form of inquiry can be. Apart from the excitement, however, there are other important reasons for studying the scientific approach to knowledge. One of them is that the scientific approach provides a powerful means for understanding the natural (as opposed to supernatural) world. Scientific research aimed at discovering the general principles underlying natural phenomena is called *basic research*. To appreciate the principles established by basic research, you need to understand the methods that led to those principles.

Another reason for studying the scientific approach is that it prepares you to evaluate the many practical claims supposedly based on "scientific" research. Research aimed primarily at practical applications is called *applied research*. The research on mystery was both basic and applied. Mystery helps us understand liking for environments in general, but it can also be used practically to design environments that are well liked. At an even more practical level, advertisements routinely make claims of a relationship between using a certain product and the satisfaction or general well being of the user. Such claims are often supported by findings from "scientific research." An understanding of the scientific approach will allow you to evaluate such claims. In fact, a basic theme of this book is that the mastery of scientific thinking can provide a valuable framework for evaluating information and for reasoning.

The final reason for studying the scientific approach is that it has been very influential in the history of humanity. You cannot claim to be truly educated if you have not studied this way of thinking, appreciated its strengths and weaknesses, and compared it with other approaches to knowledge.

APPROACHES TO KNOWLEDGE

This book is about how the scientific method is used in the social sciences. To get a feel for what the scientific method is, let us begin by contrasting nonscientific and scientific approaches to gaining knowledge.

Nonscientific approaches

Two well-known nonscientific approaches to knowledge are authority and deductive reasoning. In *authority*, knowledge is handed down by an authority figure. If the authority figure is assumed to be trustworthy, the truth or validity of the knowledge is not questioned. In other words, the knowledge is accepted on faith. In direct contrast, the scientific approach does not rely solely on authority figures. All claims are subject to independent verification. In *deductive reasoning*, knowledge is gained by moving from premises to conclusions while following the rules of deductive logic. The method is guaranteed to produce valid conclusions, but the truth of the conclusions will depend on the truth of the premises. In contrast, the scientific approach is concerned primarily with determining the truth of the premises in cases where they deal with natural, as opposed to supernatural, phenomena. Again, the method provides a way of independently verifying the truth of premises. Independent verification of the truth of propositions is a key feature of the scientific approach.

Both faith and deduction have roles in the scientific approach. Scientists have faith in the reported results of other scientists. They have faith in the integrity of other scientists and in the scientific method. If this were not so, science could not move forward in gaining new knowledge. However, you should bear in mind that any result reported by a scientist is subject to independent verification using the scientific method. Likewise, deduction is widespread in science just as it is in everyday life. Scientists use deduction to create theories, derive predictions, plan and carry out research projects, and interpret results. However, deduction is not a distinguishing feature of the scientific method.

The scientific approach

The most important distinguishing feature of the scientific approach to knowledge is *empirical verification*. The word *empirical* means, roughly, "based on experience or direct observation." Thus, a proposition is regarded as true if it agrees with what is observed. Observations may be made by the unaided senses or by using complex equipment such as brain-wave recorders. In either case, the scientist looks for sensory evidence that confirms or disconfirms the proposition under consideration. The test of truth is essentially observational.

A simple example will contrast this approach with the two nonscientific approaches described earlier. Consider the proposition "Pigs have wings." Imagine three people who lack any knowledge about pigs, trying to determine if the proposition is true. The first person relies on authority and asks, "Who says so?" If the source is someone he regards as an authority, he accepts the proposition. Otherwise, he may seek out the opinions of people believed to be authorities about pigs (e.g., Farmer Jack and Farmer McDonald). The second person uses deduction. After some library research, she says to herself, "I have learned that pigs are members of the family *Suidae*. Members of the family *Suidae* do not have wings. Therefore, pigs do not have wings." The third person goes straight to the nearest pigpen and examines a representative sample of pigs to see if they have any winglike appendages. The third person is the scientist.

There are several other features of the scientific approach that will be explored in-depth later in this book. For example, scientists strive for clear definitions of terms, they try to work under controlled conditions and to make objective or unbiased observations, and they are concerned with accurate and valid measurement. All of these features of the scientific approach serve one overriding purpose: testing for truth by making valid empirical observations.

GOALS OF RESEARCH

At a finer level of analysis, scientific research may be seen as serving a series of increasingly important goals. The most primitive goal of research is *exploration*. Exploratory research attempts to find out if something exists or occurs. For example, do people's eyes move when they sleep? One level higher is the goal of *description*. If a phenomenon exists, descriptive research tries to define its properties more fully. Under what circumstances do a sleeper's eyes move, and what is the nature of those movements? At the next highest level is the goal of *prediction*. Are a sleeper's eye movements related to anything else that might be used to predict when they will occur? For example, perhaps they always occur in conjunction with a particular kind of brain-wave pattern. In a sense, this goal is a logical extension of the previous one. A phenomenon is fully described by finding out what is related to it. The most sophisticated goal is *control*. Is it possible to find one or more causes of a sleeper's eye movements? Suppose you can show that when you play soft music into a sleeper's ears, eye movements reliably follow. If so, you could produce such movements at will. You could control when they happen.

GOALS OF SCIENCE

There is no harm in the preceding analysis of research goals, but to really appreciate what science is all about one must dig deeper. The goals of exploration through control describe the more immediate goals of the researcher-at-work. It is useful to draw a distinction between the practical goals of the scientist at work and the loftier goals of science itself. The latter may be thought of as more basic goals than the former. Two basic goals of science are generalization and understanding.

The Goal of Generalization

Whenever scientists do research, they sample various classes of objects: people, stimuli, settings, time periods, procedures, etc. *Sampling* means that scientists use only a subset of all possible objects in each class when doing a research study. Almost without exception, scientists intend for their results to apply to a larger group of objects than those sampled. The larger groups are called *populations.* The process of extending results from samples to populations is called *generalization,* or *inductive inference.* Do not worry about these technical terms now; they will be explored in detail later in the book. For now, the point is that a basic motive of scientists is to generalize their results and to do so with confidence.

The importance of generalization in the scientific approach makes it clear why students of research are required to study certain topics. One such topic is sampling procedures. A rule of thumb is that generalizations are valid whenever the sample adequately represents the population. Sampling procedures are methods for obtaining samples with known features. Thus, a scientist who uses a particular sampling procedure is in a good position to make an informed judgment about what population may be represented by the resulting sample. A related topic is inferential statistics, those strange mathematical procedures that scientists perform to make probability statements about their results. The purpose of such statistics is to allow scientists to make generalizations with known degrees of risk. Both sampling procedures and inferential statistics are tools used by scientists to attain one of their basic goals, making valid generalizations.

There is one more point to be made in defense of studying the principles of valid generalization. People make informal generalizations all the time in everyday life. Unfortunately, their generalizations are not always valid. Research shows that informal generalizations are prone to all sorts of distortions. For example, people tend to jump to conclusions on the basis of small samples. One clerk is rude, and the victim tells friends that all the clerks in that store are rude. Study of the scientific approach can help people avoid many of the pitfalls associated with informal generalizations.

Motives for research.   The generalizations that scientists want to make can be classified into two types. One is generalizations about a single phenomenon such as, "Aggression is pretty high in this crowd." The second type of generalization concerns phenomena that "go together" or are related. An example would be, "Frustration and aggression are related." Each type of generalization can be considered a basic motive for doing research.

The first type of generalization illustrates the *curiosity* motive. Scientists are very curious. When they get interested in a phenomenon like aggression, they try to measure it and find out just what the distribution of scores looks like in a population of interest. Of course, they typically measure only a sample, not the entire population. Thus, any conclusion they reach about the population is a generalization. Such generalizations concern a single phenomenon considered in isolation. This is one motive for doing research, the urge to find out everything there is to know about a single phenomenon.

A far more common and important motive for doing research is to find out which phenomena or variables "go together," that is, to establish *relationships* between variables. This involves working with two phenomena, such as frustration and aggression, rather than a single phenomenon in isolation. Typically, a scientist measures both phenomena in a sample and tries to show that their scores change together in a systematic manner. For example, the scientist will try to demonstrate that high frustration scores go with high aggression scores and vice-versa. If such evidence is obtained, then the variables are related in the sample. The inference that the variables are also related in a population is a generalization. This kind of generalization motivates most research. The concept of a relationship will be explored more thoroughly in the next chapter, but one point needs to be emphasized now. The concept of a relationship between variables is THE MOST IMPORTANT CONCEPT in this book because predicting and verifying relationships is the fundamental reason why most research is done.

Why are relationships so important to scientists? There are three reasons. First, you can understand a phenomenon deeply only by knowing its pattern of relationships to other phenomena. You cannot fully appreciate the concept of aggression until you know that it is related in certain ways to frustration, anger, childhood discipline, temperature, and a host of other phenomena. Second, relationships permit prediction. As you have already seen, prediction is one of the practical goals of research. Knowing what is related to aggression can provide advanced warning about when it is likely to occur. As you can imagine, such knowledge could be very useful. Third, there is a special category of relationships, known as *causal relationships*, so named because you know not only that two phenomena are related, but also that one of the two phenomena causes the other one. As you will see later, the explicit purpose of the experimental method of research is to establish such relationships. Causal relationships are the ultimate in understanding. To understand aggression completely, for example, you need to know what its causes are and what it causes. Moreover, causal relationships allow scientists to achieve the practical goal of control, discussed earlier. It is by manipulating known causes that you produce effects in the world. If frustration is a cause of aggression, then the likelihood of aggression can be reduced by eliminating sources of frustration.

The Goal of Understanding

It should be apparent from what has just been explained that the ultimate goal of the scientific approach is to understand natural phenomena, those that follow natural as opposed to supernatural or paranormal laws. Understanding is the second basic goal of science, and it is even more basic than the goal of generalization. To understand a phenomenon means that one has a complete account of all its properties and its relationships to other phenomena, including causal connections. In other words, one has an explanation of the phenomenon or a valid (that is, correct) *theory* of the phenomenon. Thus, it turns out that the ultimate goal of science is valid theory.

This may seem strange. It may seem to imply that theory follows or is the outcome of research. Many students, on the other hand, are accustomed to thinking of theory as something that precedes research and produces the predictions tested by research. Both views are unrealistic. The timing of theory and research is not so simple. Sometimes theory comes before research, sometimes after, sometimes during. The only certainty is that a good theory will lead to further research, which will lead to refined theory, which will lead to further research, and so on.

It is fair to say that theory is a major source of ideas for new research. Other sources are common sense, careful observation, the existing research literature, and creative thinking about both abstract and practical problems. The source that beginning students of research are least likely to be familiar with is the research literature. For that reason it deserves special emphasis. You should note that veteran researchers always scan the existing literature first, both to get ideas about new directions and to avoid duplication. With the help of computer databases, literature searches are fast and easy these days. Most libraries have developed simple procedures for on-line computer searches of many databases. Serious students of research should make it a habit to use such facilities.

Because theory is so intimately bound up with the scientific approach, it is important for you to understand what a theory is, how to evaluate one, and how to build one. Thus, the subject of theory will be examined in detail. By mastering this material you will become comfortable with theoretical thinking and will have the tools needed for proposing good theories.

THE ROLE OF THEORY IN SCIENCE

As you know, a theory is an explanation of a phenomenon. Ideally such an explanation would specify all of the important properties of the phenomenon and all of its relationships to other phenomena, including causal relationships. This approach to theory follows the treatment of Kerlinger (1986). Note two important points about this definition of theory. First, it says nothing about whether the theory is supported by research findings. It is easy to imagine theories that are complete in the sense of being all-encompassing but that cannot be supported by research findings. "Spirits determine our behavior" is an example. Second, it is important to note that in practice most explanations are partial, not complete. Such partial explanations are commonly referred to as theories, and that practice will be followed in this book. Remember, however, that such "theories" are incomplete explanations, subject to further expansion and revision. The ultimate goal is a complete and correct theory of the phenomenon of interest. Along the way one must settle for partial theories which are revised and expanded on the basis of further thought and research.

Types of Theories

One way to appreciate the variety of theories that are possible is to classify them. Two classification systems will be examined. The first, proposed by Arnoult (1976, pp. 30–35), identifies four kinds of theories. One of them represents poor theory, the sort of thing scientists should avoid. In *metaphorical* theories, a phenomenon is explained in terms of theoretical concepts that are no better understood than the phenomenon itself. An example is explaining abnormal behavior in terms of demonic possession. Demons are pretty much unpredictable and are thus less well understood than abnormal behavior. Hence, this is not a very useful theory. In general, metaphorical theories are frowned on by serious scientists. They are included here as a reminder to consider the possibility that your newly proposed theory may be metaphorical and thus useless as an explanation.

Arnoult describes three types of useful theories. The first is *analogical* theory. In this type of theory, a phenomenon is explained by analogy with another phenomenon that is already understood. An example is an explanation of brain functioning in terms of the operations of a computer. This example illustrates the major limitation of analogical theories. All analogies break down at some point. It is important for the theorist to specify which features of the analogical model (the computer) are essential and which are not. A second type of useful theory is *reductionistic*. Here one explains a phenomenon in terms of concepts that are simpler than the phenomenon to be explained. An example is any attempt to explain behavior in terms of the activity of neurons. Arnoult's third type of useful theory is *abstract*. Such theories explain a phenomenon in terms of theoretical concepts defined solely in terms of their mathematical relationships to each other and to the phenomenon in question. An example from psychology is the drive-reduction theory of motivated behavior. Drive was a theoretical concept defined solely in terms of its mathematical relationship to hours of deprivation on the one hand and its potential to produce behavior on the other hand. Many scientists consider abstract theories to be the highest form of theorizing. Note that it is common for a given theory to combine features from more than one of these theoretical categories.

An alternative classification of theories was offered by Anderson (1971), who proposed two categories. One is *Theory by General Principle*. Here the theorist tries to show that a research finding is a special case of a general principle that has already been established. For example, consider the positive relationship between time in darkness and increased visual sensitivity. If you explain this relationship as a special case of the general principle of sensory adaptation, you are using Theory by General Principle. A more common approach is *Theory by Intermediate Mechanism*. Here the theorist proposes a mechanism that serves as an intermediate link between the phenomena or variables involved in the observed relationship. The mechanism consists of a theoretical concept (or concepts) with a plausible relationship to both of the variables in the observed relationship. The mediating concept thus ties together the two observed variables and thereby explains their relationship. For example, if you explain the relationship between time in darkness and increased visual sensitivity by showing how each of them is connected to the bleaching and recovery of photopigment in the rods and cones of the eye, you are using Theory by Intermediate Mechanism.

These classification schemes do not exhaust the possible types of theories. Suppose you measure frustration and aggression in a sample of college students and find a positive relationship between the two variables. Even a simple statement like "Frustration causes aggression" is a theoretical statement because it explains why the relationship occurred and has testable implications. Note that the statement makes no appeal to either a general principle or an intermediate mechanism, nor does it fit readily into any of Arnoult's (1976) theoretical categories. Still it is a theoretical statement because it assigns cause and effect roles to the variables in the relationship. Moreover, the statement has implications for further research. It suggests that you should try to find evidence that frustration is a cause of aggression, perhaps by manipulating frustration in an experiment. As a general rule, any statement about cause, where cause is not already known, is a theoretical statement.

Although it is important to recognize theoretical statements, it is equally important to recognize and avoid nontheoretical statements posing as theory. Many students think that by restating a result they are offering a theory. When asked for a theory about the relationship between frustration and aggression, they say, "My theory is that frustration and aggression are related." Often the "theory" is a little better disguised, but it amounts to the same thing: explaining a relationship by asserting that the variables are related. Such statements sound silly when exposed for what they are, and yet they appear in the papers of students more often than you would imagine. Try to avoid this kind of pseudotheory. A real theory must go beyond the mere fact of a result to provide an explanation for why it occurred.

Evaluating Theories

How can you decide if a theory, your own or someone else's, is a good theory? What criteria should be used to evaluate a theory? Your first impulse may be to say that a good theory should meet the criterion of being correct. In some sense this must be true, for a theory that fails to be supported by research findings cannot be worth much. However, it is important not to get carried away with the notion of correctness. Partial theories, in the sense discussed earlier, cannot be completely correct explanations of a phenomenon. Does this mean that they are poor theories? Surely not. Take this one step further. Even partial theories, if they are at all complex, are unlikely to be correct in every detail. Does the fact that such theories make some incorrect predictions mean that they are poor theories? Again, surely not. Thus, what is important for partial theories is that they be generally correct and have the potential to become even more correct. The latter feature, the potential to become more correct, must mean that it is possible to find out where the theory is incorrect so that it can be changed. Clearly, then, correctness is not the only important consideration in evaluating a theory.

It is useful to give specific names to the two criteria just discussed, general correctness and the potential to become more correct. Arnoult (1976) proposed four specific criteria for evaluating theories. They are summarized in Table 1.1. Two of

Table 1.1   CRITERIA OF A GOOD THEORY

Issues Related to Correctness
        Power — Correctly explains a wide variety of phenomena
        Testability — Clear predictions that could be incorrect
Other Issues
        Simplicity — Few theoretical concepts and relationships
        Fertility — Suggests brand new ideas to explore

Arnoult's criteria deal with issues related to correctness and correspond to the criteria discussed in the preceding paragraph. The criterion of *power* refers to the number of different kinds of phenomena that can be correctly explained by a theory. All other things being equal, the broader the coverage of a theory, the better the theory. Thus, power corresponds to general correctness. The more "facts" a theory can explain, in addition to those it was set up to explain, the more powerful and the more generally correct the theory is. The criterion of *testability* means that a theory makes predictions that can be incorrect. The theorist hopes this does not happen too often, but at least it must be possible. If the theory is right no matter how the research comes out, the theory is likely to be vague, and it fails the criterion of testability. Clear theories make clear predictions, which means that there is at least one research outcome that would contradict the theory. Such theories have the potential to become more correct because it is possible to find out where they are incorrect. Fuzzy theories, on the other hand, are never "wrong" because they never make clear enough predictions to be "wrong." The issue here is clarity. Good theories should be clear enough that they make specific predictions which can be contradicted by the research findings.

Arnoult's other two criteria for theory evaluation demonstrate that correctness is not the only standard for judging theories. *Simplicity*, also known as elegance or parsimony, refers to how economical the theory itself is. In general, the fewer theoretical concepts and relationships needed to explain a phenomenon, the better. Combined with power, simplicity implies that the best theories use very little theoretical baggage (simplicity) to explain a whole lot of things (power). The last criterion, *fertility*, refers to the ability of a theory to make brand new predictions as opposed to explaining facts that are already known (power). The distinction between explaining known facts (power) and generating brand new predictions (fertility) may be impossible to maintain in practice. Both power and fertility refer to the generality of a theory—how much ground it can cover. Nevertheless, the distinction is useful in principle because fertility emphasizes the importance of a theory's potential to guide research into previously unexplored areas. Surely that is a useful property for a theory to have.

Opinions differ as to the relative importance of these criteria. Many scientists feel that testability is the most important. Their view is that a theory that cannot be falsified is worthless, and so it makes no sense to apply the other criteria unless a theory first passes the testability criterion. This is not a bad view to emphasize to beginning researchers because understanding and appreciating the testability criterion usually does not come easily to the beginner. Other scientists argue that the successful prediction of new facts, a combination of correctness and fertility, is the most valuable thing a theory can do. On the other hand, Brush (1989) has argued forcefully that the most influential theories in the history of science have been those that could explain known facts that existing theories could not explain (power). It might be better to approach the issue of relative importance from the opposite direction. Scientists would like their theories to be testable, powerful, and fertile, and they will take simplicity if they can get it. If you accept this view, then simplicity is of lesser importance than the other criteria. Of course, in an ideal scientific world, one would prefer theories that could meet all four criteria.

Before putting all this information about theories to work in a concrete example, let us clarify the meaning of some terms commonly used in the discussion of theories. Consider the terms "theory" and "hypothesis." As you know, a *theory* is a complete or partial explanation of a phenomenon. A *hypothesis*, on the other hand, is a specific prediction about a phenomenon. For example, the theory of photopigment bleaching and recovery leads to the hypothesis that time in darkness will be associated with increased visual sensitivity. For practical purposes, theories and hypotheses may be distinguished in two ways. First, theories are typically larger than hypotheses in the sense that they contain more ideas and concepts. The theory of relativity consumes volumes, but hypotheses derived from the theory (e.g., light rays that come near a gravitational field will be bent) can be stated in a single sentence. Second, hypotheses can be derived from sources other than theories. All the sources of ideas for research discussed earlier in the chapter (theory, common sense, observation, existing literature, and creative thinking) can lead to specific testable predictions or hypotheses.

Another pair of troublesome terms are "fact" and "law." "Fact" is troublesome because it has no clear definition, even among scientists. The dictionary refers to something that is true because it has been verified by experience or observation. Thus, some scientists use the word to refer to a hypothesis or a theory that has been strongly supported by research findings. Some even feel that a strongly supported theory turns into a fact. Others are comfortable regarding a strongly supported explanation as both theory and fact. Still others make a point of avoiding the word "fact." The moral is that "fact" is a tricky word, best used with caution. A scientific *law*, on the other hand, is a research finding that has been found to apply in a wide variety of situations. The "law of effect," which says that your likelihood of repeating an action depends on its consequences, has been verified in countless situations. Laws typically come from theories, which generate hypotheses, which are then found by research to have wide application. The generality of research findings will be discussed further in Chapter 13.

Theory Construction

Some research results.   Let us look at a specific example of theorizing in an area of considerable social relevance. What follows is a true account of a study carried out by the students in one of the author's research-methods courses. They constructed a questionnaire with items measuring three variables: fear of AIDS, knowledge of AIDS, and sexual promiscuity. The details of the items are not important.

The respondents were university students who completed the questionnaire anonymously. The "theory" behind the study was that fear of AIDS is affected by knowledge and promiscuity. Opinions among class members differed about the exact nature of the effects. The majority opinion was that knowledge would be negatively related to fear because knowledge would foster behavior that would reduce the risk of AIDS. Promiscuity, on the other hand, was expected to be positively related to fear for the obvious reason that promiscuity is known to increase the risk of AIDS. Note that in the last two sentences the predicted relationships are hypotheses, whereas the reasons offered for the predictions are parts of the theory.

Out of curiosity, the data were analyzed separately for males and females. There had been no prior discussion about the possibility of sex differences, nor did the class have any firm opinions on the question when it was raised. The results were stunning. The pattern of relationships differed sharply for men and women. The two predictor variables, knowledge and promiscuity, were negatively related for both sexes, implying that the more university students know about AIDS, the less promiscuous they report themselves to be, regardless of gender. Not too surprising. The shock came in the results for fear of AIDS. For men, only promiscuity predicted fear of AIDS, and the relationship was positive (more promiscuity, more fear). For women, only knowledge predicted fear of AIDS, and the relationship was negative (more knowledge, less fear). Such a fascinating difference between the sexes cried out for theoretical interpretation. After much discussion, most students felt comfortable with the following theory.

Theory.   It seems reasonable to suppose that evaluative or emotional reactions to sexual issues are affected by one's relevant knowledge, whether that knowledge is in the form of factual information, values, or knowledge of one's own behavior. Therefore, the results suggest that the kind of knowledge relied on for such reactions differs for the two sexes. Men rely on personal knowledge concerning their own behavior or experience, but women rely on so-called factual knowledge. The reason for this difference may be the differing criteria for thinking about sexual issues instilled in men and women by our culture. Men, the proposal goes, are taught to be creatures of experience in the sexual arena, whereas women are taught to heed the "principles" given to them by a male-dominated culture. Thus, men look to their personal experience when reacting to fear-of-AIDS items and rightly conclude that the more promiscuous they are, the more they have to fear. Women, on the other hand, look to the knowledge of general principles they have acquired from the "experts" in their culture and conclude that the more they know, the less they have to fear. If this scenario is correct, testable predictions follow. For example, a survey regarding the sources of moral principles for sexual behavior should reveal that women are more likely than men to report relying on cultural institutions like the church.

Moral of the story.   What kind of theory this is and whether you agree with it are not important. What matters is that you see how the class had to go beyond the research findings in order to explain them. In summary, the class proposed that culture, a theoretical mediating variable, trains the two sexes differently and that is why the pattern of relationships among the measured variables differs for men and women. The process of going beyond the findings of a study and postulating some reasons, perhaps in the form of mediating theoretical concepts, for the obtained relationships is the essence of theorizing. It is what you should do when you theorize. Note also that the proposed theory had testable predictions, and they were made explicit. You should do likewise when you theorize. Deduce testable predictions from your theory, and state them clearly.

Theories and Evidence

When the evidence, in the form of research results, supports the predictions of a theory, the researcher has cause for satisfaction. But what happens when the evidence does not support the theory? If the researcher is strongly attached to the theory, then he or she may question the evidence. Such questioning is perfectly legitimate if there is good reason for it. However, if the evidence is sound, if it has met conventional scientific standards for acceptability, then the honest researcher must conclude that the theory is wrong, at least in part. Such an outcome is NOT a bad thing. Of course, researchers would like a theory to make correct predictions most of the time or they will be inclined, with good reason, to throw it out entirely. But a theory that makes occasional incorrect predictions is not bad—it is good. Generally correct theories that make incorrect predictions can be modified to become even more correct. The point is fundamental. Scientists move closer to the truth when their theoretical predictions are contradicted by the evidence and they are thereby able to weed out false ideas. A theory that cannot be contradicted by evidence fails the criterion of testability and is scientifically worthless.

SUMMARY

The scientific approach to knowledge relies on empirical verification, that is, verification based on experience or direct observation. The two basic goals of the scientific approach are valid generalization of research findings and understanding the natural world. Scientists want to make two kinds of generalizations that may be considered basic motives for doing research: generalizations about single phenomena or variables (curiosity) and generalizations about variables that "go together" or are related. Investigating relationships between variables is the more common and important motive for doing research. The goal of understanding is achieved when one has a valid theory of a phenomenon, that is, a complete and correct explanation of its properties and relationships to other phenomena, including causal relationships. Scientists typically work with partial theories which are modified on the basis of research evidence. Good theories may be based on analogies, general principles, or intermediate mechanisms. They should meet the criteria of power, testability (falsifiability), simplicity, and fertility. Good theories generally make correct predictions, but the important thing is that they be able to learn from research experience and thereby become better theories.

FURTHER READING

The two classifications of theories are described further in Arnoult (1976) and Anderson (1971). The former also discusses the four criteria of a good theory. Brush's (1989) paper on what makes a theory influential is well worth your attention. The classic reference on how theories evolve and are eventually replaced is Kuhn (1970).

REFERENCES

Anderson, B. F. (1971). *The psychology experiment: An introduction to the scientific method* (2nd ed.). Monterey, CA: Brooks/Cole.

Arnoult, M. D. (1976). *Fundamentals of scientific method in psychology* (2nd ed.). Dubuque, IA: William C. Brown.

Brush, S. G. (1989). Prediction and theory evaluation: The case of light bending. *Science, 246,* 1124–1129.

Kaplan, R., & Kaplan, S. (1989). *The experience of nature: A psychological perspective.* New York: Cambridge University Press.

Kaplan, S., & Kaplan, R. (1982). *Cognition and environment: Functioning in an uncertain world.* New York: Praeger. (Ann Arbor, MI: Ulrichs)

Kerlinger, F. N. (1986). *Foundations of behavioral research* (3rd ed.). New York: Holt, Rinehart and Winston.

Kuhn, T. S. (1970). *The structure of scientific revolutions* (2nd ed.). Chicago: University of Chicago Press.

Basic Concepts in Research 2

The Sherman Antitrust Act was passed into law by the 51st Congress in 1890. Its apparent purpose was to discourage business monopolies and thereby encourage competition. The Act has traditionally been interpreted as proconsumer legislation; many believe that promoting consumer welfare was what motivated the 51st Congress to pass the Act. However, economist Thomas Hazlett wasn't so sure. He considered the possibility that the 51st Congress was basically anticonsumer (Hazlett, 1992)—that is, the Act was passed because the members of Congress thought it would look good on their voting record and would seldom actually be used to break up monopolies. A cynical interpretation, but perhaps it is a realistic one given the behavior of current politicians.

Hazlett tested the opposing interpretations by comparing how the members of the House of Representatives voted on the Antitrust Act and the McKinley Tariff Act, an unmistakeably anticonsumer piece of legislation. The proconsumer view predicts that the Antitrust Act should have passed, but the Tariff Act should have failed. More to the point, the proconsumer view also predicts a *relationship* between the way members voted for the two acts. Specifically, there should have been a tendency to switch votes. The proconsumer majority should have voted for the Antitrust Act and against the Tariff Act, while the anticonsumer minority should have displayed the opposite voting pattern. The anticonsumer view outlined above predicts that both acts should have passed. It also predicts a different kind of relationship between the way members voted for the two acts. Specifically, there should have been a tendency to vote the same way on both acts. The cynical majority should have voted for both acts, while the more cautious minority should have voted against both acts.

Both the proconsumer and anticonsumer interpretations of this episode in political history have one thing in common. They both predict a *relationship* between the way members of the 51st House voted for the two acts. Chapter 1 stressed that you are constantly bombarded by claims about relationships. It emphasized that the concept of a relationship is the most important one in this book and that an understanding of research methods will allow you to decide when relationships exist and when they don't. This chapter lays the foundation for such understanding by introducing the basic concepts of scientific research methods. The remainder of this book is an elaboration of the basic concepts introduced here.

Incidentally, if you are wondering which view of Congress is more plausible, you may be interested to know that both the Antitrust Act and the Tariff Act passed handily.

VARIABLES AND VALUES

The first basic concept has to do with the components of a relationship. They are called variables. The word "variable" refers to change. If you say that something varies, you mean that it changes. As a scientific concept, the term *variable* refers to a category or type of change that can occur within or among objects, events, or situations. Informally, you may think of a variable as the name of a quality that can differ from object to object. This is much easier to appreciate by example. If the objects in question are people, then variables are such things as gender, height, eye color, personality traits (like friendliness, aggressiveness, sense of humor), political or religious affiliation, and so on. In the political history example at the beginning of the chapter, one variable was how House members voted on the Antitrust Act, and a second variable was how they voted on the Tariff Act. Test yourself.

> *What is the name of the variable that describes your overall academic achievement in college? (Q1)*

(Questions posed within chapters are coded as Q1, Q2, etc. Answers may be found at the end of the chapter.)

If a variable is a GENERAL name for a quality that may differ from object to object (e.g., color), then specific examples of the quality must refer to the SPECIFIC ways that objects may differ with respect to the variable (e.g., the objects may be red, blue, green, etc.). The specific properties that objects may have with respect to a variable are called *values*. Although they may also be called levels or amounts, values is the most common term. Thus, the variable is color, and the values are red, orange, yellow, and so on. The variable is gender, and the values are male and female. The variable is height, and the values are 5-feet-1-inch, 5-feet–2-inches, and so on. In the political history example, the variable is how House members voted, and the values are for and against.

> *Question: What value do you have on the variable you named to describe your overall academic achievment? (Q2)*

As the discussion so far implies, you will be in pretty good shape if you think of a variable as a general name for a way in which objects may differ. Its values are the specific properties objects may have when they differ in that way. A common mistake made by students is to confuse values with variables. For this reason, it is a good idea for you to make a practice of separately specifying the variables of a research study and the values each variable may have.

MEASUREMENT

In the discussion of variables and values there were three players. Two of them were, of course, variables and values, but there was also repeated reference to the objects which have the values of the variables discussed. One cannot talk meaningfully about variables and values without also talking about the objects which have values. It is possible to discuss eye color in the abstract, but such a discussion has little to do with research. What the researcher needs to know is the color of Susan's eyes and Maria's eyes and Dante's eyes. This is true even if the goal is to make a general statement about the relationship between eye color and some other variable, such as attractiveness. The reason is that one cannot assess the validity of such general statements without first determining what values specific objects have on the variables involved.

A key step in the scientific approach to research is, then, determining values for objects of interest on a variable of interest. Any procedure for doing so is called *measurement*. To measure eye color, a researcher must follow some standard procedure for determining the specific color of Susan's and Maria's and Dante's eyes. The outcome of such a procedure is often called a *score* or a *measure,* but these words mean the same thing as the word "value" in the context of a measurement procedure. Susan's score, or value, for eye color is blue. What is your score for eye color, and how did you determine it?

Scientists would like their measurements to be good ones. If asked how you determined your eye color, you would probably say that you already knew it and answered from memory. But if asked to measure your eye color on the spot just to check your memory, you would probably look in the nearest mirror and report what you see. The mirror is serving as a measuring instrument, your judgment about what you see is like reading a dial or meter on such an instrument, and the process of doing so is a measurement procedure. Is the procedure any good? It is if it gives the correct answer and does so consistently. Terms like "validity" and "reliability" are used to describe these features of a good measurement procedure. They will be explored more thoroughly in the chapters on Measurement. For the moment, keep two things in mind. First, any procedure for finding out what values objects of interest have on a variable of interest is measurement. Second, measurement procedures may differ in how good they are.

OPERATIONAL DEFINITIONS

There are two procedures a researcher can do on a variable: measurement and manipulation. As you have seen, in measurement the researcher determines what values of a variable objects of interest already have. By contrast, in manipulation the researcher replaces the values that objects already have with values the researcher wants the objects to have. If a researcher was dissatisfied with Susan's measured eye color of blue, he might resort to manipulation and replace it by fitting Susan with a green-tinted contact lens. In either case, values of a variable are determined, and a procedure for determining them needs to be specified. If the procedure is described in sufficient detail that another researcher could carry it out and get the same results, then such a description is called an *operational definition.* In formal terms, an operational definition is a detailed description of the procedures or operations used to measure or manipulate a variable.

Scientific research cannot be done without operational definitions. The fundamental business of science is to measure and manipulate variables, and neither can be done without exact directions specifying what to do. Such directions constitute operational definitions. Thus, operational definitions are not a luxury in science, but a necessity.

The goal of an operational definition is clarity. A dictionary definition defines a word with other words and for that reason is sometimes vague. An operational definition, on the other hand, tells you exactly what to do to determine whether and how much the word applies to any given object. If aggression is defined as any behavior that harms another person—a dictionary definition—you may have trouble deciding whether or how much aggression occurred in a given situation. If instead aggression is defined as the number of kicks or punches administered during a five-minute period—an operational definition—it will be much easier to determine just how much aggression occurred. The difference in the two definitions is enormous. In the first case, you must make difficult judgments about whether harm occurred. In the second case, all you have to do is watch for two simple and clear indicators: kicks and punches.

Students often have great difficulty formulating good operational definitions. Their definitions tend to be closer to dictionary definitions. To appreciate the difficulty, try your hand at operationalizing a challenging psychological concept. For instance, how would you operationally define "romantic love"? If you find yourself talking in terms of "feeling attracted to someone" or something similar, you missed the point.

You need to rephrase the question as follows: How could I measure romantic love? How could I obtain scores for it? (Q3)

You must describe a specific procedure for determining romantic-love values in anyone.

Many students find an analogy with cooking helpful. An operational definition is like a recipe. A useful recipe for baking a cake must specify a lot of details: what ingredients to use, exactly how much of each ingredient, how to mix the ingredients, and the exact temperature and time for baking the mixture. An operational definition is like a recipe for baking a score for each object to be measured. It requires a similar level of detail for success.

What do you think was Hazlett's operational definition for the variable of how House members voted? His recipe was simple: look in the *Congressional Record*. Whatever the *Record* indicated as the vote for a given member was considered that member's score for the variable. Simple, clear, and guaranteed to be correct.

Like most concepts in this book, the concept of an operational definition can play a useful role in everyday reasoning. Many arguments occur because people use key words in different ways without realizing it. Consider this proposition: "Programs to help the needy should be expanded." Two people might disagree strongly about this proposition because they are making different assumptions about the meaning of the words "programs," "needy," or even "expanded." The clarity of an operational definition can be approached in this informal situation by getting both persons to specify exactly what they mean by each key word in the proposition. "Programs" might mean private-enterprise assistance to one person, while the other is thinking of public assistance. Clarifying definitions may not completely resolve such a disagreement, but at least it can eliminate misunderstanding and help pinpoint exactly where the disagreement lies.

You may have spotted a problem in defining aggression as the number of kicks and punches in a five-minute period. What about gouges, you say? Why leave them out? Why, indeed. The problem with being specific is that one runs the risk of leaving out something important, of losing some of the richness of the concept in question, or of missing the mark entirely. As with measurement, scientists would

like their operational definitions to be valid or good ones. It is often correct to criticize a single operational definition for missing something important about the concept in question. There is no perfect cure for this problem, but the use of multiple
operational definitions can help. If you operationally define the same concept a
number of ways and all of the definitions yield the same results, you can be confident of your conclusions about the concept. If the definitions yield different results,
then you may not be dealing with a single concept, which is also worthwhile to
know.

The aggression example illustrates a basic distinction among types of variables. Variables may appear as the components of theories ("Frustration causes
aggression.") or as the operationally defined products of measurement or manipulation ("Aggression scores ranged from 6 to 36."). To distinguish the two roles of
a variable, let us adopt some special terms. A variable that appears as a concept in
a theory is known as a *construct*. A variable that results from an operational definition is known as an *indicator*. Clearly, the purpose of operational definitions is to
derive indicators for constructs. This is necessary because constructs cannot be measured or manipulated directly. They are theoretical variables and are thus unavail-
able for direct control by scientists. Indicators, on the other hand, are empirical variables with concrete values derived from specific recipes (operational definitions).
Because scientists must use indicators to represent constructs, it is always important to ask how well an indicator captures or gets at its construct. That is what you
are doing when you insist that gouges should be part of the operational definition
of aggression. An indicator that is satisfactory in this sense is said to be a valid indicator. There will be much more on how to derive valid indicators of constructs in
the chapters on Measurement.

RELATIONSHIPS

As noted in the previous chapter, the most common motive for doing research is to
establish relationships. The concept of a relationship is the central organizing principle of this book. A course in research methods may be seen as a course in how
relationships are established in certain standard research settings. The previous
chapter also stressed that a relationship involves a pair of variables "going together." Thus, to establish a relationship a scientist must obtain scores on both variables
and show that the scores "go together." In formal terms, a *relationship* exists between
two variables when it can be shown that they change values together systematically.

What does this mean? Because variables change values by definition (otherwise they would be constants, not variables), the important words in the definition
must be "together systematically." To show that two variables change together systematically, it is necessary to show that specific scores on one variable tend to be
accompanied by specific scores on the other variable. When that is the case, all
objects having a particular score on one variable tend to have a limited set of particular scores on the second variable, too. In the example at the beginning of this
chapter, the evidence would have to show that the variables "vote on the Antitrust
Act" and "vote on the Tariff Act" changed values together systematically. That is,

the results would have to show that House members either consistently switched their vote or consistently voted the same way on both acts. On the other hand, if there was no relationship between the two votes, the results would show no consistency in the voting pattern of members. Those who voted for the Antitrust Act would have been likely to vote for or against the Tariff Act about equally, and the same thing would have been true of members who voted against the Antitrust Act.

Given the distinction between constructs (theoretical variables) and indicators (empirical variables), it is clear that relationships can be established directly only between indicators. Once such a relationship has been established, the question of which constructs may be related depends on which constructs are being validly represented by the indicators. The nature of the relationship may help answer this question. In the case of the 51st Congress, a relationship in which House members consistently switched their vote would suggest that both indicators were representing the construct proconsumer sentiment. In contrast, a relationship in which members voted the same way on both acts would suggest that both indicators were representing the construct political cynicism. In other words, which constructs are related depends on which theory is supported by the empirical data.

Types of Relationships

It may seem like a simple task to determine whether specific scores on one variable tend to go with specific scores on another variable. However, in practice it is often difficult. The reason is because each variable may have many possible values, and the systematic pairing of values implied by a relationship can be approximated only. That is, each value of either variable will be accompanied by a range of values on the other variable. By simply looking at pairs of scores, it may not be easy to tell whether a tendency toward systematic pairing of values is present.

In such situations, it is usually helpful to display the results in a picture known as a *scatterplot*. Several examples of scatterplots are shown in Figure 2.1. In a scatterplot, the horizontal axis represents possible scores on one variable, and the vertical axis represents possible scores on the other variable. A point is placed in the space for each object at the location where that object's scores on the two variables intersect. Imagine that the variables are frustration and aggression, each measured on a scale from 0 to 20, and that the objects are people, each of whom has been measured on both variables. The scores for three individuals on frustration (F) and aggression (A) might look like this: Susan (F = 4, A = 5), Maria (F = 17, A = 16), Dante (F = 11, A = 10). Thus, Susan's point would be located six units to the right of the origin (the 0,0 point) and 8 units up in the space, Maria's point would be at a spot 17 units right of the origin and 16 units up in the space, and so on. If the results for 100 people were put into the scatterplot, the points would form a narrow sausage-like shape that sloped up and to the right, as in Figure 2.1.a. Although the relationship is not perfect, there is a tendency for low frustration scores to go with low aggression scores (Susan), medium with medium (Dante), and high with high (Maria). The points would be well described by a straight-line function that tilts

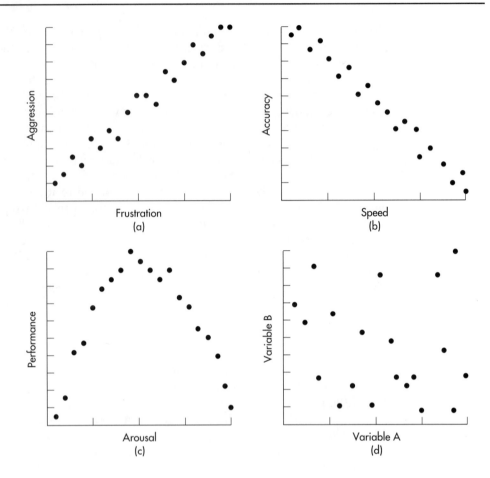

Figure 2.1
Scatterplot of a positive linear relationship (a), a negative linear relationship (b), an inverted-U curvilinear relationship (c), and no relationship (d).

upward to the right (what mathematicians call a positive slope). This is known as a direct or *positive linear relationship.*

Positive linear relationships are the most common ones seen in the social sciences. Two other types of relationship are sometimes seen. One is illustrated by the relationship between the variables speed and accuracy on many tasks. The faster you go, the more mistakes you make. Thus, as speed increases, accuracy decreases, or high scores on either variable tend to go with low scores on the other variable. The scatterplot would be well described by a straight-line function that tilts downward to the right, a so-called negative slope. This is known as an inverse or *negative linear relationship* and is illustrated in Figure 2.1.b. Less common are scatterplots where the points cluster around a U-shaped function, with the open end of the U facing upward or downward. An example of the latter type, a so-called inverted-U relationship, is the relationship between arousal level and performance on a variety of tasks, shown in Figure 2.1.c. The best performance scores occur at middle levels of arousal, with poor performance paired with either high or low arousal scores.

> *(Can you propose a good theory, using the criteria of the previous chapter, about why this should be so? (Q4))*

Relationships that require more complex functions than a straight line to describe are known generally as nonlinear or *curvilinear relationships.*

If there is no relationship, there will be no tendency for specific values of either variable to be paired with specific values of the other. In other words, any value of either variable will be paired randomly with ALL values of the other variable. The scatterplot will consist of a set of points filling the entire space, as in Figure 2.1.d.

Necessary Evidence

What is the minimum evidence necessary to determine whether or not a relationship exists? First, one must have data on each of two variables. The term *data* is a plural noun that refers to all of the information or output from a research study. Its singular form, referring to a single item of output, is datum. Second, the data must be in the form of scores or values, and there must be at least two values for each variable. If only one value for either variable occurs in a sample of scores, then the variable is not varying. In that case, it cannot change together with the other variable.

To make this concrete, imagine that the makers of Gruel, the hot breakfast cereal, have conducted a consumer taste test. One variable is the Cereal Brand tasted, and its values are Gruel and the leading competitor, Mush-O-Meal. The other variable is judged Tastiness, and its values are High and Low. Imagine that 100 hot-cereal users participated. The data are summarized in Table 2.1. Such tables are called *frequency tables* (a fancier title is contingency tables) because they show how frequently each value of one variable goes with each value of the other variable. Now you are faced with a tough challenge. With concrete results staring you in the face, how can you tell whether they satisfy the definition of a relationship? How can you tell if the values of the two variables change together systematically? It is not easy to decide, is it?

Table 2.1   FREQUENCY TABLE FOR THE VARIABLES CEREAL BRAND AND TASTINESS

		Cereal Brand		
		Gruel	Mush-O-Meal	Total
Tastiness	High	56	24	80
	Low	14	6	20
	Total	70	30	100

Let us examine this table carefully. First, it is evident from the row totals at the right side of the table that most of the sample rated their cereal High in Tastiness (80 out of 100). From the column totals at the bottom of the table, it also seems that Gruel was the Cereal Brand tasted by most of the sample (70 out of 100). The row and column totals in a frequency table are known as *marginal totals*. The numbers inside the table are called *cell frequencies*. On the question of whether the variables are related, one might be impressed with that big number 56 inside the Gruel-High cell. Someone else might object, however, that the Gruel-High cell frequency does not necessarily imply a relationship between the variables. Can you see why? Maybe the Gruel-High cell frequency is large simply because both the Gruel and High marginal totals are large (80 and 70). Clearly, you need a way of taking the unequal marginal totals into account if you are to make a correct decision about the question of relationship.

A general rule of thumb for this situation is that you must use all of the information inside the table to reach a valid conclusion. Reasoning from anything less than all four cell frequencies may lead to an erroneous conclusion about whether the variables are related. The simplest way of using all of the cell frequencies is to select one value of either variable (e.g., High Tastiness) and compute its rate or proportion of occurrence separately for each value of the other variable. Following this approach, you would compute the proportion of High Tastiness responses separately for the Gruel and Mush-O-Meal values of Cereal Brand.

Let us see how this works out in practice. Of the consumers who tasted Gruel, 56 out of 70 judged it High in Tastiness. Thus, the required proportion is 56/70 = .80. Put differently, the proportion of High Tastiness responses among those who tasted Gruel, or p(High Tastiness | Gruel), equals .80. (The vertical bar in "p(A | B)" means "given that." Thus, "p(High Tastiness | Gruel)" refers to the proportion of consumers who rated their cereal High in Tastiness "given that" Gruel was the Cereal Brand tasted.) Of the consumers who tasted Mush-O-Meal, 24 out of 30 judged it High in Tastiness, or p(High Tastiness | Mush-O-Meal) = 24/30 = .80. The "average" value of Tastiness, represented by the High Tastiness proportions, is the same (.80) for both values of Cereal Brand. Thus, there is no tendency for different values of Cereal Brand to be accompanied by different "average" values of Tastiness. In other words, there is no evidence that the variables are related.

Three points about this example should be noted. First, the example assumed that the scores contain no error. On that optimistic assumption, if the computed proportions are equal, the variables are not related, and if the computed proportions are not equal, the variables are related. On the more realistic assumption that there is some error in the scores, it might be wise to relax the decision rule a little. The new rule would be that if the computed proportions are equal or nearly equal, the variables are not related; otherwise, they are related. The assumption of no error was made solely because it simplified the presentation. The problem of error in scores and how to deal with it will be discussed in many of the following chapters.

Second, it may seem that the calculations did not follow the rule of thumb and use all of the cell frequencies in the table. After all, only the cell frequencies in the top row of the table, 56 and 24, appeared explicitly in the calculations. Be assured that the other two cell frequencies, 14 and 6, were involved implicitly in the denominators (or bottoms) of the two proportions, 70 and 30. The 14 must be added to the 56 to get the 70 in the denominator of the first proportion, and the 6 must be added to the 24 to get the 30 in the denominator of the second proportion. Thus, all four cell frequencies were used.

Third, it makes no difference which value of either variable is selected for the numerator (or top) of the proportions as long as proportions are computed separately for each value of the OTHER variable. For example, you could compute the proportion of Gruel values for Cereal Brand separately for the High and Low values of Tastiness. You would obtain the following results: p(Gruel | High Tastiness) = 56/80 = .70 and p(Gruel | Low Tastiness) = 14/20 = .70. The equal proportions are not the same as before (.80 versus .70), but they are equal, and that is what matters. If the proportions are equal when you select one value of either variable for the numerator, they will be equal if you select any other value of either variable for the numerator, provided you do the calculations correctly. The same is true for unequal proportions.

So now you know how to decide whether two variables are related in a situation where the minimum evidence necessary for such a decision is available, namely, a 2×2 (i.e., two rows and two columns) frequency table. Test yourself. Keep the same marginal totals as in Table 2.1, but insert 60 in the top left cell of the table and adjust the other cell frequencies accordingly. Now compute the proportion of High Tastiness responses separately for the two values of Cereal Brand.

Are the variables related? What is your decision? (Q5)

Now you are ready to see the actual data from the Hazlett study of voting patterns in the 51st House. They are presented in Table 2.2. The data include only members who did not abstain on either vote. If the abstainers are included as Against votes, the results are weakened somewhat but the pattern is the same. Repeat the analysis of proportions one more time using the data in Table 2.2.

Are the variables related? Which of the theories discussed at the beginning of the chapter seems to be supported? (Q6)

Table 2.2   FREQUENCY TABLE FOR THE
VARIABLES ANTITRUST VOTE AND TARIFF VOTE

		Antitrust Vote		
		For	*Against*	*Total*
Tariff Vote	For	104	3	107
	Against	14	38	52
	Total	118	41	159

Errors in Reasoning

As pointed out in the previous section, reasoning from anything less than the complete information in a frequency table may lead to an erroneous conclusion about whether the variables are related. Table 2.1 may be used to illustrate this point. The analysis in the previous section showed that the variables are NOT related. Yet it is easy to imagine that someone who does not know how to analyze frequency tables might be impressed by the large number in the Gruel-High cell. Such a person might say, "56 percent of the sample tasted Gruel and judged it high in tastiness. Clearly, Gruel and tastiness are associated." Someone else might say, "56 percent of the sample judged Gruel high in tastiness, but only 24 percent judged Mush-O-Meal high in tastiness. Gruel is more than twice as tasty." Yet a third person might say, "62 percent of the sample judged Gruel high in tastiness or Mush-O-Meal low in tastiness. It matters what cereal you eat." In each case, the statements erroneously imply that the variables are related, and yet they seem like sensible statements. Perhaps that is because the first sentence in each statement is technically correct but irrelevant to the issue of whether the variables are related. Each technically correct statement fails to use the information in all four cells of the table and thus fails to deal properly with the greatly unequal marginal totals for the two variables.

The moral of these examples is clear. Very attractive but erroneous statements about relationships are easy to make, even by those with good intentions. What about those whose intentions may be affected by self-interest? Every day you are exposed to countless assertions about relationships made by advertisers, politicians, and opinion shapers of all sorts. It is important that you be able to think clearly about such statements and to evaluate properly any evidence offered to support them. The topic of errors in reasoning about relationships has such great practical significance that an extended discussion of it will be provided in the last chapter of this book. Anderson (1971) also provides a detailed examination of such errors. For now the point to bear in mind is that the analysis described in the preceding section is the ONLY way to reach a safe conclusion about whether variables are related. Reasoning from incomplete information can easily lead you astray.

Causality

Establishing relationships is extremely important for all of the reasons discussed in the section on Motives for Research in the previous chapter. However, one thing a relationship cannot do is pinpoint cause. If you know that frustration is positively related to aggression, that fact alone tells you nothing about what may explain the relationship. Surely the relationship has an explanation, but the relationship itself does not allow one to identify the causal variable(s). Frustration may be causing aggression, either directly or through the intermediate mechanism of anger. In the latter case, frustration causes anger which in turn causes aggression. Thus, frustration indirectly causes aggression through the mediating influence of anger. Frustration as cause is essentially what is postulated by the frustration–aggression theory in psychology. However, aggression might be the cause. People who behave very aggressively may elicit a great deal of opposition from others, frustrating the aggressors from achieving their goals. It is even possible that a third variable, sunspots, is the real cause. Cosmic rays from sunspot flareups may cause both feelings of frustration and aggression. The moral is that a relationship by itself proves nothing about cause.

Cause is a very slippery concept with many meanings. Philosophers have been agonizing over it for centuries. Some social scientists (e.g., Kerlinger, 1986) believe that more harm than good is done by even using the word in the context of research methods. There is no need to be drawn into this debate. Instead, a commonly held position will be adopted: a variable qualifies as a cause when a change on that variable is reliably accompanied by a corresponding change on another variable under conditions where all other potential causes can be ruled out. Two points about this definition should be stressed. First, it corresponds to what philosophers call a "sufficient" cause. That is, the presumed cause is sufficient to produce the presumed effect, but it is not necessary to produce the effect. Other variables might also produce the same effect. Second, the definition is statistical or probabilistic. The presumed cause is "reliably" accompanied by the presumed effect. That is, the presumed cause is usually or probably accompanied by the presumed effect, BUT the presumed cause does not ALWAYS have to be accompanied by the presumed effect. This definition seems pretty reasonable for use in an uncertain world and is probably close to what most scientists have in mind when they use the word "cause." You might think of it as probable sufficient cause.

There is a special terminology for variables that are thought of as causes or effects. A presumed cause is called an *independent variable*, and a presumed effect is called a *dependent variable*. This usage highlights the notion that in a causal relationship the presumed effect depends on the presumed cause, but not vice-versa. The terminology is essentially theoretical. It refers to the theoretical role assigned to variables in a relationship.

If you wish to provide empirical evidence of cause, then you must meet the conditions implied by the definition of cause. There are three conditions. First, you must show that the presumed cause and the presumed effect are related. Second, you must show that changes on the presumed effect "accompany" changes on the presumed cause. This is usually taken to mean that changes on the presumed effect must follow in time (or be simultaneous with) changes on the presumed cause—one normally thinks of effects as unable to occur before causes. Third, you must be able to rule out the operation of all other possible causes in the situation under investigation. These conditions represent an ideal that is only approached by even the most dedicated researchers. However, there is a research method that takes special steps to meet these conditions. That research method is the experiment.

THE EXPERIMENTAL METHOD

The goal of the experimental method is to establish causal relationships. That is, the method seeks not only to establish relationships between pairs of variables, but also to pin down one of the variables in each relationship as causing the variation in the other variable. Other research methods may sometimes have similar aspirations, but the experiment is distinguished by the special techniques used to achieve its goal.

The Independent Variable

The variables in an experiment may be divided into several categories, as shown in Figure 2.2. The defining feature of an experiment is the presence of at least one manipulated variable. Recall from earlier in the chapter that *manipulation* implies two things: (1) the experimenter decides which values of the variable will occur, and (2) the experimenter decides which objects (usually people in social-science research) will have each value of the variable. In technical terms, the experimenter *produces* the values of the manipulated variable(s) and *assigns* those values to the experimental units. In the simplest good experiment, there is one manipulated variable, and it has two values because two is the minimum number of values necessary to establish a relationship.

A crucial feature of a manipulated variable in an experiment is the theoretical role it plays. The presumed cause is manipulated, and then the presumed effect is measured to see if it is affected by the manipulation. The purpose is to meet the first two conditions for cause described earlier. Because the presumed cause is manipulated in an experiment, the manipulated variable is also the independent variable. Thus, the defining feature of an experiment is the presence of a manipulated independent variable.

Manipulation requires an operational definition specifying how the values of the variable are produced and how they are assigned to the experimental units. As an example, you might manipulate frustration by giving people a paper-and-pencil maze task to work on along with instructions that any reasonably intelligent person could solve the maze in about two minutes. To produce high frustration, you hand out an unsolvable maze and let the poor victim work on it for five minutes. To produce low frustration, you hand out a very simple, easily solvable maze. Who gets which maze is determined randomly by flipping a coin. (Why randomly? Think about it for a moment. The answer is in the next section, "Other Variables.") Notice how different this is from simply finding out what values of frustration people already have (measurement). Here you are replacing the values they have with the values you want them to have (manipulation). In either case, you need an operational definition. In an experiment, the values of the independent variable produced by manipulation are referred to as *treatments* or *conditions*. In the example, there is a high-frustration and a low-frustration condition.

Other Variables

The nonmanipulated variables in an experiment may be divided into two classes. The first is the dependent variable or the presumed effect in the cause-effect relationship. In the current example, it would be aggression. The dependent variable is measured to see if its scores vary systematically with the scores on the independent variable. That is, you wish to know if the scores on the dependent variable tend to be different in the different conditions of the experiment. In the frustration

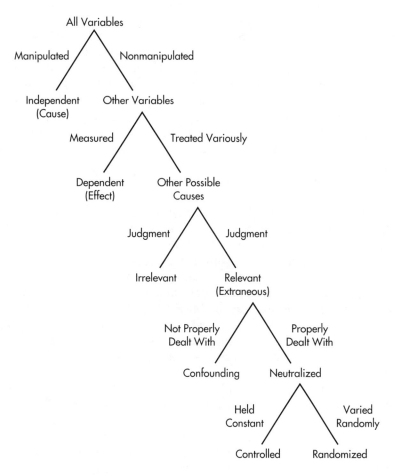

Figure 2.2
Variables in an experiment.

experiment, you would expect that the aggression scores should be higher in the high-frustration condition than in the low-frustration condition. If so, the independent variable (frustration) and the dependent variable (aggression) are related. Measuring the dependent variable also requires an operational definition. After the maze problem, you could escort each participant into an adjoining room containing a Bobo doll, a large inflated plastic doll with a weighted bottom that causes it to pop back upright whenever someone knocks it down. Then you could watch though a one-way mirror to see how many times the doll is kicked, punched, or gouged in a five-minute period. In general, the measure of the dependent variable should be valid, and more will be said about what that means in the chapters on Measurement.

The second class of nonmanipulated variables in an experiment consists of all variables in the universe except the independent and dependent variables. In order to satisfy the third condition for cause discussed earlier, every one of these variables must be ruled out as a possible cause in the current experiment. This class of variables may be subdivided three more times. The first division is into the categories of relevant and irrelevant. Relevant means that the variable is judged to be possibly related to the dependent variable. In the frustration experiment, intelligence would be an example of a relevant variable. A variable judged irrelevant has been ruled out as a possible cause by informed judgment and need be considered no further. In the frustration experiment, the position of the planet Venus seems like a reasonable candidate. Of course, informed judgment may be questioned by critics, and one must therefore be prepared to defend it. Such is the fate of any informed judgment.

Relevant variables are best dealt with procedurally. They are so important that they are usually referred to by a special name: *extraneous* variables. Extraneous variables may be subdivided into two categories: those that have been properly dealt with, and those that have not. There is no commonly accepted term for properly-dealt-with extraneous variables. You might think of them as "neutralized." However, everyone agrees that a not-properly-dealt-with extraneous variable acquires the sinister title of a confounding variable. A *confounding* variable is a variable, other than the dependent variable, that may have changed systematically along with the independent variable. Such a variable is a possible alternative to the independent variable as a cause in the experiment. Thus, it confounds the interpretation of the results. You would like to conclude that the independent variable is the cause of the results, but you cannot. The message is clear: Neutralized variables are good; confounding variables are bad.

Finally, neutralized variables may be subdivided into two categories based on how they are dealt with procedurally. They may be either *controlled* (held constant in some sense) or *randomized* (made to vary randomly or in an unpredictable way). Because it is held constant, a controlled variable cannot change values systematically along with another variable. Because its values change randomly (i.e., in a completely unpredictable way), a randomized variable likewise cannot change values systematically (i.e., in a predictable way) along with another variable. Thus, in either case, the variable cannot be involved in a relationship and is therefore ruled out as a cause in the experiment.

Intelligence probably would be randomized. Can you guess why? (Q7)

A good candidate for control would be an environmental variable like the temperature of the research setting.

Causality

There will be much more discussion about the categories and subcategories of variables in an experiment in later chapters. The purpose here was to provide a broad overview so that you could appreciate the special features of an experiment. Here is a brief summary. The purpose of the experiment is to establish a causal relationship, that is, a relationship where you can be confident that one of the two variables involved is the cause. This is accomplished by manipulating the presumed cause (the independent variable), measuring the presumed effect (the dependent variable), and using special procedures (control and randomization) to neutralize all other variables judged to be possible alternative causes (extraneous variables). If a relationship between the independent and dependent variables can be established under these conditions, you can be confident that the independent variable is the cause.

CLASSIFICATION OF RESEARCH METHODS

It is now possible to set the stage for the rest of the book by providing a broad classification of research methods. The classification is shown in Figure 2.3. Virtually all researchers agree on the distinction between experiments and nonexperimental methods. A study containing a manipulated variable is an experiment, no matter how the dependent variable is measured. Otherwise, it is not an experiment. Experiments may be divided into various experimental designs based on how the independent variable is manipulated (in particular, how its values are assigned to the experimental units). The various experimental designs will be discussed later in this book.

Nonexperimental methods may be divided into two types: observation studies and survey research. The distinction is based on how the variables of the study are measured. In observation studies, the researcher obtains scores for participants by observing their ongoing behavior and making judgments about it (so-called observational or behavioral measures). In survey research, participants make their own judgments and tell the researcher about their status with respect to the variables being studied (so-called self-report measures). Both types of nonexperimental research can be subdivided further, and various combinations are possible. These complexities will be explored later in the book.

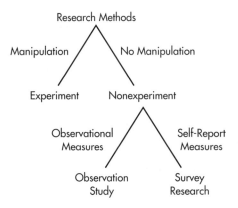

Figure 2.3
Classification of basic research methods.

In summary, there are three basic research methods: experiments, observation studies, and survey research. Largely because of the kinds of data or scores typically involved, observation studies will be examined in depth first, followed by survey research, and finally experiments.

CHOOSING A RESEARCH METHOD

The chapter concludes with a few thoughts about choosing among the basic research methods. You may have the impression that because of its special features for pinpointing cause, the experiment should always be the preferred method. Many researchers would agree although there is plenty of controversy. A more sensible approach is to realize that all research methods have both strengths and weaknesses. Thus, the researcher must make an informed and personal judgment about the match between the kinds of variables to be studied and the strengths/weaknesses of the various methods. You should avoid the attitude that if something cannot be studied experimentally, it should not be studied at all. For ethical or practical reasons, many important variables in the social sciences cannot or should not be manipulated. Two examples are child abuse and human intelligence. (For further discussion of ethical issues, see the chapter on Ethics in Research.) Variables like these make it clear that an exclusive reliance on the experimental method is a luxury science cannot afford.

Even when a variable can be manipulated, it might be preferable not to do so. Manipulated variables in an experiment typically have only a small number of values (e.g., high and low frustration). Generalization of results to all points between those values is necessarily risky. Add to that the artificial setting of the typical experimental laboratory, and there is reason to question how widely applicable the results may be in the "real" world outside the laboratory. Defenders of experiments will reply that they seek to establish causal relationships in principle and that the generality of such relationships in the "real" world is a matter for further research. Some of that research may be in the form of "field" experiments, that is, experiments carried out in natural settings. Issues like these are discussed further in the chapter on Generalizing Research Results.

The moral here is that the best method depends on the researcher's purpose. The methods complement each other, and there is no reason to regard any one as automatically superior to the others. If the purpose is to describe behavior in a natural setting, an observation study is appropriate. If you want to find out what people think, ask them (i.e., do a survey). If you want to pinpoint cause and manipulation is possible, do an experiment. If manipulation is not feasible, it may be possible to measure alternative causes in a nonexperimental study and neutralize them statistically. Such approaches are described in the second chapter on survey research. The rule of thumb is that researchers should think about their goals and then tailor the method to achieve those goals. One of the goals of this book is to prepare you to engage confidently in such tailoring.

SUMMARY

A variable is a general quality like aggression that refers to a way in which objects may differ. Its values are the specific properties (specific amounts of aggression) objects may have when they differ in that way. Measurement is any procedure for determining what values objects of interest have on a variable of interest. Manipulation is a procedure in which a researcher replaces the values objects already have with values the researcher wants the objects to have. A detailed description of the exact procedures or operations for doing measurement or manipulation is known as an operational definition.

A relationship exists between two variables when specific values of one variable tend to be accompanied by specific values of the other variable. Positive linear relationships are the most common type in the social sciences. Negative linear relationships and nonlinear or curvilinear relationships are also sometimes seen. The minimum evidence necessary to establish a relationship consists of data on at least two values of each the two variables in question. In that case, the data may be displayed in a 2×2 frequency table. To avoid errors in reasoning, one must use the data from all four cells of such a table. The most common way of doing so is to select one value of one of the variables and compute its proportion or rate of occurrence separately at each value of the other variable. Using less than the required data may lead to an erroneous conclusion about whether the variables are related.

Establishing a relationship tells you nothing about cause. Either of the variables in the relationship or some third variable could be acting as a causal agent. The experiment is a research method with special features aimed at pinpointing cause. In an ideal experiment, the presumed cause or independent variable is manipulated, the presumed effect or dependent variable is then measured, and all other potential causes are ruled out by such techniques as control and randomization. If a relationship is obtained between the independent and dependent variables, the independent variable must have been the cause of changes in the dependent variable. If relevant alternative causes are not properly ruled out, the experiment is said to be confounded. Basic research methods may be classified into experiments and two types of nonexperimental methods, observation studies and survey research, distinguished by whether scores are obtained from observations of ongoing behavior or from the self-reports of those being scored.

ANSWERS TO QUESTIONS

Q1. The variable is grade-point average, or GPA.

Q2. The value is your actual GPA. What is it?

Q3. One possibility is a self rating on, say, a 10-point scale ranging from 1 = low to 10 = high. Another possibility is mutual gazing time, the percentage of time during a standard observation period that a couple spends looking into each other's eyes.

Q4. Too little arousal produces lack of alertness. Too much arousal produces an inability to control one's thoughts or bodily movements because one is too "hyped" or "wired."

Q5. $p(\text{High Tastiness} \mid \text{Gruel}) = 60/70 = .86$, and $p(\text{High Tastiness} \mid \text{Mush-O-Meal}) = 20/30 = .67$. Therefore, there appears to be a relationship, with consumers more likely to have responded High in Tastiness if they tasted Gruel than if they tasted Mush-O-Meal.

Q6. $p(\text{For Tariff} \mid \text{For Antitrust}) = 104/118 = .88$, and $p(\text{For Tariff} \mid \text{Against Antitrust}) = 3/41 = .07$. Therefore, the actual data show a strong relationship, with members far more likely to have voted For the Tariff Act if they voted For the Antitrust Act than if they voted Against the Antitrust Act. The results support the anticonsumer theory which predicted that members would tend to vote the same way on both Acts.

Q7. The only way to hold intelligence constant would be to choose a sample of people who all had the same intelligence level. However, critics would complain that the results might not apply to people at other intelligence levels. To avoid such a criticism, intelligence probably would be randomized.

FURTHER READING

Anderson (1971) contains an extended discussion of the proper way to evaluate a 2×2 frequency table for evidence of a relationship between the variables.

REFERENCES

Anderson, B. F. (1971). *The psychology experiment: An introduction to the scientific method* (2nd ed.). Monterey, CA: Brooks/Cole.

Hazlett, T. W. (1992). The legislative history of the Sherman Act re-examined. *Economic Inquiry, 30,* 263–276.

Kerlinger, F. N. (1986). *Foundations of behavioral research* (3rd ed.). New York: Holt, Rinehart and Winston.

The Observation Study: Procedures

3

Several years ago, the author's class in research methods tried to come up with an idea for an observation study. The students had been told that they must observe in a "real" setting, that their purpose was to determine whether or not two variables of their choosing were related, and that at least one of the two variables had to involve classification of ongoing overt behavior. Armed with these criteria, the class began to think about what was available and feasible to observe.

Before long, a student noted that she had often observed a marvelous behavioral indicator of thrift—people checking the coin return of a public payphone after hanging up. The class embraced this idea enthusiastically. Of course, the student added, it doesn't happen all the time. The search was on for another variable that would predict when coin-checking might occur. Several students expressed the opinion that people in the area tended to be thrifty, presumably because of their Dutch heritage. Given the "thrift" theory, it was soon decided that area payphone users would be more likely to check the coin return if they felt they hadn't got their money's worth from the conversation just concluded. That, in turn, would depend on how long the conversation was. Short conversations would leave the users unfulfilled from a cost-benefit standpoint and would arouse their thrift motive, leading to coin-checking. Long conversations would be much less likely to have such an effect. The variables had been chosen. They were length of conversation and coin-checking behavior.

Operational definitions were next. After much debate, the class decided on two values for conversation length, short and long. Short would be any conversation lasting less than a minute, long any conversation lasting more than two minutes. Any conversation lasting from one to two minutes would not be included in the study. Omitting certain observations from a study is perfectly legitimate, provided one has good reason and the rules for doing so are stated clearly in advance. In this case, the good reason was that the students wanted a strong contrast between short and long conversations. Because it involved classifying ongoing behavior, coin-checking was much more difficult to define operationally. After much struggle, the students decided to adopt the simple rule that any movement whatsoever toward the coin return during a 30-second period after hanging up, would qualify as coin-checking and that the variable would have two values, yes and no.

The students went out into the shopping malls of the area to observe payphone conversations. They went in pairs so that the rate of agreement between observers of the same event could be assessed, an indication of how clear or reliable the operational definitions were. To avoid affecting the behavior observed, the student pairs mingled with the shoppers, sat around in conversation pits, or stationed themselves strategically behind potted plants. After each student pair had observed its allotted quota of short and long conversations, the data were brought to class and pooled across all observer pairs. The results: (1) Agreement between observer pairs was perfect for conversation length and exceeded 80 percent for coin-checking, indicating good reliability of measurement. (2) When the data for each member of the observer pairs were entered separately into two different 2×2 frequency tables like those described in the previous chapter, both tables showed a strong tendency for short conversations to go with coin-checking and long conversations with no coin-checking.

As you will see shortly, this study is an example of a systematic observation. It illustrates both the potential and the problems of observation studies. No other approach is so well suited to studying events as they happen in real-world settings outside the laboratory. On the other hand, because they deal with events as they happen in uncontrolled settings, observation studies pose special challenges to researchers interested in good measurement. Such problems will be examined in this chapter. In the process, observation studies will be categorized and the strengths and weaknesses of each type will be discussed. After covering the major types of observation studies, the advantages and disadvantages of observation studies in general will be summarized. The last section of the chapter briefly examines some related methods that may be considered variations on the basic method of observation. This chapter focuses on the procedures used in observation studies. The next chapter deals with how to analyze typical data from observation studies.

Before going on, consider a lingering problem from the payphone study. The theory behind the predicted relationship was that people in the area are Dutch, and the Dutch are thrifty. The results strongly confirmed the predicted relationship between conversation length and coin-checking.

> *Does this mean that the theory is correct or even credible? Can you think of a more plausible alternative theory that would have predicted the same result? (Q1)*

TYPES OF OBSERVATION STUDIES

There are many ways to classify observation studies. The following discussion divides them into three categories: casual, field, and systematic. This is a variation of a classification scheme proposed by Sommer and Sommer (1991). Casual observation refers to informal observation aimed at getting ideas for a more serious study to be done later. Field observation refers to in-depth observation of a social system with the goal of understanding how the system works. Systematic observation refers to observation of specific carefully defined variables with the goal of determining whether they are related.

Casual Observation

People do casual observation whenever they informally watch what is going on in a setting to get a feel for the situation. Social scientists often do something similar to get ideas for a more serious study later on. The difference is that the scientist is after more than just "a feel for the situation." The scientist tries to determine what the most important variables are and how best to operationalize them, that is, what specific features or behaviors to observe. To do this effectively may require some preparatory work such as reading whatever literature is available or talking to people who have knowledge of the setting. It may also require a series of casual observations rather than just one. In any case, it requires keen powers of observation.

There are no firm rules about casual observation. It is pretty much a do-it-as-best-you-can operation. Two general principles are probably defensible. The first is that casual observation is almost never the last step for a social scientist. It is a preliminary to more serious methods. For someone like an administrator, however, it may be a different story. One shudders to think how often administrators make important decisions based on nothing more than casual observation, however well informed. In the "real" world, casual observation is often the only method available. All the more reason for those who must rely on it to develop their powers of observation. Second, observations should be recorded in some form of permanent storage as soon as possible after making them. Memory is unreliable and easily distorted. Transferring one's impressions to a permanent record as soon as possible can largely avoid such distortions. It may be possible to record observations as they are being made. However, such activity carries great risk. It may interfere with the process of observing or alter the behavior observed. If either outcome is likely, simultaneous recording should be avoided.

Sommer and Sommer (1991, p. 51) provide an example of a casual observation in a Canadian pub. The observer spent an hour in the pub one evening, jotting down notes on such things as seating arrangements, typical behaviors of solitary patrons versus patrons in groups, type of clothes worn, and topics of conversation. Alert for useful predictors of drinking behavior, the observer noted that group members who talked mostly about family and children drank from smaller glasses and left early. Clearly the observer's rough notes contained many possibilities for more systematic follow-up research.

Field Observation

Field observation, also known as "field work" or "naturalistic observation," is a method in which the researcher studies a specific social or natural setting for an extended period of time using a variety of procedures with the goal of understanding how the system works. Sociologist Herbert Gans (Gans, 1962) went to live in Boston's West End for several months in order to understand the dynamics of a so-called "slum" neighborhood. He went to bars and public meetings, sometimes participating and sometimes merely observing. He made friends and interviewed informants of all types. Generally speaking, he kept his ear to the ground. His research report was a book, a largely narrative account of his understanding of the West End. One of his most telling findings: West Enders did not view their environment as a slum, but rather as a familiar and supportive social setting in danger of being torn apart by urban renewal.

Field observation has been used to study an astonishing variety of social groups and environments. The list includes drug users (Becker, 1953), drug dealers (Adler, 1985), Satanists (Alfred, 1976), residents of an urban ghetto (Liebow, 1967), cocktail waitresses (Spradley & Mann, 1975), and ex-mental patients (Estroff, 1978). There are more examples in the discussion below. Most of the researchers who do field observations are sociologists or anthropologists, but practitioners have come from disciplines as varied as criminology (Kirkham, 1976) and archaeology (Rathje & McCarthy, 1977).

As with casual observation, there are few firm rules for doing field observation. An important consideration is accurate record keeping. At least once a day the field observer should update the data record, either by writing down or dictating everything that happened. The data record from a field observation is usually referred to as *field notes*. The validity of conclusions depends on the accuracy of the field notes.

Monette, Sullivan, and DeJong (1990) describe five steps in a participant field observation like the one done by Gans. The first is to establish specific goals and then decide that participant observation is an appropriate research strategy. The second step is to decide which specific social group or environment to study. The third step is to gain entry into the target group or environment. This may involve delicate negotiation, or at least the offering of a plausible reason for the observer's presence. It may also involve the decision to conceal the observer's purpose. The fourth step is to establish rapport with those being observed. Depending on the situation, this step can be difficult and time consuming. The fifth and last step is to observe and record.

Distinguishing features.   Three features distinguish field observation from other forms of research. None of them does the job alone, but as a package they distinguish field observation from other approaches. The first distinguishing feature is *immersion*. The researcher immerses himself or herself in the setting, as Gans did in the West End, attempting to observe and describe accurately everything about it. Targets of observation include physical features, social interactions, typical behaviors, products or outputs produced—anything that may be relevant to the goal of in-depth understanding. Immersion means that the study requires an extended period of time, which distinguishes this approach from casual observation and from the typical systematic observation described later. It also means that the researcher uses a variety of procedures, as Gans did, supplementing observation with interviews, examination of relevant documents or other output produced in the setting, and any other technique that may be useful. Observation is the dominant procedure, but not the only procedure. Immersion also implies flexibility in use of procedures. Techniques may change during the course of the study as they are found wanting or as better approaches become evident. This would horrify the laboratory experimenter but is taken in stride by the field worker. Purity of method may give way to the goal of thorough understanding via immersion.

A second distinguishing feature is the *goal of the research*. The goal of field observation is an in-depth understanding of the dynamics of the setting as a whole, how it works as a system. Gans wanted to understand the West End as a social system. As you will see in the next chapter, this goal is often directly reflected in the kind of data typically produced by field observations and in the way the data are analyzed. Both the data (field notes) and the analysis tend to be qualitative, that is, nonnumerical and nonmathematical. The holistic system approach of the field researcher contrasts sharply with the typical experimeter's desire to tease apart the separate influences of variables.

The third distinguishing feature of field observation concerns the *role of prior predictions or hypotheses*. Most research methods, including most systematic observations, are designed to test specific predictions or hypotheses made in advance. This is not true of the typical field observation. There is a general goal of understanding the system under observation, but usually there are no specific prior predictions to be tested. In fact, some field researchers assert that the typical output of a field observation is a set of tentative hypotheses about how the system works. Chapter 1 stressed that theory and data interact over time in the research process. Here you see that a specific theory, as opposed to a general goal of understanding, typically follows the data in a field observation.

Categories. Field observations may be categorized along two dimensions, as summarized in Table 3.1. One is participation, that is, whether or not the observer is an active participant in what is going on in the social system. The second dimension is concealment, that is, whether or not the observer's purpose is concealed from those observed. Although defined as discrete categories, participation and concealment are really dimensions. An observer may not participate at all, may play only a small role in the social system, or may play one or more important roles in the system. Likewise, concealment may involve bodily concealment, blending in with the crowd, standing out from the crowd but keeping one's role as an observer concealed, making plain one's role as an observer but not revealing what one is looking for, or complete openness. To complicate matters further, a field observer may be a nonparticipant at one stage of a study and a participant at a later stage or may use different degrees of concealment at different stages of a study. Thus, the two-way classification into participant–nonparticipant and concealed–unconcealed is an oversimplification.

Having admitted this, let us make an artificial break at whether the observer participates at all and whether the observer tries to conceal his or her purpose. It will then be possible to get a feel for the various combinations by briefly considering examples of each. References for each example are shown in the appropriate cells of Table 3.1.

Participant field observation is fairly common. The Gans study described earlier is an example. Because he did not reveal his purpose, Gans was a concealed participant observer. Sociologist Laud Humphreys played the role of "watchqueen" in order to observe homosexual activity at highway rest stops (Humphreys, 1970). The watchqueen stands watch at the restroom door and warns those inside when someone approaches. Because he could not reveal his purpose and still hope to see the behavior he wanted to study, Humphreys was also a concealed participant observer. Rosenhan (1973) and several assistants faked paranoid symptoms and got them-

Table 3.1   EXAMPLES OF FIELD OBSERVATION STUDIES CLASSIFIED BY DEGREES OF PARTICIPATION AND CONCEALMENT

| | | Participation | |
		Participant	Nonparticipant
Concealment	Concealed	Gans (1962) (Living in "slum") Humphreys (1970) (Rest-stop watchqueen)	Henle and Hubble (1938) (Hiding under beds)
	Unconcealed	Rosenhan (1973) (Mental "patient")	Browne (1973) (Used car lot observer)

selves checked into mental hospitals. They intended to conceal their purpose but soon found it unnecessary. They were, therefore, unconcealed participant observers. Their open note-taking was interpreted by the staff as another symptom of paranoia, but many of the real patients realized that they were faking.

Nonparticipant field observation is relatively rare. In a classic example of concealed nonparticipant observation, Henle and Hubble (1938) had researchers hide under beds in dorm rooms to find out what college students talked about. Sociologist Joy Browne (Browne, 1973) observed used-car salesmen over a 16-month period in order to understand "the used-car game." Her study qualifies as unconcealed nonparticipant observation because Browne did not play a defined role in the situation under study, and her purpose was known to the salesmen. Browne viewed her study as participant observation, but by the definition in this book it was nonparticipant.

Systematic Observation

Systematic observation refers to the observation of a small number of carefully defined behaviors in a particular setting for the purpose of testing specific predictions about relationships among variables. A good example is the public payphone study described at the beginning of this chapter. This kind of research contrasts sharply with field observation. The differences are summarized in Table 3.2. In systematic observation, immersion is unnecessary, the time frame is relatively short, and the procedural flexibility taken for granted by the field observer is not tolerated. The outcome is not a set of tentative hypotheses about how a social system works, but rather a test of a limited set of predictions made in advance. The data are quantitative, not field notes, consisting usually of frequency counts of relevant behaviors or other features of the situation. Likewise, quantitative statistical analysis is typical.

Because systematic observation involves quantitative measurement of variables via observation, it is concerned first and foremost with good measurement. The place to insure good measurement is in the planning of the study. Two potential measurement problems strike fear into the heart of any systematic observer and therefore should be dealt with when the study is planned. The first is vagueness in operational definitions, which can lead to inconsistent results when the same event

Table 3.2   DISTINGUISHING FEATURES
OF FIELD AND SYSTEMATIC OBSERVATION

Field Observation	Systematic Observation
High Immersion	Low Immersion
Long Time Frame	Short Time Frame
Flexible Procedures	Inflexible Procedures
Goal: Understand Social System	Goal: Test Limited Hypotheses
Qualitative Data and Analysis	Quantitative Data and Analysis
Tentative Hypotheses	Specific Hypotheses
After the Study	Before the Study

is classified by different observers. The second problem is "unnatural" behavior on the part of those observed, which can invalidate all conclusions from the study. The first problem deals with reliability of measurement, the second with validity of measurement. Both reliability and validity will be examined in more detail in later chapters. For now, let us see how they apply to a systematic observation study.

Reliable measurement. When a measurement procedure is unreliable, scores obtained using the procedure may differ greatly from the true or accurate scores for the objects in question. The difference between an obtained score and a true score is measurement error. For an unreliable measurement procedure, the average size of the measurement error is large and its direction is unpredictable. In such a case, the obtained scores contain a great deal of random error or noise. Thus, the scores do not provide a very accurate or precise reading on the variable being measured. By contrast, reliable measures contain very little random error or noise and thus provide a fairly accurate account of the variable being measured. It follows that if the same object or event is measured twice with the same measurement procedure, one is likely to get pretty much the same result if the measurement procedure is reliable. However, the results may vary greatly if the procedure is unreliable. In the latter case, the obtained scores contain a large amount of noise, and they are not accurate measures of anything. You can see that reliability is essential for good measurement.

How does this kind of thinking apply to systematic observation? It implies that one should have very clear operational definitions of the variables being observed. With clear definitions, two observers using the same definition and observing the same event will classify it the same way; that is, they will come up with the same score. On the other hand, with unclear operational definitions, the two observers may be unsure about how to classify the event and will very often come up with different scores. As an example, consider aggression. If the operational definition does not specify how to classify borderline behaviors like sneering or frowning, observers will make their own interpretations of such behaviors and may often differ from each other. Such inconsistencies can render the data worthless for scientific purposes. The moral is that the road to reliable measurement in systematic observation is through clear operational definitions.

There are two ways to achieve clear definitions in a systematic observation study. One is to devise an observation checklist, that is, a list of specific criteria (behaviors, physical features, etc.) that will qualify an event for each scoring category of the variable being observed. This might be the way to go for a variable like aggression. The list should be brief so that the observer does not become overloaded with things to look for during the observation. Such overload can itself lead to unreliability. Ideally, one wants a brief list of the best or most valid criteria for the variable under study. For aggression, the list might include hitting, kicking, throwing things at an opponent, etc. You can appreciate the challenge here. Just what should be on the list, and how exactly should the list items be described for the observer? For romantic love, kissing will not do. It has to be passionate kissing, and that means an attempt to operationalize the word "passionate." There is always the fear that a really good item will be left off the list during planning only to be seen once the study is underway. The researcher cannot change the definition during the study and combine data from two different definitions. In this situation, the researcher must choose between continuing with the flawed definition or starting over. Obviously, it would have been better to have thought of the missing item in advance. Devising good checklists requires experience, sound judgment, and perhaps some casual observation to get a feel for what the best indicators are.

The second approach to clear operational definitions for systematic observation is to devise a rule for deciding how an event should be classified. The rule should be simple and clear. These conditions are met when in the researcher's best judgment two observers using the rule would be very likely to classify the same event the same way. For some variables, the simple rule is preferable to the checklist. An example is the payphone study described at the beginning of the chapter. After struggling to devise a list of good behavioral criteria for coin-checking, the class finally gave up and adopted the simple rule that any movement toward the coin return would be classified as coin-checking. The class felt that this rule was clear, and the reliability analysis of the data showed that they were right. The rule approach is even more appropriate for some nonbehavioral variables. You could go crazy trying to devise an adequate checklist for classifying gender. Better to leave it to the private judgment of the observer. Private judgment becomes the operational definition, and it works fine, meaning that the classifications turn out to be both reliable and valid. Here again, it requires experience and sound judgment to know when a checklist or a rule approach would give better results. If in doubt, a pilot study comparing the two approaches is a good idea.

With either the checklist or the rule approach, the researcher must decide how to sample relevant events. Two sampling methods are common. With *time sampling*, the researcher chooses TIMES at which observations will be made in such a way that a sample of typical behavior will be obtained. The time intervals may be chosen either randomly (the luck of the draw), according to some purposeful plan, or by a combination of the two methods. Time sampling is useful when relevant events occur very often. When such events occur less frequently, event sampling is preferable. With *event sampling*, qualifying EVENTS are sampled randomly or purposefully. The coin-checking study illustrates the last possibility. The class decided that observer pairs would sample the first two short and long phone conversations witnessed at the mall. Note that the purposeful sampling plan of the class was based on convenience. Such an approach may lead to an unrepresentative or atypical sample of events. It is always preferable to use a sampling rule that avoids any obvious sources of bias in the events to be sampled. A biased sample of events may severely limit the generality or applicability of the findings.

You may have guessed how reliability is assessed in systematic observation. Pairs of observers classify the same events independently using the operational definitions devised for the study. The observer pairs must make their judgments independently, that is, without any communication between them about their decisions. Later the proportion of agreement between observer pairs over all events observed is calculated for each variable. This figure is known as the *inter-observer agreement* rate, and it is one measure of reliability in a systematic observation study. As a rule of thumb, the inter-observer agreement rate should be about .80 or higher to justify the conclusion that measurement was reliable. Recall that in the payphone study inter-observer reliability was perfect (1.00) for conversation length and exceeded .80 for coin-checking. Reliability of measurement is so important that any serious systematic observation should include an assessment of inter-observer agreement.

Some researchers disapprove of the inter-observer agreement rate as a measure of reliability in systematic observation studies. They argue that it does not take into account the level of inter-observer agreement that would occur simply by chance. Cohen (1960) devised a reliability measure, *kappa*, that includes an adjustment for chance agreements. Because Cohen's kappa relies on the logic of chi-square analysis, its description will be deferred until the next chapter. Although kappa is frequently used, it too has detractors (e.g., Burton, 1981).

Valid measurement.   Reliability deals with whether one has measured any variable with precision. Validity deals with the more difficult question of just what theoretical variable or construct was measured and in particular whether it was the construct the researcher wanted to measure. Establishing validity of measurement is not easy. In general, a measure is regarded as valid if in the long run it performs in accordance with theoretical predictions. A valid measure of romantic love should be higher in situations where theory would predict that romantic love is higher, for instance, for an engaged couple as compared to a casually dating couple. When a result turns out as predicted, that is evidence for the validity of both the measures in the study and the theory tested. When a prediction fails, it is not clear whether the fault lies with invalid measures or an invalid theory. To avoid this problem, researchers try to build validity into their measures when planning the study.

In systematic observation, the same careful thought that leads to reliable operational definitions should also increase the likelihood of valid definitions. The discussion of the checklist approach emphasized that the list members should not only be clear but also "the best or most valid criteria for the variable under study." Similarly, the discussion of the rule approach emphasized that the rule should not only be clear, but also lead to valid classifications. Again, the preparation that leads to valid measurement should include careful thought, discussion with anyone who has knowledge of the variables being studied, thorough review of the existing literature to see what measures are already available, and perhaps even a pilot study to check out the performance of one's measures. Careful preparation can help the researcher avoid later disappointment.

There is a special threat to validity in systematic observation that cannot be countered by carefully prepared definitions. It is the fear that you will be spotted by those you are observing and that having spotted you, they will not act naturally. If awareness of being measured changes a person's behavior, the resulting measure is said to be *reactive*, a clear threat to valid measurement. When people know they are being observed, they often react in strange ways, such as wiggling their fingers, sticking out their tongues, or dancing around. Sometimes they do virtuous things, like helping other people, that they would not normally do. You may have the best operational definition in the world, but if people do not act the way they normally would, your scores will be invalid measures of their typical behavior.

For systematic observation of ongoing behavior, the way to avoid this problem is *unobtrusive measurement*. That is, you should observe in a way that does not affect the behavior being studied. The safest approach is physical concealment: Hide behind the proverbial potted plant. If that is not possible, blend in with the crowd or the nearest wall (or both) so that you do not stand out as an observer. In some situations (e.g., an adult observing on a children's playground), neither approach may be possible. Then you have no choice but to stick around until your observees get used to you. When the novelty of having you around wears off, they will return to their typical behavior. At least you hope that will happen, and it may take a long time. If you cannot afford to wait and you have been spotted, you may as well give up and return another time with a better plan for concealment. Your chances for valid observations on this occasion are zero.

As a review of field and systematic observation, what do you think is the most important similarity and difference between them? (Q2)

ADVANTAGES AND DISADVANTAGES

Like all research methods, observation studies have both advantages and disadvantages. One advantage is that observation methods do not require conversation. Observation is often supplemented by conversation with those observed, especially in participant observation, but conversation is never required. As a result, observation can be more unobtrusive than other methods. That is, people can be observed without ever knowing it and are thus more likely to act naturally than if they knew they were being studied.

A second advantage of observation methods is that they are economical in terms of money and equipment. Often the only equipment needed is paper and pencil, perhaps a clipboard, and maybe a timing device. Observation is ideally suited for researchers with a limited budget.

A third advantage of observation is that it is typically done in natural settings and is thus more likely than other methods to produce results that are valid for the so-called real world. There is a fancy phrase to describe this property: *ecological validity*. Observation methods have more ecological validity than methods carried out in laboratory settings.

There are some disadvantages to observation methods. Offsetting the economy in terms of money and equipment is the expense in terms of time. Observation typically requires long hours of waiting around for something to happen, especially in field observations. Discomfort often goes with the investment in time. Like the mail carrier, the observer may have to endure rain, sleet, snow, and sometimes even dark of night, not to mention being cooped up for long hours in an uncomfortable hiding place. Still, like the mail, the observation must go through despite all obstacles.

The discomforts just described may be seen as sources of stress for the observer. There are other stressors besides discomfort, especially for participant observers.

One observes illegal activities and must face the ethical stress of deciding what, if anything, to do about them. If an observer's cover is blown, the observer may be in the same sort of danger as an undercover police officer. The stress of emotional involvement with those observed, especially if they are disadvantaged, is a real possibility. Sometimes observers face the threat of a change in their own personalities, as might happen when an observer lives among mental patients for a long time or joins the police force for a year and witnesses a steady stream of violent crimes (e.g., Kirkham, 1976).

Finally, a problem that may accompany the immersion typical of field studies is the potential loss of scientific objectivity on the part of the observer. When one identifies emotionally with those observed, one is tempted to abandon the role of scientist and assume the role of spokesperson. As Gans (1962) discovered, this temptation is especially strong when those observed are disadvantaged. An observer must be prepared to deal with such tendencies or the validity of the observation may be compromised.

RELATED RESEARCH METHODS

This chapter concludes with a brief discussion of some related research methods. They may be considered variations on the basic method of observation. The intent is not to describe these methods in detail, but to provide an overview of possible variations on the method of observation. For more details on any of the methods described, consult the references provided.

Behavioral mapping uses observation to relate people's behaviors to specific physical settings. The goal is to produce a chart or map summarizing the behaviors that occur in specific physical locations. Such information might be useful to planners seeking to improve the fit between users and designed environments like offices, parks, etc. There are two ways to proceed. A place-centered map focuses on a particular setting and charts the behaviors of all people who enter that setting. The goal is to understand what goes on in a given setting. A person-centered map focuses on a particular group of people and follows them from setting to setting, mapping their behavior in each setting. The goal is to understand the typical behavior patterns of a particular group and perhaps to compare them to some other group. Behavioral maps have been made of libraries, hospital wards, and playgrounds (place-centered), and of residents of convalescent homes, school children, and public-housing tenants (person-centered). One enterprising observer even constructed a behavioral map of penguin behavior at an oceanarium.

Behavior is not the only thing that can be profitably observed. The discussion of systematic observation stressed the danger that behavior may be affected by the act of observing, leading people to behave unnaturally and compromising the validity of the results. The suggested cure was unobtrusiveness, that is, observing in a way that does not affect the behavior being observed. Concealment, blending in with the crowd, or waiting until the observees get used to you were suggested as ways of achieving unobtrusiveness. An alternative approach to the same problem is to observe not the ongoing behavior itself, but rather the aftereffects of the behavior. Such aftereffects are called traces, and measures based on them are known as *trace measures*. They come in two forms: accretion and erosion. *Accretion* refers to the build-up of something. Categorizing graffiti or garbage would be examples of accretion measures. *Erosion* refers to the wearing away of something. Observing unofficial pathways created by pedestrian traffic or wear and tear on floor tiles would be examples of erosion measures. Potential trace measures are limited only by the imagination of the observer.

Content analysis is another alternative to observing ongoing behavior. In content analysis, the researcher categorizes the content or form (or both) of some kind of media. Possibilities include journals, popular magazines, recordings, television programs (or ads), movies, etc. The challenge here is the same one facing the systematic observer—coming up with reliable and valid operational definitions of the categories to be used in the study. Content categories might include gender of models in ads or type of occupation depicted in ads. Form categories might include size of ad, location on the page, or proportion of space devoted to head versus torso in ad models. Again, possible categories are limited only by the imagination of the researcher. Although special problems arise, categorization of content or form may also prove useful with personal documents, such as diaries and autobiographies, and archives, that is, public records and documents.

SUMMARY

Observation studies are of three types: casual, field, and systematic. Casual observation is simply informal observation to get a feel for what is going on in a setting and to determine what the most important variables are. It is usually a preliminary to a more serious study. In field observation, the researcher studies a specific social or natural setting for an extended period of time using a variety of procedures. The goal is to understand in depth how the system works. Data and analysis are typically qualitative, that is, nonnumerical. Usually there are no specific prior predictions. Instead, a tentative theory or model follows the study. Field observations may be categorized according to the degree of participation on the part of the researcher and the degree to which the purpose of the study is concealed from those observed. In systematic observation, a small number of carefully defined variables are observed in a particular setting for the purpose of testing specific predictions about relationships among variables. Data are quantitative; statistical analysis is typical. Reliable measurement is sought through clear operational definitions and is checked by assessing the rate of agreement between independent observers of the same events. Valid measurement is also sought through careful framing of operational definitions and through unobtrusive observation. Compared to other research methods, observation has the advantages that it does not require conversation, is economical in terms of money and equipment, and is higher in naturalness or ecological validity. Observation has the disadvantages that it is expensive in terms of time, imposes a variety of stresses on the observer, and may pose a threat to the observer's objectivity. Variations on the basic method of observation include behavioral mapping, trace measures, and content analysis.

ANSWERS TO QUESTIONS

Q1. The results showed only that conversation length and coin-checking are related, not that the relationship holds only for Dutch people. It may hold for any population, a plausible alternative theory, pending further research.

Q2. Probably the most important similarity is the emphasis on accurate recording of observations. The two approaches differ in time frame, role of prior predictions, flexibility of methods, precision of measurements, and overall goals, as described in the text. It is a matter of opinion which of these differences might be considered the most important.

FURTHER READING

There are many excellent references for further reading on observation methods, including Hartmann (1982), Jorgensen (1989), Lofland and Lofland (1984), and Whyte and Whyte (1984). Sommer and Sommer (1991) provide further discussion of behavioral mapping, trace measures, content analysis, and working with archival data. Ittelson, Rivlin, and Proshansky (1976) describe how behavioral mapping is used by environmental psychologists. The definitive work on trace measures is Webb, Campbell, Schwartz, Sechrest, and Grove (1981).

REFERENCES

Adler, P. A. (1985). *Wheeling and dealing: An ethnography of an upper-level drug dealing and smuggling community*. New York: Columbia University Press.

Alfred, R. (1976). The Church of Satan. In C. Glock & R. Bellah (Eds.), *The new religious consciousness* (pp. 180–202). Berkeley, CA: University of California Press.

Becker, H. S. (1953). Becoming a marijuana user. *American Journal of Sociology, 59*, 235–242.

Browne, J. (1973). *The used car game*. Lexington, MA: D. C. Heath.

Burton, N. W. (1981). Estimating scorer agreement for nominal categorization systems. *Educational and Psychological Measurement, 41*, 953–962.

Cohen, J. (1960). A coefficient of agreement for nominal scales. *Educational and Psychological Measurement, 20*, 37–46.

Estroff, S. E. (1978). Making it crazy: Some paradoxes of psychiatric patienthood in an American community and a research/dissertation process to encounter them. Paper presented at the annual meeting of the American Anthropological Association, Los Angeles, CA.

Gans, H. (1962). *Urban villagers*. New York: Free Press.

Hartmann, D. P. (Ed.). (1982). *Using observers to study behavior*. San Francisco: Jossey-Bass.

Henle, M., & Hubbell, M. B. (1938). "Egocentricity" in adult conversation. *Journal of Social Psychology, 9*, 227–234.

Humphreys, L. (1970). *Tearoom trade: Impersonal sex in public places*. Chicago: Aldine.

Ittelson, W. H., Rivlin, L. G., & Proshansky, H. M. (1976). The use of behavioral maps in environmental psychology. In H. M. Proshansky, W. H. Ittelson, & L. G. Rivlin (Eds.), *Environmental psychology* (2nd ed., pp. 340–350). New York: Holt, Rinehart and Winston.

Jorgensen, D. L. (1989). *Participant observation*. Beverly Hills, CA: Sage.

Kirkham, G. L. (1976). *Signal zero*. Philadelphia: Lippincott.

Liebow, E. (1967). *Talley's corner*. Boston: Little, Brown.

Lofland, J., & Lofland, L. (1984). *Analyzing social settings: A guide to qualitative observation and analysis* (3rd ed.). Belmont, CA: Wadsworth.

Monette, D. R., Sullivan, T. J., & DeJong, C. R. (1990). *Applied social research: Tool for the human services* (2nd ed.). Fort Worth, TX: Holt, Rinehart and Winston.

Rathje, W. L., & McCarthy, M. (1977). Regularity and variability in contemporary garbage. In S. South (Ed.), *Research strategies in historical archeology*. New York: Academic Press.

Rosenhan, D. (1973). On being sane in insane places. *Science, 179*, 250–258.

Sommer, B., & Sommer, R. (1991). *A practical guide to behavioral research: Tools and techniques* (3rd ed.). New York: Oxford University Press.

Spradley, J. P., & Mann, B. J. (1975). *The cocktail waitress: Woman's work in a man's world*. New York: Wiley.

Webb, E. J., Campbell, D. T., Schwartz, R. D., Sechrest, L., & Grove, J. B. (1981). *Nonreactive measures in the social sciences* (2nd ed.). Boston: Houghton Mifflin.

Whyte, W. F., & Whyte, K. K. (1984). *Learning from the field: A guide from experience*. Beverly Hills, CA: Sage.

The Observation Study: Analysis

4

A generation ago it was common knowledge that in a typical middle-class American family the father was the head of the house and the mother was its heart. Social scientists used terms like "task leader" and "social-emotional leader," but they meant "head" and "heart." Although times are changing, the proposition is probably still true of most middle-class American families where the father is present. However, the proposition was never true of all cultures or even all subcultures within this country. In 1951 sociologist Fred Strodtbeck observed spouse interactions in three southwestern American subcultures (Strodtbeck, 1951). He found clear differences in the relative power of spouses when resolving differences to make a joint decision. Among Mormons, a male-dominated group, husbands won most of the disputes, but among the Navajo, a matriarchy, wives won most of the time. Husbands and wives fared about equally among Texans, perhaps a sign of things to come, although husbands still held a slight edge.

As a good sociologist, Strodtbeck wanted to know if there were any universal predictors of the outcome of spouse disputes. That is, were there any variables that predicted outcome regardless of subculture? It did not take him long to find one. When Strodtbeck combined spouses from all three subcultures and classified them according to who talked the most and who won most of the disputes, he obtained the data in Table 4.1. Clearly, the spouse who did most of the talking won most of the disputes. There is an obvious lesson here: If you want to win a marital dispute, outtalk your spouse.

Strodtbeck's study is another example of a systematic observation, as defined in the previous chapter. Two precisely defined variables were observed and quantified for the purpose of evaluating their relationship. Although in this case the results were clear, it would be nice to have methods for deciding the question of relationship when the data are not so clear. In this chapter, such methods will be explored for both field observations and systematic observations. The discussion will examine typical data for each approach, methods for describing relationships in the sample data, and methods for generalizing results to the population represented by the sample.

Table 4.1   FREQUENCY TABLE FOR THE VARIABLES
SPOUSE WHO WON MOST AND SPOUSE WHO TALKED MOST

		Won Most		
		Husband	*Wife*	*Total*
Talked Most	Husband	14	5	19
	Wife	5	10	15
	Total	19	15	34

FIELD OBSERVATION

Both the data and the analysis of a field observation are primarily qualitative rather than quantitative. This means that both the data and the analysis are primarily non-numerical and nonmathematical. Some numbers and some statistical analysis may be part of a report on a field observation, but they will usually play a relatively minor role. The data will be in the form of field notes, prose summaries of what the researcher observed. They will typically be in shorthand or abbreviated form, entered either covertly during the observation period or as soon as possible after leaving the field. Probably the most striking feature of field notes is their sheer quantity. As the weeks go by, they pile up in vast, awesome quantities. The greatest challenge facing the field researcher is to make sense of this monumental data mass.

The data analysis consists of the researcher reading and rereading the field notes, looking for valid generalizations about how the social system works. Gans, the sociologist who lived in Boston's West End for several months, found more than 2000 generalizations this way (Gans, 1962). The researcher then attempts to classify the generalizations and to find relationships among the categories. Ideally, this leads to some sort of diagram of the system, summarizing all of the important variables and processes and how they are interrelated. Joy Browne (Browne, 1973) observed used-car salesmen over a 16-month period and later produced several diagrams summarizing what she called "the used car game." Whether or not diagrams are used, the goal of the analysis is to arrive at a meaningful account of how the social system works.

Like all researchers, field workers are concerned with the validity of their observations and their generalizations. For field workers, validity begins with careful and objective observations, accurately transcribed into field notes. Problems at this stage can ruin a field observation. Given careful observation and recording, the next concern is making valid generalizations from the field notes. Two guidelines are commonly applied. One is to avoid overeagerness by insisting that a phenomenon appear consistently several times in a certain situation before it is considered "real." The second is to cross-check one's tentative generalizations by further observations or by other techniques such as interviews with multiple sources or examining archival documents. Multiple confirmation from a variety of sources increases the researcher's confidence in the validity of a conclusion.

Even with all of the safeguards just described, some social scientists are uncomfortable with field observation as a scientific method. They object to the nonquantitative nature of the data and the analysis. Most of all, they object to the after-the-fact nature of the interpretations placed on the data: Too much danger of "seeing what you want to see" and of "failing to explore plausible alternative explanations," they charge. It may be possible to counter these charges to some extent. Still, it is this kind of criticism that leads many field workers to view their conclusions as tentative hypotheses, rather than as truths set in stone. The personal journal accompanying the Gans (1962) study is an excellent example of this kind of humility. From a scientific standpoint, there is much to be said for this attitude.

SYSTEMATIC OBSERVATION

The data from a systematic observation study are typically quantitative (i.e., numerical) rather than qualitative. Data analysis for quantitative data has two goals. One is to summarize or describe the scores for the *sample*, that is, the units (usually people) actually included in the study. Statistical procedures for doing so are known as *descriptive statistics*. The second goal is to generalize conclusions to the larger set of units represented by the sample, that is, the *population*. Statistical procedures for generalization are known as *inferential statistics* because they allow inductive inferences or generalizations about the population. Chapter 1 placed great emphasis on the goal of generalization. Describing the sample may be seen as a preliminary to the basic goal of generalizing to the population. What researchers want to describe and generalize are relationships between variables. Chapter 1 also made the point that generalizations about relationships are the most common and important kinds of generalizations that social scientists want to make. A healthy attitude about statistical procedures, therefore, is to see them as a means to an end, not as an end in themselves.

Appropriate statistical procedures for a given situation depend on the kind of data one has. The coverage of statistical procedures in this chapter assumes that the data are very simple, which is often the case in a systematic observation study. Specifically, assume that a researcher has measured two variables via systematic observation and that each variable has only a small number of possible values. As a concrete example, consider the payphone study of the previous chapter. One variable was conversation length, with values of short and long. The other variable was coin-checking, with values of yes and no. As you know, data from such a study can be summarized in a frequency table which shows how frequently each value of either variable was paired with each value of the other variable.

Because pairs of observers watched the same events in the payphone study, it is necessary to split up the pairs before summarizing the results. Suppose one member of each observer pair is randomly designated (by a coin toss) as Observer #1 and the other member as Observer #2. The results for all the Observers #1 are then pooled in a 2×2 frequency table based on the variables conversation length and coin-checking. The same thing is done in a separate table for all the Observers #2. If reliability is good (and, as you know, it was), the two tables should be very similar. In fact, if reliability is perfect, they will be identical. In other words, good reliability means that the observer pairs usually agree on what they saw. From here on, consider only one of the frequency tables, say the one for Observers #1. Table 4.2 shows how the results for Observers #1 might have turned out. All the analyses described for this table could and should be done for both tables if they are not identical. First, appropriate descriptive statistics for such a table will be considered. Then inferential statistics will be discussed.

Table 4.2 FREQUENCY TABLE FOR THE
VARIABLES CONVERSATION LENGTH AND COIN-CHECKING

		Conversation Length		
		Short	Long	Total
Coin-Checking	Yes	61	19	80
	No	9	11	20
	Total	70	30	100

Descriptive Statistics

The first point to note is that the frequency table is itself a descriptive statistic. It summarizes the results from 100 separate observations in a way that allows you to begin to see whether or not the variables are related in the sample. To carry this process one step further, you should do the analysis described in Chapter 2 for using all the data in a 2×2 frequency table to decide whether two variables are related. That is, select one value of either variable and compute its proportion or rate of occurrence separately at each value of the other variable. In this table, it seems natural to compute the rate of coin-checking separately for short and long conversations. For short conversations, $p(\text{Yes} \mid \text{Short}) = 61/70 = .87$; for long conversations, $p(\text{Yes} \mid \text{Long}) = 19/30 = .63$. Thus, the rate of coin-checking is higher for short conversations, as predicted. In the sample, conversation length and coin-checking appear to be related.

Comparison of proportions is a good way of showing whether or not there is a relationship in the sample, but it has a serious drawback. When marginal totals are unequal, the size of the difference between the proportions depends on which variable is used in the numerator (top) of the proportions. If you compute the proportion of short conversations separately for the yes and no values of coin-checking, you find that $p(\text{Short} \mid \text{Yes}) = 61/80 = .76$ and $p(\text{Short} \mid \text{No}) = 9/20 = .45$. The difference between .76 and .45 is not the same as the difference between .87 and .63. So you cannot safely interpret the size of the difference between the proportions as indicating the strength of the relationship between the variables. This problem is even worse for larger contingency tables where there are more than two proportions in the set to be compared to each other.

The discussion in Chapter 2 indicated that this problem does not arise when the variables are unrelated. In that case, the proportions in each set are equal, and the difference between them is zero regardless of which variable is chosen for the numerator of the computation. However, the case of no relationship is a special case. Whenever there is a relationship and the marginal totals are unequal, the proportions in a set are not equal, but the difference between them depends on which variable is used in the numerator. Thus, comparing proportions can tell you if there is a relationship, but it is not a good way to describe the strength of a relationship.

It is possible to summarize in one number the strength of relationship between two variables in frequency tables of any size with any marginal totals. One convenient statistic for doing so is called V or Cramer's statistic. The formula for V involves chi-square (x^2), which you will learn about in the next section on inferential statistics. Thus, discussion of the formula will be deferred until later in the chapter. For now, bear in mind that V will always be a number in the range from 0 to 1 and may be interpreted as indexing the strength of the relationship between the two variables in the sample data. There are several other statistics designed to do the same job, and your instructor may want you to compute one of them instead. If so, your instructor will show you how to do the necessary computations. Some measure of the strength of the relationship between variables should be computed and reported in the write-up for a systematic observation.

Inferential Statistics

If you wanted to confine your conclusion to the sample of 100, you could pack up and go home now. However, as a social scientist, you would like to generalize your conclusion. In particular, you want to know whether the variables are related in the population represented by the sample. Because you do not have data for the whole population, you can never know the answer to that question with certainty. Your goal, then, is to make the best guess you can about the population based on the evidence provided by the sample. Statistical procedures for helping you reach that goal are called *inferential statistics*.

It is important to be clear in advance about the decision you are trying to make. With regard to the question of relationship, there are two alternatives: Either the variables are not related in the population, or they are related. In statistical terms, a statement about what might be true in a population is called a *hypothesis*. The statement that the variables are not related in the population is called the *null hypothesis* because it states that the relationship is exactly zero or null. The key feature of a null hypothesis is that it states an exact value. For no relationship, only the exact value of zero is appropriate. Thus, the only null hypothesis of interest will always be that the relationship is exactly zero (i.e., no relationship) in the population. The statement that the variables are related in the population is called the *alternative* or *research hypothesis*. It is really an umbrella statement, or an inexact hypothesis, because it includes an infinite number of nonzero relationships. Only exact hypotheses can be tested directly. Therefore, the null hypothesis is the one tested, and the outcome is a decision to reject it or not to reject it. If you reject the null hypothesis, you are implicitly accepting the alternative hypothesis that the variables are related in the population.

In Chapter 1, the term "hypothesis" was defined as a specific prediction about a phenomenon. The discussion stressed that theories are a common source of such predictions. Here it becomes clear that the "phenomenon" of most interest to social scientists is whether or not variables are related in a population. A theory typically leads to a prediction (hypothesis) that two variables are related (the alternative or research hypothesis). That hypothesis cannot be tested because it is inexact. So, ironically, the hypothesis of exactly no relationship (the null hypothesis) is tested in the hope of rejecting it. Thus, theory confirmation is achieved indirectly by means of rejecting null hypotheses.

With this terminology in place, let us see how inferential statistics can help you make a decision about the null hypothesis in the case of frequency tables, a common form of data in systematic observation studies. First, the logic of statistical inference in general will be discussed. The material here is extremely important. Ideas and concepts will be introduced that will be revisited in various forms throughout the remainder of the book. Next, you will be shown how the general logic of statistical inference is realized in a specific inferential statistic designed for frequency tables. Based on that discussion, specific indexes of the strength of relationship between two variables in a frequency table and of reliability of measurement for such variables will be presented. Finally, there will be an examination of the errors that are possible when making statistical inferences and some of the factors affecting the likelihood of such errors.

Logic of statistical inference.   The great majority of statistical inference tests are based on the same logic. The data actually obtained from the research are compared to the data that should have been obtained if the null hypothesis was true, that is, if the variables were unrelated. The latter data are called *expected data* because they are the data expected under the null hypothesis. The size of the discrepancy between the actual data and the expected data is summarized in one number, the *testing statistic*. The probability of the testing statistic, which is equivalent to the probability of the discrepancy between the actual data and the expected data under the null hypothesis, is then looked up in a table. If that probability is small, it means that the the actual data are very discrepant from what would be expected under the null hypothesis. That is, the probability of the actual data under the null hypothesis is very small. Therefore, you are inclined to reject the null hypothesis of no relationship between the variables. If the probability of the testing statistic is large, it means that the actual data are not very discrepant from what would be expected under the null hypothesis, and so you are inclined NOT to reject the null hypothesis.

You may have spotted a problem in the last paragraph. Having looked up the probability of the testing statistic, how can you tell if that probability is small (leading to rejection the null hypothesis) or large (leading to a decision not to reject the null hypothesis)? It is necessary to have some standard for evaluating probabilities, some clear dividing line between what will be considered small probabilities and large ones. This is accomplished by stating a specific probability value in advance that will serve as the dividing line. In statistical terms, this probability value is known as *alpha*, a greek letter whose symbol is α. The last step in the decision procedure is to compare the probability of the testing statistic, which was looked up in a table, to alpha. If the probability is less than or equal to alpha, it is considered small and the decision is to reject the null hypothesis. In that case, the results are said to be "statistically significant" or just "significant." If the probability of the testing statistic is greater than alpha, it is considered large and the decision is NOT to reject the null hypothesis. Thus, a clear decision is always possible.

What value is appropriate for alpha? You could decide by a rational analysis of the kinds of errors that are possible when making statistical decisions and which errors you are most eager to avoid in the current situation. This approach will be briefly discussed later. Or you could follow tradition and set alpha to whatever value is considered appropriate in your profession. For the social sciences, that usually means alpha = .05. That is, the probability of the discrepancy between the actual data and the expected data under the null hypothesis must be less than or equal to .05 before you decide to reject the null hypothesis. The rule is fairly conservative to protect you from deciding very often that two variables are related when they are not.

You may be wondering why there should be ANY discrepancy between the actual and expected data when the null hypothesis is true. The answer can be summed up in one word: CHANCE. The actual data may differ from the expected data to a greater or lesser degree as a byproduct of unpredictable and uncontrollable chance factors. Statisticians use the phrase *random error* to refer to the influence of chance factors. The previous chapter discussed one source of random error in a systematic observation study, unreliable measurement. Many other sources (sampling, settings, sloppy procedures, etc.) will be discussed in later chapters.

This discussion implies that the null hypothesis of no relationship in the population is equivalent to the assertion that any relationship seen in the sample is solely a byproduct of random error (chance factors). Good researchers try to limit the influence of random error as much as possible by running well-controlled studies, but random error can never be completely eliminated. Therefore, it is crucial to be able to assess its influence. That is exactly what a test of inference does. The probability of the testing statistic may be interpreted as the probability that random error alone could account for the discrepancy between the actual and expected data. If that probability is less than or equal to alpha, the researcher rejects the null hypothesis and decides that more than just chance (namely, a real relationship) is being reflected in the actual data. This interpretation of statistical inference as an assessment of the role of random error (chance factors) will be revisited many times in later chapters.

Note carefully that statistical significance means only that the relationship in the sample is unlikely to have occurred simply by chance. It does NOT imply that the result is important. The issue of importance can never be decided by statistical analysis. Importance is determined by the theoretical (not statistical) significance of a result, and that judgment is typically made by the scientific community.

A final way of viewing matters, which provides an opportunity for a quick review, is to note that the probability of the testing statistic, usually symbolized by the letter p, can be interpreted as the probability of obtaining the actual data given that the null hypothesis is correct. That is, the probability of the discrepancy between the actual data and the expected data under the null hypothesis is the same thing as the probability of obtaining the actual data given that the null hypothesis is correct. If D stands for the actual data and H for the null hypothesis being correct, then this is a conditional probability, $p(D \mid H)$, or the probability of "D given H." If $p(D \mid H)$ is less than or equal to alpha, then you have your doubts about H and you reject it. If $p(D \mid H)$ is greater than alpha, then D is not sufficiently different from what would be expected given H, and so you do not reject H.

In summary, tests of statistical inference typically proceed by first expressing the discrepancy between the actual data obtained from doing the research and the data that would be expected under the null hypothesis of no relationship in one number, the testing statistic. The probability of the testing statistic is then looked up in a table and interpreted as the probability of obtaining the actual data given that the null hypothesis is correct. If that probability is small (less than or equal to alpha), the decision is to reject the null hypothesis, and the results are said to be statistically significant. If the probability is large (greater than alpha), the decision is NOT to reject the null hypothesis. Now test your understanding by answering this question:

> *If p is less than alpha, is the value of the testing statistic itself large or small?*
> *(Q1)*

Logic of chi-square.   For frequency tables, the testing statistic for making inferences about the null hypothesis is called chi-square (x^2). The frequencies in such a table, the frequencies obtained from a research study, are known as *observed frequencies* and are symbolized by the capital letter O. Thus, Tables 4.1 and 4.2 contain observed frequencies. The frequencies that would be expected to appear in the table if the null hypothesis was correct and the variables were unrelated are known as *expected frequencies* and are symbolized by the capital letter E. Chi-square summarizes in one number the discrepancies between observed and expected frequencies for the entire frequency table. After chi-square has been calculated, its probability is looked up in a table. The probability is interpreted as the probability of obtaining the observed frequencies given that the expected frequencies are the correct ones, that is, given that the null hypothesis is correct. In symbols, the probability is interpreted as $p(O \mid E)$ which corresponds to the $p(D \mid H)$ in the discussion of the general logic of statistical inference. If $p(O \mid E)$ is less than or equal to alpha, reject the null hypothesis of no relationship between the variables. If $p(O \mid E)$ is greater than alpha, do not reject the null hypothesis. You can see that the logic of chi-square analysis exactly parallels the logic of statistical inference in general.

How to do chi-square.   The steps in chi-square analysis are summarized in Table 4.3. They will be applied to the data of Table 4.2. The first two steps have already been done. The cell frequencies in the table are the O values, obtained from doing the observation study (Step 1). The marginal totals and grand total shown in the table were obtained by following the instructions in Step 2.

Before chi-square can be calculated, you must determine the expected frequencies, or E values (Step 3). The formula for E for one cell of a frequency table is as follows:

$$E = [(Row\ Total)(Column\ Total)]/N. \tag{4.1}$$

The row and column totals refer to the marginal totals for the cell in question, and N refers to the grand total for all cells in the table. Thus, for Table 4.2, E for the short-no cell is $[(20)(70)]/100 = 14$. The remaining E values are calculated in the same way, taking care to use the appropriate marginal totals for each cell. For example, E for

Table 4.3 SUMMARY OF STEPS IN CHI-SQUARE ANALYSIS

1. Summarize actual data in a frequency table of observed frequencies, or O values.
2. Add across rows and down columns of the frequency table to get the marginal totals. Add either the row marginal totals or the column marginal totals to get the grand total, N.
3. Compute the expected frequencies, or E values, for each cell using Formula 4.1.
4. Compute chi-square using Formula 4.2.
5. Compute the degrees of freedom, or df, using Formula 4.3.
6. Look up the probability of the computed chi-square in Table A.1. Use the row in the table corresponding to your df. Within that row, locate your computed chi-square value relative to those given. Project to the top of the table to determine your p value relative to those given.
7. Reach a decision. If your p is less than or equal to alpha (usually set at .05), then reject the null hypothesis of no relationship between the variables in the population. If your p is greater than alpha, then do not reject the null hypothesis.

Table 4.4 EXPECTED FREQUENCIES FOR THE VARIABLES CONVERSATION LENGTH AND COIN-CHECKING

		Conversation Length		
		Short	Long	Total
Coin-Checking	Yes	56	24	80
	No	14	6	20
	Total	70	30	100

the long-yes cell is $[(80)(30)]/100 = 24$. The E values for the data in Table 4.2 are shown in Table 4.4.

Notice that the marginal totals for the two tables are identical. The E values must always sum to the same marginal totals as the O values. Thus, for a 2×2 table, an alternate method for obtaining the E values is to calculate one of them using Formula 4.1 and then obtain the rest by subtraction from the marginal totals. For example, having determined that the E value for the short-no cell is 14, you know that the E value for the short-yes cell must be $70 - 14 = 56$, the E value for the long-yes cell must be $80 - 56 = 24$, and the E value for the long-no cell must be $30 - 24$ or $20 - 14 = 6$. Test your understanding.

What are the expected frequencies for a 2×2 table of observed frequencies containing 50 and 20 in the top row and 10 and 20 in the bottom row? (Q2)

You are now ready to summarize the overall discrepancy between the O and E values in one number, chi-square (Step 4). Here is the formula for chi-square (x^2):

$$x^2 = \Sigma[(O - E)^2/E].\tag{4.2}$$

The symbol "Σ" means "take the sum of," and what you are summing across are the individual cells of the frequency table. So the formula is telling you to do the computation inside the brackets separately for each cell of the table and then sum the resulting numbers across all cells. The final sum is chi-square. What you are told to do inside the brackets, that is, within each cell of the table, is first to compute the difference between O, the observed frequency for the cell, and E, the expected frequency. Then square the difference, and then divide the squared difference by E.

For Table 4.2, the calculation of chi-square is as follows:

$$x^2 = [(61 - 56)^2/56] + [(19 - 24)^2/24] + [(9 - 14)^2/14] + [(11 - 6)^2/6]$$

$$= [5^2/56] + [(-5)^2/24] + [(-5)^2/14] + [5^2/6]$$

$$= [25/56] + [25/24] + [25/14] + [25/6]$$

$$= .4464 + 1.0417 + 1.7857 + 4.1667 = 7.4405.$$

Notice that $(O - E)^2$ is always the same. This is a special property of 2×2 frequency tables and will not generally be true for larger tables. However, for 2×2 tables, it can serve as a valuable check on your math.

Before the probability of chi-square under the null hypothesis can be looked up, it is necessary to know the *degrees of freedom*, or *df*, for the frequency table (Step 5). The degrees of freedom are related to the SIZE of the frequency table by the following formula:

$$df = (\# \ rows - 1) (\# \ columns - 1). \tag{4.3}$$

"# rows" and "# columns" refer to the number of rows and columns in the frequency table. Thus, for Table 4.2, df = (2 – l) (2 – 1) = $1 \times 1 = 1$.

Now you can look up the probability of the computed chi-square (Step 6). The probability may be found in Table A.1 in Appendix A. Table A.1 gives probability values for chi-square under the assumption that the null hypothesis is correct. Each row of the table corresponds to a frequency table of a different size, as represented by the table's degrees of freedom or df. Therefore, you are interested in row one of the table which contains chi-square values for tables where df = 1, that is, 2×2 tables.

Within row one of Table A.1, you see three chi-square values, each in a different column. The columns are defined by probability values, or p values. From left to right, the columns have p values of .10, .05, and .01. What you must do is locate your calculated chi-square value relative to the chi-square values given in row one of Table A.1. You will not usually be lucky enough to find an exact match, but you can determine where the calculated chi-square would be located within the row if it had a column of its own. Clearly, if 7.44 had a column of its own within row one of the table, that column would be located to the right of all three of the given columns. You now project to the top of that imaginary column, and ask yourself how the p value for 7.44 would compare to the three p values given at the top of the table. Because p values decrease from left to right across the columns, it follows that the p value for 7.44 must be smaller than any of those given. Thus, you can say that for $x^2 = 7.44$ and df = 1, p is less than .01, or p < .01. In other words, the chi-square value, which represents the overall discrepancy between O and E in the frequency table, has a probability of less than .01 under the null hypothesis.

The final step of the analysis is to reach a decision (Step 7). Because alpha was presumably set to .05, and p is clearly less than alpha, you decide to reject the null hypothesis and conclude that conversation length and coin-checking are probably related in the population. In other words, the results are statistically significant.

This game can be played with frequency tables of any size. Simply compute the E values for each cell using Formula 4.1, chi-square using Formula 4.2, and df using Formula 4.3. Look up the computed chi-square in the appropriate row of Table A.1, that is, the row corresponding to the df for your frequency table, project to the top of Table A.1 to determine the p value for your chi-square value, compare p to alpha, and reach a decision about the null hypothesis. In other words, follow the steps summarized in Table 4.3.

Test your understanding of how to do chi-square analysis by doing one for the frequency table described for Q2 earlier in the chapter: observed frequencies of 50 and 20 in the top row, 10 and 20 in the bottom row of a 2 × 2 table. (Q3) If you would like further practice, do a chi-square analysis of the Strodtbeck data in Table 4.1 (Q4) and of the Hazlett data on voting in the 51st Congress, presented in Table 2.2 of Chapter 2. (Q5)

Finally, remember this VERY IMPORTANT POINT. Frequency tables are fairly typical in systematic observation studies, but they are by no means necessary. If the data from a systematic observation study are more sophisticated than frequency counts of small numbers of categories for each variable, then chi-square analysis may not be appropriate. One of the more advanced methods of analysis introduced in the next chapter would be preferred. As the next chapter will make clear, it is the kind of data you have that determines the method of analysis, NOT the kind of study. This chapter emphasized chi-square analysis because it is an excellent way to introduce statistical inference and because frequency tables are probably more common in systematic observation studies than in any other form of research.

Descriptive statistics revisited. Earlier in the chapter Cramer's V statistic was mentioned as a convenient way of summarizing the strength of relationship between two variables in a frequency table. Discussion of the formula was deferred because it involves chi-square. Now you are ready to see the formula for V:

$$V = \sqrt{\{x^2/[(N)(L-1)]\}}. \tag{4.4}$$

In other words, take the square root of the quantity between the "{" and "}" brackets. x^2 means chi-square, N refers to the grand total of all frequencies inside the frequency table, and L is the smaller of the number of rows or the number of columns in the table. Thus, for Table 4.2, x^2 is 7.44 (see the preceding section), N is 100, and L is 2. The formula tells you to divide 7.44 by the product of 100 and (2 − 1), or 100 × 1 = 100. Then take the square root of the result. For Table 4.2, the whole computation amounts to taking the square root of $x^2/100$. Thus, V must be the square root of .0744, or .27.

Table 4.5 CATEGORIZATIONS MADE BY
OBSERVER PAIRS FOR THE VARIABLE COIN-CHECKING

		Observers #2		
		Yes	No	Total
Observers #1	Yes	78	2	80
	No	4	16	20
	Total	82	18	100

For practice, compute V for the data of Q3, the Strodtbeck data in Table 4.1, and the Hazlett data in Table 2.2 of Chapter 2. (Q6)

Reliability revisited. In Chapter 3, you learned that reliable measurement in a systematic observation study means that pairs of observers agree on what they see. Reliability for each variable is often assessed by computing the inter-observer agreement rate, that is, the proportion of agreement between observer pairs over all events observed. It was noted that some researchers favor a measure of reliability called Cohen's kappa because it takes into account the level of inter-observer agreement that would occur by chance. Now that the logic and details of chi-square analysis have been presented, it is a simple matter to describe Cohen's kappa.

Table 4.5 shows how coin-checking might have been seen by the pairs of observers in the payphone study. Note well that this table does NOT summarize the relationship between two different variables like conversation length and coin-checking. Rather, it summarizes the categorizations made by two different observers for a single variable, coin-checking. A similar table could be constructed for the other variable in the study, conversation length. This table shows how often the two observers agreed on coin-checking along one diagonal and how often they disagreed along the other diagonal. Let A = the sum of their agreements. Thus, A = 78 + 16 = 94 for coin-checking. Clearly A/N = 94/100 = .94 is the usual inter-observer agreement rate.

If Table 4.5 is viewed as a candidate for chi-square analysis, it is easy to determine the expected frequencies under the null hypothesis of no relationship between the categorizations of the observer pairs. Simply compute the E values for the table using Formula 4.1. The results are displayed in Table 4.6. The values in the cells with matching categorizations (yes-yes and no-no) show how often the observer pairs would be expected to agree simply by chance. Let C = the sum of their agreements expected by chance. Thus, C = 65.6 + 3.6 = 69.2. Cohen's kappa expresses the difference between A and C as a proportion of the difference between perfect agreement and C in the following formula:

$$kappa = (A - C)/(N - C). \tag{4.5}$$

Table 4.6   EXPECTED FREQUENCIES FOR TABLE 4.5

		Observers #2 Yes	No	Total
Observers #1	Yes	65.6	14.4	80
	No	16.4	3.6	20
	Total	82	18	100

Thus, for coin-checking, kappa = (94 _ 69.2)/(100 _ 69.2) = 24.8/30.8 = .8052. After adjustment for chance agreements, the original inter-observer agreement rate for coin-checking is reduced from .94 to .81.

Bakeman and Gottman (1989) suggest a lower limit of .70 for acceptable values of kappa. Thus, the coin-checking kappa of .81 indicates acceptable reliability. Whenever the inter-observer agreement rate is 1, kappa will equal 1. This was the case for conversation length, as reported in Chapter 3. As for which measure of reliability you should use, your instructor's opinion is the one that counts.

Errors of inference.   For the payphone study, the conclusion was that conversation length is PROBABLY related to coin-checking. You cannot know for sure if the conclusion is correct although the odds are favorable because of the decision-making procedure used. What is true of chi-square is also true of every other inferential testing statistic. The conclusion is necessarily probabilistic. It could be wrong. Whenever you engage in statistical inference, you leave the shores of certainty behind and launch yourself upon the sea of uncertainty.

Because the decision is binary (reject or not reject the null hypothesis), there are two ways to be right and two ways to be wrong. These outcomes are shown in Table 4.7. Imagine a world in which every time you make a decision based on a test of inference an elevator descends from the clouds, the door opens, and a disembodied voice from within says, "The TRUTH is that the null hypothesis is correct (or incorrect, as the case may be)." In this statistical paradise, you would be in a position to know what you can never know in real life, whether or not your statistical inferences are correct. Clearly, if you decide to reject the null hypothesis and the voice says that it is incorrect, you made the right decision. Likewise, if you decide not to reject the null hypothesis and the voice says that it is correct, you also made the right decision. Thus, there are two ways to be right, and they happen whenever your decision matches what the voice says. In statistical terminology, such favorable outcomes are called correct decisions.

Of course, there are also two ways to be wrong. That happens whenever your decision does not match what the voice says. In such situations, the test of inference has led you into error, and such unfavorable outcomes are called *errors of inference*. The two types of errors have both official and informal names. The error of rejecting the null hypothesis when it is correct, of concluding that there is a relationship when in fact there is none, is officially known as a *Type I error* of inference. Informally, it is called a *false alarm* because it is like turning in a false alarm, that is, claiming there is a fire when there is none. The other error, failing to reject the null

Table 4.7 POSSIBLE OUTCOMES OF A STATISTICAL-INFERENCE DECISION

		TRUTH	
		Null Hypothesis	*Alternate Hypothesis*
Decision	Reject Null Hypothesis	Type I Error (False Alarm)	Correct Decision
	NOT Reject Null Hypothesis	Correct Decision	Type II Error (Miss)

hypothesis when in fact it is incorrect, is officially known as *Type II error* of inference. Informally, it is called a *miss* because your decision led you to miss a real relationship. Just because you do not have the disembodied voice in real life does not mean that these errors will not occur. The null hypothesis is either correct or incorrect, and your decision either matches the true state of affairs or it does not. Thus, the possibility of error exists every time you make a statistical inference.

Naturally you would like to avoid errors of inference as much as possible. Thus, you need to know how probable they are and what influences them. In the case of Type I errors, you are in luck. The probability of a Type I error is exactly equal to alpha. Remember that the test of inference is based on the assumption that the null hypothesis is correct. That is, it yields the probability of obtaining the actual data GIVEN THAT the null hypothesis is correct, or $p(D \mid H)$. Thus, when the null hypothesis is in fact correct and you use alpha as the dividing line for making decisions, the proportion of times you will make the wrong decision (incorrectly rejecting the null hypothesis) must be equal to alpha.

That the Type I error rate equals alpha has the practical consequence of allowing you to control the Type I error rate directly by setting alpha wherever you please. If you wish to be conservative and minimize Type I errors, set alpha to a very small value, say .01. You might do this if you were very concerned about avoiding a reputation for crying wolf with regard to nonexistent relationships. Another situation where a low value of alpha seems appropriate is the one when you know that claiming the existence of a relationship will lead to harsh consequences for certain groups or individuals. On the other hand, in exploratory research where you want be sure not to miss any real relationships and are not much concerned about making Type I errors, you would set alpha to a relatively large value, say .10 or .15. Thus, where alpha is set should be based on a rational analysis of how important it is to avoid or allow Type I errors.

When it comes to Type II errors (misses), you are not so lucky. You cannot know exactly the probability of a Type II error. The reason is that a Type II error occurs when the null hypothesis is incorrect. Therefore, the alternate hypothesis is correct. However, the alternate hypothesis is not an exact hypothesis. It is an umbrella statement containing an infinite number of exact hypotheses about the strength of the relationship between the two variables in question. An exact probability for a Type II error cannot be determined unless you single out one of the infinite number of exact hypotheses contained in the alternate hypothesis. However, to single out one of them would be arbitrary. So you are left without knowing the exact probability of a Type II error.

However, some very insightful general statements can be made about the relationship between Type I and Type II errors. For example, if you lower alpha to avoid Type I errors, you make it harder to reject the null hypothesis, and thus you raise the probability of making the wrong decision when it is false. That is, you raise the probability of a Type II error or miss. Likewise, if you raise alpha to allow more Type I errors, as in the exploratory research example above, you do so precisely to make it easier to reject the null hypothesis and therefore avoid misses, that is, Type II errors. The general principle, then, is that lowering alpha simultaneously decreases the Type I error rate and increases the Type II error rate. Raising alpha has the opposite effect of increasing the Type I error rate and decreasing the Type II error rate. Thus, when it comes to setting alpha, you cannot simultaneously lower the probability of both types of errors. You must decide by rational analysis which type of error is most important to avoid and set alpha accordingly.

This business of setting alpha by rational analysis probably seems like the sort of thing you would like to avoid. Generally speaking, you can. Most disciplines in the social sciences have adopted a conventional value for alpha, a value that is considered appropriate to use in most situations. That value is usually .05, reflecting a pretty healthy concern with avoiding Type I errors. However, bear in mind that if you have good reason, you can and should depart from the conventional value for alpha. You have already seen one situation, exploratory research, where it makes good sense to set alpha higher than the conventional value so as not to miss possible relationships. On the other hand, if you have good reason to be cautious, if you want to be very sure that a relationship exists before saying so, then do not hesitate to set alpha lower than the conventional value of .05.

Now test your understanding. What kind of error was made by the boy who cried wolf? (Q7)

Finally, consider a point of view with strong support among statisticians and social scientists. It is this: The null hypothesis is always false in the real world. Any two variables in the universe are probably related at least to some small degree. Therefore, you should not speak of accepting the null hypothesis, but rather of failing to reject it when p is greater than alpha. The two conclusions are not the same. When you properly conclude that you cannot reject the null hypothesis (rather than concluding that you accept it), what the conclusion means is that any relationship between the variables was too small to be detected with the sample size and the test of inference used. There is a branch of statistics called power analysis that allows one to determine the sample size needed to reject the null hypothesis, provided one is willing to specify an exact alternative hypothesis and exact values for the probability of Type I and Type II errors. For relationships of modest magnitude, the computations usually yield required sample sizes that are unreasonably large as far as most social scientists are concerned. For practical purposes, the spirit of power analysis can be applied by saying that if you are satisfied with your sample size, and if you then fail to reject the null hypothesis, the proper conclusion is that any relationship between the two variables is too small to be of interest.

IN DEPTH: CHI-SQUARE

The purpose of this section is to help you gain insight into why the formulas used in chi-square analysis have the form that they do. Such insight is not necessary to do chi-square analysis, but it can enrich your understanding of the process and of statistical inference in general.

Chi-Square

Here are some brief observations on the chi-square formula. First, you may have wondered why it is necessary to square the difference between O and E. If you simply compute (O – E) for each cell, half of the differences will be positive and half will be negative, and the two sets will exactly cancel each other, yielding a sum across cells of zero. This can be proved mathematically. So the simple sum of (O – E) cannot track the discrepancy between O and E because it is always zero. To avoid that problem, the differences between O and E are squared, turning them all positive. Squared differences have the desired property: the greater the discrepancy between O and E in general, the greater the sum of squared differences between O and E will be. Second, the division by E in the formula simply scales down the size of chi-square so that it can be evaluated in terms of the theoretical values of chi-square given in Table A.1. Third, it used to be fashionable in the case of 2×2 frequency tables to include a "correction factor" in the chi-square formula, making the formula more complex. The correction factor reduced the computed chi-square, making the test more conservative than it would have been otherwise. However, Camilli and Hopkins (1978) showed that the correction does more harm than good. Thus, it was not included in this book.

Expected Frequencies

There is an important constraint on any chi-square analysis of a frequency table. The constraint is that the table being analyzed is being compared implicitly to the population of all frequency tables of the same size (number of rows and columns) and having the same marginal totals. Compared to all such tables, you want to know how discrepant your table is from the one table indicating no relationship between the variables. The constraint of being interested only in tables having the same size and marginal totals as the table of observed frequencies has important implications for developing two of the formulas used in chi-square analysis.

The first formula affected by the constraint is the formula for expected frequencies or E values, the set of frequencies that should appear in the table if the variables are unrelated. To see why this is so, you must appreciate an important property of any frequency table containing expected frequencies. Table 4.4, which contains the expected frequencies for the payphone study, illustrates this property. In Table 4.4, the proportion of coin-checking is the same for both short and long conversations (56/70 = .80 and 24/30 = .80, respectively), which is as it should be when the variables are unrelated.

Now for the BIG question. Where else in Table 4.4, other than within the two columns, can you find a .80 rate of coin-checking? If the answer is not immediately obvious, stop and think about it for a while. The answer is that the proportion of coin-checking is also .80 (80/100 = .80) in the column of marginal totals at the right side of the table. In other words, when you ignore conversation length, the rate of coin-checking in general is .80. It should be obvious that if you maintain the same marginal totals, the only way you could raise the coin-checking rate for short conversations above .80 would be to lower simultaneously the coin-checking rate for long conversations below .80. It follows that for these marginal totals, the only way the proportion of coin-checking can be equal for short and long conversations is if that proportion is also equal to the proportion of coin-checking in the marginal-totals column. This property is true for all frequency tables composed of expected frequencies. The proportions for any given value of either variable, computed separately for all values of the other variable, must be equal to the corresponding proportion computed from marginal totals.

This property of tables of expected frequencies has an important consequence. It can be used in reverse to find out expected frequencies when you do not already know them. After all, the marginal totals can be obtained from the table of OBSERVED frequencies (Table 4.2 in the current example). Once you know from the marginal totals that the proportion of coin-checking in general is 80/100 = .80, you can choose a frequency for the short-yes cell that will create the same porportion in the short-conversation column. To do so, simply take 80/100 of the marginal total for short conversations, 70, and put it in the short-yes cell. Similarly, take 80/100 of the marginal total for long conversations, 30, and put it in the long-yes cell. In this way, you produce the expected frequencies for those two cells, the frequencies that will yield equal proportions for coin-checking in the two columns. In general, then, you can find the expected frequency for any cell of a frequency table by using both marginal totals for the cell and the grand total for all cells. Because the order of doing multiplication and division makes no difference to the result, the steps just described are equivalent to the mathematical operations specified in Formula 4.1, the formula for an E value.

Degrees of Freedom

The second formula affected by the constraint of maintaining the same marginal totals as those in the original table of observed frequencies is the formula for degrees of freedom or df. To see what df means, imagine that you are tinkering with Table 4.2 in an attempt to find the expected frequencies by trial and error. Because the proportion of checking is greater for short conversations than for long ones (.87 versus .63; see the section on Descriptive Statistics), you might decide to try reducing the 61 in the short-yes cell by 3, down to 58. Given the constraint that you must maintain the same marginal totals, the moment you exercise your freedom to make the adjustment in the short-yes cell, the adjustments in the remaining three cells are completely determined. The 19 and the 9 must be increased by 3, and the 11 must be decreased by 3. Any cell in a frequency table in which you are free to make an

Table 4.8   FREE (FR) AND FIXED (FX) CELLS IN A 2 X 3
FREQUENCY TABLE AS DETERMINED BY THE STRATEGY DESCRIBED IN THE TEXT

		Value 1	Variable B Value 2	Value 3
Variable A	Value 1	FR	FR	FX
	Value 2	FX	FX	FX

adjustment of your choosing when tinkering (provided that the adjusted frequency does not exceed the smaller of the two marginal totals for the cell) is said to be free. Similarly, any cell in which the adjustment is completely determined by what you have already done is said to be fixed. Clearly, you could have chosen any cell in Table 4.2 to begin your tinkering, and it would have turned out to be free. Just as clearly, the remaining three cells would have been fixed. Therefore, for a 2×2 frequency table of observed frequencies with given marginal totals, df = 1.

For larger contingency tables, it is useful to follow a particular strategy for choosing the cells to tinker with. Always go from left to right within a row, and always start with the top row and work your way down to the bottom row. Get a piece of paper and make a 2×3 contingency table (2 rows, 3 columns), inserting any frequencies you like in the six cells. Add across each row and down each column to get the marginal totals. Now follow the strategy just described for tinkering, making small adjustments in such a way as to preserve your freedom to make such adjustments in as many cells as possible. Remember: you must keep the same marginal totals as in the original table. You will find that you are free to make adjustments in the left and middle cells of the top row but that the right cell in the top row and all the cells in the bottom row are then fixed. If you write "FR" in free cells and "FX" in fixed cells, the result should look like Table 4.8. Clearly, the fixed cells occupy the last column and the last row of the table. It follows that the free cells form a 1×2 table, smaller than the original table by one row and one column.

This strategy yields the same outcome for all frequency tables. If you repeat the exercise with a 3×3 frequency table, you will find that free cells form a 2×2 table, again smaller than the original table by one row and one column. You already know that a 2×2 table follows the same pattern; that is, the one free cell in such a table is itself a 1×1 table. The pattern generalizes to frequency tables of any size with given marginal totals, leading to Formula 4.3 for the degrees of freedom in any frequency table.

SUMMARY

In field observation, the data are qualitative, typically in the form of field notes. Data analysis consists of a careful examination of the field notes in an attempt to find valid generalizations about how the social system works. Ideally, the generalizations are tied together in a theoretical model. In systematic observation, the data are quantitative and statistical analysis is typical.

Data analysis of quantitative data has two goals: to describe what is going on in the sample (descriptive statistics) and to generalize conclusions to the population sampled (inferential statistics). Appropriate statistical procedures depend on the kind of data the researcher has. In systematic observation studies, each variable often has only a small number of possible values, and results may be summarized in a frequency table which shows how frequently each value of one variable is paired with each value of another variable. The relationship between the two variables in the sample data may be described by Cramer's V statistic, among others.

Inferential statistics help a researcher decide between two hypotheses about what is true in the population sampled. The null hypothesis is that the two variables are not related, and the alternative hypothesis is that they are related. Most inferential tests follow the same logic. The discrepancy between the data actually obtained and the data expected under the null hypothesis is summarized in one number, the testing statistic. The probability of the testing statistic is looked up in a table and treated as the probability of obtaining the actual data, given that the null hypothesis is correct, or $p(D \mid H)$. If the probability is less than or equal to a preestablished cutoff value, alpha, the null hypothesis is rejected and the results are said to be statistically significant. Otherwise. the null hypothesis is not rejected. Alpha may be established by rational analysis or by following convention which usually sets it to .05 in the social sciences. For frequency tables, the appropriate inferential testing statistic is chi-square, which summarizes the overall discrepancy between the observed frequencies in the table and expected frequencies under the null hypothesis of no relationship between the variables.

There are two ways to be wrong when doing statistical inference. A Type I error (or false alarm) consists of rejecting the null hypothesis when it is correct. A Type II error (or miss) consists of failing to reject the null hypothesis when it is incorrect. The probability of a Type I error is equal to alpha and may thus be controlled by setting alpha appropriately. Unfortunately, changing alpha has opposite effects on the two types of errors, so that one type of error can be lowered only by allowing an increase in the other type. A researcher must decide which type of error is more important to avoid or follow convention in setting alpha. Many statisticians and social scientists believe that the null hypothesis is never really correct and that failing to reject it can only mean that the relationship between the variables was too small to be detected with the sample size and the test of inference used.

ANSWERS TO QUESTIONS

Q1. If p is less than alpha, the value of the testing statistic will be large, indicating a large discrepancy between the actual data and the data expected under the null hypothesis.

Q2. Using Formula 4.1, the expected frequency, or E, corresponding to 50 (upper left cell) is $[(70)(60)]/100 = 42$. E for the upper right cell is $[(70)(40)]/100 = 28$. E for the lower left cell is $[(30)(60)]/100 = 18$. E for the lower right cell is $[(30)(40)]/100 = 12$. The last three E values could have been obtained by subtraction from the marginal totals, as described in the text.

Q3. Using Formula 4.2, $x^2 = [(50 - 42)^2/42] + [(20 - 28)^2/28] + [(10 - 18)^2/18] + [(20 - 12)^2/12] = [8^2/42] + [(-8)^2/28] + [(-8)^2/18] + [8^2/12] = [64/42] + [64/28] + [64/18] + [64/12] = 1.5238 + 2.2857 + 3.5556 + 5.3333 = 12.6984.$ From Table A.1, using row one because df = 1, p < .01. Assuming alpha = .05, you would reject the null hypothesis. In a journal article, you would express this finding as follows: "The two variables were significantly related, $x^2(1, N = 100) = 12.70, p < .01.$"

Q4. Using Formula 4.1, for the upper left cell E = [(19)(19)]/34 = 10.6176. By subtraction from marginal totals, E = 8.3824 for the upper right cell, 8.3824 for the lower left cell, and 6.6176 for the lower right cell. From Formula 4.2, $x^2 [(14 - 10.6176)^2/10.6176] + [(5 - 8.3824)^2/8.3824] + [(5 - 8.3824)^2/8.3824] + [(10 - 6.6176)^2/6.6176] = [(3.3824)^2/10.6176] + [(-3.3824)^2/8.3824] + [(-3.3824)^2/8.3824] + [(3.3824)^2/6.6176] = [11.4406/10.6176] + [11.4406/8.3824] + [11.4406/8.3824] + [11.4406/6.6176] = 1.0755 + 1.3648 + 1.3648 + 1.7288 = 5.5359.$ Thus, $x^2(df = 1, N = 34) = 5.54, p < .05.$

Q5. E = 79.4088, 27.5912, 38.5912, and 13.4088 for the upper left, upper right, lower left, and lower right cells, respectively. $x^2(df = 1, N = 159) = 90.3022, p < .01.$

Q6. From Q4, $x^2(df = 1, N = 34) = 5.5359$ for the Strodtbeck data. Thus, $V = \sqrt{\{5.5359/[(34)(2 - 1)]\}} = \sqrt{(5.5359/34)} = \sqrt{(.1628)} = .4035.$ From Q5, $x^2(df = 1, N = 159) = 90.3022$ for the Hazlett data. Thus, $V = \sqrt{\{90.3022/[(159)(2 - 1)]\}} = \sqrt{(90.3022/159)} = \sqrt{(.5679)} = .7536.$ From Q3, $x^2(1, N = 100) = 12.6984.$ Thus, $V = \sqrt{\{12.6984/[(100)(2 - 1)]\}} = \sqrt{(12.6984/100)} = \sqrt{(.1270)} = .3564.$

Q7. The boy who cried wolf made a Type I error, a false alarm, because he claimed there was a wolf when there was not. The moral of the fable is that Type I errors can get you a reputation for seeing things (i.e., relationships) that are not real. That is why scientists are eager to avoid them and usually set alpha pretty low.

FURTHER READING

For an amusing and insightful discussion of errors of inference and of many other topics related to modern statistical analysis, see Cohen (1990).

REFERENCES

Bakeman, R., & Gottman, J. M. (1989). *Observing interaction: An introduction to sequential analysis.* Cambridge: Cambridge University Press.

Browne, J. (1973). *The used car game.* Lexington, MA: D.C. Heath.

Camilli, G., & Hopkins, K. D. (1978). Applicability of chi square to 2×2 contingency tables with small expected frequencies. *Psychological Bulletin, 85,* 163–167.

Cohen, J. (1990). Things I have learned (so far). *American Psychologist, 45,* 1304–1312.

Gans, H. (1962). *Urban villagers.* New York: Free Press.

Strodtbeck, F. L. (1951). Husband-wife interaction over revealed differences. *American Sociological Review, 16,* 468–473.

Measurement: Types and Levels

5

If you were paying close attention to the research examples in previous chapters, you may have been unhappy with some of the measurement procedures. You may have felt that the studies used rather coarse measurement (few possible values) when it seemed likely that better measurement (more possible values) could have been achieved. For example, the previous two chapters discussed a study of the relationship between conversation length and coin-checking when using a payphone. You may have wondered why the payphone study had just two values of each variable, when it seemed clear that finer distinctions could have been made. Instead of "short" and "long" as values for conversation length, why not simply use the duration of the conversation in seconds? Likewise, instead of "yes" and "no" as values for coin-checking, why not simply use the number of qualifying coin-checking behaviors that occurred during the observation period? Generally speaking, why not use a finer measure when it seems readily available?

If you had these misgivings, congratulations. Your objections are legitimate. The only reason the payphone study had coarse measures instead of the finer ones that seemed available was so that the book could begin the discussion of relationships with very simple types of data. You must admit that you learned a lot about relationships by looking at the simple case of frequency tables. In practice, a researcher probably would have used the more sophisticated measures just described. Of course, as you undoubtedly know, there is no free lunch. Sophisticated measures bring with them a host of new questions and issues to consider. The purpose of this chapter is to make a transition from simple to more sophisticated measures. That will done by stepping back and considering the topic of measurement in detail. The result will be a classification of types of data, typical research situations, and typical methods of data analysis. That classification will serve as a framework for the remainder of this book.

This chapter begins by examining the types of measures that are available to social scientists. It then explores the concept of levels of measurement and its implications for interpreting measures and for selecting appropriate methods of statistical analysis. If you master the material in this chapter, you will be able to look ahead and see, in a general way, where the rest of the book is headed.

TYPES OF MEASURES

Chapter 2 defined measurement as any procedure for determining values for objects of interest on a variable of interest. The number of specific measurement procedures is virtually unlimited. However, near the end of Chapter 2, nonexperimental research methods were classified into two categories based on how the variables of the study are measured. The two categories were observation studies, which use observational measures, and survey research, which uses self-report measures. Thus, measurement procedures may be classified into two categories, observational and self-report. With the help of Figure 5.1, these two categories will now be explored to give you a feel for the variety of specific measurement procedures available to the social scientist.

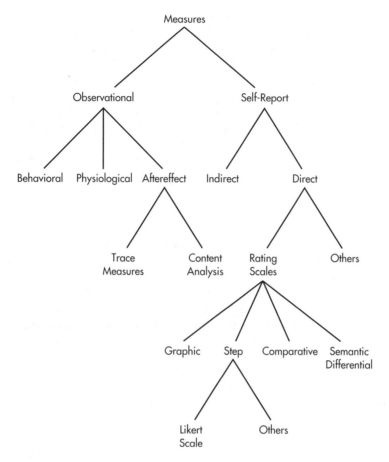

Figure 5.1
Types of measures.

Observational Measures

By definition, observational measures are derived from observation of ongoing behavior or its aftereffects. Scores are derived from the observer's judgment about which measurement category is best matched by what was observed. Clarity in defining the qualifying criteria for each measurement category is essential for this approach to be successful. The previous two chapters explored observational studies and measures at great length, so there is no need to multiply examples here. Note that it is possible to have more than two measurement categories or values for any variable in an observation study and thus possible to achieve finer measurement.

Observational measures may be subdivided further into three categories, as shown in Figure 5.1. The first is observation of ongoing visible-to-the-naked-eye behavior, a category that may be called *behavioral* measures. An example is to classify ongoing behavior according to its aggressive content. The second category is observation of ongoing but nonvisible behavior. This category includes both internal behavior, such as brain waves, and external behavior that is too subtle to be seen with the naked eye, such as slight changes in muscle tension. In these situations, the observer's naked eye must be aided by sophisticated recording equipment to render the invisible behavior visible. Such measures are usually referred to as *physiological* measures. The last category involves the observation of the aftereffects of previous behavior and includes trace measures and content analysis as described in Chapter 3. There is no agreed-upon name for this category. In this book, such measures are called *aftereffect* measures.

Self-Report Measures

By definition, self-report measures are based on reports about the participants who are being measured. Typically, the participants make their own judgments and then tell the researcher about their status on the variable being measured. In a sense, this is second-hand information because relevant behavior is not being observed directly by the researcher. Thus, there is always the danger of distortion or bias, which may result in invalid measurement. To make matters worse, some forms of self-report are really third-hand information. A third party tells the researcher about the status of the person being measured. An example is a performance evaluation by one's boss or colleague. The danger of distortion is even greater in this situation, as anyone who has ever been victimized by an unfair evaluation knows only too well. On the other hand, you should note that even observational measures rely on the judgments of the observer and therefore may be subject to distortion and confusion. In the process of measurement, the making of judgments cannot be avoided.

Self-report measures may be classified according to their purpose or their physical format. Classification by purpose yields categories like attitude scales, performance scales, consumer evaluation scales, sensory or psychophysical scales, and personality measures. As one example, consumer evaluation scales attempt to measure consumer preferences or evaluations of products and services. Several of these categories are described in more detail by Sommer and Sommer (1991).

As shown in Figure 5.1, classification of self-report measures by physical format yields two broad categories, direct and indirect. *Direct* or objective measures typically consist of clear stimuli, or questions, and responses limited to a choice among given alternatives. An example is an item asking how favorably disposed one is toward forced bussing of school children followed by a 5-point rating scale ranging from "strongly opposed" to "strongly in favor." *Indirect* or subjective measures typically consist of vague, incomplete, or otherwise ambiguous items followed by an opportunity for unconstrained or open-ended response. Examples are the so-called projective measures of personality, such as the ink-blot test. As you can imagine, scoring is much more difficult for indirect than for direct measures. Basically, the researcher must develop coding categories and do a content analysis (see "Related Research Methods" in Chapter 3) if quantification is desired. Indirect self-report measures will not be explored further.

Probably the most widely used type of direct self-report measure is the rating scale, which comes in a wide variety of formats. Some of them are shown in Figure 5.1. *Graphic* rating scales require the respondent to make a check mark anywhere along a continuous line anchored at either end (and sometimes in the middle) by descriptive adjectives such as "dislike" and "like." Fine measurement is achieved by using the distance of the check mark from one end of the line as the score. *Step* scales require the respondent to choose one of a graded series of response alternatives. The alternatives can be letters, numbers, adjectives, phrases, statements, or even simple drawings of faces with expressions ranging from frowns to smiles. The last approach might be useful for young children who cannot understand verbal and numerical alternatives. An example of a step scale is the item about forced bussing followed by the 5-point rating scale described earlier. *Comparative* rating scales provide a frame of reference or a standard of comparison for whatever is being rated. For example, if you apply to graduate school, one of your professors may be asked to serve as a reference. He or she will likely fill out a form requiring that you be compared to all undergraduates the professor has known, followed by a choice among alternative descriptions of you ranging from "outstanding" to "poor." A final example of direct ratings scales is the *semantic differential* scale, which measures the subjective meaning of a concept such as "drugs" or "romance." Respondents rate the concept on a series of 7-point scales anchored at either end by adjectives such as "good-bad," "strong-weak," and "active-passive." One can compute the average response to each pair of adjectives and thereby derive a profile of the subjective meaning of the concept in terms of the adjective pairs.

The most common use of rating scales in the social sciences is probably for the measurement of attitudes. Definitions of the term "attitude" vary, but the word roughly refers to how favorably a person feels about something. Given the importance of attitudes in the social sciences, you should not be surprised to learn that several procedures have been developed to measure them. One of these procedures, the Likert scale, is probably the most widely used attitude measure because of its simplicity.

A *Likert scale* (Likert, 1932) consists of a set of statements selected by the researcher to be clearly favorable or unfavorable toward an issue or topic. Each statement is accompanied by the same step scale for responding. A typical example is a 5-point agreement scale ranging from "strongly disagree" to "strongly agree." The statements are arranged in random order, and respondents are asked react to each statement by choosing one of the response alternatives that most closely corresponds to their feelings.

Scoring for a Likert scale proceeds in two steps. In the example above, responses to each favorable statement would be scored 1 through 5, corresponding to the alternatives "strongly disagree" through "strongly agree." Responses to each unfavorable statement would be scored in the reverse direction, with 1 assigned to "strongly agree" and 5 assigned to "strongly disagree." This approach is necessary because people with very favorable attitudes would be expected to agree strongly with favorable statements and disagree strongly with unfavorable statements. The scoring procedure thus quantifies each statement so that a favorable attitude gets a high number. Then it makes sense to take the second step, which is to sum the statement scores across all statements for each respondent. The total yields a fine measure of the person's attitude, with high numbers indicating favorable attitudes and low numbers indicating unfavorable attitudes.

An important assumption of the Likert approach is that all statements are given the same weight when they are summed. This is because all statements are assumed to be clearly favorable or unfavorable toward the issue or topic being measured. Thus, it is important for the researcher to avoid selecting items that are not clearly favorable or unfavorable. Pretesting may be necessary to achieve this goal. Given the right kind of items, the simplicity of the Likert approach accounts for its wide appeal.

LEVELS OF MEASUREMENT

The phrase "levels of measurement" refers to a classification of measurement procedures according to the kinds of information provided by the scores. Some authors use the phrase "scales of measurement" to refer to this classification system, first proposed by Stevens (1946). No harm is done as long as you do not confuse the term "scale" with the phrase "scales of measurement." The term "scale" refers to any procedure for combining responses to individual statements or items in such a way as to produce one score on the variable being measured. An example is the Likert scale described in the last section. The phrase "scales of measurement" refers to the particular classification of measurement procedures proposed by Stevens. To help you avoid confusion, the phrase "levels of measurement" will be used to refer to the Stevens classification.

As noted, the Stevens classification is based on the kinds of information provided by scores. To appreciate what this means, remember that the symbols most often used as scores are numbers. The abstract number system has several basic mathematical properties. When numbers are used as scores, it is an open question whether or not all of the mathematical properties of the number system apply to the variable being measured. A strong argument usually can be made that not all of the properties of the number system apply when numbers are used in a particular measurement situation. Thus, in any measurement situation, there are two sets of information: one is the system of numbers, and the other is the variable you are trying to measure. You are attempting to represent the variable with the number system, and you wish to know just how well the number system "fits" the variable. Varying degrees of fit correspond to different levels of measurement.

It is at times like this that students often wonder aloud why they have to study such a dull topic. There are two very good reasons for exploring this topic. The first has to do with interpreting what scores mean. If you assume that certain mathematical properties apply when in fact they do not, you may make spectacular errors in reasoning about what the scores mean. For example, if Andy and Maria have aggression scores of 20 and 10, respectively, you may be tempted to conclude that Andy is twice as aggressive as Maria. That conclusion rests on the assumption that a score of zero corresponds to no aggression, an assumption that is probably false. A second reason for studying levels of measurement is a very practical and extremely important one. The level of measurement determines the kind of statistical analy-

Table 5.1   LEVELS OF MEASUREMENT

Level	Distinguishing Feature	Example
Nominal	Identity (Same-Different) Information	Religious Affiliation
Ordinal	+ Rank Order	Product "Ratings"
Interval	+ Equal Intervals	Intelligence (as described in text)
Ratio	+ True Zero Point	Reaction Time

Note. "+" indicates that the level has all the features of the simpler levels plus the feature indicated.

sis that is appropriate for the data. Thus, you need to know what level of measurement has been achieved in order to choose the "correct" statistics for analyzing data.

Defining Characteristics

There are four basic mathematical properties of the number system that are relevant here. Each one turns out to be a distinguishing feature of one of the four levels of measurement proposed by Stevens. The discussion of these properties borrows liberally from Graziano and Raulin (1989). The four properties are identity, order, equal intervals, and a true zero. *Identity* means that each number is distinct. Thus, any number is equal only to itself, and any two different numbers are not equal to each other. It follows that numbers may be used to represent same–different information. *Order* means that numbers differ in relative magnitude and therefore may be ordered from smaller to larger. It follows that numbers may be used to represent rank-order information. *Equal intervals* means that the distance between adjacent numbers is the same for any pair of adjacent numbers. It follows that numbers may be used to represent distances between objects. *True zero* means that as far as the number system is concerned, zero truly means nothing. Therefore, the number zero may be used to represent exactly none of the variables being measured, if such a match-up is possible.

Notice that for each of the properties just described it was pointed out that the number system "may be" used to represent this or that. Whether or not such a representation is legitimate is the very point at issue. It will depend on the level of measurement achieved. That, in turn, will depend on how the scores are obtained and what kind of match between the number system and the variable being measured is justified by the measurement procedure. The four levels of measurement, their distinguishing features, and an example for each level are presented in Table 5.1.

Suppose that all the measurement procedure does is categorize objects. This might happen if you sorted cars into categories according to make or people into categories according to religion or political party. Another example from Chapter 2 is the categorization of hot breakfast cereals by brand name (Gruel versus Mush-O-Meal). You could use numbers as names for the various categories, but you could just as well use letters of the alphabet, words, or any other symbols. The only rule is that you must use a different symbol for each different category. Clearly, if you use numbers, all they are representing is same–different information about the variable being measured. If you named two of the categories "1" and "2," you would be grossly in error if you concluded that the "2" category represented more of the variable, or one unit more, or twice as much as the "1" category. The numbers are simply serving as category names, nothing more. Stevens refers to this very primitive kind of measurement as *nominal* measurement. With nominal measurement, the only valid information about the variable conveyed by the "scores" is identity information.

Suppose you asked people to rank-order five breakfast cereals in terms of how good they taste and then used numbers to represent the ranks. You would probably be confident that cereals given different numbers differed in tastiness and that the ordering of the numbers validly corresponded to the ordering of the cereals in tastiness. However, you would be hard pressed to justify the conclusion that the third- and fourth-ranked cereals differed in tastiness by the same amount as the first- and second-ranked cereals. You certainly would not believe that the second-ranked cereal was twice as tasty as the fourth-ranked cereal. Thus, the numbers convey identity, or same–different information and order information only. This kind of measurement is referred to as *ordinal* measurement. Notice that ordinal measurement has the defining property of nominal measurement, identity, plus an additional property, order. This pattern will continue to be true with more sophisticated levels of measurement. Each higher level of measurement will have all of the properties of all the lower levels, plus an additional distinguishing property.

It is easy to see that ordinal measurement is being used when people are asked to rank order objects. However, you are also probably dealing with ordinal measurement when you ask people to *rate* objects and the rating scale has only a small number of values. Suppose you ask people to rate each of twenty breakfast cereals for tastiness using the same scale: awful, tolerable, not bad, and very good. For scoring, you could use the numbers 1 through 4 to correspond to the responses "awful" through "very good," respectively. Clearly you could have confidence that two cereals with the same score were identical in tastiness as far as the raters were concerned and that cereals with different scores differed in tastiness. You could also believe that cereals with higher scores were tastier than those with lower scores. But could you justify the claim that two cereals with scores of 3 and 4 differed in tastiness by the same amount as two cereals with scores of 2 and 3? Probably not. Nor would you feel very confident about the claim that a cereal with a score of 4 is twice as tasty as one with a score of 2. In other words, you feel confident that the ratings have the properties of identity and order but not the properties of equal intervals and true zero. By definition, this means that you have achieved ordinal measurement. Thus, use of rating scales does not necessarily mean that you have achieved anything more than ordinal measurement. However, as you will see shortly, rating scales may be an excellent starting point for achieving what amounts to more sophisticated levels of measurement.

Suppose you measure intelligence by selecting a pool of test items that have been carefully pretested and shown to be equal in difficulty. The measurement procedure is to present the items in a random order and to allow only enough time so that a person of average intelligence can finish half of them. The time limit would also be determined by careful pretesting. A person's score on this test is simply the number of items correctly completed. Because you have evidence that the items are equal in difficulty, you can make a pretty convincing argument that each addition- al item correctly completed corresponds to an equal increment in intelligence. Therefore, you have confidence that the scores not only convey valid information about identity and order but also have the property of equal intervals. Such scores represent *interval* measurement.

With interval measurement, you can be confident that numerically equal dis- tances between scores represent equal distances in the variable being measured. In other words, Andy and Maria, with scores of 18 and 16 on the test described in the previous paragraph, differ in intelligence by the same amount as Juanita and Ted, with scores of 13 and 11. With equal intervals, comparison of differences is mean- ingful. However, you would still be uneasy with the claim that Andy's score of 18 represents twice as much intelligence as Bill's score of 9. You are not sure that a mea- sured score of zero corresponds to no intelligence, and making ratios is therefore unlikely to be valid. Still, being able to compare distances is quite an achievement. For reasons that will become clear shortly, interval measurement, or a reasonable approximation of it, is what most social scientists strive to achieve.

The most sophisticated measurement level is *ratio* measurement, which has all the properties of the preceding levels plus a true zero point. That is, measured zero corresponds exactly to none of the variable being measured. Latency measures or reaction times, widely used in the behavioral sciences, are a good example of ratio measurement. Zero seconds means that no time elapsed. The equal-intervals prop- erty is satisfied because one second always refers to the same amount of time. Clear- ly, latency measures also have the properties of order and identity.

(See if you can supply the reasons. Q1)

A related example of ratio measurement is the conversation-length variable in the payphone study if conversation length is measured in seconds. Generally speaking, measures of duration qualify as ratio measurement.

This discussion of properties of the number system that may or may not apply in a given measurement situation is intended to emphasize the first reason for studying levels of measurement. That is, the discussion should alert you to think about what numbers may or may not mean when they are produced by measure- ment procedures. Such critical thinking can save you from grossly inappropriate conclusions. Generally speaking, the more mathematical properties that are assumed by a conclusion, the more suspicious you should be. Thus, a conclusion that assumes ratio measurement should be treated with more caution than one that assumes interval measurement, and so on. When someone claims that Alex is twice as extroverted as George because they have scores of 20 and 10, the red flag of cau- tion should immediately go up in your mind. You must be able to satisfy yourself that all four of the properties of numbers (identity, order, equal intervals, and true zero) convey valid information about the variable based on the measurement pro- cedure used. Otherwise, the validity of the claim is suspect. On the other hand, if the claim is that Alex is more introverted than George, then all you need to do is sat- isfy yourself that the properties of identity and order are valid in this situation, an easier task. Thoughtful consideration of what scores may or may not tell you about the variable being measured is the mark of a wise researcher.

It is not always easy to tell what level of measurement has been achieved, regardless of how well informed one may be about levels of measurement. This is especially true when the decision is between nominal and ordinal measurement. The same measurement procedure may appear to be nominal measurement from one point of view and ordinal measurement from another point of view. Often it seems to depend on how the variable is named. Gender is an excellent example, although others could be given. If you use the numbers 1 and 2 as scores for the values male and female, respectively, then clearly you have nominal measurement—because females surely do not have more gender than males. However, if you rename the variable "femaleness," suddenly you have ordinal measurement, because females do have more of the variable than males. The paradox is that you are talking about the same variable and the same measurement procedure. So what's in a variable name? Apparently quite a lot when it comes to deciding about the level of measurement achieved. This disturbing example is mentioned so that you will not get too set in your ways and think that measurement decisions always have one clearly correct answer.

Despite the occasional ambiguity, it is worthwhile to try your hand at making decisions about levels of measurement.

So test your understanding by naming the level of measurement in each of the following cases: the four-star system used by movie reviewers to evaluate movies, the Fahrenheit scale for measuring temperature, running speed for the 100-yard dash, and place of birth. (Q2)

Types of Data

The second reason for studying levels of measurement is that they are related to the kind of data produced by a measurement procedure, and the kind of data determines the appropriate statistics for data analysis. Graziano and Raulin (1989) distinguish three types of data: nominal, ordered, and score. The first two correspond to the scores produced by nominal and ordinal measurement, and score data refers to the scores produced by either interval or ratio measurement. The reason for combining interval and ratio measurement into one data category is that the appropriate statistics for describing and making inferences about relationships are the same for both kinds of measurement. Meanwhile, nominal and ordinal measurement each have their own set of appropriate statistics for analysis. Collapsing four levels of measurement into three types of data for purposes of statistical analysis is typical of most books on research methods.

This book will depart from tradition and take the controversial step of collapsing categories of data even further. The category to be eliminated is ordinal data, leaving just two data categories. The two categories will be called coarse and fine for reasons that will become clear shortly. The rationale for eliminating the ordinal-data category is that it is seldom seen in its pure form in modern social-science research. Instead, the modern social scientist typically produces a refined version of ordinal data that very nearly qualifies as interval measurement. You might think of such data as near-interval data. The social scientist then treats the data as if they were score data and uses statistics appropriate for score data. The reasonableness of this approach will be discussed shortly. For the moment, two points should be emphasized. First, the position taken here is similar to the position taken by Kerlinger (1986), one of the grand masters of research methods. Second, if you ever find yourself in a position where you are convinced that you have ordinal data, nothing more and nothing less, then get competent statistical help. There are statistics designed for ordinal data and they should be used in the situation described. However, if you follow the methods of modern social science, you seldom will be in such a situation.

The reason for eliminating ordinal data rests on a very simple premise: If you have *fine* ordinal measurement, that is, ordinal measurement with a sufficiently large number of ordered categories or values, then your data are nearly identical to interval data. You have achieved what in the last paragraph was called near-interval data, and you may treat your data as though they were interval data without fear of making serious errors.

To convince yourself that this proposition makes sense, consider Figure 5.2. Each line represents the entire range of variation for some variable, say aggression. The left line has a mark at the midpoint. This line may be used to illustrate *coarse* ordinal measurement, that is, ordinal measurement with very few ordered categories. In this instance, there are only two ordered categories, represented by the two halves of the line. Assume that you can place people into one of the two ordered categories with perfect accuracy. However, because you do not know exactly where anyone falls within a category, you adopt the convention of placing them at the midpoint of the category. Of course that is not where they really fall, so your placements are somewhat in error. Question: what is the maximum error you can make with this kind of ordinal measurement? That will happen when someone really falls at the border of the category, and you have placed the person at the midpoint. As depicted, the size of the error must be one-fourth of the length of the line, because that is the distance from the midpoint to either border of a category. The maximum error you can make with your coarse two-category ordinal measurement is 25 percent—a pretty hefty error.

Now look at the right line of Figure 5.2. The marks on that line divide it into ten equal segments. The line illustrates *fine* ordinal measurement, that is, ordinal measurement with a large number of ordered categories (ten). Make the same assumptions as before: you can place people into one of the ordered categories with perfect accuracy, but you do not know exactly where they fall within a category, so you put them at the midpoint. Again, what is the maximum error you could make using this procedure? As before, the maximum error must be the distance from the midpoint to the border of a category. However, because there are ten categories this time, the distance represented by the maximum error is much smaller. As depicted, the error must be one-half of one-tenth of the line, or 5 percent of the entire range of variation in aggression represented by the line. Thus, the maximum error you can make with your fine 10-category ordinal measurement is 5 percent, a considerable improvement.

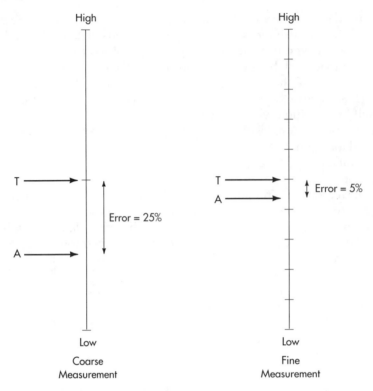

A = Assumed location of person measured.
T = True location of person measured.

Figure 5.2
Measurement errors with coarse and fine ordinal
measurement.

Perhaps you can see where this is going. With valid ordinal measurement, the finer you can do it (i.e., the more ordered categories), the smaller your error will be. In the limit, imagine an infinite number of ordered categories each having no width. Because the categories in this imaginary limiting case each have zero width, they are equal in width, which means you really have interval measurement. Thus, in the limit, fine ordinal measurement becomes identical to interval measurement. You can approach this ideal situation in practice by having valid fine ordinal measurement. With valid fine ordinal measurement, the size of the errors you can make in treating the data as though they were interval data becomes acceptably small. Thus, modern social scientists, knowing that they cannot generally achieve interval measurement, strive instead for fine ordinal measurement. They then use the powerful statistical methods designed for interval data, confident that any measurement errors will not be large enough to endanger their conclusions.

Table 5.2 TYPES OF DATA, TYPICAL
RESEARCH METHODS, AND TYPICAL STATISTICAL ANALYSIS

Types of Data		Typical Research Method	Typical Statistical Analysis
Variable A	Variable B		
Coarse	Coarse	Observation	Chi-Square
Fine	Fine	Survey	Correlation
Coarse	Fine	Experiment	Analysis of Variance
(Manipulated)			

Social scientists typically achieve fine ordinal measurement, or near-interval data, by combining trials or items, each of which involves valid coarse ordinal measurement. That is, they create scales. If you have one questionnaire item to measure aggression and respondents answer by using a 4-point rating scale, then clearly your aggression score represents coarse ordinal measurement, and it would be dangerous to treat the scores as if they were interval data. However, if you have six such items and you sum the responses for each person, then you have 19 ordered categories in your composite score. Provided you are confident of the validity of each item, your composite score, or aggression scale, represents fine ordinal measurement. By the argument presented here, you have near-interval data and you may treat the data as if they were interval data. This is the typical situation facing the modern social scientist.

For most practical purposes, then, types of data may be classified into only two categories, which may be called coarse and fine. Coarse simply means that there are a small number of possible score values, whether or not they are ordered. Fine means that there are a large number of possible score values and that interval measurement or, more likely, near-interval measurement has been achieved. If you are trying to determine whether or not two variables are related, then certain combinations of data types are typical of certain research methods and lead to typical methods of statistical analysis. This information is summarized in Table 5.2. The chapters on observation methods covered the top line of the table. The chapters on survey research will cover the middle line. The chapters on the experiment will cover the bottom line. Thus, the table provides a framework for this book, indicating both where you have been and where you are going.

Two warnings about this table should be emphasized. First, the strongest link is between the "Types of Data" and "Typical Analysis" columns. It is the kind of data, not the research method, that determines the appropriate statistical analysis. Second, "Typical Research Method" means only that the indicated combinations of data types are more likely to occur with the indicated research methods than with other research methods. There is some uncertainty here, and reasonable people might differ with the judgments about typical methods. Certainly other combinations of data types are possible with any given research method, and as pointed out above, it is the kind of data that determines the appropriate statistical analysis. Nonetheless, the table gives a reasonable picture of modern social-science research and therefore provides a useful framework for an introduction to the study of research methods in the social sciences.

SUMMARY

Measurement refers to any procedure for determining what values objects of interest have on a variable of interest. Measures may be classified into those involving observation of ongoing behavior or its aftereffects (observational) and those involving a report about the object being measured (self-report). Observational measures include those that can be made with the naked eye (behavioral) and those involving special equipment to record covert processes (physiological). Self-report measures may be classified according to their purpose (measurement of attitudes, performance evaluation, consumer preference, etc.) or their physical format. Formats range from direct (clear stimuli and constrained response choices) to indirect (ambiguous stimuli and open-ended responding). Response formats for direct self-report measures typically involve a rating scale: graphic, step, comparative, or semantic differential. In a Likert scale, commonly used in attitude measurement, all items are either clearly favorable or unfavorable, all responses use the same step scale, items are scored so that a high number reflects a favorable attitude for all items, and a final score is derived by summing or averaging item scores.

Interpretation of scores and selection of appropriate statistical methods for analysis depend on the level of measurement attained. That, in turn, depends on what properties of the number system are conveying valid information about the variable being measured. Four properties of the number system that must be considered are identity, order, equal intervals, and a true zero point. These correspond to the distinguishing characteristics of nominal, ordinal, interval, and ratio levels of measurement, respectively. Appropriate statistical methods are the same for interval and ratio measurement. Strictly ordinal measurement is rarely encountered in modern social-science research. Instead, near-interval measurement (i.e., fine ordinal measurement) is typically attained by combining responses to ordinally measured items, as in the Likert scale. Thus, two broad categories of data may be distinguished, coarse (few possible score values, whether or not ordered) and fine (near-interval measurement or better). Various combinations of data types, typical research methods, and typical statistical analyses are given in Table 5.2, and these combinations form a framework for this book.

ANSWERS TO QUESTIONS

Q1. Latency measures have the property of order because rank orders of latencies based on such measures are valid. They have the property of identity because equal scores validly indicate equal latencies and different scores indicate different latencies.

Q2. The star system for movie rating is ordinal measurement, the Fahrenheit scale is interval measurement (because measured zero does not correspond to true zero), running speed is ratio measurement, and birthplace is nominal measurement.

FURTHER READING

For more information on types of measures, including some not described here, see Sommer and Sommer (1991) and Kerlinger (1986). The latter book also contains a useful discussion of the concept of fine measurement. More advanced treatments of all issues relating to measurement may be found in Torgerson (1958) and Nunnally (1978).

REFERENCES

Graziano, A. M., & Raulin, M. L. (1989). *Research methods: A process of inquiry.* New York: Harper & Row.

Kerlinger, F. N. (1986). *Foundations of behavioral research* (3rd ed.). New York: Holt, Rinehart and Winston.

Likert, R. (1932). A technique for the measurement of attitudes. *Archives of Psychology, 140,* 1–55.

Nunnally, J. (1978). *Psychometric theory* (2nd ed.). New York: McGraw-Hill.

Sommer, B., & Sommer, R. (1991). *A practical guide to behavioral research: Tools and techniques* (3rd ed.). New York: Oxford University Press.

Stevens, S. S. (1946). On the theory of scales of measurement. *Science, 103,* 677–680.

Torgerson, W. (1958). *Theory and methods of scaling.* New York: John Wiley.

Measurement: Reliability and Validity

6

Some years ago, social psychologist Zick Rubin set out to investigate romantic love (Rubin, 1970). At the time, there was little empirical research on the subject and no established measure of romantic love. So Rubin did what all pioneers do when there is no road to travel. He blazed his own trail. That is, he developed a measure of romantic love.

It is one thing to talk about romantic love but quite another thing to measure it. Rubin knew that any attempt to measure something so romantic as romantic love would meet with plenty of skepticism from those who did not believe it could be done. He knew that he would have to provide convincing evidence that his measure was a good one. In the terminology of this chapter, Rubin would have to convince skeptics that his measure was valid.

Knowing what he was up against, Rubin developed his measure of romantic love in a series of carefully planned steps. First, based on his reading of the theoretical literature on romantic love, Rubin generated a large pool of questionnaire items that seemed relevant to the concept. He also made sure that the entire set of items sampled all aspects of the concept, such as physical attraction, idealization of the loved one, desire to share emotions and experiences, feelings of exclusiveness and absorption, etc. Thinking ahead, Rubin also generated a pool of items to measure a similar but theoretically distinct concept, friendliness. His plan was to show the world that his romantic-love measure behaved differently than did a measure of mere friendliness.

Rubin's next step was to purify his item pools, so he had two panels of student and faculty judges sort the items into love and liking categories, based on their personal understanding of the two concepts. Seventy items survived this screening as the most consistently sorted examples of each concept. Rubin then presented the seventy items in questionnaire format to a large sample of introductory psychology students. The respondents had to complete the items first with respect to a boy- or girlfriend and then with respect to a nonromantically involved friend of the opposite sex. A statistical technique known as factor analysis enabled Rubin to isolate the 13 best items for each concept. Those items formed the final love and liking scales for use in subsequent research.

Now it was time for Rubin to demonstrate empirically that his measure of romantic love was really getting at romantic love. He recruited 158 dating but nonengaged couples to complete his 26-item questionnaire, first with respect to one's dating partner and then with respect to a close same-sex friend. The love and liking items were intermixed randomly, and responses were made using a 9-point step scale ranging from "disagree completely" to "agree completely." Love and liking scores were computed by summing scores across relevant items, thus qualifying them as Likert scales.

The results showed that the love and liking scales were only moderately related to each other. So apparently the two measures were indeed getting at different things. But what where those things? An analysis of average scores showed that both sexes liked their dating partners only slightly more than their same-sex friends, but they loved their dating partners much more than their friends. Furthermore, love scores were strongly related to the respondents' independent reports of whether or not they were "in love" and with their estimates of the likelihood that they would marry their current dating partners. Finally, love scores for one's dating partner were only slightly related to love scores for one's friend and to scores on a social-desirability scale. Thus, the entire pattern of findings suggested that the love scale was tapping an attitude toward a specific other person with whom one is romantically involved.

Not yet content that he had won the day, Rubin decided to see if his measure of romantic love was good enough to predict theoretically relevant BEHAVIOR. He sorted the couples from the preceding study into two groups based on whether both partners scored above the median on the love scale (strong-love couples) or below the median (weak-love couples). Couples with mixed results were eliminated. Members of each group were invited to participate in an experiment. Half of the members of each group were paired with their own dating partners (the together condition); the other half were paired with someone else's dating partner, a stranger (the apart condition). The assignment to conditions was random within the strong- and weak-love groups. Members of each pair were seated across from each other in a waiting room and observed through one-way mirrors. The measure of interest was something called mutual focus, the percentage of total gazing time (time during which at least one partner was looking at the other's face) which was occupied by mutual gazing (both partner's looking at each other's face).

Question: What level of measurement is represented by the mutual-focus score? (Q1)

The important finding was that the average mutual-focus score was much higher for strong-love couples than for weak-love couples but only when members were paired with their own dating partners (the together condition). This was impressive evidence for the validity of the romantic-love measure.

Rubin's program of research is an excellent example of how measurement development and theory-testing research are conducted simultaneously by a serious social scientist. There are two points you should note about Rubin's approach. First, he sought to create a fine measure as defined in the previous chapter. Given the discussion there, you should not be surprised that Rubin ultimately chose a Likert-scale procedure. Having done so, he was able to use the powerful statistical methods designed for interval-level measurement in his research on romantic love. In this respect, Rubin's approach to measurement was typical of the modern social scientist. Second, Rubin had to provide convincing evidence that his new measure was a good one. In other words, he had to show that his measure possessed the two essential properties of any good measure: reliability and validity.

The concepts of reliability and validity in measurement were introduced in Chapter 3 on observation methods. There the discussion of empirical approaches to reliability and validity centered on coarse measurement in the context of systematic observation research. The purpose of this chapter is to explore the concepts of reliability and validity in the case of fine measurement, which is typical of most modern survey research. However, before that exploration can begin, it is necessary for you to become familiar with the concept of correlation. For finely measured variables, correlation is typically involved in the assessment of reliability and is often involved in the assessment of validity as well.

THE CONCEPT OF CORRELATION

The term "correlation" has been used in two senses. In a general sense, it means the same thing as "relationship." The two words are often used interchangeably. In a more specific sense, correlation refers to a particular way of describing the relationship between two finely measured variables. It is in this more specific sense that the concept of correlation will now be considered. To appreciate correlation in this narrower sense, it is helpful to review the concept of a scatterplot.

Types of Relationships

The section on "Types of Relationships" in Chapter 2 contained the one and only example of finely measured variables in the first four chapters. You may want to go back and review that section before continuing here. The variables in that discussion were frustration and aggression, and each was assumed to have been measured on a scale from 0 to 20—fine measurement, indeed. The purpose of the discussion was to show the advantages of making a scatterplot when trying to decide whether two finely measured variables are related. A scatterplot represents all possible values of one variable on the horizontal axis and all possible values of the other variable on the vertical axis. A point is placed in the space for each object measured at the location where the object's scores on the two variables would intersect. By inspecting the points for a large sample of objects, it is possible to see whether the values of the two variables tend to change together systematically, satisfying the definition of a relationship. One can also see what kind of mathematical function best describes the relationship. In fact, the scatterplot was used in Chapter 2 to illustrate the kinds of relationships most commonly seen in the social sciences.

A scatterplot is simply the logical extension of a frequency table. Both ways of displaying relationships contain essentially the same information. All possible values of one variable are represented along the horizontal dimension and all possible values of the other variable are represented along the vertical dimension. The difference is that each variable has a small number of possible values for a frequency table (coarse measurement) but a large number of possible values for a scatterplot (fine measurement). Thus, a scatterplot may be seen as a giant frequency table for displaying relationships when the variables are finely measured.

The trend of the points in a scatterplot allows one to determine the type of relationship between two finely measured variables. Figure 6.1, reproduced from Chapter 2, illustrates the possibilities. The points may fall close to a positively sloped straight line (Figure 6.1.a), a negatively sloped straight line (Figure 6.1.b), or a nonlinear (curvilinear) function (Figure 6.1.c). The most common nonlinear function encountered in the social sciences is a U-shaped function with its open end facing upward or downward. Of course, if there is no relationship between the variables, the points will be scattered randomly throughout the entire space of the scatterplot (Figure 6.1.d). For the case of frustration and aggression, one would expect the points to fall close to a positively sloped straight line because frustration–aggression theory predicts that low frustration scores will go with low aggression scores, medium with medium, and high with high.

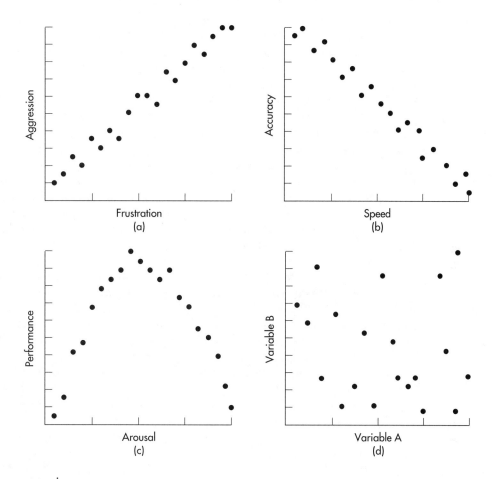

Figure 6.1
Scatterplot of a positive linear relationship (a), a negative linear relationship (b), an inverted-U curvilinear relationship (c), and no relationship (d).

The Correlation Coefficient

Suppose you wanted to further compress the description of the relationship between two finely measured variables. It would be nice if you could summarize the relationship displayed in a scatterplot by one number. That would be the ultimate in compact descriptive statistics. You know it can be done for frequency tables (Cramer's V statistic, Chapter 4), so it will probably not surprise you to learn that it can also be done for scatterplots. Assuming fine measurement, the appropriate statistic is known as the Pearson product–moment correlation coefficient or, more simply, the correlation coefficient, symbolized by the letter "r." Actually, there are several different correlation coefficients, but Pearson's correlation is usually assumed unless an author specifically indicates otherwise.

You will learn how to compute the correlation coefficient in Chapter 8. For now, it is sufficient to note that r describes the *linear* relationship between two finely measured variables. Because of the way the computational formula was derived, r is directly proportional to the slope of the straight-line function that best fits the points in the scatterplot. "Best fits" means that the straight-line function comes as close as possible to all of the points. In practice, no straight line will pass exactly through all of the points. Thus, the distance between any actual point and the straight line may be thought of as the error in predicting the point from the line. The formula for r minimizes the sum of the squared errors for all points, thereby producing the best-fitting straight line according to what statisticians call the "least-squared-error" criterion. The important point in all this jargon is that by using an objective criterion, it is possible to find the best-fitting straight-line function to describe the points in a scatterplot, and the correlation coefficient, r, is directly proportional to the slope of that best-fitting line.

The other important point you need to know about r is that the computational formula guarantees it will have a value between -1 and +1, inclusive. If the points in the scatterplot fall perfectly along a positively sloped straight line (which never happens in real life), then r = +1. If the points fall perfectly along a negatively sloped straight line (which also never happens in real life), then r = -1. If the points are scattered at random throughout the space of the scatterplot, then r = 0. To the extent that the points fall close to a positively sloped straight line, r is positive and close to +1. To the extent that the points fall close to a negatively sloped straight line, r is negative and close to -1. The last three possibilities are depicted in parts d, a, and b of Figure 6.1.

In summary, r carries two important pieces of information about the linear relationship depicted in a scatterplot. The sign of r (+ or -) tells you whether the slope of the best-fitting linear function is positive or negative. The absolute value of r (i.e., ignoring the sign) tells you how strong the linear relationship is, that is, how close the points are in general to the linear function, with a perfect fit corresponding to r = 1 (again, ignoring the sign).

Test yourself: Which correlation indicates a stronger linear relationship, r = .58 or r = -.72? (Q2)

Cautions

Three warnings are usually issued when discussing correlation. They all concern misinterpretations of what a correlations means. The first warning is that a correlation is a measure of linear relationship only. It follows that a large correlation provides clear information: the scatterplot is well described by a linear or straight-line function. However, the meaning of a small correlation is not clear because it has two possible interpretations: either the variables are not related, or they are related in a nonlinear fashion.

As illustrated by Figure 6.1.c, arousal and performance are likely to be related by an inverted-U function, with best performance at middle levels of arousal. If the scatterplot looks like an inverted U, then computing a correlation amounts to forcing a straight-line function on the data when such a function is clearly inappropriate. The best-fitting linear function in this situation, according to the least-squared-error criterion, will be flat with a slope of zero. Because the correlation is proportional to the slope of the best-fitting linear function, it follows that the correlation will also be zero. All this can mean is that there is no *linear* relationship in the scatterplot even though there may be a strong nonlinear relationship. The moral is that small correlations do not necessarily mean that the variables are unrelated. Before such a conclusion is warranted, the possibility of a nonlinear relationship must be checked out. The simplest way to do so is to examine the scatterplot. If any sign of a nonlinear trend is evident, then get competent statistical help. Advanced statistical techniques exist for describing nonlinear relationships. Remember: the only appropriate interpretation of a small correlation is that the variables are not *linearly* related.

The second warning is that if the researcher samples only a restricted range of the possible score values for either of two variables, the magnitude of the correlation may be greatly reduced. This could lead to the false impression that the variables are not correlated. Consider the strong linear relationship between frustration and aggression depicted in Figure 6.1.a. Focus on a small portion of the scatterplot near its middle, which is equivalent to looking at a narrow range of scores near the middle of each axis. If you expand that portion of the scatterplot to fill the entire space, the points will appear to be scattered throughout the space instead of falling close to a linear function. The scatterplot will look more like Figure 6.1.d than like Figure 6.1.a. The slope of the best-fitting straight line will be greatly reduced and so will the correlation. This may happen in any situation where a restricted range of possible score values is used. Presumably, this does not happen very often in practice, but it is worth keeping in mind.

The third and final warning is that "correlation does not imply causation," a famous phrase from statistics texts. What it means is that the mere fact of a strong correlation tells you nothing about what explains the correlation. Surely cause is involved somewhere, but you would not be justified in claiming that either of the two variables involved in the correlation is serving as a cause. There is always the possibility that the infamous third variable, sunspots, is the real cause. This discussion should sound familiar. The same argument appeared in Chapter 2 during the discussion of relationships and causation. It was pointed out that the mere fact of a relationship tells you nothing about cause. The current discussion is simply a special case of that general principle. The mere fact of a *linear* relationship does not allow you to pinpoint cause.

This principle is being emphasized because people commonly violate it in everyday life. If church attendance and crime rates are found to be negatively correlated over time, a moralizer will soon claim that church attendance reduces crime. Beware! It could be the other way around: high crime rates cause people to give up on church attendance. It could even be the mysterious influence of sunspots. The validity of causal claims in this situation cannot depend on the correlation alone. It must depend on other information and other arguments brought to bear on the situation. Such additional material must be examined critically to see if it is persuasive. Again, the general principle is that correlation alone does not establish causation.

> *Question: What conclusions are justified if the correlation between study time and grade-point average is .82? Same question if the correlation is .02? (Q3)*

RELIABILITY OF MEASUREMENT

The main use for correlation is to assess the linear relationship between two different variables. The concept has been introduced at this point in the book, however, because it also has something to do with measurement. As mentioned earlier, two properties that any good measure must have are reliability and validity. For finely measured variables, correlation is typically involved in the assessment of reliability and often in the assessment of validity. How that happens will be the focus of the rest of the chapter.

The Concept of Reliability

As noted in Chapter 3, a reliable measure is one that does not have much random error in it. Random error, or noise, in a measure means that the observed score may differ from the true or accurate score for the object being measured. The more noise, the bigger the difference between the observed score and the true score can be. Because noise is random error, the direction of the discrepancy is unpredictable. It follows that a noisy or unreliable measure does not provide a very accurate or precise indication of the true status of the objects being measured. A reliable measure, on the other hand, contains little noise or random error and so the observed score is close to the true score. It follows that the observed score is a pretty accurate or precise measure of the true status of the objects being measured. Fundamentally, then, reliability refers to the noise or random error in observed scores, which implies that it also refers to how accurate or precise they are as measures of some variable.

It is helpful to think of reliability in terms of a window of uncertainty around the true score. Suppose John's true IQ is 110, and that you have two different measures of IQ. This situation is depicted in Figure 6.2. Measure A, if used repeatedly, gives scores for John ranging from 108 to 112. The window of uncertainty for Measure A is narrow, only 4, and thus you can be pretty sure that any given application of the measurement procedure will produce an observed score that is close to the true score. You can trust Measure A; it is reliable. Measure B, if used repeatedly, gives scores for John ranging from 80 to 140. The window of uncertainty for Measure B is wide, a whopping 60, and you have little confidence that any given application of the measurement procedure will produce an observed score that is close to the true score. You cannot trust Measure B; it is unreliable. Without even knowing John's true score, you could examine the range of observed scores produced by repeated measurements and quickly conclude that it is much narrower for Measure

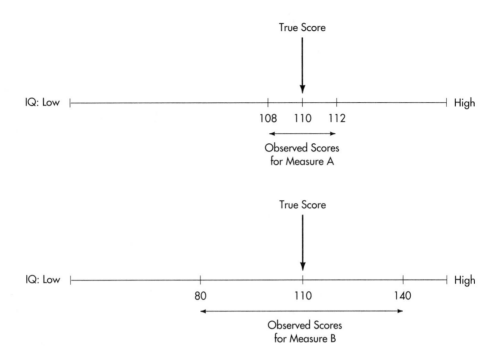

Figure 6.2
Range of observed scores for a reliable
measure (A) and an unreliable measure
(B).

A than for Measure B. Thus, you would be more inclined to trust Measure A. It has
less scatter, less noise, a narrower window of uncertainty. It is more reliable.

The example involving John's IQ has important implications for how reliability is assessed in practice. A reliable measure, one that has little noise and therefore a narrow window of uncertainty, produces stable and consistent results upon
repeated application. Reliability implies stability and consistency in observed
scores. That is, if the measure is reliable and you measure twice, you should get
pretty much the same results. For fine measurement, all procedures for assessing
reliability are attempts to quantify the stability or consistency of observed scores.
Let us now examine some of those procedures.

Assessing Reliability

As described in Chapter 3, reliability is assessed in systematic observation studies
by using independent observers of the same events and computing a measure of
how well they agree about what they see. This amounts to using two measurers
who apply the same measurement procedure to the same objects at the same point
in time. For fine self-report measures, typical of survey research, a different

Table 6.1   RELIABILITY PROCEDURES

Reliability Procedure	Time 1 (T1)	Time 2 (T2)	Reliability Measure
Stability			
Test-Retest	Measure 1 (M1)	Measure 1	r between M1T1 & M1T2
Alternate Forms	Measure 1	Measure 2 (M2)	r between M1T1 & M2T2
Internal-Consistency			
Split Half	All Items	———	Corrected r between halves
Coefficient Alpha	All items	———	Corrected average inter-item r

approach is taken. The same measurement procedure is applied to the same objects twice, and the two sets of observed scores are correlated. This amounts to correlating a variable with itself in order to check the stability or consistency of the measurement procedure. The correlation coefficient is interpreted as a reliability coefficient, and if the measure is reliable, the correlation should be large and positive. That is, if the measure gives consistent results, then a high score on the first measurement should be paired with a high score on the second measurement, medium with medium, and low with low, yielding a large positive reliability coefficient.

To apply the strategy just outlined, ideally you would like to be able to use the same measurement procedure twice on the same objects at the same point in time. Of course, that is impossible, and so you have to settle for approximations to the ideal strategy. Different approximations to the ideal strategy correspond to different reliability procedures. The approaches to reliability assessment are summarized in Table 6.1.

Stability approaches. One way of approximating the ideal strategy is to measure at two different points in time. Such an approach makes sense only for variables like intelligence that can be expected to remain stable over time. In fact, reliability coefficients from these approaches are often referred to as *stability* measures of reliability. They would be inappropriate for variables like mood where a person's true score might change between measurements.

There are two stability approaches for assessing reliability. If the same measure is used at two different points in time, the approach is referred to as *test–retest* reliability. Some researchers worry about using the same measure twice because respondents might be biased on the second measurement by their memories of how they responded the first time. An alternative is to use a different but equivalent measure of the same variable for the second measurement. This approach is known as *alternate-forms* or *equivalent-forms* reliability. In survey research, it amounts to using a different but equivalent set of items to measure the same variable. A problem with alternate forms is that it may be difficult to be certain that they are indeed equivalent.

Internal-consistency approaches. A different approach to assessing reliability involves using alternate forms at the same point in time. This may sound impossible, but it can be done whenever the measure under investigation is a composite score derived from several trials or items involving the same measurement procedure. This is typical of survey research where scale scores are derived by summing or averaging across responses to several individual items involving the same response format. The Likert scale described in the previous chapter is an example.

To assess reliability in the situation just described, the researcher splits the items measuring the same variable into subsets. Subscale scores are then derived from each subset of items. Correlations among subscale scores are treated as reliability coefficients. For example, if you had six items measuring sociableness, you could split the items into two sets of three items each. If all items are consistently measuring sociableness, then subscale scores based on the two sets of items should be strongly and positively correlated with each other. Because this approach to reliability reflects the degree to which the individual items or trials are all measuring the same variable, the reliability coefficient is referred to as an *internal-consistency* measure of reliability. Clearly this approach would be appropriate for variables such as mood, that are not expected to remain stable over time.

Historically, there have been two internal-consistency approaches for assessing reliability. The older approach involves splitting the items into two equal-sized sets, as described above. This approach is known as *split-half* reliability. The splitting may be done by using the first half of the items versus the second half, the odd versus the even items, or it may be done randomly. The correlation between the subscale scores based on the two sets of items underestimates the true reliability of the full-scale score and must therefore be corrected upward by something known as the Spearman-Brown formula, thus yielding the final reliability coefficient. The reason the subscale scores lead to an underestimate of the true reliability of the full-scale scores is that each subscale involves only half as many items as the full scale. As you will see shortly, the more items of comparable quality that go into a composite score, the higher the reliability of the composite. Thus, the reliability coefficient based on subscale scores involving half as many items as the full scale must be adjusted upward.

A more recent internal-consistency approach that has largely replaced the split-half approach is to compute the average of the correlations among all possible pairs of individual items measuring the same variable. This average is also corrected by the Spearman-Brown formula because each correlation contributing to the average is based on subscales consisting of single items. The final result is known as *coefficient alpha*. Like split-half coefficients, coefficient alpha provides a measure of the degree to which the full-scale score derived from a set of items is free from noise or random error. Fortunately, researchers seldom compute reliability coefficients. Computers do it for them.

Improving Reliability

Everyone agrees that reliability coefficients should be as high as possible. For applied purposes, the minimum acceptable reliability has often been placed at .80. For basic research, the standard is less demanding, with opinions about the minimum acceptable coefficient ranging as low as .50 (Guilford, 1954; Nunnally, 1967). Some authorities think it is a grave mistake to suggest specific guidelines for reliability because they might be applied mindlessly by lazy researchers (Pedhazur & Schmelkin, 1991). Certainly, thoughtful researchers would not be happy with a reliability of .50. The general rule for reliability is the higher the better. In his research on romantic love, Rubin's reliabilities (coefficient alpha) exceeded .80 for both the romantic-love and friendliness measures.

Given these considerations, you can see why there is great interest in how one can achieve high reliability. This topic is especially important for beginning researchers who often have to overcome some bad habits that weaken the reliability of their measures. Improving reliability amounts to reducing noise in measurement. There are three general principles that help a researcher achieve this goal. Not surprisingly, two of them focus on clarity.

First, be sure that the measurement procedure is clear and unambiguous. For survey research, this means that the items used to measure variables must be clearly worded. Ambiguous wording can be interpreted in more than one way, and if it is possible, it will happen. The result is unwanted noise in the scores. As you will see in the next chapter, good survey researchers sweat blood over the wording of their items. A corollary based on the concept of internal consistency is to make sure that all items intended to measure the same variable are indeed measuring the same thing. A common mistake of beginners is to try to build scales from items that are really measuring different things. As you can imagine, internal consistency coefficients for such scales tend to be disappointingly low. Ask yourself if all items contributing to a scale are getting at the same thing. If not, be merciless in revising the items until they meet this criterion. It will make the difference between being disappointed or thankful later on.

Second, be sure that the instructions for administering the measure are clear. You may have the clearest items in the world, but if they are administered in a sloppy fashion or under varying conditions, noise will creep into the measures. You know by now what that implies for reliability. The rule of thumb is that measuring procedures should always be administered under well-controlled standardized conditions.

Third, if a scale is not reliable enough, add more items of the same kind and quality. This often increases the reliability of the scale, but it is not guaranteed to work. The reason this approach often works is that random error in individual items tends to cancel itself out when many items are combined. Another way of saying this is that an average based on many items is likely to be closer to the true value than one based on few items. Thus, more items tend to improve reliability PROVIDED that the additional items are good ones. Of course, there is a point at which this principle breaks down. Add 200 items and the respondent's attention will begin to wander randomly long before he or she completes the survey. The researcher must be sensitive to the number of items that can safely be added before fatigue, loss of interest, and wandering attention become problems. That caution aside, it is commonly true that adding a reasonable number of quality items to a scale improves reliability.

The other side of the coin is that adding many low-quality items can create a serious problem in interpreting an internal-consistency reliability coefficient. The reason is that the Spearman-Brown correction, mentioned earlier, is based on the number of items in the full-scale composite score. The more items, the larger the upward adjustment in the uncorrected reliability coefficient. So, if you have enough items, the corrected reliability coefficient can be quite high even though the items have only weak positive correlations with each other and thus are not really measuring the same variable. In fact, with enough items, large reliability coefficients are possible when the items are really measuring DIFFERENT variables. Thus, if you are dealing with a variable measured by many items, the meaning of a large internal-consistency coefficient is unclear. Only a low coefficient provides decisive evidence. It means that you have a serious reliability problem. Pedhazur and Schmelkin (1991) provide an extended discussion of this issue and of advanced techniques for dealing with it. For now, bear in mind that what you should seek in a multi-item measure is a reasonable number of quality items.

It may be helpful for you to see a concrete example of the use of the principles just described for improving reliability. Table 6.2 contains a set of items for measuring attitude toward abortion. The set of items was generated by one of the author's research-methods classes. The items illustrate many of the principles of measurement and survey design and thus will be referred to several times in later discussions. For now, note three things. First, the set of items constitutes a Likert scale and has all the properties described for such scales in the previous chapter. In particular, each item is clearly favorable or unfavorable toward abortion, and there are an equal number of each type. The same six-point step scale for responding is used for each item. Second, the measuring procedure and the instructions are clear and simple. Third, each item seems clearly relevant to the issue of abortion, and there are a reasonable number of items. Undoubtedly, this set of items is not perfect. There may be some things about the wording of specific items that bother you, and that is understandable. Still, because the items generally follow the principles for improving reliability, you should not be surprised to learn that when they were used in a class project, coefficient alpha turned out to be .84.

VALIDITY OF MEASUREMENT

As noted in Chapter 3, reliability deals with whether any variable has been measured with precision. Validity, on the other hand, deals with the even more important question of just what theoretical variable or construct was measured and whether it was the intended construct. Establishing the validity of a measure is not an easy task. One reason is that validity itself has been conceptualized in a number of different ways. This has resulted in a number of different approaches for assessing validity.

Validity procedures fall into two broad categories. They are summarized in Table 6.3. One approach is based on informed judgment, the other on the gathering of empirical evidence. These two categories will be referred to as *judgmental* and *empirical*, respectively. As you might suspect, scientists take empirical approaches

Table 6.2 LIKERT-SCALE ITEMS FOR
MEASURING ATTITUDE TOWARD ABORTION

Instructions: Please respond to each item below by circling only ONE of the six choices.

Choices:	SA = strongly agree	MD = mildly disagree
	A = agree	D = disagree
	MA = mildly agree	SD = strongly disagree

SA A MA MD D SD	1. I approve of abortion in cases of rape.
SA A MA MD D SD	2. Abortion should NOT be used as a form of birth control.
SA A MA MD D SD	3. State-funded abortions should be available for those on welfare.
SA A MA MD D SD	4. Abortion should be a legal right.
SA A MA MD D SD	5. Abortion is murder.
SA A MA MD D SD	6. Parental consent should be required for minors to obtain an abortion.

Table 6.3 VALIDITY PROCEDURES

Validity Procedure	Basic Question Addressed
Judgmental	
Face	Does the measure appear relevant?
Content	Do the items adequately sample the construct?
Empirical	
Criterion	Does the measure predict the criterion?
Construct	Does the measure yield results predicted by theory?
Convergent	Does a variety of evidence support the measure?
Discriminant	Does the measure yield results different from measures of other constructs?

more seriously. Judgmental approaches, when used alone, do not carry much weight. However, as a preliminary to empirical validation, judgmental approaches can be quite valuable. A typical sequence is to try to build validity into one's measures using good judgment and then to follow up with an empirical assessment validity.

Judgmental Approaches

The judgmental approaches include face validity and content validity. A measure has *face* validity if it appears (on the face of it) to measure the intended construct. Obviously, this is a matter of judgment. An exam question for this chapter dealing with the definition of face validity would seem to have face validity. Rubin was aiming for face validity when he generated items that in his best judgment were relevant to the constructs of romantic love and friendliness. The items in Table 6.2 were used because the research methods class collectively judged them to have face validity for measuring attitude toward abortion.

Content validity refers to whether the measure adequately samples the construct one is trying to measure. This may seem similar to face validity, and in fact for a measure consisting of a single item, the two cannot easily be distinguished. For a multi-item measure like a scale composed of several survey items, the distinction becomes clear. One can inquire about the face validity of each item individually. However, content validity refers to whether the set of items adequately covers or samples the construct being measured. When Rubin generated items that dealt with various aspects of romantic love (physical attraction, idealization of loved one, shared intimacy, etc.), he was trying to insure the content validity of his measure. When the research-methods class generated items dealing with different aspects of the abortion issue (rape cases, birth control, welfare abortions, etc.), they too were concerned with content validity. Any student who has ever done poorly on an exam because the questions dealt with topics different from what the student expected can appreciate the idea behind content validity.

Clearly, the main weakness of face and content validity is their judgmental nature. Judgment is fallible, and a measure that appears to be a good one may prove invalid when assessed empirically. The situation is even worse if an empirical assessment is not made. Then a researcher may make serious decisions or take important actions based on an invalid measure. This is the mark of an amateur. A good researcher never makes serious use of a measure backed by nothing more than judgmental validity.

Another problem is that judgmental validity, particularly face validity, does not allow for the happy accident. Some items with no face validity are accidentally discovered to have empirical validity. An amusing example is an item from a personality test asking whether the respondent preferred cooked or raw carrots. The item was discovered to be a good predictor of academic success in college. (The author cannot remember whether the preference is supposed to be for cooked or raw carrots, so you are advised to eat plenty of both types.) If one includes only items with face validity, this kind of accidental discovery cannot occur.

Empirical Approaches

The empirical approaches to validity assessment include criterion validity and construct validity. *Criterion* validity involves showing that a new measure is strongly related to another existing measure, the criterion, which is known to be a valid measure of the variable in question. You may wonder why anyone would ever want to do such a silly thing. The most common reason is the practical need to predict future behavior. When college admissions committees use high-school grade-point average (GPA) and SAT scores to decide which applicants to admit, they do so because these measures have been shown in past research to be good predictors of college GPA. Once the relationship with the criterion (college GPA) has been established, the "new" measures (high-school GPA and SAT scores) can then be used in situations where the criterion is not currently available. Thus, criterion validity is widely used in applied research when one's major purpose is simply to predict one measure, not currently available, from another.

The most important kind of validity for basic research is *construct* validity. As you know, the word "construct" simply means a concept in a scientific theory. Therefore, construct validity refers to any research findings bearing on the question of whether a measure yields results consistent with theoretical predictions about the construct being measured. A valid measure of romantic love should be higher in situations where the theory predicts that romantic love is higher; for instance, for engaged couples versus casually dating couples. Conversely, those scoring higher on the measure should exhibit more behavior indicating romantic involvement than those scoring low. The actual evidence for the construct validity of Rubin's measure of romantic love is discussed below. By the same token, surely any sensible theory of attitude toward abortion would predict that people who are deeply involved in religious practices would be low in pro-abortion attitude. The class project discussed earlier also contained a set of items measuring involvement in religious practices. As predicted, the religious-involvement and abortion-approval variables were strongly negatively correlated ($r = -.74$, $p < .001$). Because this finding confirmed a theoretical prediction, it constitutes modest evidence for the construct validity of both the abortion-attitude and the religious-involvement measures.

As just noted, when a new measure yields results that confirm theoretical predictions, both the construct validity of the measure and the validity of the theory are simultaneously strengthened. Construct validation and theory testing typically go hand-in-hand in basic research. Thus, the construct validity of a measure usually evolves from a program of research aimed at testing the theory that led to the measure.

To avoid a possible misconception, note that the word "construct" has a broader meaning than the phrase "construct validity." "Construct" refers to any theoretical concept. "Construct validity" refers only to *empirical* evidence that a measure yields results predicted by a theory. In other words, judgmental approaches to validity do NOT qualify as construct validity. This is simply a matter of terminology. It is certainly true that judgmental approaches are attempts to achieve valid measures of constructs. Nevertheless, the phrase "construct validity" is reserved to describe *empirical* approaches to the question of whether a measure successfully taps into a construct.

Construct validity can be divided into two subcategories. Gathering evidence from a variety of studies; using different settings, participants, procedures, and predictions; and showing that measures of a construct yield theoretically appropriate results is often referred to as convergence or *convergent* validity. This is the aspect of construct validity discussed so far. It is equally important to show that measures of a construct yield results different from those yielded by measures of other similar constructs. In the case of romantic love, one would like to show that the measure yields results different from those yielded by a measure of friendliness. Such evidence would indicate that the two constructs and their measures are discriminable from one another. This aspect of construct validity is referred to as discriminability or *discriminant* validity.

A very convincing way to demonstrate convergent and discriminant validity simultaneously is the *multitrait-multimethod matrix method* or the 4M approach. It was originally described by Campbell and Fiske (1959), and a brief account may also be found in Kerlinger (1986). The essence of 4M is that at least two different methods of measuring at least two different constructs (or traits) are included in the same study. Convergent validity is demonstrated by substantial positive correlations between different measures of the same construct. Discriminant validity is simultaneously demonstrated by near-zero correlations between different constructs measured by the same method.

The ideal of 4M can be approached by showing that different measures of the same construct yield similar results while simultaneously showing that measures of a different construct yield different results. For example, in a frustration–aggression experiment, one might include two methods of measuring aggression: extent of Bobo-doll bashing and a questionnaire measuring aggressive attitude toward the researcher. The same questionnaire might include items measuring a different construct, shyness, predicted to be unrelated to the independent variable, frustration. The researcher would hope to show that both measures of aggression are strongly influenced by the frustration manipulation while the shyness measure is unaffected. Such a pattern of results would be more convincing evidence for the validity of the theory and the measures of its constructs than would be the results of a study containing just a single measure of aggression.

It is useful to reexamine Rubin's research in the light of the preceding discussion. Clearly, his primary interest was in demonstrating the construct validity of his romantic-love measure. How well did he succeed? Rubin did not fully implement the 4M approach because he had only a single measure of friendship. Nevertheless, he was able to provide an impressive array of evidence for both the convergent and discriminant validity of his measure of romantic love. The finding that the love and friendship scales were only moderately correlated supported the discriminant validity of the love scale. The finding that average friendship scores were similar for dating partners and same-sex friends but that love scores were much higher for dating partners supported both the convergent and discriminant validity of the love scale. The finding that love scores were highly correlated with respondents' independent reports of being in love with and inclined to marry their dating partners (alternate methods of measuring romantic love) further supported the convergent validity of the love scale. The finding that love scores for dating partners were only slightly correlated with love scores for friends or with social-desirability scores was further evidence for the discriminant validity of the love scale. Finally, the most impressive evidence of all for the construct validity of the love scale was that it could successfully predict theoretically relevant BEHAVIOR (mutual gazing) in an experiment. All in all, one would have to conclude that Rubin did a pretty thorough job of empirically establishing the construct validity of his romantic-love measure.

Now test yourself. What approach to validity is most likely involved in each of the following situations? (Q4)

A test for widget-making skill is developed for the hiring director of the Widget Company.

The designer of a questionnaire tries to include items covering all aspects of aggression.

The originator of stimulus-starvation theory tries to validate a paper-and-pencil measure of stimulus starvation.

Two social scientists argue about whether pupil size of the eye would be a good measure of interest in a stimulus.

SUMMARY

Linear relationships between finely measured variables may be described by the correlation coefficient, r, which can range from −1 to +1. The sign of r indicates the type of linear relationship (positive or negative), and the absolute value indicates the strength or magnitude of the relationship. Note that r describes *linear* relationships only, its value can be artificially lowered by restricted ranges of values on either variable, and it tells you nothing about what may be causing the relationship.

Correlations are often used to assess two important properties of any good measure, reliability and validity. Reliability refers to the precision of measurement, and validity refers to just which theoretical variable or variables are being measured. Reliability is typically assessed by correlating the variable with itself. This can be done either by measuring at two points in time (test-retest or alternate-forms) or, in the case of multi-item measures, correlating scores based on different subsets of items (split-half and coefficient alpha). Validity is assessed either by informed judgment (face and content) or by gathering empirical evidence (criterion and construct). Construct validity is established by showing empirically that the measure of a theoretical concept, or construct, yields results predicted by the theory in a wide variety of testing situations (convergent validity) and that it can be distinguished from measures of other similar constructs (discriminant validity).

ANSWERS TO QUESTIONS

Q1. Mutual focus involves ratio measurement. It is based on duration measures which you already know involve ratio measurement. A percentage based on durations retains all the measurement properties of the original durations.

Q2. r = −.72 indicates the stronger linear relationship.

Q3. For r = .82, one may conclude that study time and GPA have a positive linear relationship. One may not conclude that study time causes GPA. It could be the other way around, or a third variable may be involved. For r = .02, the conclusion is that the variables have no *linear* relationship. Either they are unrelated or they are related in a nonlinear fashion.

Q4. The widget example involves criterion validity. The designer of the aggression questionnaire is concerned with content validity. The stimulus-starvation theorist is pursuing construct validity. In the pupil-size example, if the arguers are relying on their own informed judgments, then it is a matter of face validity. If, on the other hand, they are citing a specific body of research findings, then a case could be made for construct validity.

FURTHER READING

Excellent discussions of reliability and validity of measurement may be found in Kerlinger (1986) and Pedhazur and Schmelkin (1991).

REFERENCES

Campbell, D., & Fiske, D. (1959). Convergent and discriminant validation by the multitrait-multimethod matrix. *Psychological Bulletin, 54*, 81–105.

Guilford, J. P. (1954). *Psychometric methods*. New York: McGraw-Hill.

Kerlinger, F. N. (1986). *Foundations of behavioral research* (3rd ed.). New York: Holt, Rinehart and Winston.

Nunnally, J. (1967). *Psychometric theory*. New York: McGraw-Hill.

Pedhazur, E. J., & Schmelkin, L. P. (1991). *Measurement, design, and analysis: An integrated approach*. Hillsdale, NJ: Lawrence Erlbaum Associates.

Rubin, Z. (1970). Measurement of romantic love. *Journal of Personality and Social Psychology, 16*, 265–273.

Survey Research: Procedures

7

Farming is among the most stressful occupations. Farmers often have to borrow heavily to finance equipment and supplies for planting. Their chances for a reasonable return depend on the whims of the weather. For family farms, the occupation and the household are so tightly connected that stresses on the former easily spill over to the latter. There is also the ever-present fear of an economic recession, which deals a double blow to farmers. Their investment in land and equipment declines in value at the same time that the market value of their products is suffering a similar fate. Recessions are well known for destroying farmers economically.

The subdiscipline of rural sociology has devoted much attention to studying the stresses associated with farming. The goal has been to understand both the causes and consequences of such stress. A typical theoretical analysis attempts to identify objective variables that may be translated into stress by way of the intermediate mechanisms (see Chapter 1) of perception and coping. An example of such an objective variable is the farmer's debt-to-asset ratio. A high ratio means that the farmer is economically vulnerable. Thus it could be a source of stress. On the other side of the equation, if perception-coping is ineffective, the outcome is stress, and its major emotional consequence is depression. This analysis of stress in farmers, with its emphasis on the mediating role of psychological processes like perception and coping, is typical of the theoretical treatment of stress in the general social science literature (e.g., Lazarus, 1966).

Michael Belyea and Linda Lobao did a study of stress in farmers based on the theoretical approach just described (Belyea & Lobao, 1990). They surveyed Ohio farmers, first using a telephone interview and later a mailed questionnaire. During the interview, the researchers collected data on three types of objective variables that might lead to stress: sociodemographic characteristics, farm-structure characteristics, and economic vulnerability. They reasoned that the first two types of variables would be directly related to economic vulnerability and that all three types might be objective sources of stress. Examples of sociodemographic characteristics are age and number of children. Younger farmers and those with larger families were expected to be more economically vulnerable. The percentage of farm land rented is an example of a farm-structure characteristic. Farmers who rent the land they work should be more economically vulnerable than those who do not. Vulnerability was measured by objective indicators such as the debt-to-asset ratio discussed earlier.

The questionnaire assessed mediating psychological variables and psychological consequences. Perception was measured by questionnaire items dealing with perceived economic hardship and perceived stress. Coping was measured by items dealing with use of coping strategies. Depression, as a psychological consequence of stress, was measured with a set of 20 items developed by the Center for Epidemiologic Studies. Responses were made using 3- to 5-point step scales, and variables were scored by summing responses to all relevant items. Thus, the psychological variables were measured via Likert scales, as described in Chapter 5. A sample item from the perceived economic hardship scale is, "During the past 12 months how often did it happen that you did not have enough money to afford the kind of medical care you thought your household should have?" Response alternatives were "not very often," "fairly often," and "very often," and they were scored 1, 2, and 3, respectively. Internal consistency reliability, discussed in the previous chapter, was assessed for each psychological variable by computing coefficient alpha. The reliability coefficients ranged from .54 (barely acceptable) for coping to .89 (pretty good) for depression.

There are two things to notice about this study. First, it is an example of survey research, as defined in Chapter 2, because all variables were measured by means of self-report. The study illustrates both types of survey research discussed later in this chapter, interviews (oral self-report) and questionnaires (written self-report). Second, scores for all variables in the study are examples of fine measurement, as defined in Chapter 5. Fine measurement is typical of modern survey research. The objective variables were finely measured to begin with (e.g., age in years, debt-to-asset ratio). Fine measurement for the psychological variables was achieved by summing item scores, each of which involved coarse (3- to 5-point) ordinal measurement.

As noted in the last chapter, relationships between finely measured variables are typically described by means of the correlation coefficient, r. As expected, in the Belyea and Lobao study, the best predictors of depression in farmers were the psychological variables, in particular perceived economic hardship (r = .49) and perceived stress (r = .52). Although only weakly correlated with depression, the objective variables also behaved as expected. The best objective predictor of perceived stress was economic vulnerability as assessed by debt-to-asset ratio (r = .25). The best predictors of debt-to-asset ratio were the sociodemographic variables (r = −.36 for age and .27 for number of children) and one of the farm-structure variables (r = .25 for percent of farm land rented). Belyea and Lobao also did some advanced analyses that will be described in the next chapter. The results described here show that objective sources of stress for farmers tend to be mediated by psychological processes, just as predicted.

This chapter explores survey research. First, general issues of definition and categorization are examined. Then the two major types of surveys, interviews and questionnaires, are covered in detail, with emphasis on the special problems of each approach. This chapter concentrates on procedural issues, the next chapter on data analysis. The last section of this chapter explores a major concern of survey researchers, how to obtain representative samples of respondents.

TYPES OF SURVEYS

Surveys are self-report measuring instruments. They consist of items composed of two types of elements, stimuli (or questions) and responses (or answers). Surveys may be classified by the way they are administered or by the physical format of their items. These two ways of classifying surveys are shown in Figure 7.1. As you can see, the mode of administration may be either oral or written. Oral surveys are known as *interviews,* written surveys as *questionnaires.* It is possible to present stimuli in one mode and obtain responses in the other mode. However, mixed-mode combinations rarely occur in practice.

The physical format of item elements may be either *structured* or *unstructured.* Structured stimuli are those in which exact wording has been predetermined and so has the order of presenting the stimuli. Unstructured stimuli are those for which

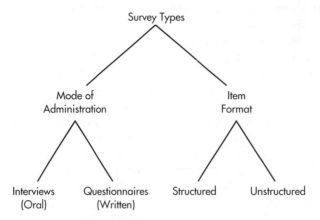

Figure 7.1
Types of surveys classified by mode of administration and physical format of items.

neither constraint applies. Degrees of stimulus structure are possible. Variation in wording but a fixed order of stimuli is one possibility. Alternate forms with identical wording but different orders of stimuli is another. Survey stimuli usually consist of words, but in some surveys (e.g., certain psychological tests) the stimuli may be nonlinguistic (e.g., ink blots or pictures). The definition of structure can be broadened to include such stimuli.

(See if you can supply such a broadened definition. Q1)

Structured responses, commonly known as *closed* or multiple-choice responses, are those in which the respondent must choose among alternatives supplied by the researcher. Unstructured responses, commonly known as *open* or free responses, are those in which the respondent may say or write anything. Combinations are possible. A common example is an "other" category followed by an opportunity to explain as part of a closed set of alternatives.

Structure is desirable when consistency across situations is important. That would be true if one wished to combine data from large numbers of respondents, as in polling, or to make comparisons across groups. An unstructured approach is desirable when exploration is the major goal, when one does not know what responses are likely and wishes to form impressions that may be tested more thoroughly in later research. The unstructured approach is also appropriate when one's goal is to understand a single respondent in depth, a typical objective in clinical applications.

The response format can make a huge difference in survey results. (So can the stimulus wording, but more on that later.) Schuman and Scott (1987) presented some startling data on this subject. In telephone interviews, respondents were asked what was the most important problem facing the country. With open responding, only 2.4 percent mentioned the energy shortage, the quality of public schools, legalized abortion, or pollution. With closed responding that included "other" and "don't know" alternatives, 60 percent of respondents chose these four problems. Respondents were also asked what national or world event over the past 50 years seemed especially important. With open responding, only 1.4 percent of the sample mentioned the invention of the computer. With closed responding, 29.9 percent chose the computer alternative. Results like these led the authors to suggest that researchers give up the idea that absolute levels of attitudes or opinions or even a valid rank ordering can be obtained from surveys. Opinions might differ on their suggestion, but there can be little doubt that response formats on surveys affect results.

When the classification of surveys based on mode of administration is combined with the one based on stimulus and response formats, some combinations are more common than others. The frequency of occurrence of the various combinations is summarized in Table 7.1. As you can see, questionnaires with unstructured stimuli are relatively rare. Sometimes alternate forms are used to guard against the possibility that stimulus order may influence responses. However, such a possibility may be reason enough to avoid alternate forms if a researcher is interested primarily in individual differences among respondents. Questionnaires with structured stimuli are more likely to have closed than open responses. The reason is that most researchers want to make statistical comparisons, and they are more likely to be valid with structured stimulus and response formats. With interviews, formats in which the stimuli and responses have similar degrees of structure are the most common. Unstructured stimuli tend to be paired with open responding, and structured stimuli with closed responding. The pairing of structured stimuli with open responding occurs less often, and the pairing of unstructured stimuli with closed responding is rarely seen.

These reflections on combinations provide a rationale for the approach to be taken in the next two sections of the chapter. The section on interviews focuses on completely unstructured interviews. The combination of unstructured stimuli and open responses seldom occurs with questionnaires and thus may be considered relatively unique to interviews. The subsequent section on questionnaires focuses on completely structured questionnaires. As noted above, the combination of structured stimuli and closed responses also occurs frequently in interviews. However, with one exception, important issues of procedure and data analysis are the same

Table 7.1 FREQUENCY OF OCCURRENCE OF SURVEYS CLASSIFIED BY DEGREE OF STRUCTURE IN ITEM STIMULI AND RESPONSES

Stimulus Format		Response Format	
		Closed	*Open*
Structured		Questionnaire (C) Interview (C)	Questionnaire Interview
Unstructured		Questionnaire (R) Interview (R)	Questionnaire (R) Interview (C)

Note: C = a common combination, R = a rare combination.

for this combination regardless of the mode of administration. The one exception is the behavior of the interviewer which can affect the validity of results. That point will be stressed in the next section, but it applies to ALL interviews. By the same token, questionnaires with structured stimuli and open responses will not be formally covered. However, what is said about the analysis of open responses in the section on interviews also applies to questionnaires.

INTERVIEWS

Unstructured interviewing may be more an art than a science. Nevertheless, there is a body of expert opinion on how to do it well. Here are some guidelines from that body of opinion.

Good Measurement

The words "reliability" and "validity" are seldom heard in the context of unstructured interviews, but they are implicit in the researcher's desire to get at the truth. Validity implies reliability. If one has true or valid information about a particular variable, then one must have achieved precise measurement of some variable. Thus, where it is difficult to address the issue of reliability directly, researchers are likely to focus on providing convincing evidence of validity, confident that reliability may then be assumed.

This abstract discussion has direct relevance to unstructured interviews with open responding. Because both stimulus and response formats lack structure, it is difficult to provide the kind of evidence for consistency that may be available when such formats are standardized. Thus, the focus is on getting valid information. This is achieved primarily by having a battle plan specifying the topics to be covered and the kind of information sought. Although flexibility in wording is allowed, the interviewer must make sure that the specified topics are covered and that information at the desired level of detail is obtained. Achieving the desired level of detail is accomplished by the careful use of follow-up questions, or probes, whenever the interviewer judges that more information is needed. The depth interview, a variant of the unstructured interview, has the goal of achieving a deeper understanding of the topics or issues under discussion than is achieved in the typical interview. Not surprisingly, probes are a prominent feature of the depth interview, but they may be used to good effect in any unstructured interview. In general, the interviewer must control the interview and follow a plan of action, preferably written out in advance, specifying the information to be obtained.

Interviewing Tips

The unique feature of the interview is the verbal exchange between interviewer and respondent. Precisely because of the lack of structure, this feature is a possible source of problems in the unstructured interview. Because one cannot directly control the respondent's behavior, most expert advice focuses on the interviewer. Such advice may be classified into three categories ranging from very general advice about planning or strategy, to more specific advice about technique or tactics, to very specific advice about particular behaviors or other issues. An example of strategic advice is the written plan of action mentioned earlier and the advice that an interviewer should typically proceed from general topics or issues to more specific ones. Tactics include the use of probes and the advice to allow enough time for respondents to answer. New interviewers are often anxious to get on with things and are not sufficiently tolerant of delayed responding.

The largest body of advice concerns specifics. Most of these tips illustrate the principle that the interviewer should be clear and neutral. Clarity avoids injecting noise, the enemy of reliability, into the responses. Neutrality avoids biasing the responses, which destroys validity. Here are some pointers from a list supplied by Smith (1991): The interviewer should not talk too fast, mumble, appear submissive, let the respondent take control by asking questions, give opinions, criticize the topics, force the respondent into certain kinds of answers, interpret the questions, apologize for the interview, answer for the respondent, skip part of the interview, or use constraining words like "just" or "only." The appearance of the interviewer may also affect the respondent's answers. In general, neat but unobtrusive dress and grooming are desirable. Most of these tips become part of the good interviewer's standard routine as a result of careful training and extensive practice.

Many of the points just raised regarding unstructured interviews also apply to structured interviews. For example, the appearance and general conduct of the interviewer can make an enormous difference in both situations. The major additional concern in the structured interview is the exact wording and ordering of items because they may also have a significant impact on responses. These topics will be covered in the section on questionnaire procedures.

Parallels With Field Observation

There are strong parallels between unstructured interviews and the method of field observation described in Chapter 3. Both approaches are distinguished by more flexibility of method and a greater emphasis on in-depth understanding than their structured counterparts (structured surveys and systematic observation, respectively). Not surprisingly, as noted in Chapter 3, interviews are often part of a field observation, and such interviews are likely to be unstructured. More parallels between the two approaches will surface in the next chapter when data analysis is discussed.

QUESTIONNAIRES

There is plenty of expert advice on designing completely structured questionnaires, including the opinion that structure is the only acceptable option for questionnaire design (Bausell, 1986). The following discussion summarizes the most common advice given by experts on questionnaire construction.

Reliable Measurement

In contrast to unstructured interviews, reliability can be dealt with directly in structured questionnaires. The key rule is to strive for clarity in the wording of items. If a word or phrase can be interpreted in several ways, respondents will adopt different interpretations on a more-or-less random basis. This creates noise in the responses, and noise reduces reliability. Clarity may often be achieved by using specific words or phrases rather than general ones. An item about alternative energy sources may yield a lot of noise. Better to replace it with one or more items about specific alternatives: nuclear, solar, geothermal, etc. Any word or phrase that respondents cannot understand will produce noise in the responses. Respondents, trying to do their job, will guess in such situations, and their guesses will vary unpredictably. So avoid technical terms and jargon. In fact, avoid complex words altogether. Bordens and Abbott (1991, p. 189) put it well: "If a word you are considering has more than six or seven letters, a simpler alternative is probably available."

Valid Measurement

The issue here is not noise, but bias. Bias occurs when the wording or context of an item systematically affects responses. In others words, a particular interpretation is made probable. The interpretation may lead to a response that is not a valid indication of the respondent's status on the variable the researcher wants to measure. This possibility strikes fear into the heart of a good survey researcher. It is similar to the systematic observer's fear of being spotted and thus producing unnatural (invalid) behavior in the person being observed. Thus, it is no surprise that survey researchers put a lot of effort into the wording and arrangement of questionnaire items. They are trying to build face validity into their items in the hope of achieving construct validity in their measures. Many survey researchers take the extra step of pretesting items for lack of clarity or bias. This can be done by asking a sample of respondents what each item means, using an open response format.

Examples of bias produced by wording or context abound. Here are two from a sobering article by Jaroslovsky (1988). Researchers found that support for free speech was 21 percent higher when respondents were asked if the United States should "forbid" public speeches against democracy versus "allow" them. This is an example of wording bias. Context effects can also be powerful. Two polls asked the same question: "Do you think it should be possible for a pregnant woman to obtain a legal abortion if she is married and does not want any more children?" The percentage of yes responses differed by 18 percent (40 versus 58) in the two polls. The apparent cause of the difference was that only the poll with the lower percentage contained another abortion item preceding the one quoted above. The other abortion item asked if a woman should be allowed to have an abortion if there was evidence of a defective fetus.

(Can you propose a theory about why the defective-fetus item may have caused an 18 percent reduction in yes responses to the quoted item? (Q2)

Clearly, responses to a questionnaire item may be biased by the context provided by preceding items.

Here are some tips from the survey research literature for avoiding the kind of bias just described. First, avoid double-barreled items that ask about two things at once. An example is, "I am opposed to wage and price controls." Split such items into as many as you need to ask about one thing at a time. Second, avoid negative wording because it is easily misinterpreted. "The president should nominate a liberal" is better than "The president should not nominate a conservative." If you must use negative wording, emphasize it, as in, "I would NOT cut in line if I was in a hurry." Respondents often miss unemphasized negatives, taking the opposite interpretation from the one intended. Third, avoid items that assume something about the respondent's opinions or behavior or that tend to push the respondent toward a certain kind of answer. Here is an example: "Aside from murder, the death penalty should never be used."

What is wrong with this item? (Q3)

Fourth, avoid sensitive material unless it is essential. If essential, place it later in the questionnaire after less sensitive material. Sensitive material sets a context, like the defective-fetus item, that may bias responses to other items. There is also the question of whether you are getting truthful answers to the sensitive items themselves. Clearly, if sensitive material is included, you must take special pains to assure confidentiality and to secure the respondent's trust. Fifth, avoid extremes of social desirability. "Citizens should vote" will not get you valid information about voting behavior. Try, "I voted in the last millage election" instead.

Item balance may also affect the likelihood of biased responding. Item balance refers to the number of favorable and unfavorable items used to measure an attitude or opinion. In general, it is a good idea to use an equal number of favorable and unfavorable items, as recommended in Chapter 5 for Likert scales. Such balance discourages the response set of tending to favor extreme response alternatives like "strongly agree." Moreover, if that response set does occur, proper scoring of negative items will neutralize it by placing extreme responders in the middle of the range of possible scores.

Reread the scoring procedure for Likert scales in Chapter 5 and see if you can explain how it would place extreme responders in the middle of the range of possible scores. (Q4)

More tips like these, having to do with the wording or ordering of questionnaire items, can be found in the references cited at the end of the chapter. The tips discussed here make the point that valid measurement is a major concern of researchers who use questionnaires. That concern is reflected in the careful construction and arrangement of questionnaire items.

A Research Example

Take another look at Table 6.2 in the previous chapter. The items provide concrete examples of many of the tips just discussed for good questionnaire items. To avoid ambiguity and thus enhance reliability, note that items avoid large words, technical terms, and jargon. The issues raised are specific rather than general. To avoid bias and thus enhance validity, each item asks about only one issue. Where possible, unfavorable items avoid negative words (Abortion is murder). Where negative words are unavoidable, they are emphasized (*NOT*). The items assume nothing about the respondent's opinions or behavior. The topic of abortion is itself sensitive, but the items avoid probing into details of the respondent's personal life (no items like, "I have had an abortion"). The issue of social-desirability bias is difficult to judge with a divisive topic like abortion. It could be argued that there is no social consensus on what is socially desirable with regard to abortion. The set of items is balanced, with an equal number favorable (items 1, 3, and 4) and unfavorable toward the issue.

SAMPLING

Chapter 3 discussed two major concerns of systematic observers, vague operational definitions and unnatural behavior on the part of those observed. There are also two major concerns that preoccupy survey researchers. One is valid measurement, particularly the problems posed by the wording and arrangement of survey items. Such problems were discussed in the previous section. The second major concern of survey researchers is sampling, the problem of getting adequate samples from specified populations. Let us now examine this concern in detail.

Chapter 1 stressed that a major goal of science is generalization. Generalizing occurs when sample evidence is used to reach conclusions about populations. A *population* consists of the entire set of objects about which one wishes to reach a conclusion. A *sample* is a subset of those objects that are included in a research study. Statistical inference consists of a set of formal procedures that help one achieve valid inferences or generalizations. However, the validity of any generalization, whether or not it is based on statistical inference, depends on the assumption that one has an adequate sample from the population of interest. Thus, all researchers should be concerned about sampling.

Ironically, in most social science research, sampling concerns are addressed after the fact. That is, samples are obtained on the basis of convenience, and the researcher worries about what population may be represented after the data have been collected. This approach reflects the fact that in many research settings "pools" of participants are available (such as introductory students in a social science discipline), and the researcher has little choice but to sample from those pools. Such an approach is workable but risky. Ultimately, the validity of conclusions depends on similar results from many studies. Although this approach to sampling is common, good survey researchers take a different approach.

Good survey researchers make a practice of naming a target population in advance of the research and then taking steps to insure that they obtain an adequate sample from that population. This approach is relatively unique to survey research and may be considering a distinguishing feature. It probably developed because of the pressure on survey researchers to deliver the goods on specific populations. Political candidates who pay a survey researcher for accurate advice about the population of likely voters will not be happy if they receive bad information. The same is true of manufacturers who need to know about consumer preferences. Word gets around about pollsters who supply bad information; only those who can deliver survive. Such pressures led to the development of sampling techniques designed to insure adequate samples. Thus, the use of such techniques has become common among survey researchers, even among those whose primary interest is basic research.

Error in Sampling

The preceding discussion stressed the desirability of adequate samples. It is time to examine what is meant by the word "adequate." A sample perfectly represents a population when relevant characteristics of the objects sampled are present in the sample in exactly the same way as they are in the population. A relevant characteristic is one that would affect responses to the survey items. For example, there might be good reason to believe that gender is relevant to the way people will answer items on a survey. A sample will perfectly represent the population with respect to gender if the proportion of males and females in the sample is exactly the same as in the population. If the same can be said for all relevant characteristics of the sampled objects, then the sample perfectly represents the population. That is, the sample is perfectly adequate.

Such an ideal situation is never achieved in practice. Samples, as SUBSETS of the population, are always imperfect. Some relevant characteristics are present in the sample in a way that does not match how they are present in the population. Such imperfections in the sample are referred to as error in sampling because they must have been produced by the sampling procedure. Error in sampling threatens the validity of generalizations. Therefore, it is important to understand such error thoroughly with a view toward either eliminating it or making it as small as possible.

Sampling error. There are two types of error in sampling, sampling error and sample bias. Sampling error is a special case of random error, a concept discussed in several earlier chapters. *Sampling error* is random error produced by the sampling procedure. The presence of such error means that at least one relevant characteristic will be imperfectly represented in the sample, but the direction and size of the imperfection are unpredictable because it was created by a random process. For example, if gender is evenly divided in the population, one might draw a random sample that consists of 75 percent females. Such an outcome is unlikely, but it could happen. If it does, then clearly the sample is in error with respect to gender. Because the error was created by a random process, it is random error, and because the random process was the sampling procedure, it is a special form of random error called sampling error. Because the error is random, its size or direction could not have been predicted in advance.

Sampling error is a form of noise. It has all the bad features of noise discussed in Chapter 6. In particular, if there is enough sampling error present, it will be impossible to reach any valid conclusion about the population. It is commonly said that random error is taken into account when a test of statistical inference is performed. It is true that the null hypothesis of no relationship between variables in the population is equivalent to saying that any relationship seen in the sample is a chance event, a byproduct of random error. Thus, the probability statement resulting from the test of inference may be interpreted as the probability that the sample relationship was a random event. However, if there is a lot of random error present in the study, it is also true that the p value from the test of inference will be high, making it difficult to reject the null hypothesis. With enough random error, it will be impossible to reject the null hypothesis. So saying that random error is taken into account in the test of inference is small comfort if there is a lot of random error. The moral is that it is desirable to make all forms of random error, including sampling error, as small as possible. That way one gets the most powerful or sensitive test of the null hypothesis in the sense that it is easier to reject the null hypothesis.

How can random error be reduced? Any time a relevant variable is controlled, all error from that variable may be eliminated. As you will see, control in sampling amounts to the researcher determining the distribution of the controlled variable in the sample. It follows that the researcher could make the distribution of the variable in the sample match that in the population, thereby eliminating any error from the controlled variable. The effect must be to reduce the overall amount of random error in the study. If you sample in such a way that males and females are equally represented in the sample, as they are in the population, you eliminate all error from gender in the sampling procedure and thereby reduce random error in the study. Thus, any time you control variables in sampling so as to make them perfectly representative of the population, you get the added bonus of reducing sampling error.

A special technique for reducing sampling error is simply to increase the size of the sample. As sample size approaches population size, sampling error must approach zero. After all, when sample size equals population size, you no longer have a sample. You have the population, which represents itself perfectly. Sampling error is inversely proportional to sample size, which implies that you get more benefit from increasing sample size when the sample is small than when it is large. It also implies that increasing sample size ultimately reaches a point where it does little good. If the sample is already very large, the reduction in sampling error achieved by further increases in sample size may not be worth the effort. Polling organizations find that they can achieve acceptable levels of precision (lack of sampling error) with samples from the general population of about 1500 to 2500 units. For basic research, where more error can be tolerated, acceptable sample sizes are typically much smaller. If you need to calculate exact sample sizes to achieve desired levels of precision, help is available from several sources, including Bordens and Abbott (1991) and Smith (1991). For present purposes, bear in mind that small samples are risky. Within reasonable limits, large samples are better because they have less sampling error.

These remarks must be tempered with the observation that sample size can be too large. The discussion of errors of inference in Chapter 4 made the point that any two variables in the universe are probably related to some small degree. With very large samples, tests of inference may result in rejecting the null hypothesis for relationships that are so small in size as to be trivial. In such cases, the test of inference is said to have too much power. The point made in Chapter 4 is relevant here. A reasonable sample size should be chosen by considering such factors as the resources available to do the research, the size of relationship one wishes to detect as statistically significant, the size of the population, and the loss of data from refusals or unusable data. If you fail to reject the null hypothesis with such a reasonable sample size, you may conclude that any relationship between the variables tested is too small to be of interest. The issue of large samples should not be overemphasized. In basic research, they are seldom a problem.

Sample bias. The second type of error in sampling is sample bias which is a special case of constant error. A constant error is one that systematically favors certain values of a variable over other values. *Sample bias* is constant error produced by the sampling procedure. As in the case of sampling error, the presence of sample bias means that at least one characteristic will be imperfectly represented in the sample. However, with sample bias the direction and size of the imperfection are, in principle, predictable because the error is produced by a systematic bias in the sampling procedure, which potentially could be identified.

To illustrate these points, let us return to the gender example, again assuming an even division between the sexes in the population. However, this scenario features a researcher who cannot resist the periodic temptation to choose females. He is supposed to sample randomly, but every now and then he abandons the random selection technique and simply chooses a female. Whenever this error in sampling occurs, it ALWAYS favors females. Therefore, it is sample bias. It follows that females will be overrepresented in the sample and males underrepresented. It could happen that the sample ends up with 75 percent females, just as in the sampling error example. However, in the current scenario, the error is caused by a systematic bias in selection. Therefore, it is a constant error, not a random error, and because the error is in the sampling procedure, it is the special form of constant error known as sample bias.

Sample bias is NOT a form of noise. Therefore, it cannot be included in the null hypothesis and taken care of by the test of statistical inference. Sample bias means that the sample does not adequately represent the target population. Period. Therefore, any generalizations from the sample to the population may be invalid. If the bias involves a relevant variable, generalizations are very likely to be invalid. Once a sample bias is present, there is no way to correct for it and no statistical means for neutralizing it. The study is flawed and cannot be rescued. Sampling error is a nuisance, but sample bias is fatal. With one exception, it must not be allowed to happen. The control techniques discussed in the next section are aimed at eliminating sample bias and simultaneously reducing sampling error.

The exception just mentioned occurs when a survey researcher wishes to make comparisons among values of variable and certain of the values are rare in the general population. An example of this situation is ethnic comparisons. The variable is ethnic group, and the researcher wants to compare minority groups with the majority ethnic group. If a certain minority constitutes a small percentage of the general population, the researcher might intentionally overrepresent that minority group in the sample. The purpose is to have a large enough sample of the minority group to justify statistical comparisons. Notice that this situation illustrates sample bias with respect to the general population, but no conclusions about the general population are to be made. The goal is to make comparisons among specific ethnic groups within the general population. Thus, the situation might better be viewed as involving several different populations, each consisting of one of the ethnic groups. The goal is to get an adequate sample from each separate population for the purpose of comparing populations. When viewed this way, there is no sample bias.

Sampling Procedures

The most common sampling procedures are presented in Table 7.2. As the table makes clear, the procedures may be classified on the basis of yes–no answers to three questions. The questions deal with whether any variables were controlled in sampling, whether controlled variables were made to perfectly represent the population, and how individual units were selected. Two terms need defining. As applied to sampling, *control* means that the values of a variable have specified proportions relative to each other in the sample and that the proportions were determined by the researcher. If the researcher specifies that the sample will be 75 percent female, then gender has been controlled. A yes answer to the second question means that the values of a controlled variable have the same proportions in the sample as in the population. Such would be the case if the researcher specifies that the sample will be 50 percent female. *Random* means that all units in the pool of potential selectees have an equal chance of being selected and that this remains true throughout the selection procedure. Throwing the names of all potential selectees into a hat and then choosing blindly would be one way of achieving randomness. The important thing about randomness is that it must be built into the selection procedure. That is, the procedure must be done in such a way that the defining conditions for randomness have been clearly satisfied. It is not appropriate to assume randomness when it is not clearly built into the selection procedure.

There are eight possible sequences of yes–no answers to the three classification questions, but two of them are impossible combinations. That occurs when the answers to the first two questions are no–yes. The remaining six sequences represent the six most common sampling procedures. The two adjectives play an important role in the classification scheme. The first adjective is determined by the sequence of answers to the first two classification questions: YY- = stratified, YN- = weighted, NY- = impossible, and NN- = simple. The second adjective is determined by the answer to the third classification question: —Y = random and —N = haphazard. Parentheses have been used to indicate where the terminology in the table differs from common usage. Stratified haphazard sampling is commonly known as quota sampling, and simple haphazard sampling is usually referred to without the "simple." Common synonymns for haphazard are convenience and accidental. Clearly, terminology varies. Table 7.2 uses a logically consistent terminology for naming the procedures.

Table 7.2   CLASSIFICATION OF COMMON SAMPLING PROCEDURES

Yes-No Questions Used for Classifying Sampling Procedures

1. Are certain variables controlled in sampling?
2. Are controlled variables made to appear in the sample in the same way as they do in the population?
3. Are individual units selected by a random procedure?

Sampling Procedures Based on Yes (Y) – No (N) Answers to Questions

Answers		Sampling Procedures
YYY	=	Stratified Random Sampling
YYN	=	Stratified Haphazard Sampling (Quota Sampling)
YNY	=	Weighted Random Sampling
YNN	=	Weighted Haphazard Sampling
NYY	=	Impossible
NYN	=	Impossible
NNY	=	Simple Random Sampling
NNN	=	(Simple) Haphazard Sampling

See text for explanations of terms.

Two points of clarification are necessary. First, not all authors agree on the definition of certain sampling procedures. Some authors define quota sampling as one of the "weighted" procedures in Table 7.2. The approach here follows the most common definitions in the literature. Second, the sampled units need not be people. They may be groups of people with something in common. This approach is called *cluster* sampling. Examples are the selection of city blocks or entire classrooms. The researcher must then decide how to choose units within the selected clusters. A common approach is to choose them all. Anything less requires a second decision about how to sample within clusters. This can go on for several levels of clustering. Such an approach is called *multi-stage* sampling.

Many authors make a distinction between probability and nonprobability sampling. With *probability sampling,* all units in the pool of potential selectees have a known probability of being chosen, and it is not 0 or 1. With *nonprobability sampling,* the probability of any unit being chosen is unknown. There are many ways of doing probability sampling, but in practice the only common method is some form of random sampling. Thus, the three random sampling procedures in Table 7.2 qualify as probability sampling. As you will see shortly, the terms "haphazard" and "nonprobability" mean the same thing. Thus, the three haphazard sampling procedures qualify as nonprobability sampling. Probability sampling by random selection is considered superior to nonprobability sampling because when properly done it is immune from sample bias.

Do you see why? (Q5)

Let us take a tour through the six sampling procedures, starting with the two that involve no controlled variables. In simple random sampling, selection is done in such a way that all individuals in the target population have an equal chance of

Table 7.3   TABLE OF RANDOM TWO-DIGIT NUMBERS

04	22	08	63	04	83	38	98	73	74	64	27	85
94	93	88	19	97	91	87	07	61	50	68	47	68
62	29	06	44	64	27	12	46	70	18	41	36	18
00	68	22	73	98	20	71	45	32	95	07	70	61
40	51	00	78	93	32	60	46	04	75	94	11	90
50	26	39	02	12	55	78	17	65	14	83	48	34
68	41	48	27	74	51	90	81	39	80	72	89	35
05	68	67	31	56	07	08	28	50	46	31	85	33
69	77	71	28	30	74	81	97	81	42	43	86	07
28	83	43	41	37	73	51	59	04	00	71	14	84
10	12	39	16	22	85	49	65	75	60	81	60	41
71	60	29	29	37	74	21	96	40	49	65	58	44
21	81	53	92	50	75	23	76	20	47	15	50	12
85	79	47	42	96	08	78	98	81	56	64	69	11
07	95	41	98	14	59	17	52	06	95	05	53	35
99	59	91	05	07	13	49	90	63	19	53	07	57
24	80	52	40	37	20	63	61	04	02	00	82	29
38	31	13	11	65	88	67	67	43	97	04	43	62
36	69	73	61	70	65	81	33	98	85	11	19	92
68	66	57	48	18	73	05	38	52	47	18	62	38
35	80	83	42	82	60	93	52	03	44	35	27	38
22	10	94	05	58	60	97	09	34	33	50	07	39

being chosen. As indicated earlier, this might be done by throwing names into a hat. In practice, it is usually done by a computer. To give you a feel for what is involved, Table 7.3 contains a list of random two-digit numbers generated by computer. Such tables are known as *random number tables*. To use the table, you assign each member of the target population a unique number by any means you like. You then enter the random number table at any point and proceed in an arbitrary direction, reading off unique numbers until you have as many as you would like for your sample. The members of the target population with those assigned numbers constitute your randomly selected sample. As an exercise, you might try this technique to select a simple random sample of your classmates.

In simple haphazard sampling, individuals are chosen on the basis of convenience, whoever is handy, and a target population may or may not be specified in advance. The only protection against sample bias is the researcher's attempt to avoid it. However, many sources of bias may be beyond the researcher's control in this situation. If you are stuck with haphazard sampling, as is often the case in student projects, the best approach is to think carefully, after the data have been collected, about what population, if any, may be represented by the sample. This amounts to thinking honestly about what features of the sampling procedure might limit your ability to generalize. Such an approach may be suitable for a class project, but it is inappropriate for serious survey research. If you ever do a serious survey project, haphazard sampling should be avoided.

When one wishes to ensure that a relevant variable is perfectly represented in the sample, stratified sampling is necessary. In sampling terminology, the variable to be controlled is called the stratification variable, and its values are called strata. The key feature of these approaches is that the researcher makes sure that the distribution of the stratified variable in the sample matches its distribution in the target population. Of course, a necessary precondition is that the researcher must know how the stratified variable is distributed in the target population. Individuals within each strata are chosen by either random or haphazard procedures. It seems silly to go to all the trouble of controlling a variable like gender and then to choose individuals within each sex haphazardly. However, it may be necessary when the researcher lacks access to the entire population. Class projects often employ quota sampling in an attempt to ensure that the sample is representative for at least one variable. Note, however, that quota sampling provides no protection against sample bias from variables other than the controlled variable. Again, the message is that stratified random sampling is preferable to quota sampling in serious survey research.

Weighted sampling is appropriate in those instances discussed earlier where the researcher wishes to make comparisons across values of a variable and some of the values occur rarely in the general population. The only difference from stratified sampling is that certain values of the weighted variable are overrepresented in the sample, and other values are underrepresented. Individuals are selected by either random or haphazard procedures, preferably random.

In the study described at the beginning of the chapter, Belyea and Lobao used weighted random sampling. The controlled variable was gross farm sales, and the purpose was to ensure adequate representation of all farm sizes. Because farms with very large gross sales are relatively rare, the researchers overrepresented such farms in their sample. They claimed that they could generalize their results to the "larger farm population in Ohio" (Belyea & Lobao, 1990, p. 65). Given the earlier discussion of sample bias, it is clear that the sample was biased in favor of large farms. Thus, if farm size is relevant to the relationships under investigation, the results of the study may provide a somewhat distorted view of what is true in the total farm population.

How To Obtain a Sample

What do you do when the first individual you have selected tells you to get lost? So does the third, the eighth, the twelfth, and so on. Clearly, you have a problem.

There is no guarantee that selected individuals will agree to participate. The percentage of those selected who also provide usable data is known as the response rate. In a survey, a low response rate means a high rate of refusal. If those who refuse differ systematically from those who participate, then you have sample bias, no matter how virtuous your sampling procedure may be. This becomes very likely when the response rate is low. Then the actual sample may not very well represent the intended target population, and the validity of conclusions is therefore in doubt. It follows that good survey researchers want to maximize their response rate. This section offers some tips for doing so.

No matter how hard you try, your response rate will not be perfect. At the very least, you should include the response rate in your research report so that readers can take it into account when evaluating your conclusions. If the response rate is low, you will also want to demonstrate that respondents did not differ from nonrespondents in relevant characteristics. If data are available for nonrespondents, a direct comparison can be made. Otherwise, it may be possible to show that respondents have characteristics similar to those known to exist in the target population.

In the Belyea and Lobao study of farmers, the initial response rate for the telephone interviews was 67 percent. Those who refused were replaced following the same sampling plan. Thus, the final sample of 940 telephone interviewees was weighted exactly as intended with respect to farm size. Unfortunately, only 503 of the interviewed farmers completed the mail questionnaire. Because the researchers collected demographic information during the interview, they were able to show that farmers who did and did not complete the questionnaire were similar with respect to age, education, number of children, and gross farm revenue.

The major factor affecting response rate is the type of contact between researcher and respondent. Face-to-face contact produces the highest response rates, followed by telephone contact. Mail contact is least effective. Face-to-face breaks down into one-on-one and group administration, with the former yielding higher response rates. As you can imagine, appropriate dress and grooming are important in face-to-face contact. So are the researcher's manner and voice, which should be friendly, courteous, and nonthreatening, but professional. Telephone contact breaks down into personal and computer calls. You should avoid computer calls if response rate is a major concern. Computer calls are dehumanizing, and the recipient may be tempted to hang up. Mail contact is popular because of its low cost. However, it also produces the lowest response rate, with estimates ranging from less than 10 percent to an upper limit of about 70 percent. Factors that increase response rates from mail contact are hand addressing the envelopes, mailing first class, and including a small financial reward or other gift.

After type of contact, the two most important factors affecting response rates for surveys are prior notification and follow-up. If a potential respondent has advance notice that a survey contact will be made, refusal is less likely. This is particularly true if the prior notification emphasizes the importance of the research and expresses the researcher's sincere appreciation. Some research suggests that prior contact is most effective when done by telephone with a female caller. Follow-up calls or postcards are also effective in increasing response rates. Some authors suggest "relentless" and "aggressive" follow-up, which is claimed to increase the response rates of mail surveys by as much as 50 percent. Of course, persistence must be combined with courtesy or the strategy may backfire.

Miscellaneous suggestions include keeping the survey as short as possible, especially for interviews, and being sure to obtain permission to administer surveys in private settings, which include such "public" places as shopping malls. Failure to obtain permission may shorten your effective life as a survey researcher and get you into legal trouble as well. More tips for combating nonresponse are contained in discussions by Bordens and Abbott (1991) and Williamson et al. (1982).

Sampling and Thinking

Chapter 2 contained a discussion of how the concept of an operational definition can play a useful role in everyday thinking. The same is true for many of the concepts in the discussion of sampling. Let us consider how sampling issues are relevant for effective thinking.

Modern humans are the result of millions of years of evolution. Our evolutionary ancestors were neither the strongest nor the fastest of the animals competing for survival on the African savannah. They had to specialize in something else to compete effectively—they specialized in thinking, living by their wits, outmaneuvering the competition. Such specialization required the storage of large amounts of information, and so natural selection favored the development of larger brains. The most valuable information was that involved in recognizing relevant situations, anticipating what was likely to happen next, figuring out what to do about it, and taking quick action. Given this scenario, it is not surprising to find modern humans with strong biases toward relying on their own experience and reaching quick conclusions so they can get on with things.

These tendencies are reflected in the way humans make generalizations in their everyday lives, and they are related to the errors in sampling discussed earlier. Recall that sampling error refers to random error or noise in the sampling procedure. A major factor affecting sampling error is sample size. When sample size is very small, sampling error may be so large that any generalization becomes risky. Yet humans persist in jumping to conclusions based on very small samples, often samples of one. As noted in Chapter 1, if one clerk is rude, the customer leaves the store in a huff and tells friends that the store is full of rude clerks. Such generalizations are understandable in terms of the human bias toward quick action. Nevertheless, they are often erroneous and unfair. The pressure to act quickly is not as prevalent today as it was in the evolutionary past. Wherever possible, you would be well advised to seek larger samples so as to reduce the risk of invalid generalizations.

Sample bias refers to any systematic distortion in the sample that renders it unrepresentative of the target population. Generalizations based on distorted samples are risky. Yet examples of such bias abound in everyday thinking. Two of them are supported by a great deal of research evidence (Nisbett & Ross, 1980). The first is a tendency to favor personal experience over "facts" when reaching conclusions, where "facts" refers to scientific evidence. This tendency is presumably a result of an evolutionary bias toward relying on personal experience. Educators, aware of this bias, strive to provide "hands-on" experiences. The other side if the coin is that erroneous conclusions are likely when personal experience is peculiar or biased in some relevant respect. If your personal contact with another ethnic group has been "strange," perhaps because both sides sent "strange" signals to each other based on mutual distrust, then you will be unlikely to credit any number of studies showing that members of that ethnic group are just as normal as you are. The problem is that your sample of interactions is biased, and you have a hard time ignoring personal experience.

A second example of sample bias in everyday thinking has been given an official name by psychologists. *Confirmation bias* refers to the tendency to favor evidence that agrees with one's current position and to discount evidence that disagrees with it. Because one's current position probably derives from personal experience, confirmation bias can be seen as a special case of the previous bias. It has the effect of reinforcing opinions based on personal experience and making it harder for contradictory evidence to have an impact. The new wrinkle is that even contradictory evidence in one's current experience may be discounted or misinterpreted so as to support existing beliefs. But that just shows how tightly humans cling to positions that develop over the course of their personal history. A dramatic example would be citing statistics about the ineffectiveness of capital punishment to a parent whose child was murdered. Imagine what would happen to those statistics in such a situation.

Although serious, the consequences of sample bias should not be overstated. It is true that generalizing about factual matters from personal experience is threatened by sample bias whenever personal experience is peculiar. But how often does one make such generalizations in situations with important consequences? Expressing an opinion among friends or blowing off steam is not a situation with important consequences, and so it does not matter if an opinion about what is true in general is biased. Taking such opinions into the arena of social action is another matter, with the gravest consequences. However, it seems likely that many generalizations humans make concern their personal lives, not what is true in general. In one's personal life, reliance on personal experience seems sensible. Bias is still possible because what is true in general may also be true for an individual, despite that person's peculiar history. Still, as a guide to living, your own experience is likely to be your most useful resource. This is not surprising, considering how humans evolved. Such a view implies that attempts to replace past experience with the facts are unlikely to succeed. Building on what is there is a more promising approach because it respects past experience.

SUMMARY

Surveys are self-report measuring instruments consisting of stimuli and responses. Mode of administration may be oral (interviews) or written (questionnaires). Stimulus format may be structured (exact wording and order of items determined in advance) or unstructured. Response format may be closed (respondent must choose from given alternatives) or open (complete freedom of response). This chapter focused on procedural issues for unstructured interviews with open responses and structured questionnaires with closed responses.

In unstructured interviews with open responses, the researcher should have a written plan specifying the topics to be covered and the level of detail to be achieved. Questioning should proceed from the general to the specific, with probes used to obtain further information where necessary. The interviewer should be clear but neutral in presenting stimuli. In structured questionnaires with closed responses, reliability is achieved by clear wording. Avoid vague words, jargon, and complex words. Validity is achieved primarily by trying to build face validity into stimulus wording. Avoid double-barreled questions, negative wording, wording that assumes something or biases the respondent, sensitive topics, and extremes of social desirability. Avoid extreme response sets by including an equal number of favorable and unfavorable items for each variable measured. Consider whether preceding items establish a biasing context. Where possible, pretest items for clarity and bias.

Survey researchers are especially interested in sampling. In a representative sample, all relevant characteristics occur in the sample in the same way as in the population. Error in sampling, or nonrepresentativeness, or comes in two forms. Sampling error is random error in the sampling procedure. Sample bias is constant error in the sampling procedure that systematically favors certain values of variables over others. Control in sampling is achieved by stratification, where the researcher ensures that a variable has the same distribution in the sample as in the population. Stratification eliminates both types of error from the controlled variable. Sample bias may also be eliminated by random sampling, that is, sampling so that all potential selectees have an equal chance of being chosen. In contrast, haphazard sampling, where individuals are chosen on the basis of convenience, offers no protection against sample bias. Random sampling creates sampling error, but it may be reduced by using large samples. Sometimes a researcher may intentionally create sample bias by overrepresenting some values of a variable in a sample at the expense of other values, a procedure known as weighted sampling. Response rate refers to the percentage of selected individuals who provide usable data. Refusals lower response rate and may create sample bias. The three major factors affecting response rate are type of contact (face-to-face best, mail worst), prior notification, and persistent follow-up. Error in sampling plays an important role in everyday thinking. Sampling error occurs when a person jumps to conclusions based on very small samples. Sample bias occurs when a person relies on biased personal experience or engages in confirmation bias.

ANSWERS TO QUESTIONS

Q1. Change the definition of structure given in the text by substituting the word "form" for "wording."

Q2. The painful situation of the woman with a defective fetus may induce a harsher attitude toward women who want an abortion just to avoid children.

Q3. The item assumes that the respondent endorses the death penalty for murder.

Q4. Imagine a 6-point step scale for responding, ranging from "strongly disagree" to "strongly agree." The Likert procedure scores favorable items so that "strongly agree" = 6 and unfavorable items so that "strongly agree" = 1. Thus, if the scale score is obtained by summing across six items, three favorable and three unfavorable, someone who chooses "strongly agree" for all six will receive a score of 6 for each of the favorable items and 1 for each of the unfavorable items, yielding an overall scale score of 21. Twenty-one is right in the middle of the range of possible scale scores which can vary from 6 to 36. A similar argument may be made for someone who always chooses "strongly disagree."

Q5. If the sampling procedure guarantees that each unit in the pool of potential selectees has an equal chance of being chosen at every step in the selection process, then it is impossible to favor systematically some units over others. Such is the case with random sampling. Thus, no bias is possible.

FURTHER READING

Further information on interviewing may be found in books by Banaka (1971) and Gordon (1975). Readable chapters may be found in Sommer and Sommer (1991) and Williamson, Karp, Dalphin, and Gray (1982). For practical help on questionnaire design, the book by Sudman and Bradburn (1982) is helpful. Sommer and Sommer (1991) have a chapter devoted to the questionnaire, and parts of chapters in books by Bordens and Abbott (1991) and Smith (1991) are also relevant. Good books on sampling include Jaeger (1984), Kish (1965), and Sudman (1976).

REFERENCES

Banaka, W. (1971). *Training in depth interviewing*. New York: Harper & Row.

Bausell, R. B. (1986). *A practical guide to conducting empirical research*. New York: Harper & Row.

Belyea, M. J., & Lobao, L. M. (1990). Psychosocial consequences of agricultural transformation: The farm crisis and depression. *Rural Sociology, 55*, 58–75.

Bordens, K. S., & Abbott, B. B. (1991). *Research designs and methods: A process approach* (2nd ed.). Mountain View, CA: Mayfield.

Gordon, R. L. (1975). *Interviewing: Strategies, techniques, and tactics* (rev. ed.). Homewood, IL: Dorsey Press.

Jaeger, R. (1984). *Sampling in education and the social sciences*. New York: Longman.

Jaroslovsky, R. (1988, July/August). What's on your mind, America? *Psychology Today*, pp. 54–59.

Kish, L. (1965). *Survey sampling*. New York: John Wiley & Sons.

Lazarus, R. S. (1966). *Psychological stress and the coping process*. New York: McGraw-Hill.

Nisbett, R., & Ross, L. (1980). *Human inference: Strategies and shortcomings of social judgment*. Englewood Cliffs, NJ: Prentice-Hall.

Schuman, H., & Scott, J. (1987). Problems in the use of survey questions to measure public opinion. *Science, 236*, 957–959.

Smith, H. W. (1991). *Strategies of social research* (3rd ed.). Orlando: FL: Holt, Rinehart and Winston.

Sommer, B., & Sommer, R. (1991). *A practical guide to behavioral research: Tools and techniques* (3rd ed.). New York: Oxford University Press.

Sudman, S. (1976). *Applied sampling.* New York: Academic Press.

Sudman, S., & Bradburn, N. M. (1982). *Asking questions: A practical guide to questionnaire design.* San Francisco: Jossey-Bass.

Williamson, J. B., Karp, D. A., Dalphin, J. R., & Gray, P. S. (1982). *The research craft: An introduction to social research methods* (2nd ed.). Boston: Little, Brown.

Survey Research: Analysis

8

If you are planning both to work for a living and get older, here is a depressing fact for you. Studies of employee performance evaluations have repeatedly shown that older employees receive lower performance evaluations. If you think of both age and performance evaluation as finely measured variables in the sense of Chapter 5, this means that the two variables are negatively correlated. Just what you needed, right? One more reason to avoid growing older.

Like most sensible people, Gerald Ferris and Thomas King, two professors of business administration, could not believe that age was a direct cause of lower performance evaluations. Nor did they believe that age produced a lower quality of performance, which would justify lower evaluations. Instead, they felt that the age-evaluation relationship resulted from the influence of a powerful mediating variable known as "subordinate ingratiation behavior" (Ferris & King, 1992). Ingratiation means to "butter somebody up" by doing favors, offering compliments or flattery, agreeing with the person's opinions, etc. Older employees are less likely to do those things because they do not feel it's something that they should have to do. As a result, their supervisors like them less, and the supervisor's liking is reflected in the performance evaluation. An additional factor is interpersonal distance. Older employees tend to be located at a greater distance, both physically and psychologically, from their supervisors than younger employees. This limits their opportunities for ingratiating behavior even if they are so inclined.

Notice that a number of variables with a complex pattern of relationships are included in the Ferris-King theoretical model of performance evaluation. Figure 8.1 is a diagram of the model in which the direction of the arrows indicates the proposed direction of influences. The model shows both a direct and an indirect (by way of interpersonal distance) influence of age on ingratiation behavior, as described in the last paragraph. The implication is that if the influence of interpersonal distance could be removed, there would still be some degree of relationship between age and performance evaluation because of the direct influence of age on ingratiation. The Ferris-King model illustrates the virtue of clarity in theory, as described in Chapter 1. Because the model was so clearly presented, a complex but testable prediction was easily derived from it.

Ferris and King tested their model on a sample of nurses and their supervisors. Both groups filled out questionnaires that allowed the researchers to derive a finely measured score for each variable in the model for each nurse. Age was measured directly, and the remaining variables were measured by means of multi-item Likert scales. Internal consistency reliability for the Likert scales was assessed by means of coefficient alpha (see Chapter 6) and ranged from .80 for interpersonal distance to .88 for both supervisor liking of subordinate and performance evaluation.

Simple correlations were computed for each pair of measured variables. The results generally supported the theoretical model. The variable with the most direct influence on evaluation in the model is supervisor liking. Thus, liking should have the strongest correlation with evaluation, and it did (r = .71). By the same reasoning, ingratiation should have the strongest correlation with liking, and it did (r = .48). Age and distance should both be negatively correlated with ingratiation, and they were (r = −.28 and −.46, respectively). Also as predicted, age and distance were positively correlated (r = .33). Finally, because of their indirect influences by way of

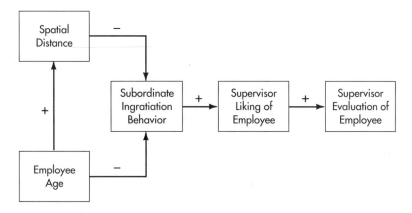

Figure 8.1
Theoretical model of performance evaluation proposed by Ferris and King.

ingratiation in the model, both age and distance were expected to be negatively correlated with evaluation, and they were ($r = -.19$ and $-.31$, respectively). All of these correlations were statistically significant according to the testing procedure described later in this chapter.

Although the simple correlations generally supported the theoretical model, simple correlations cannot provide an adequate test of the complex prediction described earlier. Recall that the model implies a correlation between age and evaluation even after the influence of distance is removed. A simple correlation has no way of removing the influence of a third variable from the relationship between two other variables. To do so requires one or more of the techniques discussed in the section on Advanced Correlation Analyses later in the chapter. So for now you will have to be patient. More of the Ferris-King results will be presented later.

The goal of this chapter is to discuss data analysis for typical survey studies. As in the previous chapter, the focus will be on unstructured interviews and then structured questionnaires. The coverage of questionnaires will explain how to do correlational analyses of multi-item scale scores and other finely measured variables typical of modern survey research. The important issue of how to combine reliability results with other results to reach sensible conclusions will also be considered. Finally, there will be a discussion of some advanced correlation techniques that are often used in the analysis of complex survey studies like the Ferris-King example.

INTERVIEWS

For unstructured interviews with open responses, a decision must be made concerning whether the data analysis will be primarily qualitative or quantitative (i.e., nonnumerical or numerical; see Chapter 4). Some mixing is possible, but the overall direction of the analysis depends on which mode is chosen as the primary approach.

Qualitative Analysis

If the decision is for qualitative analysis, then the analysis proceeds exactly as described for field observation in Chapter 4. Instead of field notes, the raw data are the record of the interview. That record may be in the form of video tape, voice recording, or interview notes. The latter approach typically relies on some kind of short-hand system, developed in advance, for recording responses. The researcher sifts through interview records looking for valid generalizations, just as the field worker sifts through field notes. The major difference is that the interviewer directed the conversation to certain topics whereas the field observer presumably did nothing to influence the ongoing events. Given the element of subjectivity in qualitative analysis, the "conclusions" in both cases are likely to be in the form of tentative hypotheses, subject to further confirmation. Note the many parallels between unstructured interviews and field observation.

Quantitative Analysis

If the analysis is to be quantitative, then the researcher must face the prospect of coding responses. *Coding* refers to the process of establishing objective response categories for open responses to a given survey item. The key feature of a good coding system is clear rules for deciding how to categorize any conceivable response. Does this sound familiar? Precisely the same problem faces the systematic observer, and Chapter 3 described possible solutions. Here is a parallel between unstructured interviews and systematic observation, and it is no coincidence that it depends on the decision to make the data analysis quantitative. Note that the same problem faces the researcher engaged in content analysis, also described briefly in Chapter 3. Whenever coding systems are used in any of these situations, it is important to check their reliability. This is done by having independent coders use the system on the same data and then computing inter-coder agreement rate or Cohen's kappa, as described in Chapters 3 and 4.

The discussion so far has assumed that coding systems are devised after data have been collected. But you know that isn't the case for systematic observation where coding systems, also known as operational definitions, must be established in advance. Is such an approach possible for unstructured surveys? Certainly. In fact, a coding system may be the short-hand system for response recording mentioned earlier. Whether a coding system comes before or after interview data are collected depends on the researcher's ability to anticipate the kinds of responses that are likely to be made.

Decisions must be made about what behavior to code. Obviously the content of the respondent's verbal answers has to be coded. Depending on the interviewer's purpose, it may also be useful to code the style of speaking, including such things as tone of voice, hesitations, etc. Then, too, body language accompanying verbal responses may be revealing and worth coding. Body language refers to such things as facial expression, eye contact (or lack of it), movements, gestures, posture, etc. Speaking style and body language constitute what Sommer and Sommer (1991) refer to as the *latent* content of a person's answers, as contrasted with the *manifest* content of the spoken words. Where the two types of content conflict, the researcher may be onto something interesting and may decide to analyze them separately. Of course, no analysis of latent content is possible unless such content makes it into the interview record.

Coding leads to a score for each coded item and each respondent. The nature of the statistical analysis depends on the level of measurement achieved. Everything said about levels of measurement in Chapter 5 applies here. If the coding system yields only same–different categories, coarse measurement in the sense of Chapter 5, then the question of whether two such items are related may be answered by frequency tables and chi-square analysis. On the other hand, if the coding system yields finely ordered categories, constituting fine measurement in the sense of Chapter 5, then correlation analysis is appropriate. Correlation analysis will be described in the section on the analysis of questionnaires. As noted in Chapter 5, one way to achieve fine measurement is to build a scale score by combining responses from several interview items. In the case of mixed measurement, one coarsely measured and one finely measured variable, it may be necessary to compare average responses on the finely measured variable across categories on the coarsely measured variable. Such an approach is identical to the analysis of experiments and will be covered in Chapter 11.

This discussion has focused on the unstructured interview with open responding. For data analysis, the case of the structured interview with open responding is exactly the same. Coding must be done, and the kind of measurement achieved by the coding determines the appropriate statistical analysis, just as described in the last paragraph. Coding systems developed in advance of data collection are more likely for structured than for unstructured interviews with open responding. However, this difference is unlikely to have any consequences for data analysis. For structured interviews with closed responding, it is also necessary to quantify responses, and it is a matter of taste whether one refers to the process as coding. In any event, scoring is likely to be much simpler because possible item scores are likely to be implied strongly by the closed response choices for each item. Statistical analysis for this situation is the same as for structured questionnaires with closed responding. That situation is next on the agenda.

QUESTIONNAIRES

Assume that scale scores for each variable of interest have been derived by combining item scores for relevant items. Thus, the analysis focuses on the question of whether pairs of finely measured variables are related. As discussed in Chapter 6, correlational analysis is appropriate for this situation. Of course, it is possible that structured questionnaires with closed responding may yield other combinations of coarse and fine data. In such cases, suggestions for data analysis would be the same as those given in the discussion of coding and analysis for unstructured interviews. In the case of finely measured variables, a researcher might want to use some of the advanced correlational techniques briefly described later in this chapter or other advanced techniques with impressive names like factor analysis, cluster analysis, and multidimensional scaling. If so, the obvious advice is to get competent help. The following sections describe the simplest possible analysis for finely measured variables, the correlation coefficient. You will be shown how to compute a correlation and how to test one for statistical significance. Before you read the next two sections, you should review the section on "The Concept of Correlation" in Chapter 6 so that you are clear about what a correlation is and about the warnings associated with its use.

Descriptive Statistics

For finely measured variables derived from questionnaires, the simplest descriptive analysis of relationships is the computation of correlation coefficients for pairs of variables or scale scores. In some situations, a researcher might also want to present scatterplots to illustrate the relationships pictorially. The formula for the correlation, r, between any two variables, X and Y, is as follows:

$$r = \frac{(N)(\Sigma XY) - (\Sigma X)(\Sigma Y)}{\{\sqrt{[(N)(\Sigma X^2) - (\Sigma X)^2]}\}\,\{\sqrt{[(N)(\Sigma Y^2) - (\Sigma Y)^2]}\}}.$$

(8.1)

This the most complex formula in the book. It is not as bad as it looks. To do the calculation, you need six quantities and a calculator with a square-root button. The six quantities needed are illustrated in Table 8.1. Let's take a close look at the table.

Table 8.1 illustrates the calculation of a correlation coefficient for a small sample of $N = 5$ subjects. Two data sets are given. For each data set, you should think of X and Y as Likert-scale scores for two variables derived from sets of questionnaire items. The complete calculation is provided for Data Set #1. The calculations for Data Set #2 are left for you to do as an exercise. For Data Set #1, the X^2 column contains the squares of the numbers in the X column, and the Y^2 column bears the same relationship to the Y column. The XY column contains cross products, that is, the X score times the Y score for a given subject. Notice that the sum of each column is one of the quantities needed in the correlation formula, as shown at the bottom of the columns. Below the data set, the relevant quantities are entered into the correlation formula, and each step of the calculation is illustrated.

The key step in the calculation is the first one where the relevant quantities are entered into the formula. The rest is just arithmetic, except for the step where the square roots are taken, and that requires a calculator with a square-root button. Note that ΣX^2 and $(\Sigma X)^2$ are NOT the same thing. The former is the sum of the X^2 column; the latter is the square of the sum of the X column. Similarly for ΣY^2 and $(\Sigma Y)^2$. If you have any doubts about why the various quantities appear where they do in the first step, talk to your instructor until you understand the step completely.

The result of all the calculations is $r = -.9833$, a strong negative correlation, which may be verified by making a scatterplot. The variables for Data Set #1 might very well be speed and accuracy because the faster you work in most tasks, the lower your accuracy. The last line for Data Set #1 presents the results of a test of inference, and it will be discussed in the next section.

Table 8.1   TWO DATA SETS ILLUSTRATING
CALCULATION OF THE CORRELATION COEFFICIENT, r,
BETWEEN VARIABLES X AND Y FOR SAMPLES OF N = 5

Subject	X	Y	Data Set #1 X^2	Y^2	XY	Data Set #2 X	Y
1	12	19	144	361	228	13	17
2	14	17	196	289	238	19	16
3	16	15	256	225	240	20	18
4	18	13	324	169	234	17	15
5	16	14	256	196	224	10	11
Sum	76	78	1176	1240	1164	?	?
	ΣX	ΣY	ΣX^2	ΣY^2	ΣXY	ΣX	ΣY

For Data Set #1:

$$r = \frac{(5)(1164) - (76)(78)}{\{\sqrt{[(5)(1176) - (76)^2]}\}\ \{\sqrt{[(5)(1240) - (78)^2]}\}}$$

$$= \frac{5820 - 5928}{\{\sqrt{[5880 - 5776]}\}\ \{\sqrt{[6200 - 6084]}\}}$$

$$= \frac{-108}{[\sqrt{104}]\ [\sqrt{116}]}$$

$$= \frac{-108}{(10.1980)\ (10.7703)} = \frac{-108}{109.8355} = -.9833.$$

Therefore, r(3) = –.9833, p < .01.

For Data Set #2: ??

Now it's your turn. What is r for Data Set #2? (Q1)

Usually you do not have to calculate correlation coefficients. A computer does it for you. The calculations are shown so that you could do the job if you ever found yourself stranded on a desert island with nothing more than a data set and a hand calculator. Alternately, your instructor may want you to have the experience of calculating an r for some data that you generate as a class project. In that case, the sample is likely to be much larger than 5, and the various sums you need will be much larger than those in Table 8.1. If so, the author recommends that your instructor give you the five sums needed for calculating r.

It would be nice if the correlation formula could be dissected in the same manner as the chi-square formula so that you could see how it does its job of quantifying a linear relationship. Unfortunately, that is not possible because it would require mathematical background that many of you probably lack. So you must take it on faith that the correlation formula produces a result with all the properties described in Chapter 6. However, two points can be made. First, the formula is derived from the calculus in such a way as to minimize the sum of the squared distances between the points in the scatterplot and the best-fitting straight-line function. Second, it is the numerator of the formula that quantifies the tendency of the variables to change together, or covary, in a linear fashion and thus determines the sign of the correlation. The denominator simply transforms the result so that it must fall in the range from –1 to +1, inclusive.

In basic research, it seldom happens that the researcher is not interested in relationships between variables. However, in some forms of survey research, such as public opinion polls, the main focus may be on single variables considered in isolation. In that case, a summary of the percentage of respondents who chose each response alternative for a structured item with closed responding may be all that is needed in the way of descriptive statistics.

Inferential Statistics

To test a correlation for statistical significance, NO FURTHER CALCULATION IS REQUIRED! There is no separate testing statistic for making inferences about correlations. Given the complex formula for calculating a correlation, the simplicity of the significance test seems only fair.

To test a correlation for significance, you simply look up the sample r in a table and find out its probability under the null hypothesis, just as you did for chi-square. The table to use is Table A.2 in Appendix A, which contains critical values of r under the null hypothesis. As usual, you will need to know the degrees of freedom, or df, to determine which row of the table is relevant. For a test of inference for a single correlation, $df = N - 2$. In the example of Table 8.1, $N = 5$, and thus $df = 5 - 2 = 3$. Now you must play the same game with r that you did with chi-square. Look in the relevant row of the table and see where the sample r of .9833 (ignore the sign of r when doing this test) would be located if it had a column of its own. Clearly, in this case the imaginary column would be to the far right. Projecting to the top of the table, note that $p < .01$. Thus, the last line of the calculation for Data Set #1 in Table 8.1 says that "$r(3) = -.9833$, $p < .01$," which means that the sample r, with 3 degrees of freedom, equals –.9833, and its probability under the null hypothesis is less than .01. Now recall the decision rule in Chapter 4 (Table 4.3, Step 7): If p is less than or equal to alpha (or, equivalently, if the value of the inferential testing statistic is greater than or equal to the critical value), reject the null hypothesis; otherwise, do not reject it. If alpha was set to the default value of .05 (setting alpha must be done *before* the data are analyzed), then this decision rule would lead you to reject the null hypothesis for Data Set #1 in Table 8.1.

What is the null hypothesis in this situation? It is that in the population r equals 0. The alternative hypothesis is that in the population r does not equal 0. In rejecting the null hypothesis, you are concluding that the variables have a linear relationship in the population sampled. Everything said about errors of inference in Chapter 4 applies here as well. For correlation, there is an additional consideration. If the test of inference yields p > .05, so that you decide not to reject the null hypothesis, it may still be true that the variables are related but in a nonlinear fashion. At the very least, one would want to check the scatterplot for evidence of such a possiblity. Remember: the correlation coefficient and its test of inference assess linear relationships only.

Although it may not be immediately obvious, the simple method of looking up the sample r in a table follows the logic of statistical inference discussed in Chapter 4. The testing statistic is the absolute value of the sample r. It may be viewed as a measure of the discrepancy between the obtained result, r, and the value that should have been obtained if the null hypothesis was true, namely 0. The larger the sample r, the larger the discrepancy from the expected value of 0, and therefore the smaller the probability under the null hypothesis. In the case of correlation, r plays the role of D, the actual data, 0 plays the role of H, the null hypothesis, and the inference test yields p(D | H), or the probability of "D given H," exactly as discussed in Chapter 4.

Unlike chi-square analysis, in the case of correlation there is no intuitively appealing interpretation of the formula for degrees of freedom. The rationale given in most statistics texts is that in general df is the number of data points minus the number of constraints on the data. Constraints refers to the number of statistical quantities that are being estimated in a given situation. In the case of a scatterplot, clearly there are N data points. The number of statistical quantities that must be estimated to fit a straight line to the data is two, namely the slope and the Y-intercept of the linear function. Thus, df = N – 2.

What do you do when you cannot find your df in Table A.2? For most situations, you may simply use the row with the df that comes closest without exceeding your df. This approach gives you a slightly conservative test (it is a little harder than it should be to reject the null hypothesis), which means that you are unlikely to be criticized for recklessness. For example, if N = 78, then df = 76, and you would use the row for df = 70 in Table A.2. Even so, you would report the proper df, 76, in a research report.

If the conservative approach yields a result that is almost, but not quite, significant, then you may wish to use interpolation. To interpolate, you compute the appropriate fractional distance between the critical values bracketing the one you seek. This may be accomplished using the following formula for CVI, the interpolated critical value:

$$\text{CVI} = \text{CVS} - [(\text{dfA} - \text{dfS})/(\text{dfL} - \text{dfS})](\text{CVS} - \text{CVL}). \tag{8.2}$$

dfL and dfS are the larger df and the smaller df bracketing dfA, the actual df, and CVL and CVS are the critical values for dfL and dfS. In the current example, with alpha set at .05, dfA = 76, dfL = 80, dfS = 70, CVL = .217, and CVS = .232. Note that critical values decrease as df increases, so CVS is greater than CVL. The calculation proceeds as follows:

CVI = .232 - [(76 - 70)/(80 - 70)](.232 - .217) = .232 - (6/10)(.015) = .232 - .009 = .223.

If your actual r, ignoring sign, is greater than or equal to CVI = .223, then p is less than or equal to .05, and you should reject the null hypothesis.

As noted in the preceding paragraph, within each column of Table A.2, the critical values of r get smaller as df gets larger. This makes intuitive sense. For a sample of 5 (df = 3), it is not uncommon for the 5 points in the scatterplot to line up near a straight line function by chance alone even when the null hypothesis is correct (no linear relationship between the variables). So it takes a very large sample r (greater than or equal to .878 for alpha = .05) to reject the null hypothesis. For large samples, it is much more unlikely that all the points will fall near a straight line by chance alone. Therefore, a much smaller sample r is needed to make the case that a linear relationship exists. Thus, smaller sample r values are associated with larger df values in the table.

What is the result of the test of inference for Data Set #2 in Table 8.1? (Q2)

Reliability, Hypothesis Testing, and the Third Option

If you are like most students, you have a pretty good idea about how correlation is used to assess the linear relationship between two variables. With allowance for forgetting, you probably also have a fair memory for how correlation is used to assess reliability for finely measured variables. However, you may have little understanding of how the two topics fit together. That problem must be addressed because it is vital for you to understand how reliability analysis contributes to the final decision about the null hypothesis of no relationship.

Consider a concrete example. Suppose that for a sample of 54 participants you have obtained a correlation of .19 between impulsiveness and compulsiveness, both measured via Likert scales. Using Table A.2, you can do the test of inference and quickly decide that p > .10, which implies that you should not reject the null hypothesis of no linear relationship between the two variables. A scatterplot indicates that there is no nonlinear relationship. Should you conclude that for all practical purposes the variables are unrelated? It would seem so.

Suppose you now learn that coefficient alpha, the internal-consistency measure of reliability discussed in Chapter 6, is .28 for impulsiveness and .78 for compulsiveness. This changes matters. Given the guidelines for acceptable reliability in Chapter 6, the alphas indicate that reliability is not adequate for impulsiveness. This must mean that your measure of impulsiveness had a lot of noise in it. In other words, you did not measure ANY variable with precision. Because you failed to measure impulsiveness, it would be unfair to reach any conclusion about impulsiveness. You have no more grounds for concluding that impulsiveness is not related to compulsiveness than for concluding that it is. The study did not provide a fair test of the null hypothesis because you failed to measure one of variables. The only responsible decision in this situation is to suspend judgment.

It is important to draw a distinction between two types of conclusions or decisions about a null hypothesis. The first, which will be called a *statistical conclusion*, is based only on the test of inference and is summarized in the p statement that accompanies the test. There are only two options for this conclusion: reject the null hypothesis (p ≤ alpha) or fail to reject it (p > alpha). The second type of conclusion which will be called the *final conclusion*, is based on ALL sources of evidence available to the researcher, including the test of inference. The final conclusion is clearly the more important of the two. It will usually be found in the "Discussion" section of a research report, after the data analysis has been presented. It indicates what the researcher, taking all sources of information into account, finally concludes about relationships among variables. The same options are available for the final conclusion as for the statistical conclusion, but the final conclusion also has a third option: suspend judgment. Such a conclusion may seem wishy-washy, but as you saw in the last paragraph, there are situations where it is the only responsible option. In any event, it is a perfectly legitimate option for the final conclusion and therefore should be used whenever appropriate.

Do not misinterpret the word "final" in this discussion. "Final" does NOT mean set in stone for all time. Ironically, the final conclusion is the more tentative of the two types. The statistical conclusion is purely mechanical, and it goes clearly one way or the other. In contrast, the final conclusion is always subject to revision based on further information or reasoned argument that may become available. All "final" means is that the conclusion represents the researcher's latest judgment, based on all sources of information, about whether the variables under investigation are likely to be related. As you know from the discussion of errors of inference in Chapter 4, statistical conclusions are not certain; they can be wrong. However, there is a meaningful sense in which final conclusions are even more tentative because of the third available option to suspend judgment.

One of the relevant sources of information that should influence final conclusions is information about reliability of measurement. Such information is so important that the following decision rule is offered for how to use it: Check reliability first; if it is unacceptable, take the third option and suspend judgment. Only if reliability is acceptable for both variables involved in the null hypothesis should the test of inference be taken seriously. In that case, one would normally accept the conclusion implied by the test of inference unless there was some other good reason to doubt it. Note that this is a two-step procedure, that the reliability check comes first, and that it may completely override the test of inference. Clearly, then, it is important to assess reliability wherever possible and to integrate that information with the results of inference tests when reaching final conclusions.

The discussion has hammered away at the importance of reliability because beginning research students often fail to assess reliability, or, if reliability information is available, they fail to use it properly in reaching conclusions, often ignoring it completely. Neither tendency should be encouraged. Unacceptable reliability carries its own distinctive message: the study has measurement problems that must be corrected before a meaningful test of the null hypothesis can be obtained. There is a world of difference between knowing this and not knowing it. Make no mistake about it: Reliability information should be obtained and used in reaching conclusions.

Some students confuse the two decision options of failing to reject the null hypothesis and suspending judgment. They are NOT the same. When you fail to reject the null hypothesis, you are concluding that any relationship between the two variables is too small to be of interest. When you suspend judgment, you are concluding that you have no idea whether or how strongly two variables are related. The second conclusion implies greater ignorance about the true state of affairs than the first one. Poor reliability is a good reason for adopting the greater-ignorance option.

One last point: Reliability evidence has similar implications regardless of the kind of research study or the type of statistical analysis. Poor reliability should make you cautious in deciding about relationships in observation studies, surveys, or experiments, and when the statistical analysis involves chi-square, correlation, or whatever.

Now test yourself to see if you understood the decision rule for using reliability evidence to reach final conclusions. Imagine a study with N = 64 and three finely measured variables: A, B, and C. The correlations are .52 for A and B, .17 for A and C, and −.39 for B and C. Reliability analysis yields coefficient alphas of .74, .68, and .26 for A, B, and C, respectively.

What conclusions are appropriate? (Q3)

A Research Example

A survey study conducted by one of the author's research-methods classes provides a concrete example of many of the topics discussed in the last several chapters. The purpose of the survey was to see if attitudes toward abortion could be predicted from two other variables: involvement in religious practices and attitude toward post-natal public-aid programs. Table 8.2 contains the entire survey used to measure all three variables. The first six items measured attitude toward abortion and are the same as the items in Table 6.2. The next six items measured attitude toward public aid, and the last six items measured religious involvement. Note that the widespread practice of Likert-scale measurement was used for all three variables. The abortion items were used in the last two chapters to illustrate suggestions for achieving reliable and valid measurement.

Clearly, no attempt was made to disguise the purpose of the survey. The class opted for what in Chapter 14 (Ethics in Research) is called an "honest-research" approach. Although ethical reasons for choosing an honest-research approach are emphasized in Chapter 14, there are also sound reasons based on measurement considerations. If you try to disguise the purpose of a survey by including filler items and randomizing the order of items, respondents will naturally try to guess what you are up to. If their guesses vary unpredictably and affect their responses, noise will be added to the data, and noise reduces reliability. Without reliability, you have nothing. Some researchers will never be comfortable with an honest-research approach, but in this case the class decided that the benefits outweighed the risks.

Responses were obtained from a quota sample of 77 participants (half of each gender, one refusal). Random sampling was not possible, but the class was fully aware of its sampling sinfulness (see the previous chapter). The class tentatively decided that their results might apply to the population of midwestern adults, but

Table 8.2   A SURVEY TO STUDY ATTITUDES TOWARD ABORTION

Instructions: Please respond to each item below by circling only ONE of the six choices.

Choices:	SA = strongly agree	MD = mildly disagree
	A = agree	D = disagree
	MA = mildly agree	SD = strongly disagree

SA A MA MD D SD   1. I approve of abortion in cases of rape.
SA A MA MD D SD   2. Abortion should NOT be used as a form of birth control.
SA A MA MD D SD   3. State-funded abortions should be available for those on welfare.
SA A MA MD D SD   4. Abortion should be a legal right.
SA A MA MD D SD   5. Abortion is murder.
SA A MA MD D SD   6. Parental consent should be required for minors to obtain an abortion.
SA A MA MD D SD   7. Government programs to aid welfare for women and children should be expanded.
SA A MA MD D SD   8. Too much money is being spent on government-funded school-lunch programs.
SA A MA MD D SD   9. The food-stamp program should be reduced.
SA A MA MD D SD   10. Tax-funded medical aid for children should be expanded.
SA A MA MD D SD   11. Tax-funded programs like Head Start are frills and should be eliminated.
SA A MA MD D SD   12. Government-funded day-care programs should be encouraged.
SA A MA MD D SD   13. I attend church at least once a week.
SA A MA MD D SD   14. I try to follow official church teachings.
SA A MA MD D SD   15. I feel that religious practice is NOT necessary for moral development.
SA A MA MD D SD   16. I seldom pray.
SA A MA MD D SD   17. I volunteer for church projects.
SA A MA MD D SD   18. Children should NOT be made to attend Sunday school.

of course that is open to question. Scores for each variable were derived following the scoring procedures for Likert scales discussed in Chapter 5. Reliability for each variable was assessed by coefficient alpha (Chapter 6). The reliability coefficients were all .80 or better, indicating good reliability.

Before discussing the results further, let's talk theory. The class wanted predictor variables that ought to be related, on theoretical grounds, to abortion attitude. They also wanted predictors that were uncorrelated with each other. That is, they sought theoretically distinct predictors of abortion attitude. That was their assignment. The last requirement, uncorrelated predictors, is often difficult to achieve in practice. After much soul searching, the class decided that attitude toward public aid and religious involvement were as likely to be uncorrelated with each other as any other pair of predictors they could imagine.

Meanwhile, there was good theoretical reason to believe that the two predictors would be correlated with abortion attitude. The reasoning for religious involvement was clearcut: Most religions are opposed to abortion, so those who are highly involved in religious practices should be low in pro-abortion sentiment. Because abortion attitude was scored so that a high score reflected a liberal attitude toward abortion, the class expected a negative correlation between religious involvement and abortion attitude.

The public-aid predictor was the interesting one. The class couldn't make up its mind what to predict because the students couldn't agree on the psychology of the anti-abortion person. On one view, the anti-abortion person respects all life, both pre- and postnatal, and thus should be in the forefront of approving postnatal-aid programs. This view predicts a negative correlation between public-aid approval and pro-abortion attitude. Another view, expressed by the pro-choice class members, is that the anti-abortion person cares only about prenatal life and could care less about aiding children in need after they are born. This view predicts a positive correlation between public-aid approval and pro-abortion attitude. Both theories had strong support. At least the class was on to something that mattered to the students.

Now for the results. As predicted (and reported in Chapter 6), religious involvement and pro-abortion attitude were strongly negatively correlated ($r = -.74$, $p < .001$). The class's quest for uncorrelated predictors also paid off. The two predictors were not significantly correlated ($r = -.19$, $p > .05$). As for the controversy about the aid-approval predictor, the pro-choice students had the better of it. The correlation between public-aid approval and pro-abortion attitude was moderately positive, but significant ($r = .29$, $p < .01$).

As you might expect, the story does not end here. The anti-abortion students were very disturbed by these findings. After seeing the results, they started thinking very deeply, much to the delight of their instructor. (If only there had been some way of putting the pro-abortion students into a similar dilemma!) Within a few days, a student who proudly proclaimed himself a right-to-lifer checked in with the following theory: Anti-abortion persons are true conservatives. They oppose public-aid programs not because they don't care about children in need but because they know that any program administered by government will shamelessly waste money. This is a good theory according to the criteria of Chapter 1 because it makes a clear prediction: If the class had used private-aid approval rather than public-aid approval, the results would have reversed, and the correlation between the predictor and pro-abortion attitude would have been negative.

There is a slight flaw in the student's theory. Do you see it? (Q4)

In any event, the follow-up study to test the student's prediction has not been done. Hint, hint.

Advanced Correlation Analyses

This chapter concludes with a discussion of some advanced uses of correlational techniques. These advanced techniques allow a researcher to home-in on possible causes. You already know that a single correlation between two variables is of no help in pinpointing cause. However, when correlations among several variables are available, it may be possible to make some progress toward isolating causes.

Partial correlation.   The simplest case in point occurs when one wishes to determine the role of a third variable, C, in explaining the correlation between two other variables, A and B. If all three variables can be measured, then it is possible to compute the so-called *partial correlation* between A and B. This amounts to a correlation between A and B with any influence of C "partialled out" or "held constant statistically." Clearly, if the correlation between A and B remains strong even after any influence of C has been removed statistically, then C cannot fully account for the simple correlation between A and B. On the other hand, if the partial correlation between A and B drops to near zero, then the mediating effects of C fully account for the simple correlation between A and B. Such an outcome implies that A and B have no direct causal effect on each other. Thus, partial correlation provides a researcher with useful information about possible causal connections among the three measured variables.

Ferris and King used partial correlation in the study described at the beginning of the chapter. Their theoretical model, illustrated in Figure 8.1, implies that age has no direct causal effect on performance evaluation. Rather, age works only through its direct and indirect effects on ingratiation behavior. Thus, the model predicts that the partial correlation between age and evaluation, with ingratiation partialled out, should be zero. In fact, it was –.01. Recall that the simple correlation between age and evaluation was –.19 (p < .05). Thus, age can be ruled out as having a direct causal effect on evaluation.

The Ferris-King model also predicts that age has an indirect influence on evaluation (via its direct influence on ingratiation) even after the influence of interpersonal distance is removed from the picture. That prediction was discussed earlier in the chapter. Unfortunately, the analysis was not kind to it. The partial correlation between age and evaluation, with distance partialled out, was –.04 (p > .05). Thus, not only does age have no influence on evaluation apart from ingratiation, it also has no influence apart from its relationship with interpersonal distance. The partial correlation results suggest that a more satisfactory theoretical model would contain no direct link between age and ingratiation, as illustrated in Figure 8.2. In this model, removing the influence of either distance or ingratiation destroys the correlation between age and evaluation.

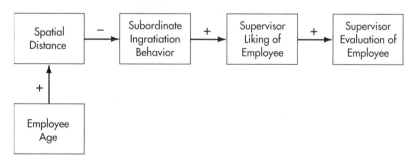

Figure 8.2
Theoretical model of performance evaluation supported by the results of Ferris and King.

If you are really sharp, you will object that any ordering of the variables between age and evaluation could have produced the partial correlation results presented above. Thus, distance could come after ingratiation in Figure 8.2 rather than before it. You are correct. One would have to compute more partial correlations to pin down the exact ordering of the intervening variables, something Ferris and King did not do. Their main goal was to show that age worked only though the mediating influence of other variables, and they achieved that goal convincingly.

Multiple regression.   An extension of the partial-correlation approach is accomplished by a technique known as *multiple regression*. In multiple regression, a single effect variable, A, is measured, and so are several possible causal variables: B, C, etc. The analysis yields the best possible combination of the causal variables, that is, the weighted sum of the causal variables that has the highest possible correlation with the effect variable, A. More to the point, the analysis also provides information about the partial influence of each of the possible causal variables. That is, the partial correlation between each possible causal variable and the effect variable, with all of the other possible causal variables partialled out, is provided. Thus, one can determine whether each potential cause is still in the running as a possible cause when all of the other potential causes have been ruled out. It is not uncommon in such analyses to find that more than one cause remains possible.

The Belyea and Lobao study of depression in farmers, discussed in the previous chapter, illustrates the use of multiple regression analysis (Belyea & Lobao, 1990). Their goal was to show that objective sources of stress (sociodemographic, farm-structure, and economic-vulnerability variables) influenced depression primarily via the mediation of psychological variables such as perceived economic hardship and perceived stress. Recall that the pattern of simple correlations among their variables agreed fairly well with their theory. However, multiple regression analysis provided much more convincing evidence. Depression was the effect variable in the analysis (also known as the dependent variable in multiple regression terminology), and all the other variables were included as potential causes (also known as independent variables). The results showed that partial correlations with depression were by far the strongest for perceived economic hardship and perceived stress, as expected. On the other hand, the partial correlations for the objective variables were either greatly reduced or eliminated.

A study of suicide in Japan provides a second example of multiple regression analysis. Kurosu (1991) wanted to explain the curious fact that the suicide rate is higher in rural than in urban areas of Japan, just the opposite of the pattern in most Western nations. Kurosu felt that the same social factors, urbanization and industrialization, influence the suicide rate in any nation. The social factors directly affect the level of social disintegration, a mediating variable, which in turn directly affects the suicide rate. High social disintegration produces a high suicide rate. The effect of the social factors on social disintegration depends on the cultural values of the particular society. In the West, urbanization and industrialization lead to high social disintegration and thus higher suicide rates. In Japan, the opposite pattern occurs. The theoretical model for Japan is shown in Figure 8.3. The model for the United States would be the same except for positive signs on all arrows.

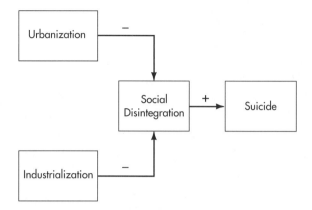

Figure 8.3
Theoretical model of factors affecting
suicide rate in Japan.

(Do you see why? Q5)

Kurosu tested the model for Japan, using prefectures (the largest units of local government in Japan) as units of analysis. The suicide rate for 1980 in each prefecture was the dependent variable. Independent variables included urbanization (the percentage of the prefecture population living in cities of 50,000 or more), industrialization (per capita income of the prefecture), and two indicators of social disintegration, the proportions of widowed and elderly in each prefecture. The latter are positive indicators; the higher the proportions, the higher the social disintegration of the prefecture. You may not believe this, but Kurosu presented an extensive rationale plus supporting evidence from the research literature.

Simple correlations among the variables showed the expected pattern. Urbanization and industrialization were negatively correlated with both indicators of social disintegration and with suicide rate. On the other hand, the social disintegration variables were both positively correlated with suicide rate. All correlations were large (minimum absolute value of .51) and significant (p < .01).

The real test of the theoretical model required multiple regression analysis, with suicide rate as the dependent variable. Figure 8.3 implies that urbanization and industrialization should have no effect on suicide apart from the mediating influence of social disintegration. Thus, if either indicator of social disintegration is entered as an independent variable in a regression analysis, along with urbanization and industrialization, the partial correlation with suicide should remain strong for the disintegration indicator but should be near zero for urbanization and industrialization. That is exactly what happened.

Structural modeling. Finally, there is a class of techniques known as causal or structural modeling that allow a researcher to fit a proposed theoretical model to the observed relationships among a set of measured variables. The theoretical model typically contains cause–effect relationships, that is, relationships in which one variable is designated as the cause and the other variable is designated as the

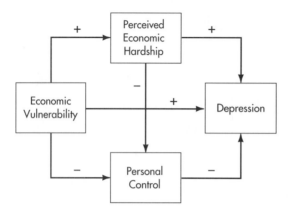

Figure 8.4
Theoretical model of depression in
farmers proposed by Armstrong and
Schulman.

effect. The model may contain a complex pattern of such causal relationships. The
analysis provides measures of how well the theoretical model fits the observed relationships. If a researcher can show that a proposed causal model fits the observed
data well or better than an alternative causal model, then the researcher is justified
in having increased confidence in the causal connections contained in the proposed
model.

An example of structural modeling is a second study of depression in farmers (Armstrong & Schulman, 1990). The study appeared later the same year in the
same journal as the Belyea-Lobao study. Sociologists Paula Armstrong and Michael
Schulman had pretty much the same theoretical orientation as Belyea and Lobao.
The Armstrong-Schulman theoretical model is presented in Figure 8.4. They eliminated the sociodemographic and farm structure variables used in the earlier study,
leaving economic vulnerability as the sole objective source of stress. Economic vulnerability, perceived hardship, and depression were measured in ways very similar to the earlier study. Personal control was measured using a subset of items from
a perceived stress scale and thus may be considered similar to the Belyea-Lobao
perceived stress variable. The intent, as in the earlier study, was to show that objective sources of stress are mediated by psychological variables. Notice, however, that
the proposed model also contains a direct link between economic vulnerability and
depression, an important departure from the Belyea-Lobao model.

Simple correlations among the variables seemed to agree reasonably well with
the theoretical model. However, when Armstrong and Schulman used a computer
program known as LISREL (which stands for LInear Structural RELations) to fit the
theoretical model to the obtained data, they got a surprise. The overall model fit the
data adequately, but two of the specific links in the model were not statistically significant. The two weak links were those between economic vulnerability and
depression and between economic vulnerability and personal control. A revised
model without those links fit the data somewhat better and was accepted by the
researchers as the best theoretical account of depression in farmers given their data.

Note that the revised model agrees fully with the Belyea-Lobao study in that there is no direct link between the objective variable, economic vulnerability, and depression. Objective sources of stress are mediated completely by psychological variables. Thus, the two studies, using different advanced correlation techniques, converged on the same conclusion.

Every one of the studies cited in this section on advanced analyses contained warnings about being cautious in reaching causal conclusions. For example, Armstrong and Schulman note that their analyses ASSUMED that depression was the effect variable. Because all variables were measured at the same point in time, nothing in their data would rule out a model in which depression develops earlier in the theoretical sequence and is a cause of perceived hardship or stress. The moral of the story is this: The advanced techniques discussed here allow a researcher to rule out some causal links and some models. However, there will typically be many models remaining that could account for the data and that have quite different causal implications. Fixing on any one of the remaining models as the best or the only adequate theoretical account is usually unwise and unjustified.

SUMMARY

In unstructured interviews with open responses, the data analysis may be qualitative, as with field observations, or quantitative. The latter approach requires coding, that is, establishing objective categories for open responses. The coding system should be checked for reliability via intercoder agreement. Statistical analysis depends on the kinds of data produced by the coding.

In structured questionnaires with closed responses, the data analysis for multi-item scale scores typically involves calculating the correlation coefficient, r, to describe the linear relationship between pairs of variables. The null hypothesis that r is 0 in the population is tested by looking up the probability of the sample r in a table and comparing that probability to alpha. Reliability coefficients should also be taken into account in reaching final conclusions. The basic rule is that if the reliability coefficient is too small, suspend judgment about the null hypothesis. Otherwise, use the test of inference and any other relevant information to decide one way or the other. This chapter concludes with a discussion and examples of some advanced correlation techniques that allow a researcher to glean some information about cause from correlational results. The techniques include partial correlation, multiple regression, and structural modeling.

ANSWERS TO QUESTIONS

Q1. $\Sigma X = 79$, $\Sigma Y = 77$, $\Sigma X^2 = 1319$, $\Sigma Y^2 = 1215$, $\Sigma XY = 1250$, $N = 5$.

$$r = \frac{(5)(1250) - (79)(77)}{\{\sqrt{[(5)(1319) - (79)^2]}\} \{\sqrt{[(5)(1215) - (77)^2]}\}}$$

$$= \frac{6250 - 6083}{\{\sqrt{[6595 - 6241]}\} \{\sqrt{[6075 - 5929]}\}}$$

$$= \frac{167}{[\sqrt{354}] [\sqrt{146}]}$$

$$= \frac{167}{(18.8149)(12.0830)} = \frac{167}{227.3404} = .7346.$$

Q2. df = N – 2 = 5 – 2 = 3. Therefore, r(3) = .7346, p > .10.

Q3. df = 62. Therefore, the tests of inference are as follows: r(62) = .52, p < .01 for variables A and B, r(62) = .17, p > .10 for A and C, r(62) = –.39, p < .01 for B and C. Reliability is acceptable (greater than .50) for A and B, but not for C. Therefore, the final conclusions are to suspend judgment on the correlations between A and C and between B and C and to reject the null hypothesis of no linear relationship between A and B. Implications: A and B have a positive linear relationship, and a better measure of C is needed.

Q4. Assuming that true conservatism is associated with high religious involvement (an assumption that might be questioned), then there should have been a negative correlation between the predictor variables. That is, true conservatism should have produced high religious involvement and low approval of public aid, which would lead to a negative correlation between the two. As noted in the text, the correlation was negative (–.19) but not significant (p > .05). How close was it? Look it up in Table A.2 at df = 75 (you will have to use df = 70) and you will find that p is approximately .10 (actual p = .095). So it was close enough to be interesting, especially if you consider the study to be exploratory.

Q5. In the United States, either high urbanization or high industrialization is supposed to go with high social disintegration, and low with low, according to Kurosu. Thus, the predicted correlations are positive. Meanwhile, in all cultures, high social disintegration is supposed to go with high suicide rate, and low with low, implying another positive correlation.

FURTHER READING

Loehlin (1987) provides an introduction to structural modeling. Lunneborg (1994) contains a general modeling approach to data analysis and features an excellent introduction to regression analysis. Kachigan (1991) provides a readable introduction to many advanced data-analysis techniques, and Pedhazur and Schmelkin (1991) cover much of the same ground in more advanced form. Thorndike (1978) provides a geometrical interpretation of advanced correlational analyses that is both readable and insightful.

REFERENCES

Armstrong, P. S., & Schulman, M.D. (1990). Financial strain and depression among farm operators: The role of perceived economic hardship and personal control. *Rural Sociology, 55*, 475–493.

Belyea, M. J., & Lobao, L. M. (1990). Psychosocial consequences of agricultural transformation: The farm crisis and depression. *Rural Sociology, 55*, 58–75.

Ferris, G. R., & King, T. R. (1992). The politics of age discrimination in organizations. *Journal of Business Ethics, 11*, 341–350.

Kachigan, S. K. (1991). *Multivariate statistical analysis: A conceptual introduction*. New York: Radius Press.

Kurosu, S. (1991). Suicide in rural areas: The case of Japan 1960–1980. *Rural Sociology, 56,* 603–618.

Loehlin, J. C. (1987). *Latent variable models: An introduction to factor, path, and structural analysis*. Hillsdale, NJ: Lawrence Erlbaum.

Lunneborg, C. E. (1994). *Modeling experimental and observational data*. Belmont, CA: Duxbury.

Pedhazur, E. J., & Schmelkin, L. P. (1991). *Measurement, design, and analysis: An integrated approach*. Hillsdale, NJ: Lawrence Erlbaum Associates.

Thorndike, R. M. (1978). *Correlational procedures for research*. New York: Gardner Press.

The Experiment: Basic Concepts and Procedures

9

One of the most famous experiments in social psychology is Philip Zimbardo's prison-simulation experiment (Haney, Banks, & Zimbardo, 1973). This experiment is often misunderstood by laypeople because they lack a firm grounding in the concepts and procedures of the experimental method. This causes them to overlook key features of the study and thus to miss its central point. After mastering the material on the experimental method in this book, you should never fall prey to such a fate.

The participants in the prison-simulation experiment were 22 male college students who had been carefully screened for high levels of physical and mental health. They were randomly assigned to play the role of either guard or prisoner in a simulated prison environment, which had been created in the basement of the psychology building at Stanford University. Guards wore khaki uniforms and reflecting sunglasses and were issued whistles and nightsticks. Prisoners wore muslin smocks, nylon stocking caps, and rubber sandals with a light chain around one ankle. Guards were told to maintain order. No specifics for how to do the job were provided other than a prohibition on physical abuse. The guards, therefore, got together with the "warden" (a research assistant) and developed a set of prison rules, which they were to enforce. The prisoners received no instructions on how to fulfill their role. To add realism to their experience, the prisoners were arrested at their place of residence by actual police officers, booked at the local police station, and then taken blindfolded to the simulated prison.

The results were astonishing. The guards became increasingly cruel in their treatment of prisoners over the course of several days. For example, three times a day the prisoners were lined up for a count that also included quizzing them on prison rules. At first the counts lasted about ten minutes, but the guards gradually increased their duration so that eventually some of them lasted several hours. In many other ways the guards treated the prisoners in an increasingly inhumane manner. The prisoners, meanwhile, tried resistance and then working within the system by setting up a grievance committee, all to no avail. Then they just gave up and tried to endure. Five of them could not, began to show signs of emotional disturbance, and had to be released from the study. The situation became so unstable that the experiment was terminated after only six days of a scheduled two weeks.

A common misinterpretation of this experiment by laypeople is that participants prone to cruelty volunteered to be guards. This interpretation overlooks an important procedural detail of the experiment, the *random* assignment of participants to roles. As you will see, the ability to randomize sources of error is a key feature that distinguishes the experimental method from other research methods. A second lay interpretation is that negative outcomes occurred because human nature is flawed and thus prone to negative reactions. There may be something to this interpretation, but other research has shown that positive behaviors like helping can also be influenced by environmental manipulations (e.g., Darley & Batson, 1973). What the interpretation overlooks is the difference in the reactions of the guards and prisoners. Cruelty and emotional disturbance are both negative outcomes, but they are quite different outcomes. The difference can be attributed directly to the assigned roles of the participants. The researchers meant to demonstrate the impact of the social environment in the form of assigned social roles, not the influence of internal factors like "human nature." In stressing human nature, the layperson overlooks the key role played by another distinguishing feature of the experimental method, the presence of a manipulated independent variable.

You are much less likely to miss the point of an experiment if you have a thorough understanding of the experimental method. Such understanding would lead you to focus on the independent variable and its effects. Likewise, it would lead you to realize the importance of random assignment to conditions for the interpretation of results. Thus, a good reason for studying the experimental method is so that you can properly interpret experimental results. As noted in Chapter 2, a second important reason for studying the experimental method is that it has special features for pinning down the causes of relationships. Because it focuses on cause, many researchers view the experiment as the most important of all research methods. Whether or not you agree, you can certainly appreciate that the experiment is a method well worth studying.

This chapter begins with a review of the basic concepts of the experimental method and its basic logic. Then the standard experimental designs used in good experiments are described and grouped into two major categories. The chapter concludes with general advice on how to plan and conduct good experiments. The next chapter deals in detail with the important subject of how to conduct sound experiments that permit clear conclusions about cause and effect.

BASIC CONCEPTS

Chapter 2 contained a description of a hypothetical experiment on the effects of frustration on aggression. Recall that high frustration was produced by giving participants an unsolvable maze problem with instructions that an intelligent person could solve it in about two minutes. Low frustration was produced by giving participants an easily solvable maze problem. Aggression was measured by counting the number of times the participant kicked, punched, or gouged a Bobo doll during a five-minute period following the maze problem. The basic concepts of the experimental method will be reviewed in the context of this experiment. The discussion will also show how those concepts apply in the Zimbardo prison-simulation experiment.

Types of Variables

Any experiment contains several different kinds of variables. They may be classified into four basic categories depending on the role they play within the experiment.

Independent Variables. The presumed cause in a cause–effect relationship is known as the independent variable. In an experiment, the independent variable is manipulated. *Manipulation* means that the experimenter produces the values of the variable and assigns the values to participants at the experimenter's discretion. The experimenter decides which participants will have which values of the variable, in effect replacing whatever values the participants already have with the values the experimenter wants them to have. The presence of at least one manipulated independent variable is the distinguishing feature of an experiment.

The values of the independent variable are also known as experimental *treatments* or *conditions.* In the frustration experiment, the independent variable was frustration, its values were high and low, they were produced by using unsolvable and easily solvable maze problems, and they were assigned to participants randomly. In the prison experiment, the independent variable was the assigned role of each participant, its values were guard and prisoner, they were produced by all of the trappings of each role described earlier, and they were also assigned randomly to participants. Note that to translate an independent variable from a general concept into concrete values in an experiment, an operational definition is necessary. That is, a recipe is needed for exactly which values are to be produced, how they will be produced, and how they will be assigned to participants.

In both of the preceding examples, there were two conditions or values of the independent variable. Two is the minimum number of conditions in a good experiment because, as noted in Chapter 2, you must examine at least two values of a variable to determine if it is involved in a relationship. Until Chapter 12, this book will focus on the simplest good experiment, one having a single independent variable with two values. Sometimes the two values or treatments in an experiment are referred to as "experimental" and "control" conditions. This terminology is usually applied when the "control" condition consists of no treatment; for example, no frustration. Thus, it would not apply to the frustration experiment described in this book where the comparison is between high and *low* frustration, rather than high and *no* frustration. Likewise, in the prison study, it is hard to see how either condition, guard or prisoner, qualifies as a no-treatment control condition.

Dependent Variables.   In an experiment, the dependent variable is the presumed effect in a cause–effect relationship. It is measured, preferably in a way that produces fine data as defined in Chapter 5. In any event, an operational definition is necessary to specify exactly how the dependent variable will be measured. The object is to find out if scores on the dependent variable change systematically with the changes in the independent variable produced by the experimenter. For drawing proper conclusions, it is crucial that the measure of the dependent variable be both reliable and valid. Thus, the operational definition of the dependent variable should be carefully considered, and perhaps more than one should be used. In the frustration experiment, the dependent variable was aggression, operationally defined as the number of times a Bobo doll was kicked, punched, or gouged during a five-minute observation period following the maze test. In the prison experiment, there were several measures of the dependent variable, "reactions to assigned roles." For example, video tapes and direct observations were content analyzed for counts of such behaviors as questions, commands, threats, insults, resistance, and help. Moods were assessed on several occasions by means of standard adjective checklists. These and other measures may be considered operational definitions of various aspects of the participants' reactions to their roles.

Extraneous Variables.   A very important class of variables consists of all variables in the universe except the independent and dependent variables. These variables are potential alternatives to the independent variable as causes of any changes found in the dependent variable. Thus, they must be ruled out as causes if the researcher wants to conclude with confidence that the independent variable is the cause of any change found across conditions in the dependent variable.

This broad class of variables may be subdivided three times based on whether and how they are ruled out as alternative causes. The outcomes are shown in Figure 2.2 of Chapter 2, beginning at the node labeled "Other Possible Causes." The first division is based on the researcher's informed judgment about whether the variable could be plausibly related to the dependent variable. If the answer is yes, the variable is considered *relevant* and must be dealt with by the researcher. If the answer is no, the variable is *irrelevant* and need be considered no further. The reasoning here is simple: For a variable to be related causally to the dependent variable, it must be related first. Thus, variables judged unrelated to the dependent variable cannot qualify as causes. As noted in Chapter 2, in the frustration experiment intelligence would be judged relevant, the position of Venus irrelevant. In the prison experiment, the personality of the participants clearly would be relevant, but hair color would probably be judged irrelevant. Note that because this is a judgment call, it may be questioned, a possibility the prudent researcher should bear in mind when planning the study.

Relevant variables are known as *extraneous* variables and may be divided into those that have been properly dealt with and those that have not. In Chapter 2, the term "neutralized" was invented to describe the former category. Everyone agrees that variables in the latter category are called *confounding* variables because they still remain as possible alternatives to the independent variable as causes in the experiment. If the researcher failed to deal with intelligence in the frustration experiment, a critic could argue that the more intelligent participants found their way into the low-frustration condition. If so, the higher aggression in the high-frustration condition might have been caused by the lower intelligence of the participants in that condition and not by the unsolvable maze problem. Thus, the ability to pinpoint frustration as the causal variable would be compromised because frustration was confounded with intelligence. To avoid such problems, the experimenter must make sure that all extraneous variables are neutralized.

Extraneous variables are neutralized procedurally either by control or randomization. A *controlled* variable is held constant in some sense. A *randomized* variable is made to vary in a random or unpredictable manner. In either case, the variable cannot change values systematically along with the independent variable and therefore cannot be confounded with it. The variable also cannot change values systematically along with the dependent variable and therefore cannot be related to it. Thus, the variable is ruled out as a cause of any relationship found between the independent and dependent variables. Controlled variables cannot be related to either the independent or dependent variables because controlled variables are not allowed to vary—a necessary condition for being involved in a relationship. Randomized variables vary unpredictably and therefore cannot vary systematically with any other variable.

Control is typically used to neutralize environmental conditions like lighting, temperature, etc. They are simply held constant across conditions of the experiment (i.e., across values of the independent variable). In the prison experiment, both prisoners and guards were exposed to the same prison environment. Only their assigned roles differed. You should imagine that similar environmental controls were implemented in the hypothetical frustration experiment. Randomization is typically used to neutralize characteristics of participants like intelligence or emotionality. In the prison experiment, such variables were dealt with by randomly assigning participants to roles as guards or prisoners. Likewise, in the frustration study, you should imagine that the participants were randomly assigned to one of the two versions of the maze problem.

Sampled Variables.   Like all research, the experiment contains sampled variables. A sampled variable has only a subset of all its possible values included in the study. The principles involved in valid generalization from samples to populations have already been discussed earlier in this book. The key issue is whether the values included in the sample are representative of the broader set of values in the population. If so, valid generalization is possible. In an experiment, some variables are sampled broadly in the hope that the sample will be representative of the population, permitting valid generalization. Examples of such variables are participants and stimuli such as words, pictures, problems, etc. Here the question is whether the sample is sufficiently large and unbiased, issues explored in Chapter 7. Other variables are sampled narrowly, sacrificing representativeness to achieve another goal, control. Examples are experimenters (one or, at most, a few are used) and environmental conditions such as location, temperature, lighting, etc., which are usually held constant. Generalizations based on these variables are risky. Sampling considerations also apply to independent and dependent variables. In each case, one may ask how well the operational definition represents the concept, that is, the population of all possible operational definitions of the concept. One may also ask how well the values of each variable represent the population of all possible values. Such questions bear on the issue of how broadly the results from an experiment may be generalized.

You should realize that generality and control are often opposing goals. The former thrives on broad sampling, the latter on narrow sampling. Because the experiment emphasizes control, it is always worth considering how the generality of the findings may be limited.

In summary, if the researcher's judgment about relevancy of variables is defensible and all extraneous variables are adequately neutralized, the experiment is procedurally sound. That is, there is no confounding, and the independent variable is the cause of any relationship found between it and the dependent variable. An experiment that qualifies for such an evaluation is said to have *internal validity*, which simply means there is no confounding. If the results may be generalized to conditions other than those actually sampled, then the experiment also has *external validity*. Internal validity is crucial. Without it, the experiment cannot be clearly interpreted. Much of the next chapter deals with how to achieve internal validity in experiments. External validity is also important. If the results do not generalize beyond the specific conditions under which they were obtained, then they are unlikely to have much theoretical or practical impact. Given internal validity, you would like as much external validity as possible. You must have some if the experiment is to be taken seriously. Chapter 13 is devoted exclusively to the topic of external validity.

Types of Validity

By now you have seen the word "validity" in so many different contexts that you are probably tired of it and perhaps confused as well. Such a reaction is understandable, but help is at hand. First, note the that term validity ALWAYS refers to the correctness of an inference. In a classic treatment, Cook and Campbell (1979) classified types of validity and their associated inferences into four categories. A slightly modified version of their classification is summarized in Table 9.1. *Statistical-conclusion validity* refers to the validity of inferences based on statistical tests of inference. The basic logic of statistical inference and the possible errors associated with such inference were discussed in Chapter 4. *Measurement-manipulation validity* refers to the validity of inferences about what variable (or variables) are involved in a particular measure or manipulation. This topic has been mentioned frequently, most extensively in Chapter 6 during the discussion of validity of measurement. As discussed in the preceding paragraph, *internal validity* refers to the validity of inferences about cause based on research findings, and *external validity* refers to the validity of inferences about the generality of research findings. So there are really only four general types of validity, and any other phrases you may encounter involving the word (e.g., "ecological validity") will be special cases of one of those four types (in this case, external validity).

Table 9.1   CLASSIFICATION OF TYPES OF VALIDITY

Validity Type	Inference Dealt With
Statistical-Conclusion	Conclusions based on tests of inference
Measurement-Manipulation	Variable(s) involved in a measure or manipulation
Internal	Cause(s) of research findings
External	Generality of research findings

Basic Logic of the Experiment

The goal of an experiment is to establish that the independent variable caused any systematic differences found in the dependent variable across conditions. Recall from Chapter 2 that a variable qualifies as a cause when a change on that variable is reliably accompanied by a corresponding change on another variable under conditions where all other potential causes can be ruled out. Such a variable may be regarded as a sufficent probabilistic cause in the sense of Chapter 2. The definition of cause implies that a candidate must meet three conditions: (1) it must precede the effect, (2) it must be related to the effect, and (3) it must be the only potential causal candidate in the situation under investigation.

The experiment is designed to meet these conditions. The presumed cause (the independent variable) is manipulated and then the presumed effect (the dependent variable) is measured (condition 1). All other potential causal candidates are ruled out either by informed judgment or by control and randomization (condition 3). The relationship between the independent and dependent variables is then assessed (condition 2). The basic logic of the experiment is that if a relationship is found when all the conditions for cause have been met, then it follows that the causal candidate (the manipulated independent variable) was indeed the cause of the systematic change in the effect candidate (the measured dependent variable). An experiment that satisfies the conditions for inferring cause has internal validity.

You would do well to keep these conditions in mind in your everyday reasoning about cause. A persistent error in everyday thinking is to find a plausible cause and then give up thinking about alternative causes. The first satisfying candidate may not be the real cause. This tendency can be countered by training yourself to ask whether all plausible alternatives have been ruled out in the situation under consideration. It is often possible to perform a simple experiment to check out a causal candidate. For example, the display panel on your stereo tuner does not light up when you turn on the power switch. Your first reaction: The tuner has died and will cost plenty to repair. Calm down and think. If the tuner is shot, then the switch on a no-tuner control component should work properly. Try the CD player. That display does not light up either. So it must be the fuse on the power strip. Check it. Hmm, it's ok. Well then, somebody must have pulled the plug on the power strip out of the wall socket. No wait; it's plugged in. Does any electrical appliance in this room work? Etc.

Here is a short self-test. Below are brief descriptions of two experiments carried out by the author's research-methods classes.

Can you name the independent variable, its values, and the dependent variable in each experiment? (Q1)

1. Participants read about an urban shooting crime. In one version, it was drug-related. In another version, it was a "drive-by" random shooting. Afterward, they rated their fear of going into the city.
2. Participants saw a campaign ad for candidate Smith. One version emphasized Smith's positive qualities, another version his opponent's negative qualities. Afterward, they rated their favorability toward Smith.

EXPERIMENTAL DESIGNS

Experimental design refers to how participants are assigned to conditions or treatments in an experiment. As discussed earlier, assignment to conditions (or values of the independent variable) is part of the manipulation of the independent variable. Good experimental designs use methods of assignment to conditions that neutralize extraneous variables, either singly or in bunches, while avoiding confounding. Thus, good designs are procedurally sound and contribute to the internal validity of the experiment.

Standard examples of good designs have evolved over the years, and they are well worth examining for what they can teach about good experimentation. This section describes and classifies the basic good experimental designs. Detailed discussion of the strengths and weaknesses of the basic designs, especially with regard to internal validity, will be presented in the next chapter.

The good designs can be grouped into two major categories, as shown in Figure 9.1. One category features random assignment to conditions without any matching of participant characteristics across conditions. The other category features matching of participants across conditions on one or more stable characteristics like intelligence. As you will see in Chapter 11, the distinction between designs with and without matching is crucial for data analysis. For reasons that will become clear shortly, designs without matching will be termed *independent-treatments designs,* and those with matching *nonindependent-treatments designs.*

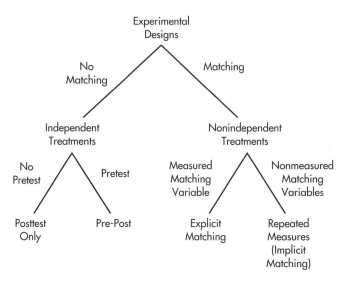

Figure 9.1
Basic experimental designs.

Independent-Treatments Designs

The distinguishing feature of this category is random assignment to experimental conditions without matching. Because assignment is random, the scores on the dependent variable in any pair of conditions should be statistically independent or uncorrelated; hence, the name of the category. Designs in this category have a number of other names or aliases. They have been called randomized-groups, between-subjects, independent-subjects, or simple-random-assignment designs by various authors. Whatever the title, the key characteristic of such designs is random assignment to conditions with no matching.

When there is no random assignment, as would be the case when working with preexisting groups, there is always the possibility that uncontrolled systematic differences between the treatments in variables other than the variable of interest may exist. The researcher may simply assume that such extraneous variables are not confounded with the independent variable, but it is well to remember that an assumption is an assumption. Thus, there is much greater risk of confounding when random assignment is not possible. Remember: statistical analysis generally cannot rescue confounded studies. So where random assignment is not possible, exercise caution in interpreting results.

Posttest-only design.   The independent-treatments category has two members. The first is the most famous good experimental design, the posttest-only design. In this design, participants are randomly assigned to conditions, and the dependent variable is measured once, after the treatment has been administered. In the frustration experiment, this would mean randomly assigning participants to either the high- or low-frustration conditions, presenting the appropriate maze problem, and then measuring aggression.

Remember that the word "random" has a specific technical meaning. The assignment of each participant to a condition must be purely a matter of chance, and the assignment procedure must guarantee that this condition is met. Either flip a coin or use a table of random numbers to determine which treatment a participant receives. With random assignment, participant characteristics (e.g., intelligence, personality, etc.) are distributed randomly across conditions and are thereby neutralized by randomization. If there is no confounding from sources other than assignment to conditions, then this design has no procedural flaws.

Two-group, pre-post design.   The second member of the independent-treatments category is the two-group, pre-post design. Some experimenters like to "improve" the posttest-only design by adding a pretest, that is, a measure of the dependent variable preceding the treatment. In the frustration experiment, this would mean measuring aggression before and after the frustration manipulation. One rationale for this strategy is that the pretest allows the researcher to verify that the groups are identical on the dependent variable at the outset. This sounds virtuous, but there are strong arguments against it. First, if assignment to conditions is truly random, there should be no need to verify the equivalence of the groups at the outset of the experiment. Second, the pretest may compromise the external validity of the experiment. That is, any differences between the groups on the posttest may occur only when there is a pretest, and surely the presence of a pretest is fairly rare in nonexperimental situations.

If external validity is not seen as a problem, then a more convincing rationale for the use of a pretest is that it may permit a better test of whether the independent and dependent variables are related. If the pre- and posttest scores are strongly correlated, as is typical, the analysis of the data can take the correlation into account. The result is a statistically more powerful test of the relationship between the independent and dependent variables. Most statisticians favor a procedure called *analysis of covariance* in this situation. Analysis of covariance is briefly described in the section on "Procedural and Statistical Control" in the next chapter. For now, the important point is that analysis of covariance is an advanced statistical procedure. Thus, if you use the two-group, pre-post design, you will need help to analyze your data properly.

Nonindependent-Treatments Designs

The distinguishing feature of this category of designs is matching. *Matching* means that participants are assigned to conditions only after having been equated (matched) on some characteristic judged relevant (e.g., intelligence). When a matching variable is relevant (i.e., strongly related to the dependent variable), scores on the dependent variable in any pair of conditions should NOT be statistically independent; hence, the name of the category. Rather, such scores should be strongly correlated because of the influence of the matching variable. The nonindependence of scores on the dependent variable across conditions means that nonindependent-treatments designs require a somewhat different method of data analysis than do independent-treatments designs.

The goal of matching is to ensure that the distribution of scores on the matching variable is the same in all conditions of the experiment. It follows that the average value of the matching variable must also be the same in all conditions. The experimenter can then argue that the matching variable has been held constant on the average across conditions and is thus eliminated as a possible source of confounding. This way of thinking about control will be explored in detail in the next chapter.

Explicit-matching design. The nonindependent-treatments category of designs also has two members. Either of the two independent-treatments designs can employ explicit matching. *Explicit-matching* means that the experimenter obtains scores on a stable participant characteristic judged relevant to the dependent variable, forms matched pairs of participants on the matching variable, and then randomly assigns one member of each matched pair to one of the experimental conditions and the other member to the other condition. The explicit prior measurement of the matching variable accounts for the name of the design. To control intelligence in the frustration experiment, the researcher would first measure intelligence, then form matched pairs of participants based on intelligence scores, and then randomly assign the members of each matched pair to the two experimental conditions, one to each condition. The result is that every time the high-frustration condition gets a participant with a given intelligence level, so does the low-frustration condition. Thus, after matching, the average intelligence in the two conditions must be equal, eliminating intelligence as a source of confounding.

Explicit-matching designs are internally valid and feature tight control of the matching variable. However, only the matching variable is controlled, and a great deal of extra work is involved in obtaining scores on the matching variable and forming matched pairs prior to the experiment. Mostly because of the extra work, these designs are seldom used.

You should know that the explicit-matching design also has some aliases. It is known among statisticians as the randomized-blocks design and has also been called the matched-random-assignment design by some authors. Whatever title is used, the distinguishing feature of the design is explicit measurement of the matching variable for the purpose of forming matched blocks of participants.

Repeated-measures design. The second member of the nonindependent-treatments category is the repeated-measures design. In this design, each participant serves in all experimental conditions. The dependent variable is measured separately in each condition for every participant. Thus, the design features repeated measures of the dependent variable, accounting for its name. In the frustration experiment, this would mean presenting both maze problems to each participant, followed in each case by the measurement of aggression.

A major advantage of this design is that it achieves *implicit matching* on all stable characteristics of participants with no need for explicit measurement. That is, participants are automatically matched with themselves across conditions on intelligence and all other characteristics that remain the same within a person for the duration of the experiment. Thus, the control exerted by the design should at least equal that of the explicit-matching design and may be superior because more participant characteristics are matched. Because of this feature, repeated-measures designs are generally preferred by experimenters who have the urge to match. Another advantage is that fewer participants are needed to generate the same number of scores in each condition; however, more time is needed to run each participant. Thus, a research environment in which participants are hard to get but time is cheap might favor a repeated-measures design.

Because of its distinguishing feature, assigning each participant to all conditions, the repeated-measures design poses some new and unique control problems for researchers. They will be discussed in detail in the next chapter. Two will be mentioned briefly now to give you an idea of what the researcher is up against. First, when each participant is exposed to all conditions, it becomes more likely that the participant will figure out the purpose of the experiment. Such knowledge may have different effects on the participant's behavior in different conditions, thus becoming a source of confounding. Second, only in repeated-measures designs does the experimenter have to worry about the order in which treatments are presented.

Do you see why this is true? (Q2)

If the order of presenting treatments is not handled properly, extraneous variables like fatigue or practice can easily become confounded with the independent variable. Thus, the high level of control achieved by repeated-measures designs does not come without a price.

Finally, you should know that the repeated-measures design has a number of alternate identities. It has also been called the within-subjects design, the identical-subjects design, and the treatment-by-subjects design. Whatever the title, the distinguishing feature of the design is that each participant serves in all conditions.

Now that the good experimental designs have been described, which of them do you think was used in the prison study described at the beginning of this chapter? (Q3)

CONDUCTING EXPERIMENTS

The chapter concludes with some general advice on how to conduct experiments.

Manipulating the Independent Variable

Broadly speaking, there are two approaches to manipulating an independent variable. In *instructional* manipulation, the values of the variable are produced by presenting written or verbal material to the participants. In *staged* manipulation, the values of the variable are produced by staging an appropriate event. You might study the effect of communicator status on persuasion by presenting the same essay, supposedly written by either an expert or a layperson, and then measuring the participant's opinion. This would be an instructional manipulation. If instead you had actors role-play either expert or layperson and deliver the same lecture, it would be a staged manipulation. Any manipulation involving the "real thing," such as drugs or other physiological interventions, would qualify as a staged manipulation. The experimenter has to decide which approach is more appropriate. Instructional manipulations are inexpensive, easy to use, and widely used in the social sciences. If there is serious doubt about whether an instructional manipulation will yield valid results, the greater cost and effort of a staged manipulation is justified.

Which type of manipulation is represented by the maze problems in the frustration experiment? (Q4)

Instructional manipulation is ideal for class projects. It allows students to investigate almost anything via the experimental method. All that is needed is a written scenario dealing with the topic of interest. Somewhere within the scenario the independent variable is manipulated. To give you an idea of what can be done, Table 9.2 contains the complete scenarios for two experiments conducted by the author's research-methods classes. The material in brackets represents the alternate versions of each scenario and constitutes the manipulation of the independent variable. Note that in each case the dependent variable was measured using multi-item Likert scales. With this approach, the author's classes have done experiments on a wide range of topics such as sexual harassment, reverse discrimination, date rape, faith healing, AIDS, televangelist misbehavior, urban violence, and political campaign tactics. In case you are curious, both experiments in Table 9.2 produced sig-

---

Table 9.2   EXAMPLES OF EXPERIMENTS WITH INSTRUCTIONAL MANIPULATIONS

Dave Miller has been convicted of murder in the first degree. Dave is [18] [58] years old, grew up in the midwest, the youngest of three children, and was an average student in high school. He has received the death sentence for his crime.

Please indicate your reaction to Dave's situation. Respond by circling only ONE of the alternatives to the left of each statement below, where

SD = Strongly Disagree	MA = Mildly Agree
D = Disagree	A = Agree
MD = Mildly Disagree	SA = Strongly Agree

SD D MD MA A SA   1. I believe the sentence was fair.
SD D MD MA A SA   2. The sentence was unjust.
SD D MD MA A SA   3. Dave deserves his sentence.
SD D MD MA A SA   4. Dave deserves a milder sentence.

Kenny Douglas is the third basemen for a major league team in the midwest. Kenny is big and strong, hits lots of home runs, and has a rifle arm. Kenny has won many awards, including rookie of the year and most valuable player (twice). [Kenny is always well mannered, is popular with teammates and fans, and does a lot of charity work.] [Kenny is short tempered, gets into a lot of fights, is not very popular with teammates and fans, and refuses to do charity work.] Last week Kenny stunned the public by announcing that he had tested positive for the HIV virus.

Please respond to the statements below using these choices:

SD = Strongly Disagree	MA = Mildly Agree
D = Disagree	A = Agree
MD = Mildly Disagree	SA = Strongly Agree

SD D MD MA A SA   1. I feel sorry for Kenny.
SD D MD MA A SA   2. I have little sympathy for Kenny.
SD D MD MA A SA   3. I think Kenny is a respectable person.
SD D MD MA A SA   4. I feel contempt for Kenny.

Note. Statements in brackets [ ] represent the alternate versions of the scenarios.

nificant results. Respondents were more satisfied with Dave's sentence when he was older and had more sympathy for Kenny when he was a nice guy.

> *Can you name the independent variable, its values, and the dependent variable for each of the experiments in Table 9.2? Which experimental design would be better for these two experiments, posttest-only or repeated measures? (Q5)*

A second decision involving the independent variable concerns the strength of the manipulation. That is, how far apart should the values of the independent variable be? Usually the manipulation should be as strong as possible. Such an approach maximizes the differences between the treatments and thus increases the chances of detecting a relationship between the independent and dependent variables. This makes sense to most students. To study frustration, compare low to high, not low to slightly higher. To assess the effect of threatened shock, compare 100 volts to 1 volt rather than to 90 volts.

Exceptions to the principle of strong manipulation occur if such a manipulation is unfeasible (e.g., too costly), unethical (e.g., extreme stress applied to humans), or unrepresentative of the real world (thereby compromising the external validity of the experiment). Another exception occurs when the expected relationship is nonlinear. If the relationship between arousal and performance is an inverted-U function, it makes little sense to compare low and high arousal. A comparison of low and moderate arousal is more appropriate. Better yet, use more than two arousal conditions and trace the shape of the arousal-performance function.

Measuring the Dependent Variable

The measure of the dependent variable should be reliable and valid. In this book, the virtues of fine measurement have been stressed several times. The next chapter points out that a fine measure of the dependent variable might be more sensitive than a coarse one for the detection of a small but real effect of the independent variable. This enthusiasm for fine measurement should be balanced with a warning. Forcing people to make very fine discriminations on single items or trials soon reaches a point of diminishing returns as far as improved reliability is concerned (Nunnally, 1978). A better strategy is to follow the advice of Chapter 5. Use several items or trials to measure the dependent variable, each one within the capacity of the respondent for making valid ordered judgments, and then build a composite scale score by combining scores from individual items or trials.

Thinking About Controls

The advice here is simple. Be your own worst enemy. When planning an experiment, assume the role of a fanatical critic and scan the experiment mercilessly for potential weaknesses. Better to do so when planning than to have an actual critic do it for you after the experiment has been completed. It is not easy to be critical of one's own pet project. Researchers identify with their projects and can become blind to potential weaknesses. A special effort is needed to overcome such blindness. Role playing your own worst enemy can be a valuable tool in this situation. So can the tips in the next section.

Good Planning

What else can be done in the planning stages to increase the chances of a successful experiment? First, write up a *research proposal*. Circulate it to peers and experts in the area of research, and actively solicit their feedback. They will see problems that you fail to see no matter how hard you try. Second, run a *pilot study* before committing yourself to the full experiment. Battlefield conditions will expose weaknesses that no one would have anticipated. Third, consider using a *manipulation check*, that is, a direct measure of the independent variable to see if you succeeded in producing the values you intended to produce. This protects you against the later criticism that the independent variable was not manipulated as intended. For example, in the arousal-performance experiment, including a measure of galvanic skin response would allow you to determine if a manipulation intended to produce high arousal actually did so. Manipulation checks are not always possible. It is hard to imagine how one could devise a direct measure of frustration for the frustration experiment. Even where possible, some researchers argue against including a manipulation check because it might affect the dependent variable or vice-versa. That problem can be solved by running the manipulation check and the experiment using two different samples from the same population.

Treating Participants

Finally, consider the following simple truth: the participants in your experiment are doing you a favor. Repeat: YOUR PARTICIPANTS ARE DOING YOU A FAVOR! They should be treated accordingly. There will be much more about humane treatment of participants in the chapter on ethics in research. The point here is that your attitude toward participants should be one of consideration and gratitude, even if they were forced to take part in your study. At the very least, you should allow participants to find out whatever they would like to know about the experiment after it is over. This is part of what is known as *debriefing*. In any event, your behavior should communicate your gratitude. Remember: your conduct will shape participants' attitudes toward all researchers. It is a considerable responsibility. Please take it seriously.

SUMMARY

The defining feature of an experiment is the presence of at least one manipulated independent variable. Manipulation means that the experimenter produces the values of the variable and assigns participants to those values. Experiments also contain at least one measured dependent variable, numerous sampled variables (participants, stimuli, conditions, etc.), and extraneous variables (those judged to be possibly related to the dependent variable). Extraneous variables must be neutralized by either control (being held constant in some sense) or randomization (being made to vary in a chance fashion). Otherwise they are confounded with the independent variable, and the internal validity of the experiment is suspect. The basic purpose of an experiment is to establish a cause–effect relationship. The presumed cause (the independent variable) is manipulated, the presumed effect (the dependent variable) is then measured, and all other possible alternative causes (extraneous variables) are neutralized as causes. If a relationship is obtained under these circumstances, the independent variable must have been the cause of changes in the dependent variable.

Experimental design refers to how participants are assigned to experimental treatments or conditions (i.e., values of the independent variable). Good designs may be divided into two categories based on whether or not any stable characteristics of participants have been matched across conditions. Designs featuring random assignment to conditions without matching are called independent-treatments designs. Those with matching are called nonindependent-treatments designs. The former category includes the posttest-only and the two-group, pre-post designs. The latter category includes the explicit-matching and the repeated-measures designs.

Among the good experimental designs, the greater control of nonindependent-treatments designs has significant costs. With explicit matching, the researcher controls one stable participant characteristic but must go to the extra trouble of obtaining measures of the matching variable before the experiment can be run. In repeated-measures experiments, each participant is assigned to all conditions, which achieves implicit matching of all stable participant characteristics. However, the researcher must deal with the greater likelihood of participants guessing the purpose of the experiment and with the problem of the order of presenting conditions.

In conducting experiments, the researcher must choose between instructional and staged manipulations of the independent variable. Within limits, the stronger the manipulation, the better. In measuring the dependent variable, a good strategy is to have a moderately fine scale for individual trials or items and to build composite scores based on several trials or items. In planning an experiment, careful thought about needed controls will pay dividends in avoiding confounding. Research proposals evaluated by others, pilot studies, and manipulation checks can also be helpful. Research participants should be treated with consideration and gratitude.

ANSWERS TO QUESTIONS

Q1. In the first experiment, the independent variable is type of urban shooting crime, and its values are drug-related and drive-by random. The dependent variable is rated fear of going into the city. In the second experiment, the independent variable is type of campaign ad. Its values are emphasis on favorable qualities of the candidate and emphasis on unfavorable qualities of the candidate's opponent. The dependent variable is rated favorability toward the candidate.

Q2. With implicit matching (i.e., a repeated-measures design), each participant is assigned to all conditions. Therefore, order of presenting the conditions becomes an issue, that is, a possible source of confounding that must be dealt with. With explicit matching or experiments without matching, each participant is assigned to ONLY ONE condition. Thus, order of presenting conditions is not an issue.

Q3. In the prison study, there was no matching or pretest measurement of the dependent variable, but participants were randomly assigned to the conditions of either guard role or prisoner role. Therefore, the experiment had a posttest-only design.

Q4. Because the maze problems were presumably presented as paper-and-pencil tasks, the frustration experiment had an instructional manipulation of the independent variable.

Q5. For the first experiment, the independent variable is age of the murderer, its values are 18 and 58, and the dependent variable is the participant's approval of the sentence. For the second experiment, the independent variable is the athlete's image, its values are positive and negative, and the dependent variable is the participant's sympathy for the athlete's medical problem. Repeated-measures designs should be avoided with scenario manipulations. In such designs, when the participants see the second scenario, they will immediately guess the purpose of the experiment, and this may influence them to respond so as to confirm the researcher's theory. This problem is much less likely, though not impossible, with a posttest-only design because the participant sees only one scenario.

FURTHER READING

Cook and Campbell's (1979) classic treatment of types of validity in research and how to achieve them is well worth your attention.

REFERENCES

Cook, T. D., & Campbell, D. T. (1979). *Quasi-experimentation: Design and analysis issues for field settings.* Chicago: Rand McNally.

Darley, J. M., & Batson, C. D. (1973). "From Jerusalem to Jericho": A study of situational and dispositional variables in helping behavior. *Journal of Personality and Social Psychology, 27,* 100–108.

Haney, C., Banks, W. C., & Zimbardo, P. G. (1973). Interpersonal dynamics in a simulated prison. *International Journal of Criminology and Penology, 1,* 69–97.

Nunnally, J. (1978). *Psychometric theory* (2nd ed.). New York: McGraw-Hill.

The Experiment: Internal Validity and Sensitivity

10

There are three properties that any good experiment should have: internal validity, sensitivity, and external validity. *Internal validity* was discussed in the previous chapter, where it was defined as the soundness of inferences about the causes of research findings. Although some progress toward pinning down cause is possible in nonexperimental research (see the section on "Advanced Correlation Analyses" in Chapter 8), the experiment is the one research method that contains specific procedures for ruling out ALL causal candidates except the manipulated independent variable. Thus, serious discussions about internal validity are usually confined to the results of experiments where the issue is whether or not all extraneous variables were properly neutralized, that is, ruled out as causes. If so, the experiment has internal validity, which means that the independent variable must have been the cause of the findings. If not, some alternative cause was confounded with the independent variable, a clear causal conclusion cannot be reached, and the experiment lacks internal validity. Because the main goal of an experiment is to achieve internal validity, the examination of experiments for possible sources of confounding is a serious business indeed. Much of this chapter is devoted to a detailed exploration of sources of confounding and procedures for neutralizing them.

Sensitivity refers to the ability of a research study to detect small but real relationships between the variables investigated. Thus, sensitivity is a desirable property of all good research, not just experiments. One way to increase sensitivity is to raise the alpha level for the test of significance. As discussed in Chapter 4, raising alpha reduces the probability of a Type II error (missing a real relationship), thereby increasing sensitivity. But raising alpha has a serious cost: the Type I error rate *increases* at the same time that the Type II error rate *decreases*. For that reason, raising alpha is not the best way to increase sensitivity.

The best way to increase sensitivity is to reduce random error from all sources as much as possible. Several previous chapters pointed out that random error (unpredictable chance effects, noise) is dealt with by tests of inference. That is, the null hypothesis of no relationship between variables in the population is equivalent to the proposition that only random error is operating in the sample. However, it was also pointed out that lots of random error makes it difficult to reject the null hypothesis. In that case, the study lacks sensitivity because a small but real relationship between the variables is unlikely to be detected correctly by the test of inference. The solution to this problem is to increase sensitivity by reducing random error. Although strategies for reducing random error have been discussed at several points in the text (e.g., Chapters 3, 6, and 7), this chapter concentrates on reducing random error (thereby increasing sensitivity) in experiments.

Sensitivity is related to a statistical concept known as power, which was briefly discussed in Chapters 4 and 7 in the context of determining sample sizes. Quite simply, *power* = 1 − (probability of a Type II error). Thus, when the probability of a Type II error (missing a real relationship) is small, the test of inference is said to have power. Clearly, anything that increases sensitivity also increases power. However, the two terms are not exactly equivalent. Sensitivity refers to a study's ability to detect *small* but real relationships, whereas power refers to a study's ability to detect *any* real relationship. Because of the slight difference in definition, there is one strategy that increases power without affecting sensitivity: increasing the strength of the independent-variable manipulation (see "Manipulating the Independent Variable" in the previous chapter).

Do you see why this is so? (Q1)

In any event, the focus in this chapter is on increasing sensitivity (and, simultaneously, power) in experiments by reducing random error.

Recall from the previous chapter that the third property of a good experiment, *external validity*, refers to the generality of research results. The generality of a finding depends on how broadly and adequately all sampled variables have been represented in a study. Limitations on generality are typically the result of sample bias, that is, constant error in sampling, as discussed in Chapter 7. For example, consider an experimenter who wonders if a result obtained with an instructional manipulation would also be obtained with a staged manipulation. That experimenter is concerned with whether the manipulation of the independent variable is a biased sample of manipulations likely to be encountered in the real world. External validity is another desirable property of all research, not just experiments, and it will be explored in detail in Chapter 13.

The concepts of internal validity and sensitivity in experiments and their relationship to each other can be neatly summarized by a simple formula. The formula lists all of the components that affect a participant's score on the dependent variable in any condition of an experiment. The formula looks like this:

$$DV = MEAN + SE + RE. \tag{10.1}$$

DV refers to the participant's score on the Dependent Variable, say, aggression. MEAN is the average of all scores in all conditions on the dependent variable. It is included in the formula because statisticians tell us that if nothing else is going on, the best guess one can make about a person's score is to guess the average of all scores. SE refers to Systematic Effects, that is, all sources that are exerting a systematic influence on the participant's score. RE refers to Random Error, that is, chance or unpredictable influences from all sources.

There are two important points regarding this formula. The first is that SE really includes two components. One is the influence of the independent variable (IV; for example, frustration), and the other is the influence all variables confounded with the independent variable (CV; for example, intelligence, temperature, etc.). In other words,

$$SE = IV + CV. \tag{10.2}$$

Thus, the original formula could be rewritten as follows:

$$DV = MEAN + IV + CV + RE. \tag{10.3}$$

You can now see clearly why it is essential for the experimenter to make sure that CV = 0. Then, and only then, can the experimenter conclude that any systematic influence on the dependent variable must have been caused by the independent variable. Given that CV = O, the null hypothesis provides a clear test of whether or not IV = O. If CV does not equal O, the experiment is confounded, and no clear conclusion about cause is possible.

Note carefully that a statistical test of inference has no way of knowing what contributes to SE. It is the experimenter's job to make sure that CV = 0 (i.e., SE = IV) by running a procedurally sound experiment. If the experimenter fails to do so, no clear conclusion about cause is possible, and no statistical magic can fix the damage. In that case, the experiment is confounded and it lacks internal validity.

The second important point regarding Formula 10.1 is that it contains a random-error component (RE). The smaller that component is, the more sensitive the experiment is. The reason is that all tests of inference implicitly or explicitly compare SE to RE. In the analysis you will read about in the next chapter the comparison is in the form of a ratio: (SE + RE)/RE. Knowing this, you can easily see that for a given SE (the effect of the independent variable in a well-run experiment), the smaller RE is, the larger is the value of the ratio. That is, the smaller the random error from all sources, the more clearly visible a small but real influence of the independent variable will be. Sensitivity refers to making a small relationship more visible by reducing the background noise of random error.

This chapter is about internal validity and sensitivity in experiments. First, the chapter examines the types and sources of error that can occur in an experiment and how errors affect the internal validity and sensitivity of the experiment. Then the special techniques used to deal with such errors are discussed. With that as background, the chapter concludes by looking at specific examples of bad and good experimental designs and noting exactly why they are bad or good.

ERROR IN THE EXPERIMENT

The kind of error that concerns experimenters is that which occurs when a change on the dependent variable is produced by any variable other than the independent variable. Such error poses a threat to the internal validity or the sensitivity of the experiment. This section categorizes such errors, examines their sources within the experiment, and discusses techniques for dealing with them.

Types of Error

Error in the experiment comes in two forms, constant and random. You have already met constant and random error in the discussion of sampling and, in the case of random error, in the discussions of observation and measurement. Now it is time to see how they apply in the context of the experiment.

Constant error. In Chapter 7, *constant error* was defined as one that systematically favors certain values of a variable over other values. In an experiment, the variable subjected to this distortion is the independent variable. Remember that the values of the independent variable are equivalent to the conditions or treatments in the experiment. Thus, a constant error in an experiment is one that systematically favors some conditions over others. Such error operates in addition to the independent variable, either adding to or subtracting from its effect on the dependent variable and doing so consistently. In the frustration experiment, a constant error would be present if the researcher systematically assigned bright people to one of the conditions (solvable or unsolvable maze problem) and less intelligent people to the other condition. Clearly, when a constant error is present in an experiment, confounding must have occurred, and the internal validity of the experiment is compromised. The only distinction between confounding and constant error in an experiment is that a confounding variable *may have* affected the dependent variable (it probably did because informed opinion judged it relevant), whereas a constant error implies that a confounding variable *did indeed* affect the dependent variable.

The importance of eliminating constant error in experiments cannot be overemphasized. As noted earlier, if such error occurs, the experiment is confounded and usually cannot be rescued. The time to deal with constant error is when planning the experiment. Such error is like a fatal disease; the only sure treatment is prevention.

Random error.   In earlier chapters, random error was defined as unpredictable error. That is, its direction cannot be predicted. In an experiment, random error sometimes favors one condition, sometimes another condition, on a chance basis. As discussed earlier, such error obscures the effect of the independent variable rather than systematically distorting it. It is like looking at the moon (the effect of the independent variable) through a cloudy haze (random error) or trying to find a radio station (the effect of the independent variable) in a background of static (random error). Random error shows up as unpredictable variation in the scores on the dependent variable. If such variation is large, then the differences in the scores *across* conditions (the effect of the independent variable, assuming no constant error) may seem small by comparison. The signal is not easily detected when there is a lot of noise (random error) present. The experiment lacks *sensitivity*, the ability to detect small but real differences across conditions. Thus, random error always contributes to a loss of sensitivity in an experiment.

Unlike constant error, random error cannot be eliminated. However, it can be reduced by the same techniques used to eliminate constant error. Also, there is a special technique aimed solely at reducing random error. Furthermore, as discussed earlier, random error is dealt with whenever a test of statistical inference is performed. However, as that discussion made clear, if there is a lot of random error, a test of inference is of small comfort because it will be very difficult to reject the null hypothesis. That is, the experiment will lack both sensitivity and power, and the probability of missing a real relationship (a Type II error of inference) will be high. Thus, the goal is to reduce random error as much as possible.

That brings us to one of the real ironies of research methods. One of the most common techniques for eliminating constant error is randomization, which by its very nature creates random error. Most techniques for eliminating constant error do not have this drawback. Fortunately, as noted in the preceding paragraph, there is a special technique aimed solely at reducing random error. However, before discussing any techniques for dealing with error in the experiment, it is necessary to examine the sources of such error. Techniques for dealing with error in the experiment depend on the source of the error.

Sources of Error

An experiment may be divided conceptually into four stages: obtaining participants (sampling), assigning them to conditions or values of the independent variable (assignment), administering the conditions (conditions), and measuring the dependent variable after a condition has been administered (measurement). Error may creep into the experiment at any of these stages, threatening either the validity or the sensitivity of the study. Thus, a researcher's concerns are the same for all four sources of error: eliminate constant error, and reduce random error as much as possible. Error in sampling and techniques for dealing with it were discussed at length in Chapter 7. You should review that material because it also applies to the experiment. Only the last three stages are unique to the experiment because they occur during or after manipulation of the independent variable. Thus, this chapter concentrates only on those stages.

Let us now look at the three sources of error that are unique to the experiment and see how they work. Table 10.1 will be helpful in this discussion. The table summarizes the sources of constant error in an experiment and control techniques for dealing with them. The left column lists the three general sources of constant error. The next column lists specific examples of each general source. As the examples are discussed, you will see how they could also be examples of random error. Later, when procedures for dealing with constant error are considered, the control techniques in the last two columns of the table will be discussed.

Assignment. When participants are assigned to conditions in such a way that a relevant stable characteristic of participants differs across conditions, error due to assignment has occurred. If the error occurs because of a systematic bias in the assignment procedure, it is constant error, and the relevant characteristic is confounded with the independent variable. For example, in the frustration experiment, if males, known to be the more aggressive sex, are assigned disproportionately to the high-frustration condition, then gender has been confounded with frustration because of the biased procedure for assigning participants to conditions. Any difference across conditions in the dependent variable, aggression, may be due to the corresponding differences in gender, the confounding variable, rather than to frustration, the independent variable. Thus, the experiment is procedurally unsound, and its internal validity has been compromised. A similar argument applies to any other relevant stable characteristic of participants, such as intelligence.

Can you state the argument for intelligence? (Q2)

The same kind of gender imbalance across conditions could occur if participants were randomly assigned to conditions. However, in this case it would be random error because it was created by a random process. Such error, as always, reduces the sensitivity of the experiment.

Conditions. Whenever conditions are administered in such a way that some variable other than than independent variable differs across conditions, error due to conditions has occurred. Constant error occurs when such a "third" variable has

Table 10.1   CONSTANT ERROR IN AN EXPERIMENT

		Control Techniques	
Source	*Example*	*Absolute*	*Balancing*
Assignment	Stable Participant Characteristics	Sample Only One Value	Matching: Explicit, Implicit
Conditions	Demand Characteristics	Single Blinds Placebo Control Unobtrusive Experiments Deception Assignment To Only One Condition	
	Experimenter Bias	Double Blinds Use Only ONE Well-Trained Experimenter Automation	Balance Experimenters Across Conditions
	Environment	Hold Environment Constant	Balance Environments Across Conditions
	Inadequate Comparison	Placebo Control Yoking	
	Order Effects	Assignment To Only One Condition	Counterbalancing
Measurement	Biased Measurement	Hold Measuring Procedure Constant	Balance Measuring Procedure Across Conditions

been allowed to differ systematically across conditions. The possibilities are almost limitless but may be broadly categorized into procedural and environmental sources. *Procedural sources* of constant error commonly involve knowledge about the study on the part of participants or experimenter. If the participants figure out the theory behind the study and thus know what is "supposed" to happen, they may try harder in some conditions than others. Cues in the situation that convey such knowledge to participants are called *demand characteristics* because they signal to participants the kind of performance "demanded" in different conditions. Likewise, experimenters with such theoretical knowledge may act differently toward participants in the different conditions, in effect creating or adding to the demand characteristics. When an experimenter behaves in such a manner, the problem is called *experimenter bias. Environmental sources* of constant error include systematic differences in temperature, lighting, time of day or year, etc., across conditions. Of course, if any of these errors result from random differences across conditions rather than systematic differences, then they qualify as random error due to conditions. If you must use two different rooms and you randomly assign participants to both conditions and rooms, then any effect of rooms on performance is random error.

Sometimes constant error due to conditions can be very subtle. If you find a difference in hand raising between children who are rewarded whenever they raise a hand and those given no reward, the conclusion that reward for hand raising increases hand raising is not clearly warranted. The reason is that receiving a reward for hand raising has been confounded with receiving a reward. That is, the "control" children not only got no reward for hand raising; they got no reward at all. In Table 10.1, this problem is referred to as *inadequate comparison*. Prudent experimeters must think very carefully about possible sources of constant error due to conditions.

The last example in Table 10.1 of constant error due to conditions, *order effects*, refers to a problem that arises only in experiments in which each participant is assigned to more than one condition. Order effects and how to deal with them will be included in the discussion of repeated-measures experiments later in the chapter.

Measurement.   When measurement procedures differ across conditions, error due to measurement has occurred. If the measurement procedures differ systematically across conditions, the result is constant error because of *biased measurement*. If you read a dial to measure the dependent variable and always round fractional readings upward in one condition but not in another, you create a constant error due to measurement. If you measure memory by a recall test in one condition and a recognition test in another condition, you have an even more blatant example of constant error in measurement. Any inconsistencies in measurement procedure that are distributed in an essentially random manner across conditions constitute random error due to measurement. If you round up or down inconsistently across conditions, that would constitute random error.

Dealing with Constant Error

As noted earlier, constant error must be eliminated, or the internal validity of the results is compromised in a way that cannot usually be repaired. There are two procedural approaches to eliminating such error.

Randomization.   One way to eliminate constant error is to turn it into random error, a technique known as randomization. A variable is randomized whenever it is made to vary in a chance fashion. The advantage of randomization is that random error is dealt with as part of the test of statistical inference. The disadvantage is that if there is too much random error present, the sensitivity of the experiment will be low, making it very difficult to reject the null hypothesis.

Randomization can be done several ways. One is to choose blindly from a container filled with slips of paper containing names of potential choices. Flips of a coin or spins of a wheel are also used. Sometimes a random number table like the one in Chapter 7 can be useful. You simply assign each potential choice a unique number arbitrarily, enter the random number table at an arbitrary point, and proceed in an arbitrary direction, reading off numbers until the desired sample has been chosen. Many computer software packages will generate random samples or orderings automatically. The procedures discussed here all satisfy the conditions of randomness: each potential choice has an equal probability of being selected, and this remains true throughout the selection process.

The exact form that randomization takes depends on the source of error being randomized. Constant error in assignment to experimental conditions is eliminated by random assignment to conditions. In the frustration experiment, you could flip a coin to decide which maze problem to give each participant. Or you could assign consecutive random numbers from a random number table to participants as they show up for the experiment. Participants who receive an odd random number get one version of the maze problem, and those who receive an even random number get the other version. In some situations, constant error in administering conditions can be randomized. As noted earlier, if it is necessary to use two rooms, randomly assigning participants to both conditions and rooms eliminates any constant error from rooms. If more than one experimenter must be used, random assignment of experimenters to conditions is one option for dealing with constant error due to experimenters. Randomization may also be used to eliminate constant error due to measurement. For example, you could always flip a coin to decide whether to round dial readings upward or downward.

Many students are confused about the distinction between random sampling and random assignment to conditions. Sampling refers to how participants are obtained from a population, and it occurs in all research, not just experiments. Sampling may be done randomly, as described in Chapter 7. Assignment to conditions refers to how participants are assigned to conditions in an experiment, and it occurs ONLY in experiments as part of the manipulation of the independent variable. Such assignment may also be done randomly. If you confuse the two procedures, then you may incorrectly refer to sampling procedures as assignment procedures or vice-versa. So it is a good idea to get them clearly apart in your head. Conceptually, they are two distict steps. Sampling comes first and then, only in experiments, assignment follows.

Good experimenters consider randomization a necessity, not a luxury. It is the only technique available for eliminating constant error from sources that have not been dealt with by control procedures. Thus, the general advice is to randomize all remaining sources of error after control procedures have been applied. Where it is possible to randomize, there is no excuse for not doing so. As noted in Chapter 7, one cannot always use random SAMPLING procedures. However, it is usually possible to randomize uncontrolled sources of error from ASSIGNMENT (note: a separate step from sampling), conditions, and measurement in an experiment. Failure to do so is grounds for justifiable criticism of an experiment.

Control. The second procedural approach to eliminating constant error in an experiment is control. Control means that an extraneous variable is held constant, in some sense, across the conditions of an experiment. There are two senses in which an extraneous variable may be held constant. It may be held constant period (*Absolute* control in Table 10.1) or it may be held constant on the average (*Balancing* in Table 10.1). In the first case, the variable is not allowed to vary. Thus, it must have the same value in all conditions. Environmental characteristics like lighting and temperature are usually controlled absolutely. In the second case, the variable is distributed across conditions in such a way that it has the same average value in each condition of the experiment. The variable is said to be balanced across conditions. Participant characteristics like intelligence are often controlled this way. Matching, as described in Chapter 9, is an example of balancing.

With either approach to control, the average value of the controlled variable is made equal in all conditions of the experiment. As you will see in the next chapter, the question of whether or not the independent and dependent variables are related in an experiment is decided by looking at whether the average values of the dependent variable differ across conditions. This focus on average values across conditions means that a variable having the same average value in all conditions cannot be involved in a relationship with the dependent variable and is thus eliminated as a source of constant error or confounding. Such is the fate of controlled variables in an experiment.

Specific Control Techniques

Let us now take a tour through the three sources of constant error in an experiment and describe some specific techniques used for controlling such error.

Assignment.   Absolute control of constant error due to assignment could be achieved by using only participants who have the same value on a relevant stable characteristic, such as intelligence. For example, you might use only people with an IQ of 100 in the frustration experiment. This would not be a very desirable approach for controlling intelligence.

Can you see why? (Q3)

The most common technique for controlling constant error due to assignment to conditions is a form of balancing called *matching*. Matching was described in detail in the previous chapter. You should reread the section on "Nonindependent-Treatments Designs" to refresh your memory on how matching is done and what it accomplishes. Remember that matching comes in two forms, explicit (the matching variable must be explicitly measured prior to assigning matched blocks of participants to conditions) and implicit (each participant is assigned to all conditions and thus matched with himself or herself). The two forms of matching are the defining features of the two nonindependent-treatments experimental designs, explicit matching and repeated measures. Whichever approach is used, matching ensures that the average value of one or more relevant participant characteristics like intelligence is the same in all conditions of the experiment.

Two important points about matching should be emphasized. First, matching should be used only for controlling relevant participant characteristics, that is, characteristics believed to be substantially related to the dependent variable. Matching on nonrelevant characteristics actually leads to a less powerful statistical analysis. Numerical examples illustrating this point will be discussed in the next chapter. Thus, matching should not be done just for the sake of doing it. Matching should always represent an informed judgment that a relevant characteristic of participants needs to be controlled.

Second, some participant characteristics cannot be controlled by matching. It works only for characteristics that remain the same within a person for the duration of the experiment. Such characteristics are considered *stable*. Examples are intelligence, gender, eye color, etc. *Unstable* characteristics, on the other hand, are those that can change from moment to moment within a person. Arousal level and fatigue are examples. Such characteristics cannot be controlled by matching because there is no guarantee that after matched groups have been formed the persons within each group will stay matched. Under such circumstances, matching is useless. Unstable characteristics must be dealt with by other means, the most common being to assume that they vary randomly within people and thus constitute random error.

Conditions. The preferred approach for dealing with constant error due to conditions is absolute control. That is, make sure that only one value of the extraneous variable is allowed to occur. It follows that the variable must have the same value in all experimental conditions and has thus been converted to a controlled variable. This is the most common way of dealing with environmental conditions like temperature and lighting.

Special cases of absolute control are used to deal with certain problems discussed earlier. They are listed in the third column of Table 10.1. For example, if demand characteristics are of concern, it may be possible to run the experiment so that participants do not know what condition they are experiencing. Thus, all participants are equally ignorant about their assigned condition. This approach is known as *blinding*. When only participants are blinded, the study is called a *single-blind* experiment. To deal with experimenter bias, it may be possible to blind the experimenter too. That is, the experimenter does not know what condition is being administered to each participant. Obviously, somebody must have this knowledge. Think of that person as the project director. Clearly, the project director and the experimenter must be different people. When both experimenter and participants are blinded, the study is called a *double-blind* experiment.

Sometimes, blinding is achieved by using a *placebo* control. The term comes from drug research in which all participants receive identical looking pills, but only those given to the experimental group contain the active ingredient. In the social sciences, the term has acquired a broader meaning and describes any experiment in which stimuli or other materials look identical but actually differ across conditions in a way that manipulates the independent variable. The frustration experiment contains a placebo control. All participants receive complex-looking maze problems, but only some get the active ingredient, unsolvability. Placebo control may be viewed as a way of achieving an adequate comparison across conditions in cases where participant knowledge about the treatments being administered is of concern. For that reason, placebo control appears as a possible antidote for both demand characteristics and inadequate comparison in Table 10.1.

Alternative absolute-control approaches to the problem of demand characteristics include *unobtrusive experiments* (in which participants do not know that they are involved in an experiment), *deception* (in which participants are misled regarding the purpose of the experiment), and assigning participants to only one condition (so that they are less likely to guess the purpose of the experiment). The goal in each case is to produce the same state of knowledge about the experiment in all participants. All three approaches have drawbacks. Unobtrusive experiments are often not possible, deception raises serious ethical issues (which will be discussed in Chapter 14), and assigning participants to only one condition means that implicit matching cannot be used.

Alternative absolute-control approaches to the problem of experimenter bias include using only one well-trained experimenter or eliminating the human experimenter altogether by completely automating the procedure. The goal in each case is to eliminate systematic differences in experimenter characteristics or behaviors across conditions. There is no drawback to the use of well-trained experimenters. Use of only one experimenter requires confidence that the experimenter is not "peculiar" in any way that would affect the results. Otherwise, the external validity of the experiment would be jeopardized. An example might be a very jovial (or threatening) experimenter in a study investigating fear reactions. Automation has the drawback that complete implementation is often impossible.

A final example of absolute control could be used in the experiment in which children are rewarded for hand raising. The problem was that control children received no reward, and thus getting rewarded was confounded with getting rewarded specifically for hand raising. The cure is to have a control condition in which children receive as many rewards as do children in the experimental condition. However, the rewards for control children do not depend on any specific behavior. The amount of reward is thus held constant across conditions, and the real variable of interest, reward for hand raising, can be evaluated. A further refinement is to run two children at a time, one in each condition (random assignment, of course), and to arrange things so that every time an experimental child gets rewarded for hand raising, the matched control child also gets a reward regardless of what he or she is doing. This is called *yoking* and refers to any experiment in which both the number and timing of participant-generated events in the experimental condition (rewards in our example) are simultaneously duplicated for a matched set of participants in the control condition.

Balancing may also be used to control certain cases of constant experimental error due to conditions, as indicated in the fourth column of Table 10.1. For example, if you must use two different rooms, you could use each room an equal number of times for each experimental condition. Subject only to the constraint of equal usage, which balances rooms across conditions, the assignment of participants to rooms and conditions should be randomly determined so as to randomize other sources of error that cannot be held constant. The same approach could be applied if more than one experimenter had to be used. In both of these situations, the temporal order in which participants are run should also be randomized to avoid confounding temporal factors (time of day, season of year, dramatic historical or social events) with conditions. When participants are run individually, never run all participants in one condition first and then all participants in the other condition. Relevant temporal factors are sure to be confounded with the independent variable if you do.

Measurement. There are no new techniques for dealing with constant error due to measurement. Absolute control is by far the best approach. The measurement procedure should be identical in all conditions. In the overwhelming majority of experiments, this is possible to achieve. If for good reason variation in measurement procedure is deemed necessary, then the variations should either be balanced across conditions (i.e., all variations used an equal number of times in each condition) or randomly assigned to conditions.

Dealing with Random Error

As noted earlier, random error cannot be eliminated, but it can be reduced. Random error should be made as small as possible because it reduces the sensitivity of the experiment. That is, it obscures the effect of the independent variable on the dependent variable, making it harder to reject the null hypothesis of no relationship between the variables. As you saw earlier, randomization, commonly used to eliminate constant error, creates random error. Thus, one problem is overcome by making another problem worse. Fortunately, there are some ways to counteract the effects of randomization and all other sources of random error in experiments.

First, use control techniques. Compared to randomization, control has the advantage of typically reducing random error at the same time that it eliminates constant error from the controlled variable. A variable that is controlled absolutely contributes no error of either type. A variable that is balanced across conditions usually contributes less random error to the experiment than one that varies freely. Numerical examples illustrating this point for the technique of matching will be presented in the next chapter. Thus, where possible, control is preferable to randomization as a way of dealing with extraneous variables.

Second, eliminate sloppy procedures. Sloppiness creates random error. Many beginning researchers do not pay enough attention to eliminating sloppiness. They tolerate small changes in procedures, testing formats, etc., after data collection has begun. The cure is consistency. Suppress any urge to vary the routine or to drift off and let automatic pilot take over. Disciplined consistency may not be romantic, but it can increase the sensitivity of experiments by reducing random error.

Third, you were promised a special technique for countering increases in random error caused by randomization. That technique has already been discussed in Chapter 7. Random error may always be countered by using larger sample sizes because it is inversely proportional to sample size. Thus, up to a point of diminishing returns, more participants, stimuli, trials, etc., are better than fewer.

Fourth, follow the tips of the section on "Improving Reliability" in Chapter 5. Improving reliability amounts to reducing random error in the measurement of the dependent variable. Any such reduction will allow the effect of the independent variable to stand out more clearly from the background noise of random variation in scores and be detected by the test of statistical significance.

Two final tips regarding measurement may be added. One is to consider using a finer measure of the dependent variable, especially in experiments where a small effect of the independent variable is expected. If a small effect of a persuasive message on rated approval is anticipated, then it is wiser to use a 6-point approval scale than a 2-point scale. The coarse scale might not allow the small effect to show itself, whereas the finer scale would. Finally, adjust the difficulty of the dependent-variable task to match the ability level of the participants. If the dependent variable involves problem solving and the problems are too easy or too difficult, the effect of the independent variable will not be detectable. Where difficulty is an issue, an intermediate level is usually best. In some tasks, the difficulty can be tailored to the ability level of each participant. For example, if the dependent variable involves the identification of briefly exposed words, exposure duration can be adjusted for each participant so that performance falls halfway between complete failure and perfect identification. Such adjustments typically require pretesting, but they pay off in measures of the dependent variable that are more sensitive to the effect of the independent variable.

Procedural and Statistical Control

The techniques discussed so far are procedures an experimenter can use to control an extraneous variable. For this reason, they are often referred to as *procedural* controls. When procedural control is not possible, an alternative may be available. In *statistical* control, the extraneous variable is not held constant, but instead it is measured before the application of the independent variable. The influence of the measured extraneous variable is then removed during the statistical analysis. The statistical technique is known as *analysis of covariance,* and the measured extraneous variable is termed a *covariate.* Stiff assumptions must be met before covariance analysis is appropriate. For example, the correlation between the covariate and the dependent variable must be the same in all conditions of the experiment. Analysis of covariance is a special case of multiple regression, which was discussed in Chapter 8. If you decide to use statistical control, you should seek competent advice. Most experimenters prefer the direct approach of procedural control to the indirect approach of statistical control.

EVALUATING EXPERIMENTAL DESIGNS

Recall from the previous chapter that the phrase "experimental design" refers to how participants are assigned to conditions or treatments in an experiment. Given the discussion of dealing with error, you can appreciate that some methods of assignment are badly flawed because they produce confounding or allow it to occur when it could be avoided. These are bad designs. Other methods of assignment are virtuous because they neutralize extraneous variables, either singly or in bunches. These are good designs. There are also in-between designs, imperfect but the best

Table 10.2 SYMBOLIC DIAGRAMS OF
BAD AND GOOD EXPERIMENTAL DESIGNS

Type	Name of Design	Symbolic Diagram
Bad	One-Shot	P–IV (1)–DV
	One-Group Pre-Post	P–DV–IV (1)–DV
	Nonequivalent-Groups	P–IV (1)–DV and P–IV (2)–DV
Good	Independent-Treatments	
	Posttest-Only	P (R)–IV (1)–DV and P (R)–IV (2)–DV
	Two-Group Pre-Post	P (R)–DV–IV (1)–DV and P (R)–DV–IV (2)–DV
	Nonindependent-Treatments	
	Explicit-Matching	P (MR) for P (R) in previous 2 designs
	Repeated-Measures	P (R)–IV (1)–DV–IV (2)–DV or
		P (R)–IV (2)–DV–IV (1)–DV

Key to Symbols
>   P = Nonrandom assignment of participants to conditions
> P (R) = Random assignment of participants to conditions
> P (MR) = Random assignment of participants to conditions following explicit matching
>   IV = Manipulation of an independent variable
>   IV (1) = Specific value of an independent variable (= condition)
>   IV (2) = A different specific value of an independent variable
>   DV = Measurement of a dependent variable
> Left-to-right sequence of symbols in each diagram indicates temporal order of events.

a researcher can do under the circumstances and therefore better than doing nothing. Let us now examine some common examples of each category to gain further insight into what constitutes good experimentation.

To help you compare the bad and good designs, they are diagrammed in Table 10.2 using a shorthand notation. IV means that an independent variable has been manipulated. Specific conditions or values of the independent variable are referred to by the symbols IV(l) and IV(2). DV means that the dependent variable has been measured. Hyphens are used to indicate the temporal order of events. Thus, IV(1)-DV means that a particular value of the independent variable was produced (e.g., high frustration) and then the dependent variable (aggression) was measured. P means that participants were assigned to a condition. P(R) means that random assignment was used. Without the (R), assume nonrandom assignment. Thus, P(R)-IV(1)-DV means that participants were randomly assigned to value 1 of the independent variable, the treatment was then administered, and finally the dependent variable was measured. In addition to diagrams, each design is given a distinctive name to help you remember it.

One last introductory point must be stressed strongly. The next two sections on bad and good designs deal only with experiments, that is, studies having a manipulated independent variable. Remember: manipulation means that the experimenter both produces the values of the independent variable and assigns the values to participants. There are nonexperimental versions of each of the designs discussed. In such studies, the researcher simply selects values of the independent variable that already exist. Few researchers are tempted to make strong claims about causality based on such research, even though these studies may yield interesting findings. The purpose of the next two sections is to show you that even when there is bona-fide manipulation, it can be either defective (bad designs) or procedurally sound (good designs) in terms of its impact on internal validity.

Bad Designs

There are three famous bad designs. The important thing to understand about each one is why it is a bad design. Then, hopefully, you will never be tempted to use it and will immediately spot it should anyone else use it.

The one-shot design.   In this design, all participants are assigned to one condition, the treatment is administered, and then the dependent variable is measured: P-IV(1)-DV. In the frustration experiment, this would be equivalent to having only the high-frustration condition. The design is worthless for pinning down cause because only one value of the independent variable occurs (hence the name one-shot). Recalling the minimum conditions necessary for evaluating a relationship from Chapter 2, you can see that it is impossible to determine if the independent and dependent variables are even related, let alone to establish causality. Rule number one: Always check to see that at least two values of the independent variable are present in an experiment. If there is only one value, it is a bad experiment.

The one-group, pre-post design.   In this design, all participants are measured on the dependent variable, then given the same experimental treatment, and then measured again on the dependent variable: P-DV-IV(1)-DV. "Pre" and "post" refer to the before- and after-treatment measures of the dependent variable. In the frustration experiment, all participants would be measured on aggression, then given the unsolvable maze (the high-frustration treatment), and then measured again on aggression. The "logic" is that if a change on the dependent variable from pretest to posttest can be demonstrated, it must have been caused by the experimental treatment. There are several problems with this design. It is important to understand them because the design, with its focus on pre-post change, is very attractive to many students.

Two important sources of confounding in this design are history and multiple measurement. *History* refers to other relevant events besides the experimental treatment that occur during the interval between measures of the dependent variable. Such events are confounded with the treatment. Consider a dramatic example. All of the participants are run as a group at the same time. Aggression is measured, then the unsolvable maze is given to everyone, then lightning strikes the room, and finally aggression is measured again. When looking at pre-post changes in aggression, it is impossible to separate the influences of the maze problem and the lightning strike.

Most historical influences are more subtle than lightning. Two of them are worth noting. First, whatever else happens during the pre-post interval, participants will get older. If the interval is long, effects of *maturation* will be confounded with the experimental treatment. Second, despite the best efforts of the researcher, the procedure for measuring the dependent variable may change over time. The observers watching for aggression directed against the Bobo doll may get tired by the postmeasurement, or they may get better at detecting signs of aggression. If an electronic instrument is used for measurement, one of its transistors may go bad during the pre-post interval. This source of historical confounding is called *instrument decay*. In either case, the change in the measure of the dependent variable is confounded with the experimental treatment.

Multiple measurement refers to the fact that there are two measurements of the dependent variable. Even if the measurement procedure remains exactly the same for both measurements, one may obtain different scores because of practice effects or participant fatigue. Another possibility is that the pretest, coupled with the experimental treatment, might cause the participant to guess the purpose of the treatment, creating demand characteristics at the time of the posttest. Any influence of multiple measurement cannot be separated from that of the experimental treatment; the two effects are confounded.

A special case of multiple-measurement confounding occurs when the pretest is used as a screening device to select participants who score either extremely high or extremely low on the pretest. Only selected participants continue in the experiment. This situation is likely to arise when special treatment programs are being investigated for effectiveness. For example, a clinical researcher might select severely depressed persons based on a pretest, then expose them to a new treatment for depression, and then measure their depression again after the treatment. Improved depression scores after the treatment are taken as evidence of the treatment's effectiveness. As a second example, imagine that a special teaching technique has been devised to help slow learners. The dependent variable is scores on a learning test. The test is administered to a large sample of participants, and only those scoring in the bottom 20 percent are selected for the experiment. They are then exposed to the special teaching technique and later are given the learning test again. Their scores show significant improvement at the second testing, which is taken as evidence for the effectiveness of the new teaching technique.

Alas, change in the desired direction could be expected in both situations regardless of the treatment technique used. Because the measure of the dependent variable is not perfectly reliable, the subgroup of participants with extreme scores on the pretest obtained those scores at least partly as a byproduct of random error or chance. When tested again, chance factors should spread them out so they are no longer bunched up at one extreme end of the distribution. Thus, they should produce less extreme scores as a group on the second measurement, regardless of what else happens. This tendency of extreme subgroups to spread out toward the center of a distribution after a second measurement is called *statistical regression*, or regression toward the mean. It is a byproduct of the unreliability of the measurement procedure. In a one-group, pre-post design, statistical regression will be confounded with the experimental treatment only when the pretest is used to select an extreme subgroup, based on pretest scores, to continue in the experiment. Pretest screening for extreme subgroups is not common in research, but when it happens the threat of confounding from regression should be kept in mind.

Regression toward the mean has an interesting application in sports. See if you can make the connection.

Why do you suppose sensational rookies often have a difficult time repeating their success the following season? (Q4)

This extended discussion of the many confoundings in the one-group, pre-post design, is meant to convince you that the design is badly flawed. Despite its apparent attractiveness, it is a bad design and should be avoided. Results from such a design should be viewed with extreme caution.

The nonequivalent-groups design. It may have occurred to you that all of the problems with the last design can be traced to the fact that, once again, there is only value of the independent variable, IV(l). What about a second treatment group, one that gets a low-frustration treatment? Wouldn't an IV(2) eliminate the confounding from all sources by allowing a direct comparison with IV(l)? It depends.

The nonequivalent-groups design has a control group: P-IV(1)-DV is compared to P-IV(2)-DV. There are two values of the independent variable, IV(l) and IV(2), and multiple measurement has been eliminated, seemingly a great improvement. In the frustration experiment, participants given the unsolvable maze problem would be compared to those given the easily solved maze problem, and measurement of aggression would occur only after exposure to the maze problem. This may not look like a bad design, but it has a serious flaw. Can you see it? Stop and think.

The problem is that assignment of participants to conditions is not random (P-instead of P(R)-). Therefore, the two groups of participants may not be equivalent on the dependent variable or an extraneous variable at the beginning of the experiment (hence the title nonequivalent-groups design). Any preexisting differences in the two groups of participants are confounded with the experimental treatment. This is a bad design when the experimenter could have used random assignment but did not. In some real-life situations researchers are forced to work with preexisting groups. In those situations, the design qualifies as one of the in-between design discussed later in the chapter because it the best the researcher can do under the circumstances. But failure to use random assignment when it is possible is inexcusable. The moral is that a second value of the independent variable is not enough to qualify an experimental design as good. How participants are assigned to conditions is also important.

Note that an experimenter may start out with random assignment of participants to conditions but still end up with nonequivalent conditions because participants drop out of the study. *Participant attrition* (loss of participants) can destroy the equivalence of treatment groups initially achieved by random assignment, especially when the attrition rate differs across conditions. Where attrition is substantial, the experimenter must be alert to the possibility that the remaining participants in the various conditions may differ systematically in ways that have nothing to do with the independent variable. Attrition rates should always be faithfully reported in research papers, and, if possible, their impact on the results should be evaluated.

Good Designs

A little reflection should convince you that the basic problem with the bad designs involves the manipulation of the independent variable. The experimenter either does not produce enough values of the independent variable (no comparison condition) or does not assign participants to the values properly. The result is a confounded experiment with questionable internal validity. The distinguishing feature of good designs is that there is no problem with the manipulation of the independent variable. Assuming no problems with constant error from sources other than manipulation of the independent variable, this means that there is no problem with internal validity. These designs are procedurally sound.

Recall from the previous chapter that good experimental designs can be grouped into two major categories. *Independent-treatments designs* feature random assignment to conditions without any matching of participant characteristics across conditions. *Nonindependent-treatments designs* feature matching of participants across conditions on one or more stable characteristics such as intelligence. The pros and cons of matching were discussed in the previous chapter and also in the "Specific Control Techniques" section of this chapter. Each design category has two members.

In the independent-treatments category, the *posttest-only design* is common. P(R)-IV(1)-DV is compared to P(R)-IV(2)-DV. The posttest-only design corrects the flaw of nonrandom assignment in the nonequivalent-groups design. Otherwise, the two designs are equivalent. The posttest-only design has two treatment groups, random assignment of participants converts any differences in stable participant characteristics across conditions into random error, and there is no pretest. The second member of the independent-treatments category is the *two-group, pre-post design*. P(R)-DV-IV(1)-DV is compared to P(R)-DV-IV(2)-DV. The distinguishing feature of the design is the presence of the pretest preceding the manipulation of the independent variable. The pretest complicates the data analysis, and perhaps for that reason the design is less widely used.

In the nonindependent-treatments category, the *explicit-matching design* requires explicit measurement of a relevant matching variable and the formation of matched blocks of participants before members of the matched blocks are randomly assigned to conditions. If the notation P(MR) is used to indicate random assignment of explicitly matched participants to conditions, then explicit matching could utilize the diagrams for either of the independent-treatments designs with P(MR) replacing P(R). Such designs are rarely used because of the extra work involved in measuring the matching variable. The more common approach is the *repeated-measures design* in which each participant serves in all experimental conditions: either P(R)-IV(1)-DV-IV(2)-DV or P(R)-IV(2)-DV-IV(1)-DV. This design achieves implicit matching on all stable participant characteristics. However, as noted in the previous chapter, the repeated-measures design poses some new and unique problems for researchers. Those problems will be the focus of the remainder of this section.

The major drawbacks of the repeated-measures design involve its distinguishing characteristic, running each participant in all conditions. Exposure to all conditions makes it more likely that participants will figure out the purpose of the experiment and thus will be more susceptible to the demand characteristics of the situation. As noted earlier in the chapter, demand characteristics may have systematically different effects in different conditions because participants may try harder in certain conditions when they know they are expected to do well. Thus, demand characteristics may lead to a confounding that compromises both the internal and external validity of the experiment. The external validity is threatened because the confounded result may not generalize to other kinds of experimental designs.

A related objection is that even if demand characteristics are not a problem, the high degree of control achieved by implicit matching is a threat to external validity. As noted earlier in the chapter, control not only eliminates constant error but also reduces random error, thereby increasing the sensitivity of experiments. Repeated-measures experiments are so sensitive, it is argued, that they are not very representative of real-life conditions, which are typically much messier. So it may be difficult to replicate results obtained with repeated-measures designs under more realistic conditions. Thus, virtue is turned into vice. Because of the potential threats to external validity, some researchers avoid repeated-measures designs as a matter of course.

The most obvious new problem in repeated-measures designs is *order effects*, that is, the effects of any variables, other than the independent variable, that change as a result of repeated measurement in different conditions. Such variables include practice, fatigue, boredom, or any other variables that might be expected to accumulate over trials. Variables like these can easily become confounded with the independent variable in repeated-measures experiments. For example, suppose you are investigating the effects of anxiety on skilled performance. If you always present the high-anxiety condition first, superior performance in the low-anxiety condition may be caused by either the lower anxiety or the additional trial of practice preceding the low-anxiety condition. Clearly something needs to be done about the order of presenting the anxiety conditions. Thus, the effects of variables like practice are referred to as order effects.

Order effects come in two forms, and the distinction is crucial. *Symmetrical* order effects are unrelated to the independent variable. Thus, they are the same regardless of the order in which conditions (values of the independent variable) are presented. Practice effects often work this way when the dependent variable involves skilled performance. That is, the performance benefit from one trial of practice is the same regardless of the experimental condition preceding the measurement. Another example might be boredom in the frustration experiment. If it can be safely assumed that boredom from repeated exposures to the Bobo doll accumulates the same way over trials regardless of the kind of maze problem preceding each exposure, then the build-up of boredom is a symmetrical order effect.

Asymmetrical order effects, on the other hand, are related to the independent variable. Thus, they depend on the order in which conditions are presented. That is, they differ in size for different orders of presenting conditions. In the frustration experiment, fatigue is a plausible example. It seems likely that fatigue and aggression affect each other: aggression causes fatigue, and fatigue inhibits aggression. Thus any fatigue remaining from a previous trial inhibits aggression on the next trial. If frustration causes aggression which, in turn, causes fatigue, then the amount of fatigue present on a given trial depends on the frustration condition of the preceding trial. Thus, the change in fatigue level over trials is different for a high-low order of frustration conditions than for a low-high order. This is an asymmetrical order effect.

What can be done to neutralize order effects? Here is where the distinction between the two types of order effects becomes important. Symmetrical order effects can be neutralized, but asymmetrical order effects cannot. Both of the standard neutralization techniques, control and randomization, can be used to neutralize symmetrical order effects, but neither technique works for asymmetrical order effects.

To appreciate these points, consider boredom in the frustration experiment. Assume that the build-up of boredom is unrelated to frustration and thus qualifies as a symmetrical order effect. Then boredom can be controlled by a technique called *counterbalancing,* which means that each possible order of presenting conditions is used for an equal number of participants. Thus, in the frustration experiment, the high-frustration condition would be presented first half of the time and second half of the time, and the same would be true of the low-frustration condition. Because the boredom level during a trial depends only on the number of trials preceding it and not on the frustration condition during those trials, and because each frustration condition occurs first and second half of the time (counterbalancing), the distribution of boredom scores must be the same in both frustration conditions. Thus, the average boredom level must be the same for both frustration conditions. Boredom has been successfully balanced across conditions. Counterbalancing is thus a special form of balancing, used for controlling symmetrical order effects in repeated-measures experiments. As an alternative, an experimenter could randomize the order of presenting conditions. In that case, any resulting difference in average boredom levels across conditions would be part of the overall random error in the experiment.

As was the case with balancing settings or experimenters across conditions, the temporal order in which participants are run must also be considered when counterbalancing is used. Never run all participants receiving one presentation order (say, low frustration followed by high frustration) first and then all participants receiving the other presentation order (high-low) first. If you do, temporal factors will be confounded with presentation order. The simplest solution is to randomize the temporal order in which participants are run, subject to the constraint that half of them receive each order of presenting conditions (counterbalancing).

Now consider what happens for asymmetrical order effects. Earlier it was assumed that the level of fatigue depends on the order of presenting conditions in the frustration experiment. Specifically, there is more fatigue following the high-frustration condition than following the low-frustration condition. In other words, the fatigue level is ALWAYS higher in the low-frustration condition than in the high-frustration condition when either condition is presented second. Therefore, presenting each condition first and second half of the time (counterbalancing) must produce an average fatigue level that is higher for the low-frustration condition than for the high-frustration condition. The attempt to balance fatigue across conditions has failed, and fatigue is confounded with frustration.

Randomizing the order of conditions does not help in this situation. Randomization typically works because the expected value of the randomization process is a constant error of zero. However, if the expected value of the randomization process is a nonzero constant error, then the process is producing random variation on top of a nonzero constant error rather than eliminating the constant error. If you randomize the order of conditions in the frustration experiment, the expected percentage of high-low and low-high orderings is 50 percent of each, which is equivalent to the percentages produced by counterbalancing. But you just learned in the last paragraph that counterbalancing produces a difference in average fatigue levels across the two conditions, that is, a nonzero constant error due to fatigue. Thus, for an asymmetrical order effect, the expected value of randomizing order of conditions is the same constant error produced by counterbalancing.

The moral of this lengthy discussion of order effects is simple. If you are not interested in studying order effects for their own sake and have reason to believe that asymmetrical order effects may be a problem in your planned repeated-measures experiment, you should abandon the repeated-measures design. Such effects cannot be eliminated, and your experiment will be confounded. Choose one of the other good designs. Presumably, such a sad state of affairs does not happen very often because repeated-measures experiments are fairly common.

In-Between Designs

Some experimental designs are less clearly good or bad. They have flaws that cannot be ignored, but they are also the best that can be done under the circumstances. On the good-bad continuum, they are in-between. Because they are the best that can be done, they are clearly preferable to doing nothing. Because of their shortcomings, results from such designs should be treated with caution. Generally, confidence in such results may be strengthened by replicating the results in a variety of circumstances and by using statistical control to deal with measurable extraneous variables. Here is a brief survey of the most common in-between designs.

Field experiments. Any study with a manipulated independent variable carried out in a nonlaboratory setting qualifies for this category. A nonlaboratory setting usually implies a noncontrived "real-world" setting like a school, streetcorner, or park. The appeal of these designs is that they are high in *ecological validity*, that is, the extent to which the results should generalize to real-world settings. The chief limitation of field experiments is their greater potential for error compared to laboratory experiments. Error from environmental variables is especially likely because the experimenter cannot usually control what goes on in the real-world setting of a field experiment. The error is more likely to be random (i.e., unpredictable) than constant. Consider the effect of unpredictable bursts of jackhammer noise on dependent-variable performance in a field experiment, and you will appreciate this point. The lack of control over environmental "noise" is the reason for classifying field experiments in the in-between category.

Single-subject designs.   These are experiments carried out with a sample of one participant. Researchers in the operant-conditioning and behavior-modification traditions tend to favor these designs. The typical study begins by measuring a single participant's behavior (the dependent variable) over time during a "baseline" control period. The manipulation or treatment is then introduced while the participant's behavior continues to be measured. A change in behavior from baseline to treatment periods is taken as evidence for the effectiveness of the treatment. For example, you might monitor an aggressive child for aggressive behavior toward a Bobo doll during a baseline control period. You then introduce the treatment, a reward delivered after every thirty seconds of nonaggression, while continuing to measure the child's aggressive behavior. If the rewards are valuable, the child's aggression should decline during the treatment period. This is very similar to the one-group, pre-post design with a sample of one. The difference is that it is actually a pre-during design. It is commonly called an *AB design*, where A refers to the baseline period and B to the treatment period. Whatever it is called, the design suffers from the same major problem as the pre-post design: What else may have changed along with the treatment during the treatment period?

Variations on the basic design are intended to deal with this problem. In *reversal designs*, also known as *ABA designs*, baseline and treatment periods are alternated. The object is to show that the behavior change can be reversed and reinstated at the discretion of the experimenter. It seems unlikely that the very same confounding could have occurred during each treatment period. An alternative approach is the *multiple-baseline design*. In such a design, the treatment is administered under multiple circumstances with the object of showing that the behavior change occurs only when the treatment is administered. Here, too, the argument is that the same confounding could hardly have occurred under all the circumstances in which the treatment was administered. Both reversal and multiple-baseline designs offer some reassurance against confounding, but another problem remains with all single-subject designs.

The basic objection to such designs is their small sample. With a sample of one, the external validity of results is necessarily compromised. No amount of reversals or multiple baselines can change that. Some conditioning researchers claim that they use a "typical" subject or that they have no desire to generalize. There is no good reason to accept either claim. Some researchers claim that replication of the results with a few more typical subjects will solve the problem. More subjects are indeed better, but the sample is still small. Fortunately, there has been a tendency to study larger samples with "single-subject" designs and to compare average scores during baseline and treatment periods (Barlow & Hersen, 1984).

Quasi-experiments.   These are "experiments" in name only because the independent variable is not fully manipulated by the experimenter. Either the experimenter does not produce the values of the independent variable or does not assign participants to the values or both. Such studies are not "true" experiments; hence they are called quasi-experiments. Usually they represent the best the researcher can do under the circumstances, and so they are tolerated despite their flaws. As usual, the best medicine for increasing confidence in the results from such studies is replication in a variety of circumstances. Here are some examples of quasi-experiments.

In *natural experiments* (also known as *selection studies*), the researcher compares preexisting groups. Presumably, nature manipulated the independent variable, and the researcher is unable to override that manipulation. When this is true, the research is tolerated as an in-between design even though it has the same structure as the nonequivalent-groups design, one of the bad designs discussed earlier. Examples are gender comparisons or comparisons between cities struck by natural disasters and similar cities that were spared. Note well that natural experiments suffer from all of the internal validity problems that plague the nonequivalent-groups design. Results from such studies should be treated with extreme caution.

Add a pretest to the nonequivalent-groups design (described in the "Bad Designs" section) and you have the *nonequivalent-groups, pre-post design:* P-DV-IV(1)-DV compared to P-DV-IV(2)-DV. An example would be giving the unsolvable maze problem to one preexisting group and the easily solvable maze problem to another preexisting group, with aggression measured before and after the maze problem in both groups. Of course, a researcher would do this only if forced to work with preexisting groups. Because assignment to conditions is not random, the two groups of participants may not be equivalent at the outset, with all that implies. However, because there is a pretest measure of the dependent variable, it is possible to determine if the groups are equivalent at the outset on that variable. The bad news is that the researcher cannot determine if the groups are equivalent on any other participant characteristic that may be related to the dependent variable. Also, the presence of the pretest raises questions about the external validity of the findings. This design is a step up from the nonequivalent-groups design. When the researcher cannot use random assignment to conditions, it is a good idea to check for group equivalence on the dependent variable before treatments are administered despite the external validity question raised by the pretest. Hence, this design qualifies as an in-between design.

A final example of quasi-experiments is *time-series designs.* In the *interrupted time-series design,* a potential causal event is embedded within a series of measures of the presumed effect. An example would be the adoption of a seat-belt law with a comparison of auto fatalities for several years both before and after passage of the law. This design may be seen as a nonexperimental version of the one-group, pre-post design, improved by adding several pre- and postmeasures. It is also similar to what single-subject researchers do when establishing a baseline, only here extended pre- and postmeasures are obtained rather than pre (baseline) and during measures. Although several pre- and postmeasures are an improvement over single pre- and postmeasures, this design still has a serious flaw: no control for other relevant events that may have occurred during the same time interval as the presumed causal event. Adding a nonequivalent-comparison series improves matters somewhat. An example would be comparing auto fatalities for several years before and after the seat-belt law in the state which enacted it and in a neighboring state with no such law. Now the study is a nonexperimental version of the non-equivalent-groups pre-post design, improved by having a series of pre- and post-measures of the dependent variable. This *control-series design* is about the best one can achieve for studying events that cannot be manipulated by the researcher.

SUMMARY

Two types of error may occur in an experiment, constant (which systematically favors some values of the independent variable or experimental conditions over others) and random (which sometimes favors one experimental condition, some-times another, on a chance basis). Three sources of constant error in an experiment are assignment of participants to conditions, administering the conditions, and measurement of the dependent variable. Constant error from these sources affects the internal validity of the experiment because an extraneous variable has been con-founded with the independent variable. Random error from any source adds noise to the scores, making it harder to reject the null hypothesis. The result is a loss of sensitivity, the ability of the experiment to detect a small but real effect of the inde-pendent variable.

Constant error in an experiment may be neutralized by randomization or control, but randomization creates random error. Control in assignment to con-ditions involves matching, explicit or implicit. Control in administering con-ditions involves holding an extraneous variable absolutely constant or balanc-ing to create equal average values across conditions. Special cases of absolute control include blinding, placebo controls, and yoking. Where multiple settings, experimenters, or measurement procedures are necessary, they may be bal-anced across experimental conditions. Random error is reduced by most con-trol techniques, by clarity and consistency in all procedures, by increasing sam-ple sizes, and by increasing the sensitivity of the measure of the dependent variable.

Bad experimental designs such as the one-shot; one-group, pre-post; and non-equivalent-groups designs, contain serious flaws in the manipulation of the inde-pendent variable. Either not enough values of the independent variable are pro-duced (one is not enough), or the assignment of participants to conditions is inadequate, leading to possible confounding. Good designs have proper controls and may be divided into two categories. Designs without matching (posttest-only and two-group, pre-post) are called independent-treatments designs. Those with matching (explicit-matching and repeated-measures) are called nonindependent-treatments designs. In-between designs, which have some flaws but are the best that can be done under the circumstances, include field experiments, single-subject designs, and quasi-experiments.

In repeated-measures experiments, the researcher must deal with the problem of order effects or changes in any variable, other than the independent variable, with repeated measures of the dependent variable in different conditions. Order effects come in two forms, symmetrical and asymmetrical. The former do not depend on the order in which experimental conditions are presented, but the latter do. Symmetrical order effects can be randomized or controlled by counterbalancing, that is, using each possible order of presenting experimental conditions for an equal number of participants. Neither technique neutralizes asymmetrical order effects. The only cure for asymmetrical order effects is not to use a repeated-measures design. Some researchers also feel that problems with demand characteristics and difficulties in replicating results are greater with repeated-measures designs. Nonetheless, they are popular.

ANSWERS TO QUESTIONS

Q1. Increasing the strength of the independent-variable manipulation typically increases the magnitude of the relationship between the independent and dependent variables. Thus, it is no longer a question of detecting a *small* but real relationship, that is, a question of sensitivity.

Q2. If, for example, less intelligent participants are systematically assigned to the high-frustration condition, then any increase in aggression in that condition could be attributed to their lower intelligence rather than to their higher frustration. Intelligence and frustration have been confounded because of the biased method of assigning participants to conditions.

Q3. If you use only people with one value of IQ, you will never know if the results apply to people with other values of IQ. This is a case where internal validity is purchased at too high a cost in external validity. There are better ways to deal with characteristics like intelligence.

Q4. The measure of their success (batting average, winning percentage, etc.) has some random error in it. Thus, when measured a second time (i.e., the following season), sensational rookies tend to spread out toward the center of the distribution as a group. This is known as the sophomore jinx, and only the truly sensational can survive it.

FURTHER READING

The definitive work on quasi-experiments is a book by Cook and Campbell (1979). Likewise, Barlow and Hersen (1984) will tell you all you need to know about single-subject experimental designs.

REFERENCES

Barlow, D. H., & Hersen, M. (1984). *Single case experimental designs: Strategies for studying behavior change* (2nd ed.). New York: Pergamon Press.

Cook, T. D., & Campbell, D. T. (1979). *Quasi-experimentation: Design and analysis issues for field settings.* Chicago: Rand McNally.

Simple Experiments: Analysis

11

This chapter examines simple experimental designs in considerable detail. The focus is on the analysis of data from the two major categories of simple experimental designs (Chapter 9) and a comparison of the strengths and weaknesses of the categories.

The coverage in this chapter is limited in two ways. First, only the simplest good experimental designs are considered—those having one independent variable with two values and one dependent variable. An example is the much-discussed experiment on frustration. It has one independent variable, frustration, with two values, high and low, and one dependent variable, aggression. See Chapter 2 for details of manipulation and measurement. As you know, the values of an independent variable are also called treatments or conditions in an experiment. Complications arising from more than two values of an independent variable or from more than one independent or dependent variable will be discussed in the next chapter.

Second, only the combination of data types described as typical of the experiment in Table 5.2 are considered. That is, the discussion assumes that the independent variable is coarsely manipulated (very few values, only two in this chapter) and the dependent variable is finely measured. The latter assumption amounts to assuming at least near-interval measurement for the dependent variable which justifies use of interval-level statistics for data analysis. Finely manipulated independent variables are extremely rare. Thus, the only other data combination from Table 5.2 that is likely to occur is the coarse–coarse combination. In that case, frequency tables and chi-square analysis might be appropriate, but the best advice is to get competent statistical help. In any event, the coarse–fine combination is typical of most modern experiments in the social sciences, and that combination is the focus of this chapter and the next one.

Recall that two of the good designs, posttest-only and two-group, pre-post, involve random assignment to conditions without any matching of participant characteristics across conditions. The other two designs, explicit-matching and repeated-measures (implicit matching) involve matching participants across conditions on one or more stable characteristics like intelligence. Designs without matching are called *independent-treatments designs*, and those with matching *nonindependent-treatments designs*. As you will see, the distinction between the two categories is crucial for data analysis.

As noted in Chapter 9, one member of each category is used less frequently than the other member. In the independent-treatments category, the two-group, pre-post design is less frequent because of controversy about its external validity and complexities in data analysis. In the nonindependent-treatments category, the explicit-matching design is rare because of the extra work necessary to obtain prior measures on the matching variable. Regardless of frequency of use, the major distinction among the designs involves matching and its implications for data analysis.

This chapter begins with a discussion of the general logic of statistical inference in simple experimental designs. Then the chapter examines the descriptive statistics for such designs which, fortunately, are the same for both categories of designs. That is followed by a detailed treatment of the inferential statistical analysis of independent-treatments designs and then of nonindependent-treatments designs. Finally, the two types of design are compared, with emphasis on the effects of matching on the outcome of the data analysis.

LOGIC OF STATISTICAL INFERENCE

As usual, the goal of data analysis in an experiment is to find out if the variables of interest are related. In a properly run experiment, establishing a relationship between the independent and dependent variables allows one to draw a causal conclusion. Before the logic of making inferences to the population can be pursued, it is necessary to discuss the kind of evidence used to decide the question of relationship in the sample. Then you will be able to see how the sample evidence is used to make inferences.

Sample Evidence

Look at Table 11.1. The numbers in the "Low" and "High" columns are aggression scores for the low- and high-frustration conditions of the frustration experiment. How would you decide if frustration and aggression are related in this sample? If the answer is not immediately obvious, stop and think about it. The problem is similar to the one you face when trying to decide if two variables are related given the data in a 2×2 table of observed frequencies. Chapter 2 described special procedures designed to take into account the information from all four cells of the frequency table. Reasoning from anything less leaves you open to serious errors when deciding about the relationship between the variables. The situation is similar here, except that one of the variables, aggression, is finely measured. Nevertheless, you must take into account all of the information in both columns of numbers if you are to reach a sound judgment on the question of relationship. How can this be done?

When faced with scores like those in Table 11.1, it seems natural to compute an average or mean score within each column and then compare the means. That is exactly how the question of relationship is decided for the sample data of most experiments. The researcher checks to see if the mean score on the measured or dependent variable changes systematically along with the changes produced by the experimenter on the manipulated or independent variable. In the current example, you want to know if aggression changes on the average when the experimenter produces changes in frustration. If so, the data satisfy the definition of a relationship given in Chapter 2: the two variables change values together systematically. On the other hand, if the mean aggression score is the same or nearly so in both conditions, then aggression has not changed along with frustration, and you conclude that the variables are not related. So the crucial sample evidence for the question of relationship in the typical experiment consists of mean scores on the dependent variable, computed separately within each condition. These treatment means are compared across conditions to see if they are the same or not.

In Table 11.1 the treatment means are in the row labeled "Mc" which stands for "Mean of a column of scores." The means are 4 and 5 for low and high frustration, respectively. They do not differ very much, especially when compared to how much the scores within each column differ from each other. Thus, you may have trouble deciding whether frustration and aggression are related. If so, you are already going beyond the sample data and trying to reach a general conclusion.

Table 11.1 ANOVA I: ANALYSIS OF VARIANCE FOR INDEPENDENT-TREATMENTS DESIGN, ONE INDEPENDENT VARIABLE

Frustration Condition				
Low	*High*	*Tr*	*Nr*	*Mr*
4	3	7	2	3.5
3	7	10	2	5.0
5	7	12	2	6.0
2	5	7	2	3.5
6	5	11	2	5.5
2	6	8	2	4.0
6	3	9	2	4.5
4	4	8	2	4.0

Tc   32   +   40   =   72   =   G
Nc   8   +   8   =   16   =   N
Mc   4   5   M   =   4.5
$\Sigma X^2 c$ 146   +   218   =   364   = ΣX^2

$SST = \Sigma X^2 - (G^2/N) = 364 - (72^2/16) = 364 - 324 = 40$

$SSC = \Sigma \left[(Tc)^2/Nc \right] - (G^2/N)$

$\qquad = (32^2/8) + (40^2/8) - (72^2/16) = 328 - 324 = 4$

$SSE = SST - SSC = 40 - 4 = 36$

$dfT = N - 1 = 16 - 1 = 15 \qquad\qquad dfC = c - 1 = 2 - 1 = 1$

$dfE = dfT - dfC = 15 - 1 = 14$

$MSC = SSC/dfC = 4/1 = 4 \qquad\qquad MSE = SSE/dfE = 36/14 = 2.5714$

$F (dfC, dfE) = MSC/MSE$ or $F (1, 14) = 4/2.5714 = 1.5556, p > .10$

Inferential Reasoning

If you wish to generalize from the sample evidence to reach a conclusion about a relationship in the population, you run into a familiar problem. Even if the independent and dependent variables are not related in the *population*, there will be some difference in the *sample* means across conditions as a byproduct of chance or random error. Thus, for generalizing to the population, the question of interest shifts somewhat. You now wish to know if the variation among the sample treatment means exceeds what could expected from chance factors or random error. This new question is not easy to answer by informal judgment. How can you tell if the variation between the treatment means of 4 and 5 in Table 11.1 is greater than what could be expected from chance factors? A formal procedure would be helpful.

Let us begin by formalizing some terms. The null hypothesis for an experiment is that the independent and dependent variables are not related in the population. Because the question of relationship is decided by evaluating the variation among treatment means, an equivalent statement of the null hypothesis is that the population means for the dependent variable are the same in all conditions. In other words, the null hypothesis is that the population treatment means do not vary across conditions. Even so, you know that the sample treatment means will vary somewhat as a natural byproduct of random error. Thus, another equivalent statement of the null hypothesis is that the variation in the sample treatment means is a byproduct of random error only. The alternative hypothesis is that the independent and dependent variables are related in the population. That is, the population treatment means do vary, and the variation in the sample treatment means is caused by random error plus the real variation in the population treatment means. As always, the statistical question is whether or not to reject the null hypothesis, whichever way it is worded.

Informally, you might reason as follows. If the sample treatment means are not very different, then their variation most likely can be attributed to random error only, and the null hypothesis should not be rejected. On the other hand, if the sample treatment means differ greatly, then their variation most likely was caused by real differences in the population treatment means added to any effect of random error. Thus, the null hypothesis should be rejected. This line of thought is reasonable but not specific enough. Exactly how much variation among the sample treatment means is sufficient to decide against the null hypothesis? Where do you draw the line for making a decision?

The problem here is similar to the one posed for frequency tables in Chapter 4 when the topic of statistical inference was first introduced. There the challenge was to decide how much discrepancy could be tolerated between observed and expected frequencies before rejecting the null hypothesis. The solution was to formalize the degree of discrepancy in the chi-square calculation and then look up the probability of chi-square in a table. The current situation is similar, and so is the solution. The main difference is that in the current situation you do not yet have a quantity like the expected frequencies. The variation among the treatment means corresponds to the observed frequencies, but you have no idea how much variation could be expected from random error only, which corresponds to the role played by the expected frequencies in chi-square analysis. This comparison provides a valuable hint about what to do next.

A standard of comparison is needed in the current situation, an estimate of how much variation could occur in the sample treatment means when only random error is operating. With such a standard, you could compare the actual variation in the sample treatment means to the standard, summarizing the comparison in one number, just like you did with chi-square. You could then determine the probability of the summarized comparison or testing statistic under the null hypothesis (assuming that statisticians have constructed appropriate tables for doing so) and compare that probability to alpha to reach a decision about the null hypothesis.

As you have probably guessed, a formal procedure of the sort needed already exists. It is called the *analysis of variance* or *ANOVA* (ANalysis Of VAriance). The word variance refers to the fact that ANOVA compares the actual variability among the sample treatment means to an estimate of the variability expected from random error only. The comparison is summarized as a ratio, with the actual variability among the sample treatment means in the numerator and the standard of comparison in the denominator. The ratio is called the F ratio, in honor of Ronald Fisher who invented it.

The numerator of the F ratio is often called *systematic* variance because it contains random error plus any systematic effect of the independent variable on the sample treatment means. The denominator is called *error* variance because it contains random error only, regardless of which hypothesis is true. So the F ratio in ANOVA compares systematic variance from the sample treatment means to error variance from random error only to see how many times greater the systematic variance is. As suggested earlier, statisticians have produced tables of the F ratio. Thus, after calculating an F ratio, you can look up its probability under the null hypothesis and reach a decision following the rules of Chapter 4.

You may be wondering where in the data you get an estimate of error variance for the denominator of the F ratio. It depends on the category of experimental design. When all sources of systematic variance have been removed from the data, whatever variability is left is used to calculate the estimate of error variance. The number of sources of systematic variance is different for independent- and nonindependent-treatment designs. Thus, there are two forms of ANOVA, which in this book will be named ANOVA I and ANOVA II. When each ANOVA is discussed, you will see that the calculations for the estimate of error variance are reasonable for estimating random error only. For now, you must take it on faith.

One thing you need not take on faith is the expected value of F. Under the null hypothesis, variability among the sample treatment means (the numerator of F) is a byproduct of random error only. The denominator of F is always an estimate of how much variability could be expected among the sample treatment means when only random error is operating, regardless of which hypothesis is true. Thus, under the null hypothesis, the F ratio consists of two independent estimates of the same thing. Therefore, its expected value should be 1. (For technical reasons, the expected value is slightly greater than 1, but you may think of it as roughly 1.) Under the alternate hypothesis, variation among the sample treatment means results from random error plus the real variation in the population treatment means. Thus, the numerator of F should be larger than it would be under the null hypothesis. Therefore, under the alternative hypothesis, you have a larger numerator divided by the same denominator as under the null hypothesis. Hence, the expected value of F is substantially greater than 1.

The discussion so far implies that one way to increase the odds of reaching the correct conclusion when the alternative hypothesis is correct is to increase the sensitivity of the experiment by reducing random error. Using the symbols of Chapter 10, if RE stands for variation associated with random error and SE for variation caused by differences among the population treatment means (assuming no confounding or constant error), then the previous paragraph established that F = (SE + RE)/RE. It follows that for a given SE, a reduction in RE will increase F, making it more likely that the researcher will reject the null hypothesis and correctly conclude that SE is not zero. Because SE represents only the effect of the independent variable in a properly run experiment, this means that reducing random error increases the sensitivity of an experiment to small but real effects of the independent variable, as discussed in Chapter 10.

The key question in ANOVA, then, is whether the calculated value of F is sufficiently greater than 1 that it is unlikely to have resulted from only random variation among sample treatment means. The probability you look up in a table is the probability that you could have obtained an F value equal to or greater than the calculated value given that the null hypothesis is true. Following the guidelines of Chapter 4, if that probability is less than or equal to alpha, you decide to reject the null hypothesis.

In Chapter 4, you learned that the probability associated with a calculated value of chi-square could be interpreted as the probability of obtaining the observed frequencies (O) in a frequency table given that the expected frequencies (E) are the correct ones, that is, given that the null hypothesis is correct. In other words, the probability may be interpreted as $p(O \mid E)$. Because the observed frequencies correspond to the obtained or actual data (D) and the expected frequencies correspond to the data expected under the null hypothesis (H), $p(O \mid E)$ is equivalent to the more general $p(D \mid H)$.

Similar reasoning applies to ANOVA. The numerator of F contains systematic variance (SV, where SV = SE + RE), the actual variability among the sample treatment means. The denominator of F contains error variance (RE), the expected variability among the sample treatment means when only random error is operating, that is, given that the null hypothesis is correct. The probability of F, the ratio SV/RE, may thus be seen as the probability of obtaining SV, given that only RE is expected, or $p(SV \mid RE)$. However, SV corresponds to the obtained or actual variability among the sample treatment means (D), and RE corresponds to the variability expected under the null hypothesis (H). Thus, $p(SV \mid RE)$ also corresponds to the more general $p(D \mid H)$. As noted in Chapter 4, all inferential tests have the property that the probability of the testing statistic can be interpreted as the probability of obtaining the actual data given that the null hypothesis is correct, or $p(D \mid H)$. You now see that the F test in ANOVA is another example of this general principle.

Some texts prescribe a test of inference known as the t-test for the analysis of simple experiments with two treatments. In such a situation, the t-test and the F ratio from ANOVA always yield the same conclusion (in fact, $t^2 = F$). The t-test is appropriate ONLY for experiments with two treatments, but ANOVA may be used for any number of treatments. For that reason, this book focuses on the more general method of analysis, ANOVA.

To summarize, the procedure for making inferences about the relationship between the independent and dependent variables in a typical experiment (coarsely manipulated independent variable, finely measured dependent variable) is the analysis of variance or ANOVA. The testing statistic in ANOVA is F, a ratio obtained by dividing a variance estimate based on the actual variability among the sample treatment means by a variance estimate based on the variability expected among the sample treatment means when only random error is operating, that is, given that the null hypothesis is true. Under the null hypothesis, the expected value of F is near 1. Under the alternate hypothesis, F should be substantially greater than 1. After the F ratio has been calculated using the data from an experiment, its probability under the null hypothesis is looked up in a table. That probability is compared to alpha to decide whether or not to reject the null hypothesis. Like all inferential tests, F may been seen as a comparison of the obtained sample data (D) to the expected data under the null hypothesis (H), and its probability may therefore be interpreted as the conditional probability p(D|H) or the probability of the obtained data given that the null hypothesis is correct. If that probability is less than alpha, the decision is to reject the null hypothesis.

DESCRIPTIVE STATISTICS

You know that the key statistic for describing the relationship between the independent and dependent variables in the sample is the treatment mean, that is, the average of the scores on the dependent variable within a given condition of the experiment. Such means are computed separately within each condition and compared to each other to see whether or not they appear to be identical—but why use the mean for this purpose? The earlier discussion suggested that it seems like the natural thing to do, but it is important to ask why. The answer is that the mean represents the most typical score in the sample, and what you really want to know is whether or not the typical score on the dependent variable is identical in all conditions.

To appreciate the notion of typicality, you must understand distributions of scores. Unlike the example in Table 11.1 which has only eight scores in each condition, most actual experiments have much larger samples of scores in each condition. One way to see what is going on is to form a frequency distribution within each condition. A *frequency distribution* is a table in which each possible score value (X) is listed in rank order and paired with its frequency of occurrence (f) in the sample. For large samples, looking at the frequency distribution can give you a fairly good idea of the shape of the distribution of scores. An even better idea may be obtained by drawing a picture or graph of the frequency distribution. If you plot the frequencies (f) on the vertical axis against the possible score values (X) on the horizontal axis and connect the points in the space, you will have a *frequency polygon* depicting the shape of the distribution. What shape will you see?

Figure 11.1 illustrates an idealized bell-shaped distribution. Clearly, in such a distribution the most typical score is located in the center. Score values in the center of the distribution are closest to all the other scores, they have the highest frequencies, and they are in the middle, all of which makes them prime candidates for typical scores. Until recently, it was commonly assumed that most variables of interest to social scientists had distributions similar to the bell-shaped curve. However, it now appears likely that the distributions of most variables depart substantially from the idealized bell shape (Micceri, 1989). Regardless of the shape of the distribution, it still makes sense to think of the center or middle of the distribution as the location of the most typical score. So when statisticians try to describe the most typical score in a distribution, they end up estimating where the center of the distribution is located. Such descriptive statistics are known as measures of *central tendency*. As you will see, the mean is such a measure, and there are others.

The center is not the only important characteristic of a distribution. For an adequate description, it is also necessary to indicate how spread out the scores are around the center. Clearly the most typical score is more typical when all the scores

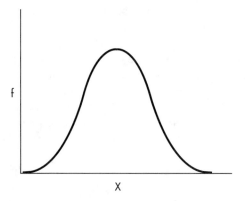

Figure 11.1
Frequency polygon for an idealized bell-
shaped distribution.

are bunched up near the center of the distribution than when they are spread out
far away from the center. Thus, the issue of spread, or variability around the center, cannot be ignored. Statistics designed to describe the spread of scores in a distribution are known as measures of *variability* or dispersion. There are several candidates, and one of them plays a central role in ANOVA.

Central Tendency

Three well-known descriptive measures of central tendency are the mode, median,
and mean. The *mode* is the score value with the highest frequency. Unfortunately,
there may be more than one mode, or the mode may not be located near the apparent center of the distribution. The *median* is the score value that falls at the 50th per-
centile when the scores are rank ordered. Thus, half of the scores in the distribution
fall below the median, and half fall above the median. The median is insensitive to
just how far above and below it the scores are located. It depends solely on a frequency count of how many scores fall above or below it. The *mean* is the average
score value, obtained by adding up all the scores in a distribution and dividing by
the number of scores. The mean is sensitive to how far away from the center scores
are located. For *skewed distributions,* those with a long tail at one end, the mean may
be pulled well out into that tail. In such cases, the median would be a better descriptive measure of central tendency.

The mean is the most widely used measure of central tendency for finely measured variables. Conceptually, the mean is the balance point of a distribution. That
is, if you placed the whole distribution on a pivot point and located that pivot point
directly below the mean, the distribution would neither teeter nor totter. It would
balance perfectly. Such a result is not guaranteed with either the median or mode.
In a symmetrically shaped distribution with one mode, all three measures of cen-

tral tendency are identical. Because inferential statistics are more fully developed for the mean than for the other measures of central tendency, this book focuses on the mean.

The formula for the mean, M, of a sample of scores is as follows: $M = \Sigma X / N$. ΣX means to add all the individual scores in the sample, and N is the number of such scores. Some texts present an alternate formula for grouped data, that is, data in the form of a frequency distribution. In practice, because of the ready availability of computers, you probably will never have to construct frequency distributions or calculate descriptive statistics from them. Thus, statistical formulas for grouped data will not be presented.

In Table 11.1 the treatment sums are given in the row labeled "Tc," which means "total of the scores in a column." The number of scores in each condition are in the row labeled "Nc," or "number of scores in a column." Thus, in the formula for a sample mean, Tc corresponds to ΣX and Nc corresponds to N. Mc, the mean for a column, equals 32/8 or 4 and 40/8 or 5 for the low- and high-frustration conditions, respectively. The grand sum of all scores in all conditions, G, is the sum of the treatment sums, or $32 + 40 = 72$. The grand N is the sum of the Nc values, or $8 + 8 = 16$. Therefore, the grand mean of all scores, M, is 72/16 = 4.5.

Variability

How could you quantify the variability or spread of scores around the center of a distribution? Several measures have been proposed, but some of them have drawbacks. An obvious measure is the *range*, the difference between the highest and lowest scores in a distribution. The range has the drawback of being sensitive only to the two most extreme scores in the distribution and completely insensitive to the spread of all the rest of the scores. Still, the range is often used as a rough measure of variability.

Measures of variability that are sensitive to the spread of all the scores in a distribution are based on the concept of a deviation score. A *deviation score*, x, is the difference between a raw score, X, and the mean of the distribution of scores. Thus, in a sample of scores, $x = X - M$. A deviation score can be computed for each score in a sample, and in each case it indicates how far above or below the mean the raw score is. You might think that a good measure of variability for the whole sample would be the sum of all the deviation scores, Σx. However, Σx fails as a measure of spread because it is always zero. This can easily be proved mathematically, but you may view it as just another way of saying that the mean is the balance point of a distribution. That is, the negative deviations from the mean exactly equal or balance the positive deviations from the mean in any distribution. So Σx cannot track spread because it is always zero.

How can deviation scores be used to develop a meaningful measure of spread? The answer is simple: square the deviations and then sum them. Squared deviations are always positive and therefore cannot cancel each other out. More to the point, squared deviation scores have the desired property: the farther away from the mean the scores in a distribution are, regardless of direction, the larger the sum of squared deviation scores will be. Thus, the sum of squared deviation scores, Σx^2, tracks the variability or spread of scores in a distribution.

The sum of squared deviations is not only a descriptive measure of the variability of scores in a distribution, but it also plays a prominent role in the analysis of variance. This important quantity has been given a shortened name, *sum of squares,* and a special symbol, SS. The formula for a sum of squares is as follows:

$$SS = \Sigma x^2 = \Sigma(X - M)^2 \qquad\qquad\qquad (11.1.A)$$

$$= \Sigma X^2 - [(\Sigma X)^2 / N]. \qquad\qquad\qquad (11.1.B)$$

The first version of the formula (11.1.A) is given in terms of deviation scores and tells you what SS is conceptually, a sum of squared deviation scores. Unfortunately, M is usually a decimal quantity, and thus so are all the deviation scores. Squaring and summing such quantities can be painful. The second version of the formula (11.1.B) is known as the computing formula and is much easier to deal with if you must compute SS by hand.

Let us apply the computing formula (11.1.B) to the data of Table 11.1. SS may be computed separately for each experimental condition. In that case, the column total, Tc, corresponds to ΣX in the computing formula for SS and the number of scores in the column, Nc, corresponds to N. The sum of squared scores in a column is given in the row labeled "$\Sigma X^2 c$." Thus, $\Sigma X^2 c$ corresponds to ΣX^2 in the computing formula for SS. So the computing formula for SS for a single experimental condition becomes $SS = \Sigma X^2 c - [(Tc)^2 / Nc]$. For the low-frustration condition,

$$SS = 146 - [(32)^2 / 8] = 146 - 128 = 18.$$

Your turn. What is SS for the high-frustration condition? (Q1)

SS has a drawback as a description of the spread of scores in a distribution. Because of the squaring and summing, SS is usually very large. It can be much larger than the range, as in Table 11.1. For the low-frustration condition, the range is 6 $- 2 = 4$, and SS is 18, over four times as large. For descriptive purposes, it would be nice to have a measure of spread that makes more sense in terms of the original units of measurement.

To undo the inflation in SS, first take an average (to counteract the summing), and then take a square root (to counteract the squaring). The first step yields another famous quantity, the *variance,* which is defined as the average of the squared deviations in a distribution. The sample variance, S^2, has the formula $S^2 = SS/N$. The second step yields yet another well-known quantity, the *standard deviation,* which is defined as the square root of the variance. The sample standard deviation,

S, has the formula $S = \sqrt{S^2}$. For the low-frustration condition of Table 11.1, $S^2 = 18/8$ = 2.25, and $S = \sqrt{2.25} = 1.5$. For roughly bell-shaped distributions, S will be typically about one-third as large as the range. Many journals in the social sciences require descriptive statistics for both central tendency and variability. For finely measured variables, the quantities usually required are means and standard deviations. Your turn again.

What are S^2 and S for the high-frustration condition of Table 11.1? (Q2)

You might suspect that the variance has something to do with ANOVA, the analysis of variance. You are correct. However, ANOVA uses variance *estimates*, not sample variances, and the two are not quite the same.

Variance Estimates

Suppose your goal was not to describe the variability in a sample of raw scores but rather to estimate the variability of raw scores in the population represented by the sample. Can this be done using only the sample data? The answer is yes. Your first impulse might be to nominate the sample variance for this purpose. However, statisticians have shown that the sample variance, $S^2 = SS/N$, is biased because it underestimates the population variance. Fortunately, the bias is easily corrected by dividing SS by N – 1 instead of N. In other words, the expected value of $SS/(N – 1)$ is the population variance, that is, the variance of scores in the population represented by the sample. To distinguish between the sample variance, S^2, and the unbiased estimate of the population variance, the symbol "s^2" will be used for the latter. Thus, $s^2 = SS/(N – 1)$, is the unbiased estimate of the population variance. Because its goal is to make inferences about the population based on sample data, ANOVA uses unbiased estimates of the population variance (s^2) rather than sample variances (S^2).

Let us calculate s^2 for the low-frustration condition of Table 11.1. For this application, $s^2 = SS/(N – 1)$ where N = Nc. Thus, $s^2 = 18/(8 – 1) = 2.57$.

What is s^2 for the high-frustration condition? (Q3)

The quantity N – 1 in the denominator of the formula for s^2 is an old friend, df, or degrees of freedom. In this situation, df = N – 1 makes sense. If you have a set of finely measured scores with a known sum or mean, how many of them are free to vary? All but one of them may be assigned any value you choose, but the last one is then completely determined by the constraint that the sum or mean must equal the known value. This is just another way of saying that Σx, the sum of the deviation scores, must always equal zero for any set of scores. Thus, all but one of the deviation scores can be anything you like, but the last one is fixed so that the sum equals zero. Because df = N – 1 for a sample of finely measured scores, the unbiased estimate of the population variance has the general form $s^2 = SS/(N – 1) = SS/df$.

Therefore, any time a sum of squares is divided by its degrees of freedom, something done often in ANOVA, the result is a population variance estimate.

The building blocks for ANOVA are now in place. You are ready to see exactly how ANOVA works for each of the two major categories of simple experimental designs.

THE INDEPENDENT-TREATMENTS DESIGN: ANOVA I

As you know, this category of experimental designs features random assignment of participants to experimental conditions without any matching. If assignment is truly random, the scores on the dependent variable in any pair of conditions should be statistically independent or uncorrelated. To simulate such a situation, the scores within each of the two treatment columns (Low and High) of Table 11.1 were entered in a random order. Thus, the correlation between the two columns of numbers should not differ significantly from zero. In fact, there is no rational basis for pairing any score in the Low column with any score in the High column. However, if you arbitrarily assume that the scores in the same row of each column ought to be paired and then compute a correlation between the two columns of scores using formula 8.1, you get r = −.33. Using the test of significance described in Chapter 8, you have r(6) = −.33, p > .10. Thus, the scores in Table 11.1 are typical of the kind of data to be expected in an independent-treatments design.

You are now ready to tackle the inferential statistical analysis for independent-treatments designs. The data of Table 11.1 will be used. The scores could represent posttest scores from a posttest-only design. They could also represent posttest scores or pre-post difference scores from a two-group, pre-post design. However, for reasons given in Chapter 9, the approach described here is not recommended for pre-post designs. Thus, you should think of the scores in Table 11.1 as posttest scores from a posttest only design. Earlier, the appropriate analysis of variance was named ANOVA I.

The presentation of ANOVA I will be influenced by two guidelines. The first is that the testing statistic is F, a ratio of variance estimates. In the context of ANOVA, such variance estimates are called *mean squares*, or MS for short. As you know from the preceding section, a variance estimate is a sum of squares (SS) divided by its degrees of freedom (df). Thus, in general, MS = SS/df. Reversing these steps provides an agenda for doing ANOVA: (1) compute sums of squares, (2) compute degrees of freedom, (3) compute mean squares, (4) compute F, (5) look up computed F in appropriate table and reach conclusions.

The second guideline is that the general approach in any ANOVA is to compute the total variability in all of the scores, then to compute the variability from each possible source of systematic variability and remove it from the total, and finally to consider what is left over to be variability associated with random error only. In a properly run independent-treatments experiment, the only source of systematic variability is the independent variable which is represented by the columns of the data table. Thus, you must remove the variability represented by the central

Table 11.2   SUMMARY OF STEPS IN ANOVA I

1. Compute SST, the total sum of squares for all scores, ignoring the column variable.
2. Compute SSC, the sum of squares for columns, based on the column means and representing the systematic variability contributed by the column (independent) variable.
3. Compute SSE, the sum of squares for error, representing left-over variability after SSC is subtracted from SST.
4. Compute dfT, dfC, and dfE.
5. Compute MSC and MSE.
6. Compute F.
7. Look up F in appropriate table to determine p.
8. Reach a decision by comparing p to alpha.

Formulas for all computations are in Table 11.1

tendencies of the columns from the total variability of the scores in Table 11.1 and treat what is left over as an estimate of random error only.

Combining the two guidelines yields a set of steps for doing ANOVA I. Those steps are summarized in Table 11.2. Formulas and computations for SS, df, MS, and F are in the bottom half of Table 11.1

Let us look at the ANOVA I formulas to see what is going on. The formula for SST is simply Formula 11.1, the general formula for a sum of squares, applied to all sixteen scores in the data table. In this application, the scores are treated as a single sample, ignoring the column variable, and so $N = 16$. The first term in the formula is the sum of all sixteen squared scores, or $4^2 + 3^2 + 5^2 + \ldots + 6^2 + 3^2 + 4^2 = 364$. The second term is the grand sum (G) of all sixteen unsquared scores, which is then squared and divided by the total N for the table. G is thus the sum of the column totals or Tc values, $32 + 40 = 72$, and it corresponds to ΣX in Formula 11.1. In the second term of the SST formula, $G^2/N = 72^2/16 = 324$. Thus, $SST = 364 - 324 = 40$.

The formula for SSC amounts to computing a variance estimate using the two treatment means as raw scores. Thus, the variability contributing to SSC is the variability among the treatment means. The formula is expressed in terms of treatment totals, Tc values, which are easier to work with than treatment means, Mc values. The formula tells you to square each column total, Tc, and then divide by the number of scores in the column, Nc. Thus, you have $32^2/8$ and $40^2/8$. You must then sum these quantities across columns and finally subtract G^2/N from that sum. Thus,

$$SSC = (32^2/8) + (40^2/8) - (72^2/16) = 328 - 324 = 4.$$

SSE is simply SST minus SSC, the variability left when SSC is removed from SST. Thus, $SSE = 40 - 4 = 36$.

The approach for df is similar to that for SS. You first apply the general formula, $df = N - 1$, to the total sample of scores to get $dfT = 16 - 1 = 15$. For dfC, it is important to note that the "scores" are the treatment means, and there are as many of them as there are columns of raw scores. If "c" equals the number of columns of raw scores or experimental conditions, the formula for dfC must therefore be c – 1. Thus, dfC = c – 1 = 2 – 1 = 1 for the frustration experiment or any other experiment with two values of the independent variable. dfE is what is left over when dfC is removed from dfT. Thus, dfE = dfT – dfC = 15 – 1 = 14.

From here on, the total variability of the scores is of no further interest. You want to compare the variability based on the column means, which contains random error plus any systematic effect of the column (independent) variable, to the left-over variability, which contains random error only. First you form mean squares, or MS values, by dividing each relevant SS by its own df. Thus, MSC = SSC/dfC = 4/1 = 4, and MSE = SSE/dfE = 36/14 = 2.5714. Then you form the F ratio, MSC/MSE. Unlike previous inferential statistics, F has two separate degrees-of-freedom values associated with it, one each for its numerator and denominator. Because the numerator of F is MSC, the df for the numerator is dfC. Similar reasoning leads to dfE for the denominator. For the data of Table 11.1, the result is F(dfC,dfE) = MSC/MSE, or F(1,14) = 4/2.5714 = 1.5556.

You still have to do the final step, look up the calculated F value in an appropriate table to determine its probability, p, under the null hypothesis and then make a decision about the null hypothesis. The appropriate table is Table A.3, which contains critical values of F. Critical values are F values associated with p values of interest for various combinations of dfC and dfE, assuming the null hypothesis is correct. Under that assumption, the expected value of F is about 1. (Can you remember why?) Thus, the table allows you to determine the probability of obtaining an F equal to or greater than the critical value, given that the expected value is approximately 1. Notice that you must select both the correct row and column for entering the table. The correct column is the one headed by dfC (the numerator of F), and the correct row is the one for dfE (the denominator of F). If the dfE you need is not listed, which can happen for large sample sizes, follow the strategy of Chapter 8 and use the largest dfE given that does not exceed your actual dfE.

For the data of Table 11.1, you want column 1 and row 14 which contains four F values: 1.44, 3.10, 4.60, and 8.86. They correspond, respectively, to four p values in the column labeled "p": .25, .10, .05, and .01. Now you play an old familiar game. Locate the calculated F, 1.56, among the four critical values of F, noting that it falls between the values of 1.44 and 3.10. Projecting to the p column, you see that the probability value for F must be between .10 and .25. You then compare the p value to the predetermined value of alpha, presumably .05, and make a decision. You would express the decision this way: F(1,14) = 1.56, p > .05. That is, F is not significant, and therefore you cannot reject the null hypothesis of no relationship between the independent and dependent variables.

Modern researchers recognize the desirability of describing the strength of the relationship tested by ANOVA. According to Keppel (1991), the most popular measure for this purpose is *omega squared*, w^2, which reflects the proportion of the total population variance accounted for by the variation among the experimental treatments. For ANOVA I, w^2 may be estimated as follows:

$$est-w^2 = [(SSC) - (dfC)(MSE)]/(SST + MSE). \tag{11.2}$$

Thus, for Table 11.1,

$est-w^2 = [(4) - (1)(2.5714)]/(40 + 2.5714) = 1.4286/42.5714 = .0336.$

Normally a researcher would not report est-w^2 for nonsignificant results. The calculations for Table 11.1 are shown to demonstrate how the formula for est-w^2 works. In principle, est-w^2 can vary from 0 to 1. In practice, it can actually be negative (when $F < 1$) and is unlikely to be extremely large because of the amount of noise in most social science research. Keppel suggests that an est-w^2 value of .15 or greater should be interpreted as a large effect of the independent variable.

It is time to tackle the question of just what variability is represented in the denominator of the ANOVA-I F ratio. You know it is an estimate of random error only, regardless of which hypothesis is correct. You also know that it is the variability left over after the variability in the sample treatment means has been subtracted from the total variability in all of the raw scores. Look at the raw data in Table 11.1 and see if you can figure out exactly what variability is being described. You might reason that the only variability left after removing the variability from the column means is the variability of the raw scores *within* each column. Good thinking. The variability of the raw scores within each column is clearly part of the total variability of all the scores in both columns, and it is unaffected by how far apart the column means are from each other. It must, therefore, be the left-over variability that is attributed to random error.

Notice that variability within a single column of Table 11.1 corresponds to individual differences in performance among participants when the value of the independent variable is held constant. In psychology, such variability is called individual differences. In statistics, it is called random error. Whatever it is called, the important fact is that no one knows what causes it, and so it is assumed to be random error. Because the estimate of random error is derived from the variability of raw scores within each condition in ANOVA I, some texts refer to it as the mean square within (MSW) and to its formula components as the sum of squares within (SSW) and the degrees of freedom within (dfW). Such usage is equivalent to MSE, SSE, and dfE.

There are three columns in Table 11.1, labeled Tr, Nr, and Mr, that have not been discussed. Rest assured that they have nothing to do with ANOVA I. They will be discussed later. If you would like to try your hand at ANOVA I, then consider a posttest-only experiment with scores of 4, 3, 5, 2, and 6 in the low-frustration condition and scores of 5, 8, 4, 7, and 6 in the high-frustration condition.

What are the treatment means and standard deviations, what are the SS, df, MS, and F values for ANOVA I, what is p, and what is est-w^2? (Q4)

IN DEPTH: ANOVA I

If you have had a statistics course and you paid very close attention to the discussion of ANOVA I, you may have noticed something strange. The numerator of F is based on the variability of the treatment MEANS, but the denominator is based on the variability of RAW SCORES within each condition. This may seem like comparing apples and oranges because surely means, especially when based on large samples, cannot vary as much as raw scores. In fact, you may even recall a formula relating the estimated variance of sample means for samples of size N, s_M^2, to the estimated variance of raw scores in the population, s^2: $s_M^2 = s^2/N$. The formula clearly shows that the variance of sample means must be N times smaller than the variance of raw scores. So how can the two kinds of variability be meaningfully compared in an F ratio.?

The answer is simple. The formula for s_M^2 permits easy conversion from one kind of variance estimate to the other. The ANOVA formulas automatically make the necessary conversions so that the same kind of estimate goes into both the numerator and the denominator of F. Conceptually, it makes more sense to think of both components of F as estimates of the variance among treatment means, or s_M^2-type estimates, and that is how the logic of ANOVA was developed earlier. In fact, however, the formulas most commonly used in ANOVA (and the ones presented in this book) yield s^2-type estimates. No matter. As long as the same type of estimate goes into the numerator and the denominator of F (and the ANOVA formulas accomplish this), the ratio is the same regardless of which type is used.

In case the discussion of ANOVA I failed to convince you, it is easy to show numerically that the denominator of F (MSE) is based on the variability of raw scores within conditions. Earlier in the chapter, SS for the low-frustration condition of Table 11.1 was computed, and you were invited to compute SS for the high-frustration condition. The result was 18 for both conditions. If you pool those two values, each based only on variability within one condition, you get 18 + 18 = 36, which is exactly the SSE for the data of Table 11.1. Likewise, the df within each condition, used earlier to compute s^2 for each column, was 8 - 1 = 7. If you pool the two df values, each based only on the scores within a condition, you get 7 + 7 = 14, which is exactly the dfE for the data of Table 11.1. Thus, the MSE in the ANOVA for Table 11.1 consists of the pooled within-column SS values divided by the pooled within-column df values.

THE NONINDEPENDENT-TREATMENTS DESIGN: ANOVA II

The distinguishing feature of this category of designs is matching, explicit or implicit. When a matching variable is relevant (i.e., strongly related to the dependent variable), scores on the dependent variable in any pair of conditions should NOT be statistically independent. Rather, they should be strongly and positively correlated. That situation is simulated in the two treatment columns (Low and High) of Table 11.3. The numbers in the two columns are the same as in Table 11.1, and thus so are the column statistics (Tc, Nc, etc.). The difference between the two tables is that the numbers in the High column of Table 11.3 have been rearranged to create a strong positive correlation between the High and Low scores. These data are thus typical of what can be expected with relevant matching in either an explicit-matching or a repeated-measures design. The rows of the table can be seen as either matched pairs of participants (explicit matching) or the same participant contributing scores in

Table 11.3 ANOVA II: ANALYSIS OF VARIANCE FOR NONINDEPENDENT-TREATMENTS DESIGN, ONE INDEPENDENT VARIABLE

| P# | Frustration Condition | | Tr | Nr | Mr |
	Low	High			
1	4	6	10	2	5.0
2	3	4	7	2	3.5
3	5	5	10	2	5.5
4	2	3	5	2	2.5
5	6	7	13	2	6.5
6	2	3	5	2	2.5
7	6	7	13	2	6.5
8	4	5	9	2	4.5

Tc	32	+	40	=	72	=	G	
Nc	8	+	8	=	16	=	N	
Mc	4		5		M	=	4.5	
$\Sigma X^2 c$	146	+	218	=	364	=	ΣX^2	

SST = Same = 40   SSC = Same = 4

SSR = $\Sigma [(Tr)^2/Nr] - (G^2/N)$

    = $(10^2/2) + (7^2/2) + ... + (9^2/2) - (72^2/16)$ = 359 − 324 = 35

SSE = SST − SSC − SSR = 40 − 4 − 35 = 1

dfT = Same = 15   dfC = Same = 1

dfR = r − 1 = 8 − 1 = 7   dfE = dfT − dfC − dfR = 15 − 1 − 7 = 7

MSC = SSC/dfC = 4/1 = 4   MSE = SSE/dfE = 1/7 = .1429

F (dfC, dfE) = MSC/MSE or F (1, 7) = 4/.1429 = 28.0000, p < .01

both conditions (repeated measures). Thus, "P#" may be read as either "pair number" or "participant number." The correlation between the High and Low columns is $r(6) = .94$, $p < .01$, compared to $r(6) = -.33$, $p > .10$ for Table 11.1.

To appreciate fully what successful matching buys an experimenter, you must understand how a strong correlation between a matching variable and the dependent variable leads to a strong positive correlation between scores on the dependent variable in any two conditions. The frustration experiment can show how this works. Suppose participants are explicitly matched on the basis of measured IQ scores. Thus, the rows of Table 11.3 represent different values of IQ. Surely intelligence is NEGATIVELY correlated with aggression because intelligent people find better ways than aggression to solve their problems. To simplify matters, assume a perfect negative correlation between IQ and aggression, $r = -1$. What are the consequences of this correlation?

The perfect negative correlation between IQ and aggression must mean that the matched pair of participants with the two highest IQ scores also have the two lowest aggression scores. Thus, these two participants must end up with the lowest aggression scores in each condition. If no other sources of random error are operating, the only difference between the pair would be the effect of the independent variable, frustration, which would produce a slightly higher aggression score for the participant in the high condition. The same reasoning leads to the conclusion that the pair of participants with the lowest IQ scores must end up with the highest aggression scores in each condition. Likewise, the pair of participants with the most middling IQ scores must end up with the most middling aggression scores in each condition. Thus, the strong negative correlation between IQ and aggression causes high aggression scores in one condition to go with high aggression scores in the other condition, middle with middle, and low with low. That is, the negative correlation between IQ and aggression produces a positive correlation between aggression scores in the two conditions. The same thing happens in a repeated-measures design because the paired scores in each condition are implicitly matched on IQ.

So relevant matching creates a strong positive correlation between scores on the dependent variable in any pair of conditions. So what? The point is that the correlation of .94 between the two columns of Table 11.3 represents systematic variance that can be attributed to the row variable, that is, to the matching variable. All sources of systematic variance must be removed from the total variability of the scores before what is left over can be attributed to random error only. Now there are two sources of systematic variance to be removed, the column effect (the independent variable) and the row effect (the matching variable). If the row effect is sizable (relevant matching), what is left over will be small compared to the case of no matching. Thus, the denominator of F will be smaller, F will be larger, and the sensitivity of the experiment will have been improved. You are about to see this happen in a numerical example.

The appropriate analysis for a nonindependent-treatments design is ANOVA II, and it is illustrated in Table 11.3. The only change from ANOVA I is that the row effect, which represents the variability due to matching, is computed and removed from the total variability in the raw scores. Thus, both column and row effects are removed, and whatever variability is left over is regarded as an estimate of random error only. As shown in the bottom half of the table, SST, SSC, dfT, and dfC are computed the same way as in ANOVA I. Because the scores in the columns of Table 11.3 are the same as in Table 11.1, the computed values for these quantities are the same in both tables.

The only new computations are for the row effect. Those computations are exactly the same as for the column effect, except that rows are substituted for columns. In the top half of the table, the last three columns contain row totals (Tr), the number of scores in each row (Nr), and row means (Mr = Tr/Nr). As you can see in the bottom half of the table, the formula for the sum of squares for the row effect (SSR) tells you first to square each Tr value and then divide by Nr. You must then sum the resulting eight quantities (one per row) and subtract G^2/N. Thus,

$$SSR = (10^2/2) + (7^2/2) + \ldots + (9^2/2) - (72^2/16) = 359 - 324 = 35.$$

Following the same logic as for columns, the df for rows is the number of rows, r, minus 1, or dfR = r − 1 = 8 − 1 = 7.

Now the analysis can be quickly finished. SSE is what is left over when both the row and column variability have been removed from the total variability. Thus,

SSE = SST – SSC – SSR = 40 – 4 – 35 = 1. Likewise, dfE is the left-over degrees of freedom, or dfE = dfT – dfC – dfR = 15 – 1 – 7 = 7. MSC will be the same as in Table 11.1, because it uses the same quantities. Thus, MSC = SSC/dfC = 4/1 = 4. MSE will be different because the removal of the row effect has reduced both its numerator and denominator compared to the corresponding quantities in Table 11.1. Because of relevant matching, the new numerator has been reduced much more than the new denominator. Thus, MSE = SSE/dfE = 1/7 = .1429, a much smaller quantity than the MSE in Table 11.1. Finally, F(1,7) = 4/.1429 = 28.0000, p < .01. Notice that you must look in column 1 and row 7 of the F table to determine p. You find that the calculated F (28.0) exceeds the largest critical value of F (12.2), and so p must be less than .01. In other words, the same difference in the treatment means that was not significant in Table 11.1 is now significant in Table 11.3, and the reason is clearly the reduction in error variance due to matching.

You may wonder if a second F ratio should be calculated to test the row effect: F(dfR,dfE) = MSR/MSE. Expert opinion differs, but the recommendation here is no. The purpose of the experiment is to test the effect of the independent variable, the column effect, and not the effectiveness of matching, the row effect. As you will see in the next section, with ineffective matching you actually lose statistical power or sensitivity when you do ANOVA II. Nonetheless, if you have matching, explicit or implicit, ANOVA II is the proper analysis. To test the row effect in order to decide which ANOVA to use for the column effect is unethical. The moral is that you should use matching only when you are confident that it will be effective, and then there should be no need to test its effectiveness.

Earlier, w^2 was suggested as a measure of the magnitude of the treatment effect based on ANOVA analysis. For ANOVA II, there is some disagreement about how to calculate est-w^2, the estimate of w^2. The problem is that w^2 is defined as the proportion of the total population variance accounted for by the treatment effect or the column variable in ANOVA II. The disagreement arises over whether the estimate of the total population variance should include all the sources of variance in the ANOVA (columns, rows, and error) or just the treatment effect and error (columns and error). Keppel (1991) recommends the latter approach for all experimental designs, no matter how many separate sources of variance they contain. Thus, consistency in the definition of w^2 is maintained no matter how complex the experimental design. Following Keppel's advice, the estimate of w^2 for ANOVA II is as follows:

$$A = (dfC)(MSC - MSE), \text{ and } est-w^2 = A/[A + (N)(MSE)]. \tag{11.3}$$

For Table 11.3,

$$A = (1)(4 - .1429) = 3.8571, \text{ and } est-w^2 = 3.8571/[3.8571 + (16)(.1429)] = 3.8571/6.1435$$
$$= .6278.$$

Thus, ignoring other sources of systematic variance (in particular, the row effect or matching), the estimate is that 63 percent of the total population variance is accounted for by the effect of the independent variable. According to the earlier guideline for interpreting the magnitude of est-w^2, this one represents a very strong relationship indeed.

You might like to try your hand at ANOVA II. Suppose you have a repeated-measures experiment in which participants 1 to 5 produce scores of 4, 3, 5, 2, and 6,

Table 11.4 REMOVAL OF COLUMN
AND ROW EFFECTS FROM DATA OF TABLE 11.3

P#	Column Effect Removed		Row Effect Removed	
	Low	High	Low	High
1	4.5	5.5	4.0	5.0
2	3.5	5.5	4.5	4.5
3	5.5	4.5	5.0	4.0
4	2.5	2.5	4.5	4.5
5	6.5	6.5	4.5	4.5
6	2.5	2.5	4.5	4.5
7	6.5	6.5	4.5	4.5
8	4.5	4.5	4.5	4.5

respectively, in the low-frustration conditions and scores of 6, 5, 7, 4, and 8, respectively, in the high-frustration condition.

> *What are the treatment means and standard deviations, what are the SS, df, and MS*
> *values for ANOVA II, and what are F, p, and est-w² for the treatment effect? (Q5)*

IN-DEPTH: ANOVA II

Consider the question of what variability is represented in the denominator of the
ANOVA-II F ratio. You cannot simply look within each column of raw scores, as
you did in Table 11.1, because the variability within each column of Table 11.3 contains both random error and the row effect, that is, the systematic variability caused
by matching. If you wish to see the random error variability directly, you must
remove both the column and row effects from the raw scores.

You must proceed in two steps. First, remove the column effect by adjusting
the scores in each column so that the new column mean is equal to the grand mean,
4.5. Thus, you must add 0.5 to all of the scores in the Low column and subtract 0.5
from all of the scores in the High column. This adjustment will not change the row
means. Second, remove the row effect by adjusting the CURRENT scores in each
row so that the new row mean is equal to the grand mean. Thus, you must subtract
0.5 from both scores in the first row, add 1 to both scores in the second row, subtract
0.5 from both scores in the third row, and so on. This adjustment will not change the
column means. The final set of scores contains unexplained variability, which is
assumed to estimate random error only. You could do the steps in the reverse order
and would obtain the same final set of scores. The steps have been done for you in
Table 11.4, and you can see that there is little variability left in the final set of scores.
The variability in these doubly adjusted scores is what goes into the denominator
of the ANOVA-II F ratio.

To convince yourself that the final set of adjusted scores contains only error
variability, compute its sum of squares directly using Formula 11.1. You will have

$$SS = 4^2 + 4.5^2 + 5^2 + \ldots + 4.5^2 + 4.5^2 + 4.5^2 - (72^2/16) = 325 - 324 = 1$$

which equals SSE from the ANOVA. The df for the adjusted scores is N minus 1, minus the df for all effects removed in the adjustment process. Thus

$$df = N - 1 - (c - 1) - (r - 1) = dfT - dfC - dfR = 15 - 1 - 7 = 7$$

which equals dfE from the ANOVA.

COMPARISON OF DESIGNS

This chapter concludes with a brief comparison of the independent- and nonindependent-treatments designs and their ANOVAs. If you have followed the discussion up to now, most of these points will seem obvious to you. They are included for review and to strengthen your understanding.

The distinguishing feature of nonindependent-treatments designs is matching, either explicit or implicit. The proper ANOVA, which takes account of the matching, is ANOVA II. If the matching is relevant, ANOVA II will provide a more powerful or sensitive test of the null hypothesis (no relationship between the independent and dependent variables) than ANOVA I. You have already seen these points illustrated in the analyses of Table 11.1 and Table 11.3.

Relevant matching means that some matching variable is strongly related to the dependent variable. When that is the case, there will be several observable effects on the raw data, each of which can be illustrated by a comparison of Table 11.1 and Table 11.3. You can think of these effects as visible indicators of relevant matching. Some are easier to see than others, but all are effects of the same cause, relevant matching.

The first indicator of relevant matching is the correlation between the scores on the dependent variable in any pair of conditions. Such correlations should be strong and positive with relevant matching and should not differ significantly from zero otherwise. The two tables illustrate this effect, with a correlation between high- and low-frustration scores of –.33 in Table 11.1 (no matching) and .94 in Table 11.3 (relevant matching).

The second indicator of relevant matching is the variability or spread among the row means of the data table. There is no reason for computing such means in Table 11.1, but it has been done anyway in the Mr column. As you know, Mr = Tr/Nr. Tr and Nr columns are also shown in Table 11.1 so that you can verify the Mr values. The range of Mr values is 6.0 – 3.5 = 2.5 in Table 11.1, and 6.5 – 2.5 = 4.0 in Table 11.3. The greater variability of row means in Table 11.3 also shows up in the sum of squares for rows. Again, there is no reason for computing SSR for Table 11.1, but if you do so anyway, using the formula for SSR in Table 11.3, you get SSR = 12 as compared with SSR = 35 for Table 11.3. SST, the total variability, is 40 in both tables because they contain the same 16 scores. So SSR is 12/40 or 30 percent of the total variability in Table 11.1, and 35/40 or 87.5 percent of the total variability in Table 11.3. The greater spread of row means in Table 11.3 should come as no surprise because it reflects the influence of random error plus the systematic differences in the matching variable across rows. In Table 11.1, on the other hand, the rows means vary only as a by-product of random error.

The third indicator of relevant matching is the variability in the column effect, the effect of the independent variable, across rows. You can see this variability by calculating difference scores (High minus Low) for each row of both tables. The row effect (matching) is removed from difference scores, and so you see only variability in the column effect (the independent variable). For Table 11.1, the eight difference scores are –1, 4, 2, 3, –1, 4, –3, and 0. For Table 11.3, they are 2, 1, 0, 1, 1, 1, 1, and 1. With relevant matching, there is much less variability in the effect of the independent variable across rows because a significant contributor to that variability, the matching variable, has been removed. Without relevant matching, removing the row effect accomplishes little.

These comparisons were presented so that you will thoroughly understand what relevant matching can accomplish. However, you have been warned several times that there is danger in making believe you have relevant matching when you do not. You end up with a less powerful, less sensitive analysis when you do ANOVA II on data for which ANOVA I is appropriate. This can be illustrated by doing ANOVA II on the data of Table 11.1. A few paragraphs back, SSR = 12 was calculated for Table 11.1. Thus, SSE = 40 – 4 – 12 = 26. dfR is r – 1 = 7, and so dfE = 15 – 1 –7 = 7. Thus MSE = 26/7 = 3.7143. Notice that this MSE is actually larger than the MSE for ANOVA I, 2.5724. Thus, F = MSC/MSE must be smaller, and it is. For ANOVA II, F(1,7) = 4/3.7143 = 1.0769, compared to the earlier value of 1.5556 for ANOVA I. You actually lose ground by doing ANOVA II inappropriately.

There are two reasons for this loss in sensitivity. First, ANOVA II involves an automatic reduction in dfE compared to ANOVA I. Automatic means that you suffer the loss whether or not you have relevant matching. A glance at Table A.3 will convince you that when dfE is smaller, critical values of F are larger, making it harder to reject the null hypothesis. Thus, the loss in dfE in ANOVA II makes for a less sensitive analysis. However, there will also be a reduction in SSE for ANOVA II as compared to ANOVA I, which brings us to the second and decisive reason for the loss in sensitivity. When there is relevant matching, the reduction in SSE in ANOVA II will more than make up for the reduction in dfE, resulting in a smaller MSE, and a more sensitive analysis. On the other hand, when there is not relevant matching, the reduction in SSE in ANOVA II will NOT offset the automatic reduction in dfE, resulting in a larger MSE and a less sensitive analysis. So doing ANOVA II when you should not actually results in a penalty. Sometimes the universe is just.

SUMMARY

In a typical experiment (coarsely manipulated independent variable, finely measured dependent variable), the question of relationship is decided by examining treatment means. Sample means for the dependent variable are computed separately within each condition or treatment and then compared to see if they are equal. If the treatment means are not equal, then the dependent variable is changing, on the average, when the experimenter changes values of the independent variable, which satisfies the definition of a relationship. The treatment mean is used because it is the most common statistic for describing central tendency, that is, the most typical score in a set of scores. For descriptive purposes, researchers will usually also report a statistic describing the spread or variability of scores within each condition. The most common statistic for this purpose is the standard deviation, the square root of the average squared deviation from the mean in a set of scores.

For making inferences about the relationship between the independent and dependent variables in the population, it is necessary to decide whether the sample treatment means differ or vary from each other more than would be expected if only random error were operating. The inferential statistical procedure for making such decisions is the analysis of variance or ANOVA. In ANOVA, an estimate of the actual variability among the treatment means is compared to an estimate of the variability expected from random error only. The comparison is in the form of a ratio, the F ratio, with the estimate of the actual variability among the treatment means in the numerator. Under the null hypothesis, the variability among the sample treatment means is a byproduct of random error only, and thus the value of F should be near 1. Under the alternate hypothesis, the variability among the sample treatment means results from random error plus the real differences in the population treatment means, and the value of F should be substantially greater than 1. The calculated value of F from the sample data is compared to critical values of F to determine its probability under the null hypothesis. As usual, that probability is then compared to alpha in order to decide whether or not to reject the null hypothesis of no relationship between the variables.

The appropriate ANOVAs are slightly different for the two categories of simple experimental designs. ANOVA I is used with independent-treatments designs (although it is not the best approach for pre-post designs; see chapter 9), and ANOVA II with nonindependent-treatments designs. In ANOVA I, the denominator of the F ratio, which contains the estimate of variability expected from random error only, is based on the variability of raw scores within each condition around the sample mean for that condition. In ANOVA II, the denominator of F contains whatever unexplained variability is left in the raw scores after the systematic variability caused by the independent variable and by matching have been removed. If there is a strong relationship between a matching variable, explicit or implicit, and the dependent variable, then the denominator of F in ANOVA II will be much reduced by removing the variability due to matching. The result is a larger F ratio and a more sensitive test of the null hypothesis than would be the case with an ANOVA I analysis.

ANSWERS TO QUESTIONS

Q1. SS $= 218 - (40^2/8) = 218 - 200 = 18$.

Q2. $S^2 = 18/8 = 2.25$, and $S = \sqrt{2.25} = 1.5$.

Q3. $S^2 = 18/(8-1) = 2.57$.

Q4. The means are 4 and 6 for the low and high conditions, and the standard deviations are 1.4142 (i.e., $\sqrt{2}$) in both conditions. SST $= 280 - (50^2/10) = 30$; SSC $= (20^2/5) + (30^2/5) - (50^2/10) = 10$; SSE $= 30 - 10 = 20$; dfT $= 10 - 1 = 9$; dfC $= 2 - 1 = 1$; dfE $= 9 - 1 = 8$; MSC $= 10/1 = 10$; MSE $= 20/8 = 2.5$; F(1,8) $=$

$10/2.5 = 4$, $p > .05$ but $< .10$. Est-$w^2 = [10 - (1)(2.5)]/(30 + 2.5) = 7.5/32.5 = .2308$. Thus, there is a "large" effect (est-$w^2 = .23$), which is not significant ($p > .05$), an apparent contradiction. The reason is that est-w^2 is not affected by sample size, but F is. You can be sure that if you obtained the same size effect with a larger sample, F would be larger and significant. However, the test of inference (F) is telling you that you probably would obtain a smaller effect with a larger sample, resulting in another nonsignificant F ratio.

Q5. The means and standard deviations are the same as in Q4. So are SST, SSC, dfT, dfC, and MSC. SSR $= (10^2/2) + (8^2/2) + (12^2/2) + (6^2/2) + (14^2/2) - (50^2/10) = 20$; SSE $= 30 - 10 - 20 = 0$; dfR $= 5 - 1 = 4$; dfE $= 9 - 1 - 4 = 4$; MSE $= 0/4 = 0$; F(1,4) $= 10/0$, a mathematical embarrassment, but the result can be said to approach positive infinity, and $p < .00000000000$ etc. The spectacular sensitivity resulted from a correlation between the low and high scores of +1, something you will never see in real life. If you can produce data like these without cheating, you will be much in demand as a researcher. Meanwhile, A $= (1)(10 - 0) = 10$, and est-$w^2 = 10/[10 + (10)(0)] = 10/10 = 1$ because MSE $= 0$ with perfect matching.

FURTHER READING

Keppel (1991) discusses the analysis of just about any experimental design imaginable. A readable introduction to statistics is provided by Wike (1985). Step-by-step instructions for most commonly used statistics and analyses are contained in Bruning and Kintz (1977).

REFERENCES

Bruning, J. L., & Kintz, B. L. (1977). *Computational handbook of statistics* (2nd ed.). Glenview, IL: Scott Foresman.

Keppel, G. (1991). *Design and analysis: A researcher's handbook* (3rd ed.). Englewood Cliffs, NJ: Prentice Hall.

Micceri, T. (1989). The unicorn, the normal curve, and other improbable creatures. *Psychological Bulletin, 105,* 156–166.

Wike, E. L. (1985). *Numbers: A primer of data analysis.* Columbus, OH: Charles E. Merrill.

Complex Experi-mental Designs

Elaine Walster and her colleagues (Walster, Walster, Piliavin, & Schmidt, 1973) wanted to test the folk maxim that the woman who plays hard to get is perceived as more desirable than the woman whose affection is easily won. The researchers tried five times, in different ways and in different settings, to obtain data in support of the hard-to-get hypothesis. They failed every time. It began to get through to them that maybe the hypothesis was wrong. So they humbly backed up and conducted some open-ended interviews with male college students on their perceptions of hard- and easy-to-get women. They found out that each type of woman had both advantages and disadvantages. This discovery led the researchers to a new hypothesis: A woman who has all the advantages of both the hard- and easy-to-get types and none of the disadvantages will be seen as most desirable. What kind of woman would she be? She would be *selectively* hard to get, that is, hard for other men to get but easy for the man in question.

Walster and colleagues set about to test this new hypothesis. They created a fake dating service. College men who answered their ad were invited to come to the "dating center" to choose a date. The men were given background information on five potential dates. Included in the background information for three of the women were ratings that they had supposedly made for their own potential dates, one of whom was the current male research participant. This manipulation allowed the researchers to create three kinds of women: uniformly hard- or easy-to-get, and selectively hard-to-get (high rating for the participant and moderate ratings for other potential dates). The background information of the other two women contained no ratings of their own potential dates. They served as no-information controls. Each male participant then rated all five of his potential dates for desirability and selected one of them for a date. This time the researchers struck gold. The selectively hard-to-get woman was rated significantly more desirable than any of the others and was selected as a date significantly more often.

By today's standards, this experiment seems sexist. Males chose females who were treated as objects, and the word "get" clearly has sexual connotations. Ironically, the experiment was a sincere effort by a female social psychologist to investigate relations between the sexes. Times change, and so do interpretations. However you may view the topic of the experiment, please be assured that it was not included here to offend any readers, especially female readers. The experiment was included because it has special (possibly unique) features: This single study clearly illustrates all of the ways in which an experiment can qualify as complex, and one of the ways in which it may be viewed as complex reveals a very instructive flaw in the experimental design.

The Walster experiment can be viewed conceptually in two ways, but either way qualifies it as a complex experiment. So far this book has considered only the simplest possible good experiment: one independent variable with two values and one dependent variable. Any additions to this simple scenario create a complex experiment. It follows that a complex experiment can arise in one or more of three ways: (1) more than two values of a single independent variable, (2) more than one dependent variable or more than one measure (operational definition) of a single dependent variable, and (3) more than one independent variable. Clearly the Walster experiment qualifies under (2) because it included both desirability ratings and date choices as measures, plus a few others not mentioned. However, to set the stage for this chapter, let us focus on the independent variable.

The independent variable of the Walster study may be viewed in two ways. One way is to treat it as one variable with four values. The variable is hard-to-getness, and the values are selective, uniformly high, uniformly low, and no information. This is how the authors viewed the experiment for purposes of data analysis. Their analysis was geared to show that the selective condition produced higher desirability than the other conditions. On this view, the study qualifies as complex under (1) because it had four values of the single independent variable, hard-to-getness.

A second way of viewing the experiment comes through in the theory offered by the authors. After five failures followed by open-ended interviews of college males, it became clear to the researchers that a woman's perceived desirability is influenced by two separate factors. The first is how hard she is for the participant to get, and the second is how hard she is for other men to get. The first factor will be called Hard to Get Self (HGS) and the second Hard to Get Others (HGO). Factor, of course, is just another name for an independent variable. Thus, on this view, there are two independent variables, HGS and HGO. Each independent variable may have two values, high and low. The selectively hard-to-get woman is low in HGS and high in HGO. The uniformly hard-to-get woman is high in both variables; the uniformly easy-to-get woman is low in both variables. The status of the no-information woman cannot be determined for either variable. On this view, the study qualifies as complex under (3) because it had two independent variables.

You may have noticed something strange about this second view of the Walster experiment. Three of the four possible combinations of HGS and HGO values were included in the study, but the fourth combination was missing. The low-high, high-high, and low-low combinations defined the selectively hard-, uniformly hard-, and uniformly easy-to-get conditions, respectively, but the high-low combination was nowhere to be found. It is a wicked combination. Such a woman is hard for the participant to get but easy for other men. The participant might well wonder, "Why does she hate me? Why am I being singled out?" What effect do you think this perception would have on his desirability rating for this woman? You can speculate about it until you turn blue, but the answer cannot be known because the high-low combination was not included in the Walster experiment. Instead, the researchers opted for the no-information control woman whose status on HGS and HGO cannot be determined.

This analysis implies that although the Walster experiment was brilliantly conceived and executed, in one respect it was a failure. The authors clearly implicated two separate causal variables, HGS and HGO, and yet failed to show how they work together in affecting desirability. They showed that one combination, low-high, produces high desirability, and that is what is brilliant about the study. However, without the missing high-low combination, they were unable to show how the two variables combine in their effect on desirability. Do the effects of HGS and HGO simply add together, or do they combine in some more complicated manner? There is no way to know without the missing condition.

The problem is one of conceptualization. The researchers failed to conceptualize their experimental design as a member of the third category of complex designs. The result was that they failed to include all the conditions necessary to answer the broad theoretical question of how their separate causal variables combine in their influence on the dependent variable. You may not fully understand this criticism now, but by the end of the chapter it should make sense. In fact, mastering the material in this chapter will enable you to spot such problems in published research and to avoid them in any research you carry out.

This chapter explores the three ways an experiment can be made complex. It examines the additional issues raised by each of them regarding conceptualization, interpretation, and data analysis. In contrast to the previous chapter, details of data analysis will not be presented. The purpose here is primarily conceptual. However, you will be alerted in a general way to the choices you face in terms of data analysis and to the new kinds of information that can be obtained from complex experiments. The vast majority of experiments in the social sciences qualify as complex. It is important that you understand the new issues raised by such experiments.

MORE VALUES OF A SINGLE INDEPENDENT VARIABLE

A simple way to increase the complexity of an experiment is to have more than two values of a single independent variable. What new information is gained by this maneuver? Figure 12.1 contains plots of the mean score on a dependent variable, performance, on the vertical axis against values of the independent variable, arousal, on the horizontal axis. Figure 12.1a shows what can happen with two conditions or values of the independent variable. As you can see, there can be only two points in the graph. Any relationship between the independent and dependent variables must therefore appear to be a straight-line function. However, that appearance could be deceiving. With more values of the independent variable and thus more points in the graph, it might become clear that the shape of the function relating the variables is not linear. That possibility is illustrated in Figure 12.1b. So by adding more values of the independent variable, you get a more accurate picture of the nature of the relationship between the independent and dependent variables. Even when the independent variable is categorical (nominal data in the sense of Chapter 5) and there is no basis for ordering its values for purposes of making a graph, having more than two values can give the researcher a better idea of what is going on. Knowing that cola gets a higher preference rating than water is interesting, but knowing how cola's rating compares to that for several other types of soft drink is even more interesting.

The possibility of more than one kind of relationship between the independent and dependent variables creates new problems for the data analysis. Suppose you are investigating the effect of arousal on performance, using three values of the independent variable: low, medium, and high arousal. When the data have been collected and you have performed the appropriate ANOVA, if the F ratio is significant, you know that arousal and performance are probably related. However, the analysis reveals nothing about the exact nature of the relationship. Is the function relating performance to arousal linear or U-shaped? The ANOVA cannot answer that question because the null hypothesis it tests is no relationship between the variables. Rejection of that hypothesis means there is some kind of relationship between the variables, nothing more. If you wish to pin down the exact nature of the relationship, further data analysis is required.

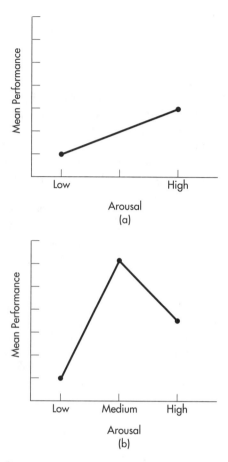

Figure 12.1
Mean performance scores as a function of arousal condition for an experiment with (a) two and (b) three arousal conditions.

Post-Hoc Comparisons

The appropriate follow-up analysis in this situation is known as *post-hoc comparisons*. They are "post-hoc" because they are performed only "after the fact" of a significant F ratio from an ANOVA. Such comparisons allow the researcher to find out if the mean score on the dependent variable for any subset of conditions differs significantly from the mean score on the dependent variable for any other subset of conditions. For example, you could find out if the medium-arousal condition differs from the combined low- and high-arousal conditions. If so, you could conclude that the function relating performance to arousal is probably U-shaped. As you can see, post-hoc comparisons permit a more fine-grained analysis of the exact nature of the relationship once the fact of a relationship has been established by an ANOVA.

There are almost as many post-hoc comparison procedures as stars in the sky. The wide variety of techniques arises because there are so many kinds of comparisons that can be made and because there are different viewpoints about how best to make them. Details of individual procedures will not be presented. To do one of the post-hoc procedures requires study of the specific techniques (which are not difficult), expert help, or both. What you should understand is when post-hoc comparisons are appropriate so that you will know when you need them. Post-hoc comparisons are used when a researcher has no SPECIFIC PRIOR prediction to make about the nature of the relationship between the independent and dependent variables. In such a situation the appropriate analysis to test the general hypothesis that the variables are not related is an ANOVA (as described in the last chapter). If and only if that hypothesis is rejected because the F ratio is significant, follow-up post-hoc comparisons are performed to further explore the exact nature of the relationship.

One distinguishing feature of virtually all procedures for post-hoc comparisons is that they tend to be conservative. Because many comparisons may be made in a single experiment, there is a need to protect against making too many Type I errors of inference, that is, falsely rejecting the null hypothesis. (See Chapter 4 for a review of errors of inference.) Thus, most approaches to post-hoc comparisons make adjustments so that it is harder to reject the null hypothesis for any given comparison than it would be if only one comparison was being made.

Planned Comparisons

The situation of no specific predictions in advance is very common, but obviously another scenario is possible. What if the researcher is explicitly testing the optimal-arousal theory discussed in Chapter 2? As depicted in Figure 12.1b, the theory predicts that the best performance will occur at middle levels of arousal. In this scenario, the researcher is predicting a SPECIFIC kind of relationship IN ADVANCE rather than probing around in the data after finding out that there is some sort of relationship. In this situation it does not seem fair or even wise to test the general null hypothesis of no relationship followed up by conservative comparisons to establish the exact nature of the relationship. What to do?

The proper approach is to test specific prior predictions directly with the most powerful statistical test available. This is a job for *planned comparisons*. The main thing you should understand about planned comparisons is that they are NOT to be confused with post-hoc comparisons. Post-hoc comparisons are generally conservative procedures used in conjunction with ANOVA to explore the nature of a relationship when no prior predictions have been made. Planned comparisons are statistically powerful procedures used INSTEAD OF ANOVA when prior predictions of specific relationships have been made. If you do enough of any kind of comparisons, you get into trouble with Type I errors of inference. With post-hoc comparisons, conservative adjustments are made. With planned comparisons, the number of comparisons permitted is limited. The advice most often given is to limit the number of planned comparisons to the df for the treatment effect from an ANOVA analysis of the same data. For the arousal experiment, there are three conditions, and so dfC = c – 1 = 3 – 1 = 2. Thus, you could do two planned comparisons. You have only one prior prediction and therefore need only one planned comparison. You would compare the medium-arousal condition with the other two conditions combined.

The Walster experiment on playing hard-to-get made good use of a planned comparison. As mentioned earlier, the authors analyzed the data as though the experiment had one independent variable with four values. Because they were able to make the prior prediction that the selectively hard-to-get woman should be most desirable, they set up a planned comparison pitting the selectively hard-to-get condition against all three of the other conditions combined. The F ratio for the comparison was highly significant (p < .001), confirming the prior prediction.

The details of how to do planned comparisons will not be presented. Suffice it to say that even though they should be done instead of ANOVA, planned comparisons are intimately related to ANOVA. The testing statistic for each comparison is an F ratio, and it always has 1 df in the numerator. For this reason, planned comparisons are sometimes called single-df contrasts. The main point is that planned comparisons are available when specific prior predictions have been made, and they provide powerful tests of such predictions.

To sum up, when there are more than two values of the independent variable, a series of questions must be answered to determine the appropriate data analysis. The first question is: Do I have specific prior predictions about the relationship between the independent and dependent variables? If yes, perform planned comparisons testing those specific predictions. If no, do ANOVA. In the latter situation, the next question is: Do I have a significant F ratio? If yes, do post-hoc comparisons to pin down the exact nature of the relationship. To do so will require answers to further questions about what type of comparisons you need to perform and what post-hoc procedure is best suited to your situation. If the F ratio from the ANOVA is not significant, your analysis is finished and your conclusion is that you cannot reject the hypothesis of no relationship between the independent and dependent variables. For a discussion of how to do post-hoc and planned comparisons, see Keppel (1991).

MORE DEPENDENT VARIABLES

A second way to make an experiment more complex is to include more than one dependent variable or more than one measure of a single dependent variable. A statistical analysis cannot tell the difference between the two cases because all it sees is more than one score or measure for the participants in each condition. This situation also creates data-analysis problems. One cannot simply do a separate ANOVA for each separate measure. The problem, of course, is the same one faced with comparison procedures. If you do enough of them, your risk of Type I errors of inference rises. If you have twenty measures for the participants in each condition and perform a separate ANOVA for each one, you can expect at least one "significant" result (assuming alpha = .05) even though the null hypothesis is true in all cases. Multiple tests of inference increase the risk of Type I errors.

The most widely used approach to data analysis in this situation is *multivariate analysis of variance* or MANOVA. MANOVA is not a perfect solution to the problem of Type I errors, but it does provide some extra protection against them. MANOVA proceeds in two steps. The first step contains MANOVA's distinctive feature, a multivariate test of the relationship between the independent variable and the entire set of dependent variables. In fact, most MANOVA programs provide several such tests in their output. Fortunately, they usually agree with each other. The second step in MANOVA is a set of univariate significance tests, that is, F ratios from separate ANOVAs for each separate measure.

A common rule of thumb for interpreting MANOVA results is not to reject the null hypothesis unless all of the multivariate tests indicate rejection (p less than alpha). This is where you get the extra protection against Type I errors. The data must first pass the hurdle of the multivariate tests before you even consider the univariate tests (Bock, 1975). If the multivariate tests fail to reject the null hypothesis, the analysis is finished and you conclude that the null hypothesis cannot be rejected. If the multivariate tests reject the null hypothesis, you then examine the individual univariate tests and may choose to follow up those that are significant with post-hoc comparisons. If you have prior predictions about specific types of relationships, MANOVA allows for multivariate and univariate tests of planned comparisons.

As noted earlier, MANOVA is not a perfect solution to the problem of Type I errors in experiments with multiple measures. Some authors (Harris, 1985; Huberty & Morris, 1989) recommend downward adjustment of alpha instead of or in addition to the MANOVA approach. The most common method of adjusting alpha is called the Bonferroni procedure. In the simplest version of the Bonferroni adjustment, if you want to perform k univariate significance tests (because you have k dependent variables or measures), you reset the original alpha to alpha/k. Thus, for alpha = .05 and four significance tests, the adjusted alpha for declaring a result significant would be .05/4 = .0125. Each of the four tests would have to meet the criterion of p < .0125 to be considered significant. With this approach, the entire set of four tests has a combined Type I error rate equal to the original alpha, .05. More sophisticated versions of the Bonferroni procedure permit different adjustments for the univariate tests in a set based on their relative importance to the researcher (Rosenthal & Rubin, 1984).

The Walster experiment had several measures for each participant in each condition and thus would have been a good candidate for MANOVA. The researchers did not use MANOVA, presumably because its use had not yet become standard practice when their research was published. The use of multiple measures is widely advocated nowadays, and so you may encounter more and more research using MANOVA analysis. The point to remember is that MANOVA is designed to deal with the situation in which there is more than one score or measured variable for the participants in each condition.

MANOVA is never done by hand calculation because the mathematics are too complex. If you need MANOVA, the best advice is to get competent help in using any of several MANOVA computer programs and in interpreting their output. MANOVA can be used with either independent- or nonindependent-treatments designs and with any of the factorial designs described in the next section. It is truly an all-purpose approach to the analysis of experimental data.

MORE INDEPENDENT VARIABLES

The third way to make an experiment more complex is to include more than one independent variable. When done properly, such an experiment can be very efficient in supplying useful information. The researcher can learn not only about the separate effect of each independent variable but also about how the independent variables work together in all possible combinations. Separate experiments, each with a single independent variable, cannot supply information on how independent variables work together. As you will see, such information can be both insightful and theoretically important.

Factorial Design

An experimental design with more than one independent variable is known as a *factorial design*. In a complete factorial design, all values of each independent variable, or factor, are combined with all values of the other independent variables to create experimental conditions. Thus, each condition consists of a combination of values, one from each independent variable. This situation is depicted in Figure 12.2. If you combine three values of the independent variable arousal (low, medium, and high) with two values of the independent variable task complexity (low and high), you will have a complete factorial design with six conditions: low arousal-low complexity, medium arousal-low complexity, high arousal-low complexity, low arousal-high complexity, medium arousal-high complexity, and high arousal-high complexity. The six conditions are represented by the cells in Figure 12.2. Incomplete factorial designs, with some of the combinations of values missing, are possible, but they are difficult to analyze and may not provide complete information on how the independent variables work together. For that reason, the discussion here focuses on complete factorial designs.

The simplest complete factorial design has two independent variables each with two values. This 2×2 factorial design has four conditions. In general, the number of conditions in a complete factorial experiment equals the number of values of the first independent variable times the number of values of the second independent variable and so on for however many independent variables the experiment has. Thus, a 2×3 factorial design has six conditions and a 3×4 design has twelve.

How many conditions does a $2 \times 3 \times 4$ complete factorial design have? (Q1)

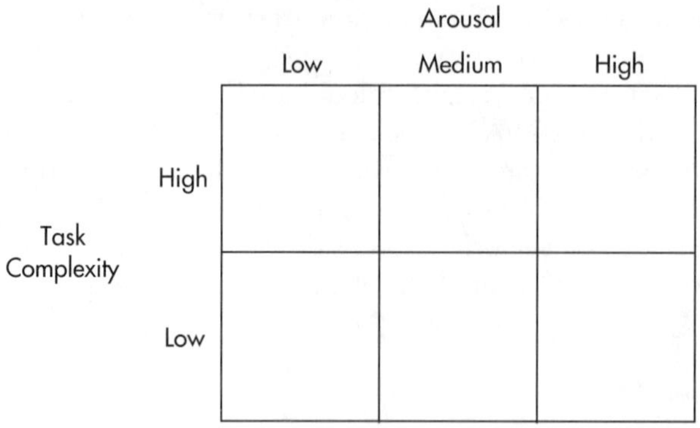

Arousal

	Low	Medium	High
High			
Low			

Task Complexity

Figure 12.2
Diagram of a factorial experiment with three values of the independent variable arousal and two values of the independent variable task complexity.

Most of what you need to know about factorial designs can be learned from the 2 × 2 design.

A concrete example of a 2 × 2 factorial design may be helpful. This book has repeatedly discussed the relationship between frustration and aggression. One example of a simple experiment had frustration as the independent variable, with values of low and high, and aggression as the dependent variable, finely measured. Frustration was manipulated by varying the difficulty of a maze problem along with some ego-involving instructions. Aggression was measured as the number of kicks-gouges-punches inflicted on a Bobo doll during a standard observation period. Let us now add a second independent variable, temperature, with values of cool and hot.

Temperature is known to affect aggression. However, Baron and Bell (1976) found that, contrary to popular assumption, really hot temperatures (92–94°F) decreased aggression in participants who had been made angry. Cool temperatures (71–72°F), on the other hand, increased aggression in angry participants. The researchers explained their finding by suggesting that the need to escape from really hot temperatures dominates any aggressive tendencies. Suppose you wish to know if temperature would work the same way for people who have been frustrated by working on an unsolvable maze problem. To find out, you could run the 2 × 2 factorial experiment depicted in Figure 12.3. As you can see, the experiment has four conditions: low frustration-cool temperature, high frustration-cool temperature, low frustration-hot temperature, and high frustration-hot temperature.

Like all factorial designs, this one yields two kinds of information. First, you can find out how each independent variable, considered in isolation, affects the dependent variable. This kind of information is referred to as a *main effect*. There are as many main effects in a factorial experiment as there are independent variables.

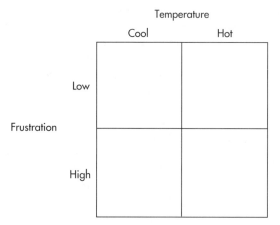

Figure 12.3
Diagram of a 2 × 2 factorial experiment involving the independent
variables frustration and temperature.

Thus, the proposed experiment has two main effects, one for frustration and one for temperature. Second, you can find out how various combinations of the independent variables work together in affecting the dependent variable. In the proposed experiment, only one combination is possible, frustration and temperature. In particular, you can find out if frustration and temperature interact in their effect on aggression.

An *interaction* between two independent variables means that the effect of either one of them on the dependent variable is different at different values of the other independent variable. Thus, if frustration has a different effect on aggression at cool and hot temperatures, then frustration and temperature interact in their effect on aggression. To say the same thing a different way, if temperature affects aggression differently in conditions of low and high frustration, then frustration and temperature interact. The study by Baron and Bell (1976) suggests that an interaction is likely: aggression should *increase* with hot temperatures for participants low in frustration but should *decrease* with hot temperatures for participants high in frustration. On the other hand, if each independent variable has the same effect on aggression at all values of the other independent variable, then there is no interaction. Do not worry if the concept of interaction is not completely clear at this point. It will be explored in considerable detail shortly. For now, the point is that factorial designs provide information on the separate or main effect of each independent variable and also provide information on whether or not combinations of independent variables interact.

Thus, in the expanded frustration experiment, you will find out three things. First, you will learn if frustration and aggression are related, ignoring temperature. This is the main effect of frustration. Second, you will learn if temperature and aggression are related, ignoring frustration. This is the main effect of temperature. Third, you will learn if frustration and temperature interact in affecting aggression. This, of course, is the interaction of frustration and temperature.

ANOVA provides a separate F test for each of these three effects. In each case, the null hypothesis is that the effect does not exist in the population: no relationship between frustration and aggression, no relationship between temperature and aggression, and no interaction effect. The details of the ANOVA need not be explored except to note that they differ depending on the types of independent variables included in the factorial design. Various combinations of independent variables representing independent and nonindependent treatments, as defined in the last three chapters, are possible, and each combination has a different ANOVA. But they all have one thing in common: a separate test of inference or F ratio for each main effect and each possible interaction. Thus, a great deal of useful information is packed into a single experiment.

Interaction

The one new type of information provided by factorial designs is information about interactions. Information about main effects can be obtained from separate experiments, each having only a single independent variable. Only when independent variables are combined in a factorial design can information about interactions be obtained. Thus, interaction is a new concept, and you should understand it thoroughly. Interaction is the most important concept in this chapter.

The standard definition is that an interaction between two independent variables exists when the effect of either one of them on the dependent variable is different at different values of the other independent variable. Thus, when an interaction is present, the relationship between either independent variable and the dependent variable is different at different values of the other independent variable. A concrete example will help you understand this definition.

Possible results of the factorial experiment on aggression are presented in Table 12.1 and displayed graphically in Figure 12.4. Look first at the graph. It plots mean aggression scores against values of frustration and provides separate functions (lines) for the two values of temperature. You can see that aggression rises with increased frustration for cool temperatures but falls with increased frustration for hot temperatures. Thus, the relationship between frustration and aggression is very different for cool and hot temperatures. This pattern of results fits the definition of interaction given in the last paragraph. Note that because of the different effect of frustration on aggression for cool and hot temperatures, the two functions (lines) in Figure 12.4 are not parallel. In fact, they cross over each other, indicating a very strong interaction between frustration and temperature.

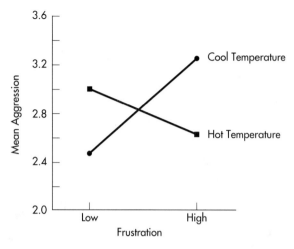

Figure 12.4
Graphs of the frustration-aggression relationship at low and high temperatures illustrating a strong interaction.

Table 12.1   RESULTS OF A 2 X 2 FACTORIAL EXPERIMENT ON AGGRESSION ILLUSTRATING A STRONG INTERACTION

		Cool	Hot	Mean
		Temperature		
Frustration	Low	2.47	3.00	2.74
	High	3.21	2.60	2.90
	Mean	2.84	2.80	2.82

The graphical approach is probably the easiest way to spot an interaction. As Figure 12.4 illustrates, the graph is constructed with dependent-variable means on the vertical axis and one of the independent variables on the horizontal axis. Separate functions are plotted for each value of the other independent variable. It does not matter which independent variable is placed along the horizontal axis and which one defines the separate functions. If the independent variables interact, the functions will NOT be parallel. Thus, strongly nonparallel functions suggest that an interaction is likely. By contrast, if there is no interaction, the functions will be parallel. Figure 12.5 illustrates how the results of the aggression experiment would look with the same main effects but NO interaction. The identical effect of frustration at both temperatures is reflected in the identical slopes of the two functions.

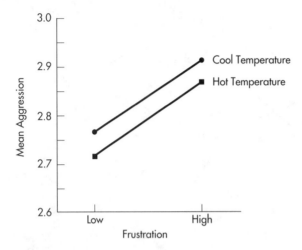

Figure 12.5
Graphs of the frustration-aggression
relationship at low and high temperatures illustrating no interaction.

The identical effect of temperature at both values of frustration is reflected in the
constant difference between the two functions.

Now look at Table 12.1. This kind of table is a standard way of presenting the
results of a factorial-design experiment. Each dimension of the table corresponds
to one of the independent variables. The rows and columns are defined by specific values of the independent variables. Thus, each cell of the table represents a particular combination of the values of the two independent variables, that is, a particular condition in the factorial experiment. The numbers inside the cells and along
the margins are means scores for the dependent variable. With equal sample sizes
in all conditions, each row and column marginal mean is the simple average of the
two cell means for that row or column. The mean at the lower right where the row
and column margins intersect is the grand mean for all raw scores. With equal sample sizes, the grand mean may also be obtained by computing the simple average
of the four cell means, the two row-marginal means, or the two column-marginal
means.

As you may have already realized, the two row-marginal means in Table 12.1
are the sample means for the main effect of frustration, and the two column-marginal means are the sample means for the main effect of temperature. The reason
is that in each case the pair of marginal means show the effect of one independent
variable collapsed across, or ignoring, values of the other independent variable. The
cell means provide sample evidence about the interaction effect. The reason is that
the cell means allow you to see how each independent variable affects the dependent variable at different values of the other independent variable.

Let us examine the table closely. The main effect of frustration is a mean
increase of 0.16 (2.90 – 2.74) when frustration is high. However, concentrating on the

main effect is misleading. The cell means within each column inside the table show that high frustration *increases* aggression 0.74 (3.21 – 2.47) when the temperature is cool but *decreases* aggression 0.40 (2.60 – 3.00) when the temperature is hot. Thus, frustration has a very different effect on aggression (+0.74 versus –0.40) at cool and hot temperatures. This outcome satisfies the definition of an interaction: One independent variable, frustration, has a different effect on the dependent variable, aggression, at different values of the other independent variable, temperature. Of course, this is the same conclusion that followed from the examination of Figure 12.4. Table 12.1 and Figure 12.4 are simply two different ways of presenting the same results.

The same conclusion is reached if you look at the effect of temperature in Table 12.1. Overall, not much seems to be going on (2.84 versus 2.80), but such a conclusion would be misleading. The hot temperature produces a 0.53 (3.00 – 2.47) *increase* in aggression in the low-frustration condition but a 0.61 (2.60 – 3.21) *decrease* in aggression in the high-frustration condition. Thus, the effect of temperature is very different (+0.53 versus –0.61) in the low- and high-frustration conditions, which satisfies the definition of an interaction. Interactions are symmetrical: You can examine either independent variable, and you will reach the same conclusion about whether or not there is an interaction.

The discussion of Table 12.1 suggests a second method of determining whether an interaction exists (the decisive evidence is the F test for the interaction from the ANOVA) and of interpreting its nature. If you compute the difference between the cell means separately within each column of the 2 × 2 table and then compare those differences, you can quickly see whether an interaction is probable. For example, in the cool column you have 3.21 – 2.47 = +0.74, and in the hot column you have 2.60 – 3.00 = –0.40. Thus, the frustration effect is very different for cool and hot temperatures, meaning that an interaction is likely. Of course, you can do the same thing using the cell means within each row, and you will reach the same conclusion.

This example has an important implication. When there is an interaction, it can be misleading to interpret the main effects. The interaction is more important, and it should be interpreted first. An interaction means that either main effect must be qualified because neither main effect applies across-the-board at all values of the other independent variable. In such a situation, the interaction is the most important finding and should be the focus of any theoretical analysis. Of course, if there is no interaction, then any main effects should be the focus of theoretical analysis.

What would the results in Table 12.1 look like if there was no interaction? Specifically, given the same marginal means, what would the cell means look like? If you can appreciate the answer to this question, then you truly understand the concept of interaction. The approach to finding the correct answer is based on the following insight: For the effect of frustration to be the same within each column (no interaction), the cell means within each column must have the same difference as the means in the marginal column. Thus, you must create the same difference within each column of the table as exists within the marginal column while preserving the given set of marginal means.

Applying this insight, note that the marginal column has a difference of 2.90 – 2.74 = 0.16. If you now center that difference of 0.16 around each of the cool and

Table 12.2 RESULTS OF A 2 X 2 FACTORIAL EXPERIMENT ON AGGRESSION ILLUSTRATING NO INTERACTION

		Temperature		
		Cool	*Hot*	*Mean*
Frustration	Low	2.76	2.72	2.74
	High	2.92	2.88	2.90
	Mean	2.84	2.80	2.82

hot marginal means (2.84 and 2.80), you will have cell means corresponding to no interaction. Centering amounts to splitting the marginal column difference of 0.16 in half within each column of the table. Thus, for the cool column you have 2.84 ± 0.08 = 2.76 and 2.92 for low- and high-frustration, respectively. For the hot column, you have 2.80 ± 0.08 = 2.72 and 2.88 for low- and high-frustration, respectively. The outcome of these calculations is presented in Table 12.2. The same method could be used within each row, and it would produce the same results. This procedure maintains the same marginal means and produces the one set of cell means that indicates exactly no interaction. The graph for this situation is given in Figure 12.5. Note that creating the same frustration effect within each column of the 2 × 2 table produces parallel functions, indicating no interaction, when the results are plotted graphically. Here again, Table 12.2 and Figure 12.5 are simply two different ways of presenting the same results.

Try your hand at finding the expected cell means for a 2 × 2 factorial design with no interaction. Imagine marginal means of 13 and 10 for low and high frustration, respectively, marginal means of 12 and 11 for cool and hot temperatures, respectively, and equal sample sizes in all cells.

What are the cell means if there is no interaction? (Q2)

Now let us return to the factorial interpretation of the Walster experiment on playing hard-to-get. The experiment is diagramed as a 2 × 2 factorial design in Table 12.3. You can see that there are two independent variables, Hard-to-Get for Self (HGS) and Hard-to-Get for Others (HGO), each with two values, low and high. The means in the table are the actual means for desirability from the Walster experiment. The measure of desirability was such that the means had to fall in a range from 2 to 12. As you can see, the cell mean for the high HGS-low HGO condition is missing because that condition was not included in the experiment. Therefore, you cannot determine either marginal mean corresponding to that condition, nor can you determine the grand mean. (The no-information control condition, which does not fit into the 2 × 2 conceptualization, had a mean desirability rating of 8.58.)

It should now be clear why it was impossible to determine how the independent variables worked together. Without the missing cell mean, you cannot know whether or not HGS and HGO interact. The woman who is Selectively Hard-to-Get for Others (SHGO) is clearly the most desirable of those tested, but what about the woman who is Selectively Hard-to-Get for Self (SHGS)? Without results for her, you

Table 12.3   RESULTS OF A 2 X 2
FACTORIAL EXPERIMENT ON PLAYING HARD TO GET

		HGO Low	HGO High	Mean
HGS	Low	8.53	9.41	8.97
	High	?	7.90	?
	Mean	?	8.655	?

cannot determine whether the independent variables interact. That is, you cannot determine if the difference between the high and low HGS means is the same within each column of the table or, equivalently, if the difference between the high and low HGO means is the same within each row of the table.

It is possible, however, to determine what the missing cell mean would have to be if there were exactly no interaction. The approach here must be modified because all of the marginal means are not available. However, the information in one complete row and column exists, and that is enough for our purpose. What must be done is to create the same difference within the low HGO column as exists within the high HGO column. The difference within the high HGO column is 9.41 − 7.90 = 1.51. Thus, the expected mean for the missing cell under the hypothesis of no interaction must be 8.53 − 1.51 = 7.02. If you insert 7.02 into the missing cell, the difference within each column is constant (1.51) and so is the difference within each row (0.88). The variables do not interact.

If the variables do not interact, how are they working together? Clearly they are combining their effects somehow because the low HGS-high HGO or SHGO combination is the most desirable (9.41), and the high HGS-low HGO or SHGS combination is the least desirable (7.02). When there is no interaction, the independent variables are combining their effects *additively*. When there is an interaction, the independent variables are combining their effects *nonadditively*. What does this new jargon mean? Quite simply, it means that when there is no interaction, you can determine the cell means by adding together the main effects. (To see how this works with a numerical example, see the "In-Depth" section.) However, such an approach will not work when there is an interaction. With an interaction, something systematic is going on within each condition (or cell) over and above what can be accounted for by simply adding together the separate main effects. The extra systematic something that is happening within the cells IS the interaction effect.

One last observation about the Walster experiment. You now see clearly that the SHGO woman is the most desirable when there is no interaction. The presence of the SHGO effect does not require an interaction. It requires only that the SHGO cell have the highest mean. What if there was an interaction? All that is required for an interaction is that the missing cell mean be significantly above or below 7.02.

How would you interpret the interaction theoretically if the missing cell mean was, say, 7.90, 6.50, or 11.02? (Q3)

Finally, note that the concept of interaction is not confined to experiments. Interactions can occur in nonexperimental research as well. A broadened definition is that an interaction occurs whenever the relationship between two variables differs for different values of a third variable. This definition applies equally well to manipulated or measured variables. However, when you are dealing with only measured variables (nonexperimental research), it is a bit more difficult to specify which variables are interacting. For example, if the correlation between measured frustration and measured aggression differs for the two sexes (it might be higher for males), then clearly the variables are interacting. But how should you talk about the interaction? It seems most natural to say that the relationship between frustration and aggression interacts with gender, but there is no standard format for talking about interactions among measured variables. However one talks about the interaction, it is the most important finding and should be the focus of any theoretical discussion.

Varieties of Factorial Design

To fully comprehend factorial design, you must consider the types and number of independent variables that can be included in such a design. The previous chapters distinguished between two categories of simple experimental designs, independent and nonindependent treatments. The distinction, you will recall, was based on whether or not matching of stable participant characteristics across conditions occurred. That distinction is relevant for each independent variable in a factorial experiment. To carry out the factorial experiment and analyze the data, the researcher must specify whether each independent variable falls into the independent- or nonindependent-treatments category. This usually comes down to whether each independent variable will be treated as an example of the more common member of each category, namely the posttest-only design for the independent-treatments category and the repeated-measures design for the nonindependent-treatments category. In the context of factorial design, a posttest-only independent variable is usually called a *between-subjects* variable because its values are randomly assigned to different subjects or participants. Likewise, a repeated-measures independent variable is usually called a *within-subjects* variable because all of its values are assigned to every subject or participant.

With this new terminology, you can see that a 2×2 factorial design has three possible combinations of independent-variable types: both between-subjects, both within-subjects, or one of each. The actual manipulation of the independent variables will be affected by the combination chosen because the appropriate method of assigning participants has to be followed. In the both-between-subjects factorial, participants are randomly assigned to only one of the four cells or conditions of the design. In the both-within-subjects factorial, each participant is assigned to all four conditions, and order effects must be dealt with by counterbalancing or randomization, as described in Chapter 10. In the one-of-each factorial, also known as a mixed design, each participant is randomly assigned to only one value of the between-subjects independent variable but receives all values of the within-subjects variable. Order effects must be neutralized for the within-subjects independent variable. There is nothing new here conceptually except that you must think in terms of combinations of independent-variable types.

The data analysis is also affected by the type of factorial design. The differences show up in the error terms of the ANOVAs. In the both-between-subjects factorial, there is one error term for all three effects tested, the two main effects and the interaction. In the both-within-subjects factorial, there is a separate error term for each of the three effects tested. In the mixed factorial, there are two error terms, one for the main effect of the between-subjects independent variable and a second for the other two effects tested. These details of analysis are unimportant because computers do the actual work nowadays. What is important is to give the computer the correct information about whether each independent variable is between subjects or within subjects.

Many factorial designs contain one or more nonmanipulated independent variables. Gender is a favorite, followed closely by personality traits like introversion-extroversion. In a 2×2 table of results, such a variable will look no different from a manipulated independent variable, but it is well to keep the distinction in mind. As stressed in Chapter 10, nonmanipulated independent variables carry a much greater risk of confounding than manipulated independent variables. Thus, caution is always in order when interpreting either main effects or interactions involving nonmanipulated independent variables.

There can, of course, be more than two independent variables in a factorial design. In such cases, the number of possible combinations of between- and within-subjects independent variables is much greater than in the 2×2 factorial. There will also be more main effects and interactions. Some of the interactions will involve more than two independent variables. By definition, such interactions are known as *higher-order interactions*. For example, in a $2 \times 2 \times 2$ factorial design, there will be three main effects, three two-way interactions (involving two independent variables), and one three-way higher-order interaction (involving all three variables). There will thus be seven F tests in the ANOVA, and any subset of them may be statistically significant. In a four-way factorial design (four independent variables), there will be four main effects, six two-way interactions, four three-way interactions, and one four-way interaction. Any subset of the fifteen F tests may turn out significant.

Clearly, the more independent variables there are in a factorial design, the more difficult it will be to interpret the overall pattern of results simply because there will be so many results. It may be virtually impossible to make sense of significant higher-order interactions beyond three-way interactions. The rule for interpreting an interaction of any complexity is simple: an n-way interaction means that any (n – 1)-way interaction involving a subset of the n independent variables is different in nature for different values of the nth independent variable. Thus, following the earlier rule of thumb, a higher-order interaction should take precedence in interpretation over a lower-order interaction because it means that the lower-order interaction needs to be appropriately qualified. However, knowing this is useless when you actually try to interpret a significant four- or five-way interaction. The moral is that complex factorial designs quickly reach a point of diminishing returns. There is not much to be gained by having more than three or four independent variables in a factorial design.

IN-DEPTH: INTERACTION AND ADDITIVITY

The concept of additive main effects (no interaction) is easy to see in a simple numerical example. Table 12.3 will do nicely. The earlier discussion determined that the missing cell mean must be 7.02 for the case of no interaction. At this point, you should get a sheet of paper and make your own version of the table. Do it now before going any further. Include the value of 7.02 in the high HGS-low HGO cell. Assuming equal sample sizes in each cell, you can now determine the missing marginal means by averaging the appropriate cell means. Thus, the low HGO marginal mean must be the average of 8.53 and 7.02, or 7.775, and the high HGS marginal mean must be the average of 7.02 and 7.90, or 7.46. The grand mean must be the average of either pair of marginal means, or 8.215.

Now you are ready to play. Additivity (no interaction) means that you can determine any cell mean by starting with the grand mean and simply adding to it the deviation of the relevant row marginal mean from the grand mean (the main effect of the row variable) and the deviation of the relevant column marginal mean from the grand mean (the main effect of the column variable). It sounds like a mouthful, but it is easy to do. Let us try it for the upper left cell of the table. The relevant row marginal mean is 8.97, and its deviation from the grand mean is 8.97 − 8.215 = +0.755. The relevant column marginal mean is 7.775, and its deviation from the grand mean is 7.775 − 8.215 = −0.44. If you start with the grand mean, 8.215, and then simply add on these two deviations representing the relevant row and column main effects, you should obtain the cell mean if the independent variables combine additively (no interaction). You have 8.215 + 0.755 − 0.44 = 8.53. Thus, there is nothing going on in the upper left cell beyond what can be accounted for by simply adding the relevant main effects to the grand mean. If you try the same exercise with any of the other cells, you will obtain the same result: additivity, no interaction.

If you try this same exercise with Table 12.1, which contains a strong interaction, you will obtain a very different result. For the upper left cell, the relevant row marginal mean is 2.74, and its deviation from the grand mean is 2.74 − 2.82 = −0.08. The relevant column marginal mean is 2.84, and its deviation from the grand mean is 2.84 − 2.82 = +0.02. If the variables combine additively (no interaction), the expected cell mean is 2.82 − 0.08 + 0.02 = 2.76. The actual cell mean is 2.47. Something systematic is happening within this cell or condition beyond what can be accounted for by simply adding together the relevant main effects. In other words, the independent variables combine nonadditively. They interact.

You may have noticed that the procedure for determining expected cell means under the assumption of additivity is simply a slightly altered version of the procedure presented earlier for determining expected cell means under the hypothesis of no interaction. This should not be surprising because additivity is equivalent to no interaction. The additivity procedure was presented here to deepen your understanding of interaction by demonstrating that no interaction amounts to independent variables combining by simply adding their main effects. Interaction, on the other hand, means that something more than a simple addition of main effects is happening when independent variables combine.

COMBINATIONS AND COMPLICATIONS

This chapter concludes with a few items of unfinished business. The first is to note that the three ways of making an experiment more complex can occur in any combination. Thus, the data-analysis options associated with the three ways of making an experiment more complex can also occur in any combination. For example, no matter what else is going on in an experimental design, if you have more than one dependent variable, you should use MANOVA to analyze the data. MANOVA can be used with factorial designs of any complexity, and most MANOVA programs provide options for both planned and post-hoc comparisons. Thus, a researcher can either make specific predictions in advance and test them via planned comparisons or simply test a general null hypothesis of no effect and follow up significant results with post-hoc comparisons. These options apply to interactions of any complexity as well as to main effects. Thus, a researcher may have a specific prior prediction about the exact nature of an interaction. If so, the researcher should set up the appropriate planned comparison in order to achieve the most powerful statistical test of the specific prediction. Expert advice may be required to set up complex planned comparisons, but it is well to know that they are available for predictions of any complexity. Every possibility discussed in this chapter might actually occur in a $2 \times 3 \times 4$ factorial design with three dependent variables.

The major complication that arises in actual research situations is unequal sample sizes in the different conditions of an experiment. The discussion so far has assumed equal sample sizes. Unequal sample sizes have serious drawbacks. They can raise Type I error rates under certain conditions (that is, the p values for a given F ratio are actually higher than those given in the F table), and in factorial designs unequal sample sizes usually destroy the statistical independence of the main effects and interactions (i.e., the various sums of squares no longer add up to the total sum of squares). Thus, where possible, it is best to design experiments so that they have equal sample sizes.

Where sample sizes are nearly equal, the researcher may elect to discard participants randomly (it MUST be done randomly to avoid bias) from the conditions with the larger samples to achieve equal sample sizes. Most researchers cannot bring themselves to do this because of overly severe training. A second approach is to try for proportional sample sizes. That is, the ratio of sample sizes across the values of an independent variable is maintained at all values of other independent variables. In the frustration experiment, this condition would be satisfied if you had 18 and 12 participants for low and high frustration at the cool temperature and 15 and 10 participants at the high temperature. Thus, the ratio for low and high frustration is 3/2 at all values of temperature. The advantage of proportional sample sizes is that the statistical independence of main effects and interactions is maintained.

Finally, if you must accept unequal sample sizes that are nonproportional, there are statistical approaches for analyzing the data, but they are messy. Keppel (1991) and Winer (1971) provide detailed discussions of the options for dealing with unequal sample sizes. As usual, the best advice is to be alert to the available options and then get expert help to select and use them.

SUMMARY

An experiment can be more complex than the simplest good experiment in one or more of three ways: (1) more than two values of a single independent variable, (2) more than one dependent variable or more than one measure of a single dependent variable, and (3) more than one independent variable. Number (1) allows a researcher to determine more precisely the exact nature of the relationship between the independent and dependent variables. The appropriate analysis depends on the hypothesis to be tested. The general null hypothesis of no relationship is tested by the appropriate ANOVA, with a significant F ratio followed up by post-hoc comparisons to pin down the nature of the relationship. Post-hoc comparisons are generally conservative tests to protect against the increased risk of Type I errors from unrestricted snooping around in the data. If a specific type of relationship is predicted in advance, the appropriate analysis is planned comparisons, which are very powerful tests of a restricted set of prior hypotheses. Either version of (2) is handled by multivariate analysis of variance or MANOVA, possibly supplemented by a conservative adjustment of alpha (as in the Bonferroni procedure). Number (3) allows a researcher to test the separate or main effects of each independent variable and also to see how independent variables work together in combination. A complete factorial design is one in which experimental conditions are created by pairing every value of each independent variable with every value of all other independent variables. The appropriate ANOVA or MANOVA will depend on the mix of independent variables representing independent and nonindependent treatments.

An interaction between two independent variables means that the relationship between either independent variable and the dependent variable differs at different values of the other independent variable. Thus, when an interaction is present, the main effects of either independent variable cannot be generalized across values of the other independent variable. It follows that an interaction is the most important finding and must be the focus of any theoretical account of the results. In factorial experiments with more than two independent variables, higher-order interactions can occur, but they may be difficult to interpret. The three ways of making an experiment more complex can occur in any combination. The analysis usually involves a similar combination of the analyses appropriate to each component of the combination. Unequal sample sizes can cause statistical problems in any of the analyses discussed. Various strategies have been devised to deal with the problem.

ANSWERS TO QUESTIONS

Q1. A $2 \times 3 \times 4$ complete factorial design has $2 \times 3 \times 4 = 24$ conditions.

Q2. The difference between the marginal means for low and high frustration is 13 – 10 = 3, favoring low frustration. Under the hypothesis of no interaction, the expected cell means for the hot temperature are 11 ± 1.5, or 12.5 and 9.5 for low and high frustration, respectively. The expected cell means for the cool temperature are 12 ± 1.5, or 13.5 and 10.5 for low and high frustration, respectively.

Q3. Briefly, here are some possibilities.

Theory #1 (missing cell mean = 7.90) : When a woman is hard-to-get for self, the man does not like her and does not care or even notice how hard she is to get for others. When she is easy-to-get for self, she is generally seen as more desirable, but her worth peaks when she is also hard for others to get.

Theory #2 (missing cell mean = 6.50) : The SHGO woman is highly prized, but the SHGS woman is even more virulently hated than the SHGO woman is prized. This could be the ultimate ego-involvement theory.

Theory #3 (missing cell mean = 11.02) : The SHGO woman is prized, but the SHGS woman is even more highly prized. In other words, the woman who is selectively nice to a man is liked, but the woman who is selectively mean to a man is liked even more. This would make sense if men generally enjoyed pain.

FURTHER READING

Keppel (1991) and Winer (1971) discuss data analysis for factorial designs of any complexity. An insightful discussion of the concept of interaction may be found in Kerlinger (1986). Aiken and West (1991) and Lunneborg (1994) extend the concept of interaction to nonexperimental research and show how to analyze the data properly.

REFERENCES

Aiken, L. S., & West, S. G. (1991). *Multiple regression: Testing and interpreting interactions*. Newbury Park, CA: Sage.

Baron, R. A., & Bell, P. A. (1976). Aggression and heat: The influence of ambient temperature, negative affect, and a cooling drink on physical aggression. *Journal of Personality and Social Psychology, 33*, 245–255.

Bock, R. D. (1975). *Multivariate statistical methods in behavioral research*. New York: McGraw-Hill.

Harris, R. J. (1985). *A primer of multivariate statistics* (2nd ed.). Orlando, FL: Academic Press.

Huberty, C. J., & Morris, J. D. (1989). Multivariate analysis versus multiple univariate analyses. *Psychological Bulletin, 105*, 302–308.

Keppel, G. (1991). *Design and analysis: A researcher's handbook* (3rd ed.). Englewood Cliffs, NJ: Prentice Hall.

Kerlinger, F. N. (1986). *Foundations of behavioral research* (3rd ed.). New York: Holt, Rinehart and Winston.

Lunneborg, C. E. (1994). *Modeling experimental and observational data.* Belmont, CA: Duxbury.

Rosenthal, R., & Rubin, D. B. (1984). Multiple contrasts and ordered Bonferroni procedures. *Journal of Educational Psychology, 76,* 1028–1034.

Walster, E., Walster, G. W., Piliavin, J., & Schmidt, L. (1973). "Playing hard to get": Understanding an elusive phenomenon. *Journal of Personality and Social Psychology, 26,* 113–121.

Winer, B.J. (1971). *Statistical principles in experimental design* (2nd ed.). New York: McGraw-Hill.

Generalizing Research Results

13

Chapter 10 introduced the distinction between internal and external validity. The former refers to whether or not a study is procedurally sound and thus free from confounding influences. The latter refers to how broadly the results may be generalized. Previous chapters have dealt mainly with issues of internal validity. This chapter concentrates on external validity, or the generalizability of results.

Results that generalize are desirable for three reasons. First, a result with no generality is unlikely to have much theoretical or practical impact. Its range of application is simply too limited. Second, one of the basic goals of science described in Chapter 1 is generalization. A result that does not generalize frustrates this basic goal. Third, it is the generality of a result that ultimately confers on it the status of a scientific law. Chapter 2 described the inverted-U relationship between arousal level and performance in a variety of tasks (see Figure 2.1.c). In psychology that relationship is known as the Yerkes-Dodson law, named after its discoverers. It is a law precisely because it has been found to apply across a wide range of tasks, settings, people, and measures. In other words, it is a law because of its generality.

Generalizability and sampling are intimately related. To question the generality of a research result is to ask how broadly the result applies across values of one or more variables of interest. For example, many people who hear about the Walster experiment on playing hard to get wonder if the major finding applies to females as well as males. That is, would the selectively hard-to-get date be as highly regarded by females as by males? To pose this question is to ask whether the selectively hard-to-get phenomenon generalizes across values of the gender variable. The answer is not known because female raters of potential dates were not included in the study, nor is it known whether the result applies to other types of males besides college students because other types of males were not included in the study. These examples illustrate the first rule of generalization: To determine if a result generalizes across the values of a variable, a research study must contain an adequate or representative sample of those values.

This rule is not new. It first appeared in Chapter 7 during the discussion of sampling procedures. The rule specifies the minimum conditions that must be met to decide whether a result applies to a given population. The sample must adequately represent the population with respect to all relevant variables. Adequate representation means that the sample must be large enough to reduce random error within reasonable bounds. The sample must also be unbiased, that is, free of any systematic tendency to favor certain values of relevant variables over other values. If these conditions are not met for any given relevant variable, the question of whether a result generalizes across values of the variable cannot be answered. To offer an answer anyway is to assume what has not been demonstrated. Such an assumption carries a high risk of error. Moreover, it is well to remember that many different kinds of variables are sampled in any research study: participant characteristics, researcher characteristics, stimuli, procedures, settings, measures, etc. The question of generality can be raised with respect to any of these kinds of variables.

One of the main reasons for questioning the generality of a research result is that the researcher chose to control a relevant extraneous variable by holding it absolutely constant. Such control means that only one value of the variable was sampled—clearly a systematic bias in sampling. This is typically done for the best of reasons, control, but it means that the generality of the results cannot be determined for the controlled variable. You can see that control and generality may be in conflict: The tighter the control, the weaker the evidence for generality. Fortunately, not all approaches to control have this problem. The method of balancing or holding constant on the average, discussed in Chapter 10, often allows a researcher to have the best of both worlds, a broad sampling of values of a relevant extraneous variable plus a guarantee that the variable has the same average value in all conditions of the study. For any extraneous variable where both control and generality are desired, balancing should be the method of choice for control.

Although generality is desirable, you should not get the impression that a study with limited generality is worthless. A healthier view is that such a study makes a worthwhile but limited contribution. Limited generality is perhaps best seen as an opportunity for further research rather than a reason for devaluing the contribution of a study. The Walster study illustrates this point. The fact that the study did not determine whether the results generalize to females or noncollege males takes nothing away from its cleverness, value, or theoretical contribution. It simply means that somebody ought to do the research to explore the generality of the results with respect to these variables.

Suppose someone does the necessary research. For example, suppose a researcher does a follow-up to the Walster study in which college and noncollege males are compared. According to the first rule of generalization, such a study would provide the evidence necessary to decide whether the selectively hard-to-get phenomenon also applies to noncollege males. What will the evidence look like if the result generalizes or does not generalize across values of educational status of male raters? The answer can be summed up in one word: interaction. If the selectively hard-to-get phenomenon does not generalize across educational category, the results will be different for college and noncollege males. In other words, educational status will interact with the independent variable of the experiment, hard-to-getness. By the same token, if the phenomenon does generalize, hard-to-getness will work the same way for college and noncollege males. That is, educational status will not interact with hard-to-getness. Thus, the second rule of generalization is that generality with respect to a variable means no interaction involving the variable. Lack of generality means that the variable interacts with the independent variable or variables of the study.

These two generalization rules provide the framework for this chapter. It first surveys the kinds of variables a researcher might wish to generalize across. They are summarized in Table 13.1 and will be discussed in the next two sections. In each case a key issue concerns the sort of evidence that would cause a researcher to qualify the generality of a result. You will see that a limitation on generality is equivalent to an interaction involving the variable under consideration. In the process, you will be alerted to the very real possibility of limited generality with respect to variables like participant characteristics, researcher characteristics, procedures, settings, and measures. The chapter then discusses the value of replication in deciding questions of generality. Next, issues involved in generalizing across existing studies are considered. Finally, there is a brief discussion of the relationship between the generality of research results and their application in nonresearch settings.

Table 13.1 CHECKLIST OF FACTORS
FOR EVALUATING EXTERNAL VALIDITY

Participant Variables
      Educational level
      Volunteer versus nonvolunteer status
      Place of residence
      Gender
      Personality
      Social Status
Researcher Variables
      Gender
      Personality
      Personal appearance
Procedures
      Operational definitions
      Presence-absence of pretest
Settings
      Laboratory versus "real life"
      Mundane and experimental realism
Measures
      Single versus multiple measures

GENERALIZING TO PARTICIPANT POPULATIONS

As noted in Chapter 7, random sampling of participants from a prespecified target population, although ideal, is the exception rather than the rule in social sciences research. Researchers commonly choose from available pools of potential participants and worry later about what population their sample might represent. The nonrandom nature of selection can lead to sample biases that may affect the generality of results. This possibility should always be kept in mind by the careful researcher.

What are some participant characteristics that may limit the generality of results from a typical research study in the social sciences? Three come to mind immediately. The typical participant is a college student at a specific school and is also a volunteer. College students differ systematically from the general population in a number of ways. For example, they are more intelligent (Sears, 1986). Likewise, volunteers differ from nonvolunteers. For example, volunteers are more highly educated and higher in need of approval (Rosenthal & Rosnow, 1975). There is even evidence that different kinds of people volunteer for different kinds of studies (Hood & Back, 1971). College campuses differ in their social and intellectual atmospheres and therefore tend to attract different kinds of students. Differences among campuses are a special case of the broader variable of geographic location. It is always worth considering whether the results obtained in your research study would apply to Tibetan monks or residents of New York City. Some kind of geographic restriction on the generality of results is usually justified.

Then there is gender. Many researchers have gone mad trying to find gender differences where there was no good theoretical reason to expect them. Males and females are probably more alike than different in general, but if you happen to research a gender-related issue, it is a good bet that the two sexes will react differently. Consider the relationship between type of humor, hostile versus sexual, and rated funniness. Mundorf, Bhatia, Zillmann, Lester, and Robertson (1988) found that sexual humor was rated as funnier. Does this result apply to both sexes? Yes and no. Both sexes found the sexual humor funnier, but the difference was greater for males. In other words, there was an interaction. Both sexes found hostile humor equally funny, but males liked sexual humor more than females did. There is more. The humor was also classified on the basis of the victim's gender. A three-way interaction resulted. Each sex rated hostile humor funnier when the opposite sex was the victim, but males rated sexual humor funnier than did females regardless of the victim's gender. You can see that any generalization based on the main effect of humor type conceals some important qualifications based on the gender of rater and humor victim.

Personality and sociological variables include numerous plausible candidates that might produce interactions and thus limitations on the generality of main effects. For example, consider the aggressiveness of a rater's personality or whether a rater is a member of a street gang. Can you see how these variables might interact with type of humor, sexual versus hostile? It seems likely that aggressive personalities (presumably including members of street gangs) might be more sensitive to hostile humor than nonagressive personalities but show no difference in sensitivity to sexual humor.

As an exercise, consider a modification of the humor study. The modified study examines the relationship between the rated sexual content of cartoons and their rated funniness. In general, the correlation is positive, but is it the same for male and female raters?

What do you think Love and Deckers (1989) found when they investigated this question? (Q1)

The moral of this discussion of participant characteristics and generality is that a wise researcher tries to anticipate which such characteristics are likely to be most relevant to the variables under investigation. The researcher can then plan to gather data on such characteristics and find out whether they interact with the main independent variables of the study. As usual, forethought may yield richer data and a deeper understanding of the phenomena under investigation.

OTHER SAMPLED VARIABLES AND GENERALIZATION

This section briefly reviews some of the other sampled variables in a research study, and indicates how they may affect the generality of results.

Researchers

Most research studies in the social sciences employ a single researcher. The object is to control for any peculiarities of the researcher that might affect results. Such a concern implies that results might not always generalize across researchers. *Experimenter effects* involving the personality, gender, or experience of the researcher have been documented (Kintz, Delprato, Mettee, Persons, & Schappe, 1965). Personal appearance of the researcher is also likely to be relevant. Extremes of attractiveness or grooming will probably produce results that do not generalize to other researchers. Sometimes researcher and participant characteristics interact, making generalization even riskier. For example, Stevenson and Allen (1964) found that participants tend to perform better on a sorting task when tested by a researcher of the opposite sex.

There are two approaches to the problem of generalizing across researchers. One is to use two or more researchers to run a study and to either balance them across conditions to control for experimenter effects or (better yet) to treat the researchers as one variable in a factorial design. The latter strategy allows one to test explicitly for interactions involving the researcher variable. A modification of the factorial strategy is to designate a specific researcher characteristic as relevant and then make it an independent variable in a factorial design. Gender of researcher is often treated this way. The second approach to generalizing across researchers is replication. If similar results are obtained in a variety of studies involving different researchers, the evidence for the generality of the finding is strong. Replication will be discussed in more detail shortly.

Procedures

Given the same independent variables, it is always worth asking whether similar results would be obtained if different procedures were used. How well do the findings generalize across variations in procedure? One of the most theoretically interesting ways to vary the procedure is to vary the operational definition of the independent variables. In the frustration experiment, frustration was manipulated by having participants work on either unsolvable or easily solvable maze problems. Suppose the predicted positive relationship between frustration and aggression is obtained. It would then be legitimate to ask whether a similar finding would be obtained if frustration was manipulated by a direct insult or by some other means. One way to find out is to run a second study, a replication involving the alternative manipulation of frustration. A second approach is to anticipate the question, and thus to include more than one operational definition of the independent variable in the original experiment. The kind of manipulation could be one factor in a factorial design, which would allow the researcher to examine directly potential interactions involving the kind of manipulation. Again you see that anticipation of generality questions may lead to modification of the research design to include additional independent variables.

A procedural variation that has produced much controversy is whether or not a pretest should be used. That is, should the dependent variable be measured both before and after the independent variable is manipulated? This issue was discussed in Chapter 10. The conclusion was that because pretests are seldom found in the real world and because they increase the risk that demand characteristics will come into play, the generality of results obtained with pretests is questionable. Pretests are best avoided unless the researcher is specifically interested in the effect of pretesting. If so, the presence or absence of a pretest can be built into a factorial design along with the independent variable of interest. In the frustration experiment, the pretest variable, with values of present and absent, could be combined factorially with frustration, with values of high and low. The resulting 2×2 factorial design allows the researcher to examine the interaction of pretesting and frustration and thus to obtain a direct answer to the question of whether the frustration results generalize across values of the pretesting variable. The 2×2 factorial design with pretesting as one of the independent variables has been named the *Solomon four-group design* after the psychologist who first suggested it as a way of dealing with the pretesting problem (Solomon, 1949).

> *Do you think there would be an interaction of pretesting and frustration in the frustration experiment, and if so, what form would it take? That is, how would the relationship between frustration and aggression differ in the pretest present and absent conditions? (Q2)*

Settings

As with procedures, it is always worth asking whether the same results would be obtained in a different setting. A common criticism of social science research deals with the generality of results across settings. The criticism is that results obtained in a laboratory setting may not generalize to real-life settings. The laboratory allows the researcher to gain a great deal of control over extraneous variables, but it is also an artificial environment. Thus, the question is raised as to whether the researcher buys control at the expense of generality.

There are several ways of dealing with this criticism. One is to note that the ultimate purpose of laboratory research is to establish relationships in principle and then subsequent research explores the generality of such relationships. In this approach, the generality of a finding is established by a body of research and not in any single study. As will be evident shortly, this approach is equivalent to replication across settings, and it is perhaps the best way to explore the generality of any finding.

It should be pointed out that many laboratory findings do generalize to real-life settings. Laboratory findings concerning basic psychological processes have found wide application beyond the laboratory. The basic principles of learning and conditioning have been used to improve both teaching and the treatment of physical and mental disorders. Laboratory findings on basic perceptual processes have been applied to problems ranging from airplane cockpit design to improved street lighting to the teaching of reading. A book by Stanovich (1992) contains many more examples like these.

A second approach to the problem of generalizing from the laboratory is to do research in real-life settings. This approach emphasizes the importance of field research of all kinds, including field experiments. The argument is that the "ecological validity" of results can be assured only if they are obtained in real-life settings. Perhaps the most colorful advocate of this approach in the social sciences was Egon Brunswik. His idea of the proper way to do research was to follow a person around all day and, at randomly determined times, obtain judgments of things like the perceived size and distance of objects in the environment. He could then determine the relationship between these judgments and physical measures of the objects' properties, thereby deriving what he called the "ecological cue validity" of the stimulus information used for perception in real-life settings (Brunswik, 1956). Notice that a researcher devoted to ecological validity does not care what results are obtained in laboratory settings. Such results are considered irrelevant. The issue of generality is sidestepped by the value judgment that only results obtained in the "real world" have any meaning. You need not accept this extreme view to appreciate the value of research in nonlaboratory settings. Such research can be seen as a valuable supplement to laboratory research, a means of checking the generality of findings across settings.

It should be noted that just because a study is carried out in a real-life setting does not mean that the results have real-world relevance. Even field studies can be contrived and artificial. The important ingredient, according to Aronson, Brewer, and Carlsmith (1985), is *mundane realism,* which refers to whether the research deals with events similar to those in real life. The frustration experiment is low on mundane realism because most people do not spend much time working on unsolvable maze puzzles. Doing the same experiment on a street corner would not help much. To achieve mundane realism would require finding a more realistic way of frustrating people. A nonfunctioning coin-operated soft-drink machine might be just the ticket. Not only does the uncooperative machine have mundane realism, it also has *experimental realism.* That is, it has a real impact on participants, and it makes them take the study seriously. The best research, according to Aronson et al., has both mundane and experimental realism. Results from such research are likely to have broad generality.

A third approach to the problem of generalizing across settings may be feasible when field research is not. Perhaps the next best thing to a real-life setting is a simulation. A *simulation* is an imitation, intended to resemble the real setting in all important functional characteristics. You saw a dramatic example in the Stanford prison experiment, described in Chapter 9. Few would doubt that the simulated prison was effective or that similar results would be obtained in a real prison setting. Other forms of simulation include games, role playing, and scale models. To be effective, a simulation must be realistic. That is, it must evoke the same reaction that the real thing would. Where there is doubt on this point, research is necessary to compare reactions to the simulation and the real thing. Once the external validity of a simulation has been established, it can be an economical way to learn about the setting being simulated.

Measures

Just as a researcher might want to use more than one operational definition of an independent variable to explore the generality of results, the same is true of a dependent variable. The use of multiple measures of dependent variables is often suggested as a way of finding out how strong or "robust" a relationship is. The Walster experiment on playing hard-to-get used both desirability ratings and date choices as dependent measures to see if the results would agree with each other.

Strength or robustness in these situations is equivalent to generality. That is, how well does the finding generalize across different measures of the dependent variable?

The discussion of construct validity in Chapter 6 distinguished between convergent and discriminant validity. Convergent validity means that evidence from different sources using different measures of a theoretical variable or construct yields similar results for the same construct. Discriminant validity means that measures of a construct behave differently from measures of other constructs. The 4M approach, in which at least two different methods of measuring at least two different constructs are included in the same study, was described as an efficient and convincing way of demonstrating convergent and discriminant validity simultaneously. In the present context, note that whenever convergent validity is demonstrated by using multiple measures of the same construct, the results necessarily also provide evidence for generality across different measures of the same variable. Thus, the 4M approach, with multiple measures of different dependent variables, allows a researcher to pursue theory validation, construct validity, and generality simultaneously.

REPLICATION

A replica is a copy. To replicate a research study is to copy that study. The goal is to see if the earlier results can also be duplicated. If the same results are obtained a second time, confidence in the statistical reliability of the findings is greatly increased. Sommer and Sommer (1991, p. 231) assert that "two independent studies represent a more powerful test of a hypothesis than a single study involving twice as many subjects." The reason has to do with the relationship between replication and generality.

Exact Replication

There are two kinds of replication, exact and conceptual. You might think that an exact replication means an exact copy of an earlier study. A little reflection will convince you that such a thing is impossible. Any attempt at replication will involve a different researcher, participants, setting, time period, and probably minor variations in procedure as well. In other words, there is no such thing as an exact copy of a research study. By definition, an *exact replication* is an attempt to copy exactly the *procedures* of an earlier study. The most common reason for an exact replication is to show that one can replicate earlier results before going on to do further work in a given area of research. Given the inevitable differences in an exact replication, the findings necessarily have implications for generality. If the same results are obtained, not only is confidence in the reality of the phenomenon increased, but some indication of its generality has also been demonstrated.

Failure to replicate a previous finding is more difficult to interpret. Given the inevitable differences in a replication study, a single failure to replicate might mean that the original results were a fluke, a Type I error of inference. However, it might also mean that one or more of the differences in the replication attempt were crucial. The first possibility suggests that the original finding was invalid, a chance occurrence. The second possibility suggests that the finding was valid but of limited generality. Although a single failure to replicate is inconclusive, repeated failures strongly suggest that the original finding was invalid, a fluke.

Conceptual Replication

Even more common than exact replications are replications in which the same variables are investigated using procedures that differ on purpose from those of a previous study. Here the focus is directly on the issue of the generality of a previous finding. Such studies are called *conceptual replications* because the same conceptual variables are explored using different methods. A common form of conceptual replication is the use of different operational definitions. If one frustration experiment uses unsolvable maze problems to manipulate frustration and a subsequent experiment uses direct insult, the latter study is a conceptual replication. Conceptual replication is a powerful way of exploring the generality of relationships because it focuses on validity at the conceptual level.

Sometimes procedural changes are introduced to correct weaknesses in an earlier study that failed to find a relationship. The goal is to obtain a different result from that of the earlier study, to succeed in finding a relationship where the earlier study failed. Generality is explored because the boundary conditions for obtaining the relationship are being determined. For example, Wright and Contrada (1986) felt that the general failure of the Walster group to find a relationship between hard-to-getness and desirability was caused by flaws in the earlier study. They set up a dating situation similar to that of the Walster study but with two key differences. First, information on potential dates included no data on their reaction to the participant. The purpose was to avoid any influence of personal ego involvement on the part of the participant. Second, potential dates with medium values of hard-to-getness were included in addition to those with low and high values. Wright and Contrada found that the potential date with medium hard-to-getness was rated most desirable, while potential dates with high and low values did not differ from each other. Thus, even when a conceptual replication fails to duplicate the findings of an earlier study, valuable information about the generality of a phenomenon can be obtained.

As you can see, replication, exact or conceptual, makes a valuable contribution by providing evidence on the important issue of generality. In addition, replication research typically leads to many good ideas for an expanded program of further research. Thus, replication should be seen as a highly desirable starting point by beginning researchers.

GENERALIZING ACROSS EXISTING STUDIES

The inevitable result of conceptual replication is a body of research on the same general phenomenon using numerous variations in procedure. What conclusions can be drawn from such a body of research, and how does one go about drawing them? The problem here is to extract valid generalizations from a collection of studies that may be very large. There are two approaches, one traditional and one modern. Each has advantages and disadvantages.

The traditional approach is the literature review. The reviewer reads the existing literature on a particular topic and then writes a paper summarizing the findings. Typically, the findings are sorted into three categories: those strongly supported by numerous conceptual replications, those less strongly supported, and those where the literature contains contradictory findings. In the best literature reviews, the writer also provides a conceptual or theoretical framework for organizing the findings. The advantage of a literature review is that it allows a researcher to find out what is going on in an area of research without having to do his or her own review. The drawback is that any such review will reflect the subjective judgments of the reviewer. It is very difficult to attain objectivity when attempting to summarize a vast and contradictory literature because all human beings are subject to problems with information overload. Still, literature reviews provide a valuable service to researchers. In each of the social sciences, one or more journals are devoted primarily or solely to literature reviews.

If you would like to get a feel for the task confronting a reviewer trying to integrate the findings from several studies, consider the following question. How might one reconcile the findings of the Walster and Wright-Contrada experiments on playing hard to get? The Walster study found that selective hard-to-getness (high for others, but low for the participant) produced increased desirability. The Wright study found that medium values of hard-to-getness for others produced increased desirability compared to either high or low values.

Can you think of a theoretical framework that could explain both results? (Q3)

The more recent approach for generalizing from large numbers of existing studies is called meta-analysis (Rosenthal, 1984). In *meta-analysis,* the results of a number of studies are combined statistically to provide an estimate of the strength of relationships across all of the studies. The element of subjectivity is largely removed from conclusions. However, not all relevant studies may provide enough information to be included in the meta-analysis, and thus the sample of included studies might be biased. Also, the analyst must devise a way of assessing the relative quality of the various studies included in a meta-analysis. Despite these problems, meta-analysis is becoming increasingly common and has been favorably compared with traditional literature reviews (Beaman, 1991).

GENERALIZATION AND APPLICATION

No discussion of generalization would be complete without a brief consideration of how well results of scientific studies can be applied to solve practical problems. Chapter 1 distinguished between basic and applied research. The former seeks to discover general principles, the latter to solve practical problems. Even though such a distinction can be made, one dimension of generality for all scientific research is the extent to which the results may be applied to the problems of real life.

The social sciences have fared well in this respect. Psychological research has provided practical means for reducing stress, conquering undesirable habits or behaviors, improving educational and work environments, and reducing intergroup conflicts. Sociological research has led to the development of social indicators for assessing the noneconomic quality of life and to survey techniques that have provided knowledge about a variety of subjects not easily approached by other methods (e.g., the incidence of sexual behaviors). Anthropologists have uncovered many differences among cultures, such as differing norms for personal space, that have permitted cultures to interact without misunderstanding. Economists have developed models for forecasting economic trends. Finally, social scientists of all persuasions have pooled their talents in *program evaluation research* to provide an assessment of social programs and interventions before, during, and after they are implemented. Despite the many limitations on generality covered in this chapter, the findings of social science have generalized broadly to the problems of everyday life.

SUMMARY

External validity refers to the extent that a finding generalizes beyond the circumstances under which it was obtained. To determine whether a finding generalizes across values of a given variable, one must have a representative sample of values for that variable. If so, the question of generality becomes one of interaction. If the evidence shows that the finding remains essentially the same across values of the variable in question (no interaction), then the finding generalizes with respect to the variable. If the finding changes substantially in nature across values of the variable (interaction), then the finding does not generalize with respect to the variable.

One can raise the question of generality with respect to several classes of variables involved in any research study: participant characteristics, researcher characteristics, procedures, and measures. In each case, common variables that may lead to limited generality can be identified. For example, participant characteristics such as educational status, volunteer status, and gender may limit the generality of findings. Procedures such as the use of a pretest raise concerns about the generality of results. The issue of whether laboratory results apply in the "real" world is a common concern. The generality of results with respect to different operational definitions of independent and dependent variables is another common question. Special approaches have been developed to address these issues: including participant and researcher characteristics as treatment variables in factorial designs, the Solomon four-group design, multiple manipulations and measures of the same variables within one study, field research, and simulation. Perhaps the best approach of all is replication, exact and (especially) conceptual.

Generalizing across an existing body of literature on a topic has traditionally been accomplished by a literature review, a subjective approach that relies on the judgment of the reviewer. A more recent approach is meta-analysis, an objective statistical approach for combining results across studies. If the generality of research in the social sciences is judged by how widely research results have been applied to everyday problems, then it is fair to say that social-science research has demonstrated a great deal of generality.

ANSWERS TO QUESTIONS

Q1. This result does not generalize across gender of rater. The researchers found that rated sexual content predicted rated funniness only for male raters, not for female raters. Ratings of sexism, on the other hand, predicted funniness only for females, another result that failed to generalize across gender of rater. The relationship between rated sexism and funniness for females was negative.

Q2. A plausible prediction is that the relationship between frustration and aggression would be stronger with a pretest than without one. With an aggression pretest, there is little reason for participants to deduce that increased aggression is expected after working on an easily solved maze problem, but they would very likely make such a deduction after working on an unsolvable maze problem. Thus, demand characteristics would be greater in the high-frustration-pretest condition than in the low-frustration-pretest condition. This should produce a stronger relationship between frustration and aggression when a pretest is present than when it is not.

Q3. The selectively hard-to-get theory should be able to handle both results. You already know how it accounts for the Walster findings. For the Wright study, we need only assume that the participant desires a selectively hard-to-get date, but has only hard-to-get-for-others (HGO) information to work with. Clearly potential dates with high and low HGO values are ruled out. Only dates with medium HGO values could possible qualify as selectively hard-to-get. Thus, they are rated higher in desirability.

FURTHER READING

Sommer and Sommer (1991) have an informative chapter on simulation. In addition to Rosenthal (1984), standard references on meta-analysis include Glass, McGaw, and Smith (1981), Hedges and Olkin (1985), and Hunter and Schmidt (1990). For students who wish to know more about program evaluation research, Monette, Sullivan, and DeJong (1990) and Smith (1991) have up-to-date chapters. Standard references include Putt and Springer (1989), Rossi and Freeman (1985), and Tripodi (1983). An excellent book to sharpen your thinking about issues of generality and about the implications of social-science research is Stanovich (1992).

REFERENCES

Aronson, E., Brewer, M., & Carlsmith, J. M. (1985). Experimentation in social psychology. In G. Lindzey & E. Aronson (Eds.), *Handbook of social psychology* (2nd ed., pp. 441–486). Hillsdale, NJ: Lawrence Erlbaum Associates.

Beaman, A. (1991). An empirical comparison of meta-analytic and traditional reviews. *Personality and Social Psychology Bulletin, 17,* 252–257.

Brunswik, E. (1956). *Perception and the representative design of psychological experiments.* Berkeley and Los Angeles: University of California Press.

Glass, G. V., McGaw, B., & Smith, M. L. (1981). *Meta-analysis in social research.* Beverly Hills, CA: Sage.

Hedges, L. V., & Olkin, I. (1985). *Statistical methods for meta-analysis.* Orlando, FL: Academic Press.

Hood, T. C., & Back, K.W. (1971). Self-disclosure and the volunteer: A source of bias in laboratory experiments. *Journal of Personality and Social Psychology, 17,* 130–136.

Hunter, J. E., & Schmidt, F. L. (1990). *Methods of meta-analysis: Correcting error and bias in research findings.* Newbury Park, CA: Sage.

Kintz, N. L., Delprato, D. J., Mettee, D. R., Persons, C. E., & Schappe, R. H. (1965). The experimenter effect. *Psychological Bulletin, 63,* 223–232.

Love, A. M., & Deckers, L. H. (1989). Humor appreciation as a function of sexual, aggressive, and sexist content. *Sex Roles, 20,* 649–654.

Monette, D. R., Sullivan, T. J., & DeJong, C.R. (1990). *Applied social research: Tools for the human services* (2nd ed.). Fort Worth, TX: Holt, Rinehart and Winston.

Mundorf, N., Bhatia, A., Zillmann, D., Lester, P., & Robertson, S. (1988). Gender differences in humor appreciation. *Humor: International Journal of Humor Research, 1,* 231–243.

Putt, A. D., & Springer, J. F. (1989). *Policy research: Methods and applications.* Englewood Cliffs, NJ: Prentice-Hall.

Rosenthal, R. (1984). *Meta-analytic procedures for social research.* Beverly Hills, CA: Sage.

Rosenthal, R., & Rosnow, R. L. (1975). *The volunteer subject.* New York: Wiley.

Rossi, P., & Freeman, H. (1985). *Evaluation: A systematic approach* (3rd ed.). Beverly Hills, CA: Sage.

Sears, D. O. (1986). College sophomores in the laboratory: Influence of a narrow data base on social psychology's view of human nature. *Journal of Personality and Social Psychology, 51,* 515–530.

Smith, H. W. (1991). *Strategies of social research* (3rd ed.). Orlando, FL: Holt, Rinehart and Winston.

Solomon, R. L. (1949). An extension of control group design. *Psychological Bulletin, 46,* 137–150.

Sommer, B., & Sommer, R. (1991). *A practical guide to behavioral research: Tools and techniques* (3rd ed.). New York: Oxford University Press.

Stanovich, K. E. (1992). *How to think straight about psychology* (3rd ed.). New York: HarperCollins.

Stevenson, H. W., & Allen, S. (1964). Adult performance as a function of sex of experimenter and sex of subject. *Journal of Abnormal and Social Psychology, 68,* 214–216.

Tripodi, T. (1983). *Evaluation research for social workers.* Englewood Cliffs, NJ: Prentice-Hall.

Wright, R. A., & Contrada, R. J. (1986). Dating selectivity and interpersonal attraction: Toward a better understanding of the 'elusive phenomenon'. *Journal of Social and Personal Relationships, 3,* 131–148.

Ethics in Research

14

Ethics and morality both deal with what is good and right, as opposed to what is bad and not right. In the dictionary the two words are listed as synonymns. This chapter is about ethics in research, that is, about what researchers in the social sciences ought to do and ought not to do. More important, it is about the development of principles and procedures for guiding decisions about what researchers should or should not do in the conduct of their research. The word "ethics"will be used to describe the topic of this chapter, with no implication that a distinction is being drawn between ethics and morality.

Some ethical decisions are easy for researchers to make, but most are not. A researcher will quickly reject the option of killing humans as part of a research project because it will lead to much harm and little good. However, for many ethical decisions, the balance of good versus harm, benefits versus costs, good features versus bad features, is not so easy to see. What about spying on someone through a one-way mirror? Perhaps something extremely useful could be learned that could help 9.6 million people annually. Does that justify invading the privacy of people who do not know they are being watched? No? Then what if the results could benefit 26.6 million people? How much justification is needed? Most ethical decisions involve a delicate balancing act and therefore are often not easily made. No ethical question arises unless there is at least some potential for harm in the proposed course of action. The question then becomes whether or not sufficient good can be secured through the action to offset the harm and thereby justify taking the action.

To compound the problem, researchers are not neutral parties when it comes to making ethical decisions. They are biased toward carrying out the research they have proposed. Thus, without guiding principles and perhaps even formal social controls, it is a safe bet that ethically questionable practices would commonly occur in social-sciences research. Certainly the history of research in the social sciences offers plenty of examples of ethically controversial research. Here is a brief sample:

> Student volunteers are randomly assigned the role of prisoners in a simulated prison and are then subjected to so much stress by the "guards" that many of prisoners begin to show symptoms of emotional breakdown (Haney, Banks, & Zimbardo, 1973).

> A social scientist poses as a homosexual so that he can observe what homosexual men do in public restrooms (Humphreys, 1970).

> Social scientists hide under beds in college dorms to find out what college students talk about (Henle & Hubbell, 1938).

> A psychologist orders research participants to deliver what they incorrectly believe are painful electric shocks (the researcher lied to them) to victims in the next room (Milgram, 1963).

You will recognize some of these examples as research projects described earlier in this book. Such examples could be multiplied endlessly. Common ethical dilemmas emerge: stress, deception, invasion of privacy. This chapter covers some of the most common ethical dilemmas that arise in the course of social-sciences research. The chapter also describes the procedures that have evolved to deal with them.

TREATMENT OF PARTICIPANTS

The largest set of ethical issues involves the interaction between researchers and the participants in their research projects. There is an interaction between human beings going on here, and it should be guided by the same ethical considerations that apply to any such interaction. At the very least, researchers should observe the physician's maxim of doing no harm. Most researchers would agree, however, that the bare minimum is not good enough. A much better ideal to aim for is the golden rule: Do unto others as you would have them do unto you. In other words, the welfare of participants should be a major consideration in the planning of a research project. Not only should harm be avoided, but the researcher should try to make the participant's experience as positive and beneficial as possible. With these general considerations as background, let us examine some of the specific ethical problems that arise in the context of the researcher-participant interaction.

Stress

Perhaps the first concern of any researcher should be to avoid harmful procedures. The word "stress" will be used to refer to the immediate negative consequences, physical or psychological, of research procedures. The potential benefits of stress-inducing research must be weighed carefully against the negative consequences to the participants. The potential for stress in social-sciences research is very real, as some of the examples above illustrate. The prison-simulation experiment created so much stress for some of the prisoners that the experiment had to be terminated ahead of schedule. As a result, one of the researchers (Haney, 1976) subsequently wrote that his altered views about harming participants might well prevent him from performing such research.

Probably the most famous stress-inducing research of all time is Milgram's research on obedience (Milgram, 1963, 1965). Participants were ordered by an authority figure, the researcher, to deliver increasingly painful electric shocks to a "learner" whenever the latter made a mistake. No shocks were actually administered, but the participants did not know that. A film of the participants' reactions leaves little doubt that they experienced a great deal of stress. Protests, sweating, and nervous laughter were common. There are many other examples of harmful procedures in social-sciences research.

Largely as a result of studies like those just described, professional organizations representing various social sciences have adopted codes of ethical conduct for researchers. Excerpts from three of the more prominent codes are presented in Table 14.1 to give you an idea of what they are like. The complete codes are in the following references: American Anthropological Association (1983), American Psychological Association (1990), American Sociological Association Committee on Professional Ethics (1989).

Table 14.1   EXCERPTS FROM PROFESSIONAL CODES OF
ETHICS OF THREE NATIONAL ORGANIZATIONS: THE AMERICAN
ANTHROPOLOGICAL ASSOCIATION (AAA), THE AMERICAN PSYCHOLOGICAL
ASSOCIATION (APA), AND THE AMERICAN SOCIOLOGICAL ASSOCIATION (ASA)

Protection from Harm

Anthropologists must do everything in their power to protect the dignity and privacy of the
people with whom they work, conduct research or perform other professional activities. Their
physical, social, and emotional safety and welfare are the professional concerns of the anthropologists who have worked among them. (AAA)

The investigator protects the participant from physical and mental discomfort, harm and
danger that may arise from research procedures. . . . Research procedures likely to cause serious or lasting harm to a participant are not used unless the failure to use these procedures might
expose the participant to risk of greater harm, or unless the research has great potential benefit
and fully informed and voluntary consent is obtained from each participant. (APA)

The process of conducting sociological research must not expose respondents to substantial
risk of personal harm. (ASA)

Informed Consent

The aims of all their professional activities should be clearly communicated by anthropologists to those among whom they work. . . . They should inform individuals and groups likely to
be affected of any consequences relevant to them that they anticipate. (AAA)

. . . the investigator establishes a clear and fair agreement with research participants, prior
to their participation, that clarifies the obligations and responsibilities of each. . . . The investigator informs the participants of all aspects of the research that might reasonably be expected to
influence willingness to participate and explains all other aspects of the research about which the
participants inquire. . . . The investigator respects the individual's freedom to decline to participate in or to withdraw from the research at any time. (APA)

Informed consent must be obtained when the risks of research are greater than the risks of
everyday life. Where modest risk or harm is anticipated, informed consent must be obtained. . .
. Sociologists should take culturally appropriate steps to secure informed consent and to avoid
invasions of privacy. (ASA)

Protection of Privacy

The right of those providing information to anthropologists either to remain anonymous or
to receive recognition is to be respected and defended. . . . It should be made clear to anyone
providing information that despite the anthropologist's best intentions and efforts anonymity may
be compromised or recognition fail to materialize. . . . Anthropologists should not reveal the
identity of groups or persons whose anonymity is protected through the use of pseudonyms.
(AAA)

Information obtained about a research participant during the course of an investigation is
confidential unless otherwise agreed upon in advance. When the possibility exists that others
may obtain access to such information, this possibility, together with the plans for protecting confidentiality, is explained to the participant as part of the procedure for obtaining informed consent. (APA)

Subjects of research are entitled to rights of biographical anonymity. . . . To the extent possible in a given study, sociologists should anticipate potential threats to confidentiality. Such means as

the removal of identifiers, the use of randomized responses, and other statistical solutions to problems of privacy should be used where appropriate. (ASA)

Sources: American Anthropological Association. (1990).
Statements on ethics: Principles of professional responsibility (As amended through October 1990). Washington, DC: American Anthropological Association. Reprinted by permission.
American Psychological Association. (1990). Ethical principles of psychologists (amended June 2, 1989). *American Psychologist, 45,* 390–395.
American Sociological Association Committee on Professional Ethics. (1989). Code of ethics. Washington, DC: American Sociological Association. Reprinted by permission.

The main protection against harmful procedures in professional codes of ethics is the principle of informed consent. *Informed consent* means two things: (1) Participants must be given an accurate account of the potential risks before they consent to take part in a research study, and (2) they must be allowed to withdraw from a study at any time without negative consequences. The intent is to allow participants to know what they are getting into and to permit them to change their minds later if it looks like they made a bad choice. Most institutions in which research is conducted encourage the use of informed-consent forms. Such forms allow participants to express their understanding of the two aspects of informed consent and their willingness to proceed by means of a written signature. A sample informed-consent form is presented in Table 14.2. Informed consent has the advantage that it does not preclude stress-inducing research. Rather, it allows potential participants to make a free and informed choice to take part for the common good that may ensue from the knowledge generated by the research. Thus, the research becomes a virtuous experience for both researcher and participants. Meanwhile, those who do not care to subject themselves to stress are free to avoid participation.

Informed consent sounds pretty reasonable, but it is not without controversy and serious problems. On the one hand, there are those who think it necessarily creates biased samples and thus endangers the generality of results. On the other hand, there are those who think informed consent does not go far enough and that additional procedures are needed to protect participants from harm. One such procedure, review of proposed research by an ethics committee, will be described near the end of this chapter. Perhaps the main problem with informed consent is that it normally precludes another ethically questionable practice that researchers sometimes feel is necessary for valid results: deception.

Deception

Although less blatant than in the past, deception is probably the most common ethically questionable practice in social-sciences research. Examples include Milgram's lying to his participants about the electric shocks in his obedience studies, Humphreys (1970) misrepresenting himself as a homosexual, and Walster's (1973) misrepresentation of her research as a computer dating service. Deception is so

Table 14.2   SAMPLE INFORMED CONSENT FORM

INFORMED CONSENT FORM

I have been informed that the study in which I am about to participate is investigating factors that influence interpersonal attraction. I have also been informed that I will be asked to read descriptions of potential dates and then to rate each potential date for desirability. This will require one 60-minute session. This study is being conducted by Dr. Susan Smith, professor of psychology, whom I may contact at any time for additional information about the project. The study has been approved by the University Ethics Committee. I understand that the anticipated benefits of my participation are an opportunity to gain insight into social-science research methods and a chance to find out later about the factors that influence interpersonal attraction. I will also receive extra credit in my introductory psychology course for participating in this study, the amount of credit to be determined by my instructor.

I have been informed that there are no known risks to me from participation in this study.

I understand that my responses will be kept confidential and that no names will be used.

I will be free to ask questions about the study, and I may refuse to participate or withdraw from the study at any time without penalty.

My signature indicates that I have given my informed consent to participate in this study, that I have been allowed to ask questions about the study, that all such questions have been answered to my satisfaction, that I have been permitted to read this document and have been given a signed copy of it, that I am at least 18 years old and legally able to provide consent, and that to the best of my knowledge I have no physical or mental condition that would be harmed by my participation in this study.

Name (printed)_____
I hereby give my written consent to participate in this study.

Signature _____ Date _____

Witness Signature _____ Date _____

widespread that it even crept into the proposed frustration experiment. The plan was to give participants an unsolvable maze problem with the instructions that a reasonably intelligent person could solve it in a couple of minutes.

In the not-so-distant past, researchers seemed bent on outdoing each other in the cleverness of their deceptions. Rubin (1970) described the situation as "jokers wild in the lab" and Ring (1967) referred to a "fun and games" mentality among researchers. Rubin described the ultimate example of this mentality: a large complex-looking machine, a researcher who claimed that his entire future depended on the machine working properly, an explosion followed by billows of smoke from the machine, an emotional breakdown by the researcher, and finally a request for the participant to sign a petition. This elaborate deception increased the likelihood that the participant would sign.

The justification for deception is that it ensures natural behavior on the part of participants in situations where they might not behave naturally if they knew the truth. There can be no doubt that this justification has merit. As pointed out in Chapter 3, a major concern in observation research is that the observees will notice the observer and then act unnaturally. Validity of results is the strongest card a researcher can play to justify deception. Even so, that justification must be weighed against the harmful consequences of deception. Such consequences include not only the loss of trust between specific researchers and their participants but also the loss of trust in social scientists generally. Social scientists acquire a reputation as tricksters, and future generations of participants come to research settings expecting to be tricked, unwilling to believe anything they are told. Such an attitude may lead to unnatural behavior. Thus, if for no other reason than self-interest, social scientists have a stake in curbing deception in research as much as possible.

A number of alternatives to deception have been proposed. Kelman (1967) suggested role playing and simulation as possibilities. In role playing, participants assume an "as if" attitude, pretending they are in a certain situation and responding as they think they or someone else would respond. The problem, of course, is that the situation is not real and the participant knows it. Thus, a critic can always question the external validity of the results. As described in the previous chapter, a simulation is an imitation of a real-world situation, designed to resemble the real-world situation in all important functional characteristics. Putting participants in a simulated prison requires no deception. However, as the Stanford prison simulation study shows, simulations may have other problems. If they are too realistic, they may produce unacceptable levels of stress; if not realistic enough, the validity of the result may be questioned. Still, simulations are worth considering whenever a middle path between these problems can be charted.

Rubin (1973) suggested a different approach to avoiding deception, "honest" research. A number of honest research strategies are possible. One is simply to make participants fully aware of the purpose of the research. It may be possible to obtain valid data under such conditions more often than you would think, especially if the researcher is willing to make some extra effort. For example, instead of a bogus computer dating service, Byrne, Ervin, and Lamberth (1970) actually computer matched male and female students on high or low attitude similarity and then sent the couples on campus dates. The study measured how much the members of each couple liked each other and involved no deception whatever. A second strategy is to do research on real behavior-change programs, such as programs for quitting smoking or losing weight. Because the program is real, no deception need be involved. A third approach is field studies or field experiments in which participants may not even know that they are participating in research. Clearly, no deception is necessary, and such studies may also have a high degree of generality because of their realistic settings. Such studies may have other ethical problems, such as invasion of privacy (discussed below), but deception need not be a problem.

Despite the availability of alternatives, the plain fact is that sometimes deception is necessary. No alternative will do. If participants know the truth, they simply will not act naturally. Presumably, given the concern about ethical issues within the social sciences, such occasions will arise less often than they used to. That is, social scientists will decide that research involving serious deception simply is not worth doing. Even so, the ethical balancing act will sometimes land on the side of going forward with the research. In such cases, what can be done to minimize the negative consequences of deception?

The traditional procedure for dealing with cases where deception has been used is debriefing. *Debriefing* means two things: (1) a thorough explanation of the study, including justification for any ethically questionable practices like stress induction or deception and (2) removal or treatment of the effects of any harmful procedures. Most students understand that debriefing includes (1), but many are surprised to learn that it also includes (2). Researchers have an ethical obligation to remove, as nearly as possible, any harmful effects they have created. Studies have shown that proper debriefing is an effective way to remove the harmful effects of deception (Ring, Wallston, & Corey, 1970; Smith & Richardson, 1983).

Milgram's obedience studies illustrate how far a researcher may have to go in dealing with harmful effects. Participants were given a full explanation of the study, including reasons for the deception. They were made aware of the pressures imposed on them and were assured that their responses were normal. They were allowed to express themselves fully and to unload any emotional reactions they may have had. A friendly reconciliation with the victim followed. Some time later Milgram mailed a report to participants of the research, which included survey items asking about their reactions. The overwhelming majority were glad they participated and claimed to have benefited from the experience. A year later participants were interviewed by a psychiatrist. No ill effects of their participation were found. Most research studies would not have to go to the lengths that Milgram did to deal with harmful effects. The obedience studies illustrate the point that when serious stress is imposed on participants, serious follow-up obligations are incurred by the researcher.

Although it is imperative to remove harmful effects, researchers can and should aim for more. A research study provides an opportunity to achieve an ethical positive by making the experience educational for participants. That is the major goal of providing a thorough explanation of the study, preferably in the form of written feedback. Good feedback is written in a way that laypeople can understand, is brief and to the point, and contains information on how the participants can find out more about the study if they so desire. The latter should include some background references and information on how to contact the researcher for follow-up conversation on the study. A final point is that feedback should be made available but not forced on participants. If they do not want it, that is their business. In the matter of feedback, researchers should respect the participant's right to a free choice.

Invasion of Privacy

How would you like it if, unknown to you, someone observed your sexual behavior for research purposes? Perhaps you would prefer someone watching you urinate. Can't happen, you say? Guess again. Both of these scenarios have happened in actual research. Humphreys (1970) posed as a homosexual and observed homosexual behavior at highway rest stops. He played the role of "watchqueen," one who stands guard at the restroom door and warns those inside when someone approaches. If a social scientist can rationalize spying on homosexuals at rest stops, can you be certain that there is not one at the other end of a high-powered telescope just down the block from your bedroom window? Middlemist, Knowles, and Matter (1976) used a periscope concealed in a toilet stall to watch males urinate in college restrooms. The purpose was to investigate the effect of personal-space invasion by a confederate who used either the adjacent urinal or one farther away. Social scientists have even stooped to hiding under beds. As noted earlier, Henle and Hubbell (1938) had researchers hide under beds in dorm rooms to find out what college students talked about.

Clearly the ethical issue in these cases is the invasion of privacy represented by concealed observation. But concealed observation is not the only way that privacy may be invaded. After a researcher has collected data on any topic, however innocent, privacy is invaded if the data are accessed by anyone other than the researcher, especially if the participant's identity is part of the data. The threat of such invasion is real. There are cases in which courts have ordered social scientists to release their data for use in a lawsuit (Marshall, 1993). Should researchers refuse to reveal any part of a participant's data even under threat of death? What are the researcher's ethical obligations with respect to the safeguarding of data?

On the issue of concealed snooping and when it may be justified, little can be added to what has already been said. Researchers must carefully weigh the benefits to be gained from the research against the ethical costs and decide if the research is really worth doing on balance. They should note that the costs include not only the potential embarrassment or other harm that might occur to participants if they should ever find out that they were observed. There is also the harm done to the principle of the right to privacy itself whenever it is violated. Finally, there is the harm done to the reputation of social scientists when they acquire the reputation of peeping toms. The more intimate or sensitive the behavior in question, the more these considerations should weigh against concealed observation. A mature awareness of such considerations should lead to less hiding in bedrooms or bathrooms than in the past.

On the issue of safeguarding data, including the identity of participants, two procedures have evolved among social scientists for dealing with the problem. The cadillac of privacy techniques is *anonymity*, which means that the researcher does not know the identity of the participants in the study. Whenever anonymity is possible, it is the preferred approach because there is no way a researcher can reveal a participant's identity if that information was never collected. But anonymity is often not possible. The researcher may be required to keep a record of participants' names for administrative purposes, such as ensuring that participants are paid. In such a situation, the fallback strategy is *confidentiality*, which means that the identity of participants is known to the researcher but protected from public exposure. Confidentiality implies that a participant's name cannot be paired with his or her other data by unauthorized individuals.

Confidentiality comes in two forms. Strong confidentiality means that the names of participants are separated from their other data during or after data collection. The separation is done in such a way that names and other data cannot be reunited. Strong confidentiality is almost always possible when names must be collected and is thus the preferred form. Weak confidentiality means that names and other data remain paired, but the researcher refuses to reveal data-name pairs to unauthorized persons. With weak confidentiality, the participant's protection is only as good as the moral strength of the researcher. Still, weak confidentially is better than nothing, and it is the minimum that should be expected of an ethical researcher.

Harmful Consequences

Harm to participants can occur after a research study has been completed. Such harm has two forms. One is the aftereffects of harmful procedures. Such effects were covered in the discussion of debriefing. The researcher is ethically obliged to provide whatever follow-up may be necessary to counteract harmful aftereffects. The second form of harmful consequence occurs when a third party uses the results of the research to harm the participants.

As an example of the latter situation, suppose you do a research project in a certain school district and find, as you probably would (Benbow & Stanley, 1983), that by age 13 females have lower mathematical ability than males. Your results are used by the school board as justification for a policy of discouraging females in that district from taking advanced math courses in high school. An unlikely turn of events, but stranger things have happened. What should you do? As a researcher, you have an obligation to speak out publicly against improper interpretation and application of your results. What you are doing is known as *advocacy*, taking a public position regarding the interpretation and use of your results. There will be more about advocacy below because it is clear from this example that not only the participants in the research study but also all future female students will be harmed by the proposed use of the results. Here the point is that researchers must be prepared to take public action to defend participants against harmful uses of research results.

Exploitation

Exploitation means using others for selfish purposes. There is necessarily an element of exploitation in research because the researcher has a personal interest in the research project but no clear interest in the welfare of the participants. Thus, the researcher has an ethical obligation to be on guard against unnecessary exploitation. Such exploitation often shows up in the power relationship between researcher and participant. In many settings, such as universities and colleges, researchers have the power, directly or indirectly, to pressure people to participate in research. The temptation to use such pressure should be vigorously resisted. One way to resist it is to adopt formal rules that allow potential participants a range of choices, one of which is research participation. Another approach is to make research participation an extra-credit option rather than a requirement. The important point is to respect the potential participant's right to make a free choice. In other settings, such as prisons and certain hospitals, researchers work with captive samples, made available by those in charge. In such situations, the researcher has an obligation to remember that the participants are humans and should be treated accordingly.

Even when participation is completely voluntary, the participant is in the position of accepting the conditions laid down by the researcher. Thus, the researcher should not only plan the research to avoid harming the participant but also be on the alert for unforseen developments that might produce harm. The Stanford prison simulation shows how easily things can get out of hand. Avoidance of unnecessary exploitation is one of the primary goals of the codes of professional ethics. You are urged to become familiar with the code for your area of specialization.

The issue of exploitation is posed most acutely by the use of animals in research. Animals never have a free choice regarding participation, and they cannot defend themselves against abuse in research settings. Thus, they require special consideration from ethical researchers. The American Psychological Association has published detailed ethical guidelines for the use and treatment of animals (American Psychological Association, 1986). They deal with such topics as compliance with laws and regulations, proper training and monitoring of individuals using animals, minimizing pain and discomfort to animals, and appropriate methods of terminating an animal's life. The intent is to address some of the valid concerns raised by animal-rights activists. Abuse of animals is unethical and intolerable, and it is equally unethical to look the other way when witnessing abuse. On the other hand, some opponents of animal research take extreme positions that would prohibit any research using animals. It is also an ethical obligation of responsible scientists to resist such efforts.

PARTICIPATION

The word "participants" has been used in this book to describe those who produce the data in research projects. The traditional word, of course, is "subjects." That word was avoided because it devalues and deemphasizes the humanity of research participants. It implies that they are merely objects to be manipulated or measured and are best kept in the dark about what is going on so as not to bias their responses. In contrast, "participants" implies active human beings helping the researcher solve a common problem.

The distinction is not merely one of style. It has practical implications for researchers interested in obtaining valid data. Kaplan and Kaplan (1982) point out that the basic human need to comprehend what is going on will operate regardless of attempts by a researcher to maintain secrecy. If humans are not given useful information, they will invent their own explanations, and those explanations might not be anything like what the researcher would have preferred. Thus, by frustrating the human need to comprehend, the researcher may achieve the opposite of the intended goal, valid data.

Both ethical considerations and concern for valid data argue for viewing participants as partners in research. Such a view raises many questions about how to make the best use of their cognitive abilities. Those questions lead to an emphasis on presenting information to participants in a way that is easy to understand. The Kaplans have many useful suggestions for achieving this goal in the last two chapters of their book. Here let us simply note that viewing those who generate data as participants can be beneficial to all parties in the research setting. It also raises the interaction between researcher and participant to perhaps the highest ethical level possible.

OTHER ETHICAL ISSUES

The interaction between researcher and participant is the most direct interaction in the research process. However, when the process is viewed broadly, there are other interactions that raise ethical issues. Let us briefly review some of them.

Fraud

Fraud refers to dishonest reporting of data, methods, or results. It is, of course, imperative that scientists be honest in these matters. Fortunately, science has powerful deterrents against fraud. First, there is the knowledge that one's methods and findings will be carefully scrutinized by other scientists. Second, there is the possibility that replication will be attempted. Finally, there is the certain knowledge that one's career will be damaged if the scientific community concludes that fraud was committed.

As you might suspect, serious allegations of fraud are rare in the social sciences. A famous case involved Sir Cyril Burt who reported evidence suggesting a strong genetic influence on IQ. Careful examination of the data by Kamin (1974) uncovered suspicious regularities such as correlations for different samples that were exactly the same to the third decimal place. Further digging revealed that some of Burt's reported coworkers did not exist. Ironically, other research on intelligence supports a significant genetic influence. Nonetheless, Burt's data and his reputation suffered severe damage. Not everyone believes the case against Burt, and the matter is still being disputed.

It is not easy to prove fraud. Even repeated failures to replicate may indicate nothing more than that the original finding was an honest error or a chance occurrence. There are documented cases in the social sciences where fraud was suspected but not proved (Marlatt, 1983). Unfortunately, the mere suggestion of fraud is usually enough to damage a scientist's career. Thus, those who suspect fraud have an ethical obligation, too. Their obligation is to refrain from damaging someone's career unless the evidence of fraud is strong. Such evidence might consist of clear indications of wilfull carelessness or a deliberate attempt to deceive. Certainly negative emotional reactions to a researcher's findings is no excuse for alleging fraud.

Probably the most dangerous temptation a scientist faces is the temptation to cheat in small things. What harm could possibly come from changing just one or two scores from participants who obviously misunderstood the instructions because they produced the wrong results? There can be only one reply to this question. Fudging data is unethical. It can never be justified. If you have good reasons, you may be justified in omitting participants from your sample, provided that you report your reasons for inspection by the scientific community, but altering data can seldom be justified. If you think you are in an exceptional situation, you would be well advised to seek wise counsel. The road to fraud is paved with good intentions.

Use of Results

The danger here is misuse of results, including misinterpretation. The ethical obligation of the scientist is to resist such misuse. Often that means advocacy, taking a public position regarding the interpretation and use of one's results. Because scientific findings often have social or public policy implications, scientists cannot afford the luxury of an ivory-tower or hands-off attitude. They must try to protect not only their research participants but also anyone else who may be harmed unnecessarily by their results. The study of homosexual activity at highway rest stops is an example. Humphreys (1970) took the position that his results provided no excuse for the forces of social control to crack down on the "tearoom trade." Whether or not you agree with Humphreys is beside the point. The point is that he felt obliged to take a public position on the use of his results.

Distribution of Benefits

An intriguing ethical problem arises when a researcher wishes to study the effectiveness of an untested but potentially beneficial treatment like a new drug or a new therapy. The ideal approach would be to compare the new treatment to the currently accepted treatment in an experiment, with random assignment to conditions. The problem is that one would not be testing the new treatment unless there was good reason to think it might be superior. So how can one ethically justify withholding the treatment from participants in the control condition?

There are three approaches to this dilemma. One is to reason that assignment to conditions is a matter of the luck of the draw and that participants in the control condition are receiving the currently accepted treatment. Thus, no harm is being done to them relative to the current status quo. This approach works pretty well if one is not dealing with a life-or-death situation and the currently accepted treatment has some demonstrated effectiveness. For these situations, adding a second approach usually resolves the problem completely. The second approach depends on the outcome of the experiment. If the new treatment is found to be more effective than the current treatment, then the new treatment is made available to the control participants after the experiment has been completed. That way all participants realize its benefits.

Life-or-death situations are another matter and call for a third approach. An example would be a new treatment for cancer or AIDS. Thus, social scientists rarely face such situations. In any event, one cannot easily rationalize withholding the new treatment until after the study because there is a good chance that control participants may be dead by then. In such a situation, the researcher would have to use one of the quasi-experimental approaches described in Chapter 10. For example, the researcher could compare otherwise similar groups differing only in that one of them had received the new treatment and the other had not.

ETHICS COMMITTEES

Most universities and research centers require researchers to submit proposals to an ethics committee or an "institutional review board." The committee's function is to determine if the proposed research conforms to accepted ethical guidelines and to applicable laws and regulations. The amount of detail required in the proposal depends on the type of research, which in turn depends on the degree of potential risk to participants. The committee may allow the project to proceed as proposed, may ask for further information and perhaps modifications to reduce unacceptable risks, or may veto the project altogether. The latter outcome is rare because the very presence of an ethics committee inhibits researchers from proposing ethically irresponsible projects. You can see that an ethics committee serves a valuable purpose. It provides a formal step of ethical monitoring which examines all of the ethical issues discussed in this chapter.

The federal Department of Health and Human Services (HHS) requires every institution that receives funds from HHS to have an ethics committee. HHS regulations (Department of Health and Human Services, 1981, January 26) also categorize research according to the degree of risk for participants. The three categories are "at risk," "minimal risk," and "no risk." Review by an ethics committee is required for all proposed research in the first two categories. Most institutions go one step further and require review even for no-risk projects. The purpose is so that the ethics committee can agree in writing that the proposed research is indeed risk free. The good news is that much proposed research in the social sciences falls into the no-risk category, which includes most survey procedures and most studies involving observation of public behavior. The majority of the remaining proposals fall into the minimal-risk category, which includes studies of individual or group behavior using noninvasive measuring procedures that do not involve stress to participants. Review of no-risk and minimal-risk studies is fairly simple, but a more thorough examination of at-risk studies is made. This is reasonable given the importance of protecting the welfare of research participants.

Review by an ethics committee protects the researcher as well as participants. Written notice of approval from an ethics committee is formal proof that an officially designated body has examined the proposed research and pronounced it ethically fit. Provided the researcher satisfies all conditions imposed by the committee, such written proof can be produced later if participants should allege unethical treatment. Approval of the research proposal cannot guarantee victory in a legal battle, but it can certainly help one's chances.

Clearly, review by an ethics committee is good for all parties in the research process. Thus, it is something to be embraced, not avoided. However, it has one practical drawback that should be pointed out to the beginning researcher. It takes time, and like just about everything else in research, it takes more time than you think. So in setting up a timetable for a research project, it is wise to allow several weeks for the research proposal to clear the ethics committee.

SUMMARY

Research ethics deals with what researchers ought or ought not to do. This chapter surveys common ethical dilemmas in research and approaches for dealing with them. One set of ethical issues involves treatment of research participants. The two most common concerns in this category are harmful effects during research and deception. The accepted procedure for dealing with harmful effects is informed consent. Potential participants are given a full account of possible risks and then permitted a free choice regarding participation. They are also free to change their minds any time during the research procedure. Sometimes deception may be necessary. Although always desirable, debriefing is essential when deception is used. Debriefing includes a full explanation of what was done, including reasons for deception, and restoration of the participant's former physical and psychological states. Alternatives to deception should be considered, including role playing, simulation, and "honest research." Perhaps the highest form of honest research is to view participants as partners in solving a common problem. This implies making full use of their cognitive abilities by providing them with complete and easy-to-understand information.

Researcher have an ethical obligation to protect the privacy of participants. The identity of participants can be protected either by anonymity (the researcher does not know their identity) or by confidentiality (the researcher knows but will not reveal their identity). Harmful consequences following the research procedure may need to be dealt with by appropriate follow-up and possibly by advocacy, taking public positions on the use or interpretation of one's results. To avoid exploitation, the use of others for selfish purposes, researchers must beware of using their official status to pressure participants. Special guidelines have been formulated to prevent exploitation of animals used in research.

Other ethical issues encountered by researchers include fraud, use and interpretation of results, and distribution of benefits from research. Fraud, the dishonest reporting of data, methods, or results, can never be justified. Whenever improper uses or interpretations of results harm anyone, researchers are obliged to take public positions against such activities. Likewise, researchers should conduct studies in such a way that benefits of the research are not withheld from any participants. Ethics committees ensure that proposed research conforms to accepted ethical guidelines.

FURTHER READING

Among many excellent references on ethical issues in social-science research are the following: Beauchamp, Faden, Wallace, and Walters (1982), Blumer (1982), Keith-Spiegel and Koocher (1985), Kimmel (1988), and Steininger, Newell, and Garcia (1984).

REFERENCES

American Anthropological Association. (1983). *Professional ethics*. Washington, D.C.: American Anthropological Association.

American Psychological Association. (1986). Guidelines for ethical conduct in the care and use of animals. *Journal of the Experimental Analysis of Behavior, 45*, 127–132.

American Psychological Association. (1990). Ethical principles of psychologists. *American Psychologist, 45*, 390–395.

American Sociological Association Committee on Professional Ethics. (1989). *Code of ethics*. Washington, D.C.: American Sociological Association.

Beauchamp, T., Faden, R., Wallace, R. J., & Walters, L. (Eds.). (1982). *Ethical issues in social science research*. Baltimore: Johns Hopkins University Press.

Benbow, C. P., & Stanley, J. C. (1983). Sex differences in mathematical reasoning ability: More facts. *Science, 222*, 1029–1031.

Blumer, M. (Ed.). (1982). *Social research ethics*. London: Macmillan.

Byrne, D., Ervin, C. R., & Lamberth, J. (1970). Continuity between the experimental study of attraction and real-life computer dating. *Journal of Personality and Social Psychology, 16*, 157–165.

Department of Health and Human Services. (1981, January 26). Final regulations amending basic HHS policy for the protection of human research subjects. *Federal Register, 46*(16), 8366–8392.

Haney, C. (1976). The play's the thing: Methodological notes on social simulations. In M. P. Golden (Ed.), *The research experience* (pp. 177–190). Itaska, IL: F. E. Peacock.

Haney, C., Banks, W. C., & Zimbardo, P. G. (1973). Interpersonal dynamics in a simulated prison. *International Journal of Criminology and Penology, 1*, 69–97.

Henle, M., & Hubbell, M. B. (1938). "Egocentricity" in adult conversation. *Journal of Social Psychology, 9*, 227–234.

Humphreys, L. (1970). *Tearoom trade: Impersonal sex in public places*. Chicago: Aldine.

Kamin, L. G. (1974). *The science and politics of IQ*. New York: Wiley.

Kaplan, S., & Kaplan, R. (1982). *Cognition and environment: Functioning in an uncertain world*. New York: Praeger. (Ann Arbor, MI: Ulrichs)

Keith-Spiegel, P., & Koocher, G. P. (1985). *Ethics in psychology: Professional standards and cases*. New York: Random House.

Kelman, H. C. (1967). Human use of human subjects: The problem of deception in social psychological experiments. *Psychological Bulletin, 67*, 1–11.

Kimmel, A. J. (1988). *Ethics and values in applied social research*. Newbury Park, CA: Sage.

Marlatt, G. A. (1983). The controlled-drinking controversy: A commentary. *American Psychologist, 38*, 1097–1110.

Marshall, E. (1993). Court orders 'sharing' of data. *Science, 261*, 284–286.

Middlemist, R. D., Knowles, E. S., & Matter, C. F. (1976). Personal space invasion in the lavatory: Suggestive evidence for arousal. *Journal of Personality and Social Psychology, 33*, 541–546.

Milgram, S. (1963). Behavioral study of obedience. *Journal of Abnormal and Social Psychology, 67*, 371–378.

Milgram, S. (1965). Some conditions of obedience and disobedience to authority. *Human Relations, 18*, 57–76.

Ring, K. (1967). Experimental social psychology: Some sober questions about frivolous values. *Journal of Experimental Social Psychology, 3*, 113–123.

Ring, K., Wallston, K., & Corey, M. (1970). Mode of debriefing as a factor affecting reaction to a Milgram-type obedience experiment: An ethical inquiry. *Representative Research in Social Psychology, 1*, 67–88.

Rubin, Z. (1970, December). Jokers wild in the lab. *Psychology Today*, pp. 18, 20, 22–24.

Rubin, Z. (1973). Designing honest experiments. *American Psychologist, 28*, 445–448.

Smith, S. S., & Richardson, D. (1983). Amelioration of deception and harm in psychological research: The important role of debriefing. *Journal of Personality and Social Psychology, 44*, 1075–1082.

Steininger, M., Newell, J. D., & Garcia, L. T. (1984). *Ethical issues in psychology*. Homewood, IL: Dorsey.

Walster, E., Walster, G. W., Piliavin, J., & Schmidt, L. (1973). "Playing hard to get": Understanding an elusive phenomenon. *Journal of Personality and Social Psychology, 26*, 113–121.

Research Methods and Critical Thinking

15

Early in Chapter 1, you will find the following statement: ". . . a basic theme of this book is that a mastery of scientific thinking can provide a valuable framework for evaluating information and for reasoning. . . ." The discussion there pointed out that in contrast to other approaches to truth, the scientific approach relies on *empirical verification.* That is, propositions are regarded as true if they agree with what one observes. Using observations made under controlled conditions to reach conclusions is at the core of the scientific method. The observations are *samples* of whatever one is trying to understand. The name of the game is to use the sample evidence to reach valid general conclusions about the phenomenon under study. The crucial step of *generalization* is aided by the techniques of statistical inference. They provide a formal procedure for valid generalization based on sample evidence, but statistical inference is a special case of *inductive inference*—reasoning from the particular to the general. Thus, inductive inference is at the core of the scientific approach. The quotation at the beginning of this paragraph amounts to an assertion that inductive inference should be a major focus of an introductory research methods course and that it also has valuable applications to everyday thinking.

The purpose of this chapter is to show you how inductive inference, as practiced in the scientific method, can aid you in thinking critically about everyday matters. Applications of scientific thinking to everyday thinking have been discussed throughout this book. The purpose here is to remind you of those applications by pulling them all together in one place. In the process, you will also get a review of the basic concepts and principles of research methods.

GENERALIZATION REVISITED

As noted in Chapter 1, inductive inference or generalization can be seen as a major goal of science, second only to the goal of understanding natural phenomena. There are three reasons why generalization, via statistical inference, should be a major focus of the introductory research methods course. First, generalization can be found virtually everywhere in the typical research methods course. The next paragraph expands on this assertion. Thus, it is not a question of whether generalization is present throughout the course material. Rather, it is a question of whether the instructor makes its presence clear and thereby takes the opportunity to teach a valuable thinking skill. Second, generalizing is something people do constantly in everyday life. Often it has important consequences. Stereotyping is one example, and surely you can provide many others. Thus, there is the added benefit of learning a thinking skill that is clearly relevant to your everyday life. Third, research evidence suggests that statistical inference, as a form of inductive inference, is more readily teachable to humans than other kinds of thinking such as deductive inference (Nisbett, Fong, Lehman, & Cheng, 1987). In fact, it seems that people naturally acquire statistical rules of thumb in the course of solving everyday problems. Ironically, such rules of thumb are generalizations derived by inductive inference from repeated experiences with similar situations.

The reason generalization is present throughout the research methods course is that scientists never want to limit their conclusions only to the objects they have actually measured in a given study. The goal is always to generalize the results to whatever larger body of objects is represented by the objects actually measured. Every topic covered in the course is aimed directly or indirectly toward making such inferences safely. Even techniques for simply describing the data in a sample should be understood as preliminary steps. The point is not merely to describe the sample but to use the sample evidence in the process of reaching a conclusion about the population. Thus, generalization, or inductive inference, casts its shadow over the entire research endeavor.

Certainly, valuable thinking skills other than generalization are involved in the scientific method. Two such thinking skills, deductive inference and creative thinking, were discussed in Chapter 1. It was pointed out that scientists need to develop both their deductive reasoning abilities and their creative thinking skills. Nevertheless, neither deduction nor creative thinking are distinguishing features of the scientific method. The chief distinguishing feature is empirical verification, which proceeds by way of inductive inference.

TYPES OF GENERALIZATION

Researchers typically want to make one of two types of inductive inferences or generalizations. In Chapter 1, they were referred to as motives for doing research. One is far more common than the other. First, and less commonly, a researcher may want to reach a conclusion about a single variable. Some authors call these inferences "state descriptions" because the goal is to decide about the state of a given variable in a certain population. For example, one might want to determine the state of the variable, "preference for candidate Smith," in the population of voters. In statistics, this sort of inference is covered under the topics of point estimation or single-sample hypothesis testing. Informally, one wants to know what the distribution of scores looks like for a single variable in a population of interest. This is the curiosity motive for doing research. It is probably more common in applied than in basic research.

The second and more common type of generalization, especially in basic research, is a generalization about a relationship between variables. For example, one might wish to find out whether frustration is related to aggression in the population of college undergraduates. The ultimate goal of research is to understand variables in terms of their relationships with other variables. A special case of generalization about relationships is when the researcher also wants to reach a conclusion about cause. For example, the frustration-aggression theory says that frustration causes aggression and thereby explains the relationship between the two variables. As you know, one must satisfy certain conditions to reach a safe conclusion about a relationship and even stricter conditions to reach a safe conclusion about a causal relationship. As noted in Chapter 2, one can get into murky philosophical waters with the concept of cause. In any case, the focus of scientific interest is on relationships, and thus the concept of a relationship ought to be the core concept of a course in research methods. It follows that fully explaining the concept and the conditions that must be satisfied to reach safe conclusions about relationships should be the most important task in such a course.

In addition to its central position in research methods, the concept of a relationship between variables has great practical use. In everyday life, you are bombarded by claims of such relationships. Sources of these claims range from advertisers and politicians to preachers and teachers, all claiming a relationship between doing what they want you to do and some form of satisfaction. In learning about the conditions that must be met for such claims to be legitimate, you are providing yourself with an extremely valuable thinking tool.

RULES OF GENERALIZATION

It seems fitting to conclude this book by reviewing four "rules" of inductive inference or generalization. These rules specify the conditions that must be met for safe or valid generalizations. They also further illustrate the point that generalization is a central concept in the research methods course. The rules were borrowed from a book by Anderson (1980) entitled *The Complete Thinker.* The first two rules apply to all generalizations. The last two apply only to generalizations about relationships. You will see that these rules encompass much of the material commonly found in an introductory research methods course.

Operational Definitions

The first rule is known as the *Operational Definitions rule.* It stresses the importance of clear definitions of terms when making generalizations. Basically, the rule says that (a) one must be clear in using words that make reference to the world and (b) a good way to do so is to define key words in terms of what one must do to determine where they apply and where they do not. In the scientific method, this is accomplished by defining variables in terms of the specific operations necessary to measure or manipulate them. Chapter 2 used the metaphor of an operational definition as a recipe to bring home this point. That is, one must list all ingredients, amounts, how to mix them, and all other details of cooking temperature, time, etc., needed to cook up a specific value of the variable for any object one wants to measure or manipulate. This kind of thinking readily transfers to everyday life. It alerts you to the importance of clarity in use of terms when making informal generalizations so that all parties can be sure they are talking about the same thing.

Clarity of definitions influences the process of generalization at two points. The first is during the gathering of evidence. As you saw in the chapters on observation and measurement, the fuzzier the variable definitions, the greater the likelihood of disagreement about the data. The same behavior is seen as patriotism by one person but as treason by another. The formal term for describing disagreement in data caused by fuzzy definitions is unreliability. Whatever you call it, such disagreement can lead to one person's "evidence" showing a relationship between variables, while another person's "evidence" shows no relationship. The problem is sloppy evidence resulting from sloppy definitions.

The second point at which clarity of definitions can influence the generalization process is when the results are interpreted after the data have been gathered.

Even if clear definitions were used by those who gathered the data, others who later interpret the results may use their own definitions. Obviously, this can lead to sharp disagreements about what the results "really mean." Was the latest military venture a success or a failure? It may depend on whether you define success in terms of enemy forces killed or innocent civilians killed. At least the source of disagreement can be pinpointed if all parties are forced to make their definitions clear.

Sampling

The second rule is the *Sampling rule.* It says that to make a safe generalization about a population of objects one must obtain a sample from the population that is both adequate in size and unbiased. The adequate-size criterion is aimed at reducing random error in sampling or, equivalently, increasing precision of estimation. The bias criterion is aimed at eliminating constant error in sampling which can completely invalidate a generalization. The specialized sampling techniques discussed in Chapter 7 are designed primarily to eliminate sources of bias in sampling.

The concepts of precision and bias in sampling have wide application in everyday life. Most students coming into the research methods course are willing to make informal generalizations based on grossly inadequate sample sizes (often from a sample of one) and to overlook common sources of bias in sampling. Alerting you to the issues of sample size and bias can help you make better generalizations in your own lives. Two good rules of thumb would be these: (1) Always resist the impulse to jump to a conclusion whenever there is time to gather more evidence, and (2) be on the lookout for common sources of bias in your informal sampling. A good research methods course will make you aware of the many kinds of objects that are simultaneously sampled in both formal research and informal decision making. People, environments, stimuli, and time periods are just a few examples of the types of "objects" typically sampled when making a single generalization. All are potential sources of bias.

Chapter 7 discussed two common sources of bias in informal sampling. One is the tendency to rely on personal experiences when reaching conclusions about facts in general. Reliance on personal experience is usually a sensible way to generalize about one's personal life, but it can cause trouble when used as a basis for reaching conclusions about facts in general. The reason is that personal experience may be peculiar or biased. Armed with this knowledge, you should be leery of using your personal experience to reach conclusions about the world in general. If external sources of evidence are available, particularly if they are in the form of scientific data, bend over backward to give them due weight and a sympathetic hearing. This is especially important when the external evidence conflicts with your personal experience. Seriously consider the possibility that your experience may be biased, and actively search for possible sources of such bias.

The second common source of bias in informal sampling is confirmation bias—the tendency to favor evidence that agrees with one's current position and to discount evidence that disagrees with it. Researchers are not in agreement about the causes of confirmation bias. The discussion in Chapter 7 suggested that it may be a byproduct of the bias toward relying on personal experience. That is, people usually arrive at their current positions on issues that matter to them after long and sometimes painful personal experience. Thus, they are reluctant to alter their positions. Whatever its causes, confirmation bias makes it very difficult for people to be changed by relevant evidence, and it can lead to the worst kind of close-mindedness. Again, armed with this knowledge, you should bend over backward to give opposing viewpoints an open-minded and sympathetic hearing. A good approach is to make a habit of sincerely role playing someone who holds an opposing point of view. It will not be easy. You will have to force yourself to argue persuasively against your cherished beliefs. You may need the help of a friend who will monitor you against backsliding. If you can successfully counter the tendency toward confirmation bias, then whatever position you emerge with is likely to be a fair and valuable one.

Relationships

The third rule is the *Comparison rule*. It spells out the conditions that must be met to infer that a relationship between two variables exists. The rule states that one must be able to find out what happens to each variable as one looks across values of the other variable. The rule implies that an adequate number of instances of at least two values for each of the two variables must exist. Only then can one show that the two variables change values together in a systematic fashion, or covary, which is the definition of a relationship.

This chapter has already stressed how important the concept of a relationship is to a course in research methods. You should also bear in mind that it is possible to make a fairly convincing case for the existence of a relationship when in fact there is none. One does this by reasoning from inadequate evidence, that is, by using data from fewer than two values on each of the two variables. Advertisers and other persuaders sometimes engage in such cognitive sleight-of-hand. Chapter 2 contained a few examples of errors in reasoning about relationships. The subject is of such great practical importance, however, that it is worthwhile to examine it in more detail. A thorough understanding of errors in reasoning about relationships will prepare you to deal with incorrect and possibly fraudulent claims about relationships.

Errors in Reasoning. Suppose you have been hired by the makers of Gruel, the hot breakfast cereal, to make their cereal look good to the public. You do a taste test on a representative sample of 100 hot-cereal users and obtain the data in Table 15.1. The observed frequencies are the same as in Table 2.1 in Chapter 2. The analysis in Chapter 2 made it clear that the variables are NOT related. (You may wish to review that discussion before continuing here.) Thus, the data indicate no relationship between brand of hot breakfast cereal and judged tastiness. Nevertheless, your job is to use the data selectively to make it appear that there is a relationship favoring Gruel without coming right out and saying so.

There are four ways to use less than the full information in a 2×2 frequency table to make it appear that the variables are related when in fact they are not. These represent errors in reasoning about relationships, and all four of them have been

Table 15.1 FREQUENCY TABLE FOR THE
VARIABLES CEREAL BRAND AND TASTINESS

		Cereal Brand		
		Gruel	*Mush-O-Meal*	*Total*
Tastiness	High	56	24	80
	Low	14	6	20
	Total	70	30	100

known to appear in advertising. The following discussion of these errors is similar to Anderson's (1971).

The first error occurs when you focus on a single cell of the table, usually the cell with the largest frequency. By doing so, you might be able to make a convincing statement implying a relationship. For example, you might say, "In our recent survey of hot-cereal users, 56 percent said Gruel had great taste. That's a majority in any crowd! Shouldn't you be eating Gruel?" Because it uses the information from only one cell of the table, this is known as the *single-cell* error. In modern advertising, it is considered fashionable to attack the competition directly. Here is the single-cell version of attack: "In our recent survey, only 24 percent of those sampled liked the taste of Mush-O-Meal. Need a change? Try Gruel." Two single-cell errors side by side can be powerfully misleading: "In our survey, 56 percent liked Gruel, but only 24 percent liked Mush-O-Meal. Gruel wins by better than two-to-one!" Forming percentages by dividing both cell frequencies by the common grand total (100) ignores the fact that the column marginal totals are greatly unequal, which is equivalent to ignoring the cell frequencies in the bottom row of the table (14 and 6). What is really happening, then, is two single-cell errors strung together. It looks like a legitimate comparison, but it is really a compound single-cell error.

The single-cell error may seem beneath contempt because it seems so simple and easy to spot. However, it is far more common than you might think. Whenever people focus on instances that support their current beliefs, they are making the single-cell error. Prejudice and superstition are often sustained this way. When a prejudiced person claims that all members of an ethnic minority group are uncouth because he has met a lot of uncouth members, he is considering only the uncouth-member cell. When a superstitious person says, "You just wouldn't believe how often my horoscope is correct," that person is considering only the horoscope-predicted-and-it-actually-happened cell. From a research methods standpoint, there are probably other problems as well in both cases, which shows that more than one thing can easily go wrong in "informal" research. In each case, however, there is a clear component of single-cell reasoning.

The second type of error is the *single-row* or *single-column* error. In research methods, this problem is often referred to as lack of a control group or a comparison group. In this error, only the frequencies from a single row or column of the frequency table are used. For example: "Eighty percent of those who tasted Gruel judged it high in tastiness. Shouldn't you join the crowd?" This is a single-column error (See Table 15.1) because only Gruel tasters are considered (56/70 = .80). A proper comparison would reveal that the same percentage of Mush-O-Meal tasters liked their cereal too, but it serves the advertiser's purpose to omit this information. Or: "Seventy percent of those who liked their cereal were eating Gruel. Shouldn't you join them?" This is a single-row error because only those who judged their cereal high in tastiness are considered ($56/80 = .70$). In fact, the same percentage of those who didn't like their cereal also ate Gruel, but it wouldn't do to bring that up. The problem with the single-row or column error is that there is no comparison with the value of the variable in the other row or column.

The third error is called the *diagonal* error because only the cells from one diagonal of the frequency table are used. The diagonal with the larger total, called the main diagonal, is usually more convincing. In Table 15.1, the upper-left and lower-right cells form the main diagonal. The diagonal error simply sums the frequencies in the diagonal cells and expresses the sum as a percentage of the grand total, ignoring the row and column marginal totals, which is equivalent to ignoring the frequencies in the other two cells. For Table 15.1, the diagonal error would look like this: "Sixty-two percent of those surveyed either liked Gruel or didn't like Mush-O-Meal. Buy Gruel!" Because both cereals were mentioned, it may seem like a comparison was made. But there was no comparison (the two cell frequencies were lumped together to yield one percentage), and the unequal marginal totals were ignored.

The last error is the ultimate in nerve because NO information from inside the frequency table is used. Only marginal totals are used, and so this is called the *marginal* error. If you say "Seventy percent of our sample tasted Gruel and 80 percent of our sample liked their cereal, so get some Gruel right away," you have committed the marginal error. The 70 and the 80 are marginal totals, each expressed as a percentage of the grand total (100). The "and" in the statement seems to imply a connection between the propositions that precede and follow it, but in fact there is no logical connection. All the statement really says is that one of the values of each variable occurred a lot. It actually says nothing that would allow one to decide if the variables are related.

You should study these examples thoroughly so that you can spot each type of error whenever you encounter it. The moral is that very convincing statements that imply a relationship often can be made, when there is really no relationship. The way to analyze apparent assertions about relationships is to recast such statements in terms of a 2×2 frequency table. Ask yourself what the variables are, what the values are, and just how much information from the table you have actually been given. A good practice exercise is to rename the variables and values of Table 15.1 and then work through some examples of your own. Try to form both a statement corresponding to each type of error and a valid statement about the degree of relationship. As an example, suppose the column variable is regular church attendance, with values of yes (left column) and no (right column), and the row variable is charitable contribution (monetary, other than to the church, within the last two weeks), also with values of yes (top row) and no (bottom row).

Compare your answers with those at the end of the chapter. (Q1)

Cause

The final rule for generalization is the *Controlled Comparison rule*. It specifies the conditions that must be met to infer a causal relationship. The rule says that to infer a causal relationship, one must compare values of the presumed causal variable that differ only with respect to the presumed cause. All other potential causes of the effect in question must be ruled out as causes. This is typically accomplished by either controlling or randomizing alternative causal variables. Achieving this state of affairs is precisely the purpose of the experimental method: Manipulate the independent variable or presumed cause, measure the dependent variable or presumed effect, and ensure that all other potential causes are not allowed to change systematically along with the presumed cause. Under these conditions, one can identify what in Chapter 2 was called "probable sufficient cause." That is about as close as the scientific method can come to pinning down cause. In practice, this means that a research methods course should include extensive coverage of control and randomization techniques. You may have noticed plenty of material on these subjects in Chapter 10. The ultimate purpose of such extensive coverage is the making of "good" generalizations about causal relationships.

The principle of controlled comparison can be applied to informal reasoning about cause in two ways. The preferred approach is to consider the possibility of actually doing a controlled comparison. The experimental method would be ideal, but even where it is not possible one can often approach the ideal by systematically examining one variable at a time under comparable conditions. You saw an example of this approach in Chapter 9 in the case of the stereo tuner that did not light up when the power was turned on. By checking one potential cause at a time (other switches, the power strip, the wall plug, the fuse box, etc.) under comparable conditions, the owner was able to zero in on the probable cause. People like auto mechanics, electricians, and others who have to diagnose causes for a living are accustomed to this kind of disciplined thinking. However, everyone could benefit from considering this strategy as a first option when trying to evaluate causal claims.

If a direct test is not possible because one cannot maintain comparable conditions, the principle of controlled comparison can still be used in evaluating the evidence offered to support causal claims. A second approach is to think hard about possible alternative causes that were not adequately ruled out. Once a plausible causal candidate has been suggested, many people are satisfied and simply do not try to think of alternatives. It is often amazing how many alternatives you can think of if you will just make the effort. Consider the advertising claim that "Mush-O-Meal gives you quick energy in the morning." The advertisement may then go on to cite research showing an energy gain after eating Mush-O-Meal.

> *The implication is that Mush-O-Meal is the cause of the energy burst. Maybe, but how many plausible alternative causes can you think of? (Q2)*

Finally, please bear in mind that there is a fine line between thinking of plausible alternative causes and making up rationalizations to defend against unwelcome information. The first is responsible critical thinking, but the second is irresponsible. The connection between smoking and cancer is a good example. The ideal experiment cannot be done with humans because it would be unethical. Instead, there are countless studies showing a relationship in humans plus controlled experiments on lower animals demonstrating a causal connection. Some people can confront this mountain of evidence and still deny a causal connection in humans because experimental evidence is lacking for humans. Technically, they are correct, but is this responsible critical thinking or rationalization? The same thing could be said about the relationship between wearing seat belts and traffic fatalities. Like almost any general principle, the controlled comparison rule can be abused. It is abused when it it used to deny the obvious implication of massive evidence obtained under the best scientific conditions attainable. There is something to be said for responsible critical thinking about cause.

IN CONCLUSION

This chapter made the point that generalization lurks almost everywhere in the introductory research methods course. Because this is so, because this thinking skill already occupies so much time in the course implicitly, why not make it explicit? The purpose of the preceding discussion has been to draw out the parallels between the statistical inference practiced in the scientific method and the informal generalizations people make every day. The goal is to improve your skills and abilities in everyday thinking. In that way, the research methods course explicitly becomes what it already is implicitly, a cornerstone of a truly general education.

SUMMARY

The ultimate goal of the scientific method is to understand natural phenomena by making generalizations based on empirical data. There are two kinds of generalizations of interest to the scientist: those dealing with single variables and those dealing with relationships between variables. This chapter describes four rules for making such generalizations validly and shows how the rules may be applied in everyday critical thinking.

The Operational Definition rule stresses the importance of clarity in the definition of key terms. Without such clarity, disagreement about how to measure the key variables and about how results should be interpreted is likely. The Sampling rule states that valid generalizations require samples that are adequate in size and unbiased. Thus, one should avoid jumping to conclusions based on small samples as well as common sources of bias in informal sampling. Examples of the latter include relying on personal experience to reach conclusions about the world in general and favoring evidence that agrees with one's current position (confirmation bias). The Comparison rule states that to establish a relationship between variables one must be able to compare at least two categories or values of either variable. The practical application is to make sure that such a comparison accompanies any claim of a relationship and to avoid the very convincing errors in reasoning (single cell, single row/column, diagonal, and marginal errors) that can arise based on incomplete evidence. The Controlled Comparison rule states that to establish cause one must compare values of the causal variable that differ only with respect to the causal variable. Thus, in everyday life one might try to evaluate causal claims either by setting up a controlled comparison or by examining existing evidence to see if plausible alternative causes have been convincingly ruled out.

ANSWERS TO QUESTIONS

Q1. Single-cell error: "Fifty-six percent of the sample were both church-goers and charitable. Therefore, church-goers are charitable." Single-column error: "Eighty percent of the church-goers were charitable. Therefore, ... " Single-row error: "Seventy percent of the charitable people were church-goers. Therefore, ... " Diagonal error: "Sixty-two percent of the sample were either charitable church-goers or noncharitable nonchurch-goers. Therefore, ... " Marginal error: "Seventy percent of the sample were church-goers, and 80 percent of the sample were charitable. Therefore, ... " Valid statement: "Eighty percent of both church-goers and nonchurch-goers are charitable. Therefore, church-going and charitableness are not related." Or: "Seventy percent of both charitable and noncharitable people are church-goers. Therefore, church-going and charitableness are not related."

Q2. Plausible alternative causes may include a certain ingredient in Mush-O-Meal (e.g., farina) that could just as easily be obtained in other cereals, any ingredient at all that has some nutritional value, or junk additives like sugar that give you a brief burst of energy, which does not last long. Barring evidence to the contrary, it is even possible that just sitting at the breakfast table has a placebo effect, providing a brief burst of energy.

FURTHER READING

The two books by Anderson (1971, 1980) contain extended discussions of how to use the evidence in 2×2 frequency tables to decide whether variables are related.

REFERENCES

Anderson, B. F. (1971). *The psychology experiment: An introduction to the scientific method* (2nd ed.). Monterey, CA: Brooks/Cole.

Anderson, B. F. (1980). *The complete thinker.* Englewood Cliffs, NJ: Prentice-Hall.

Nisbett, R. E., Fong, G. T., Lehman, D. R., & Cheng, P. W. (1987). Teaching reasoning. *Science, 238*, 625–631.

Statistical Tables

A

Table A.1   CRITICAL VALUES OF CHI-SQUARE

Degrees of Freedom	Probability level		
	.10	.05	.01
1	2.706	3.841	6.635
2	4.605	5.991	9.210
3	6.251	7.815	11.345
4	7.779	9.488	13.277
5	9.236	11.070	15.086
6	10.645	12.592	16.812
7	12.017	14.067	18.475
8	13.362	15.507	20.090
9	14.684	16.919	21.666
10	15.987	18.307	23.209
11	17.275	19.675	24.725
12	18.549	21.026	26.217
13	19.812	22.362	27.688
14	21.064	23.685	29.141
15	22.307	24.996	30.578
16	23.542	26.296	32.000
17	24.769	27.587	33.409
18	25.989	28.869	34.805
19	27.204	30.144	36.191
20	28.412	31.410	37.566

Source: Adapted from Table 8 (pp. 130–131) in E.S. Pearson and H.O. Hartley (Eds.), *Biometrika tables for statisticians,* Volume 1 (2nd ed.). New York: Cambridge University Press, 1958. Reprinted by permission.

Table A.2 CRITICAL VALUES OF r
(PEARSON PRODUCT-MOMENT CORRELATION COEFFICIENT)

	Level of significance for two-tailed test		
df	.10	.05	.01
1	.988	.997	.9999
2	.900	.950	.990
3	.805	.878	.959
4	.729	.811	.917
5	.669	.754	.874
6	.622	.707	.834
7	.582	.666	.798
8	.549	.632	.765
9	.521	.602	.735
10	.497	.576	.708
11	.476	.553	.684
12	.458	.532	.661
13	.441	.514	.641
14	.426	.497	.623
15	.412	.482	.606
16	.400	.468	.590
17	.389	.456	.575
18	.378	.444	.561
19	.369	.433	.549
20	.360	.423	.537
25	.323	.381	.487
30	.296	.349	.449
35	.275	.325	.418
40	.257	.304	.393
45	.243	.288	.372
50	.231	.273	.354
60	.211	.250	.325
70	.195	.232	.303
80	.183	.217	.283
90	.173	.205	.267
100	.164	.195	.254

The significance level is halved for a one-tailed test.

Source: Adapted from Table 13 (pp. 138) in E.S. Pearson and H.O. Hartley (Eds.), *Biometrika tables for statisticians, Volume 1* (2nd ed.). New York: Cambridge University Press, 1958. Reprinted by permission.

Table A.3　CRITICAL VALUES OF F

| df for denomi-nator (error) | p | \multicolumn{12}{c}{df for numerator (systematic)} |
		1	2	3	4	5	6	7	8	9	10	11	12
1	.25	5.83	7.50	8.20	8.58	8.82	8.98	9.10	9.19	9.26	9.32	9.36	9.41
	.10	39.9	49.5	53.6	55.8	57.2	58.2	58.9	59.4	59.9	60.2	60.5	60.7
	.05	161	200	216	225	230	234	237	239	241	242	243	244
2	.25	2.57	3.00	3.15	3.23	3.28	3.31	3.34	3.35	3.37	3.38	3.39	3.39
	.10	8.53	9.00	9.16	9.24	9.29	9.33	9.35	9.37	9.38	9.39	9.40	9.41
	.05	18.5	19.0	19.2	19.2	19.3	19.3	19.4	19.4	19.4	19.4	19.4	19.4
	.01	98.5	99.0	99.2	99.2	99.3	99.3	99.4	99.4	99.4	99.4	99.4	99.4
3	.25	2.02	2.28	2.36	2.39	2.41	2.42	2.43	2.44	2.44	2.44	2.45	2.45
	.10	5.54	5.46	5.39	5.34	5.31	5.28	5.27	5.25	5.24	5.23	5.22	5.22
	.05	10.1	9.55	9.28	9.12	9.01	8.94	8.89	8.85	8.81	8.79	8.76	8.74
	.01	34.1	30.8	29.5	28.7	28.2	27.9	27.7	27.5	27.3	27.2	27.1	27.1
4	.25	1.81	2.00	2.05	2.06	2.07	2.08	2.08	2.08	2.08	2.08	2.08	2.08
	.10	4.54	4.32	4.19	4.11	4.05	4.01	3.98	3.95	3.94	3.92	3.91	3.90
	.05	7.71	6.94	6.59	6.39	6.26	6.16	6.09	6.04	6.00	5.96	5.94	5.91
	.01	21.2	18.0	16.7	16.0	15.5	15.2	15.0	14.8	14.7	14.5	14.4	14.4
5	.25	1.69	1.85	1.88	1.89	1.89	1.89	1.89	1.89	1.89	1.89	1.89	1.89
	.10	4.06	3.78	3.62	3.52	3.45	3.40	3.37	3.34	3.32	3.30	3.28	3.27
	.05	6.61	5.79	5.41	5.19	5.05	4.95	4.88	4.82	4.77	4.74	4.71	4.68
	.01	16.3	13.3	12.1	11.4	11.0	10.7	10.5	10.3	10.2	10.1	9.96	9.89
6	.25	1.62	1.76	1.78	1.79	1.79	1.78	1.78	1.78	1.77	1.77	1.77	1.77
	.10	3.78	3.46	3.29	3.18	3.11	3.05	3.01	2.98	2.96	2.94	2.92	2.90
	.05	5.99	5.14	4.76	4.53	4.39	4.28	4.21	4.15	4.10	4.06	4.03	4.00
	.01	13.7	10.9	9.78	9.15	8.75	8.47	8.26	8.10	7.98	7.87	7.79	7.72
7	.25	1.57	1.70	1.72	1.72	1.71	1.71	1.70	1.70	1.69	1.69	1.69	1.68
	.10	3.59	3.26	3.07	2.96	2.88	2.83	2.78	2.75	2.72	2.70	2.68	2.67
	.05	5.59	4.74	4.35	4.12	3.97	3.87	3.79	3.73	3.68	3.64	3.60	3.57
	.01	12.2	9.55	8.45	7.85	7.46	7.19	6.99	6.84	6.72	6.62	6.54	6.47
8	.25	1.54	1.66	1.67	1.66	1.66	1.65	1.64	1.64	1.63	1.63	1.63	1.62
	.10	3.46	3.11	2.92	2.81	2.73	2.67	2.62	2.59	2.56	2.54	2.52	2.50
	.05	5.32	4.46	4.07	3.84	3.69	3.58	3.50	3.44	3.39	3.35	3.31	3.28
	.01	11.3	8.65	7.59	7.01	6.63	6.37	6.18	6.03	5.91	5.81	5.73	5.67
9	.25	1.51	1.62	1.63	1.63	1.62	1.61	1.60	1.60	1.59	1.59	1.58	1.58
	.10	3.36	3.01	2.81	2.69	2.61	2.55	2.51	2.47	2.44	2.42	2.40	2.38
	.05	5.12	4.26	3.86	3.63	3.48	3.37	3.29	3.23	3.18	3.14	3.10	3.07
	.01	10.6	8.02	6.99	6.42	6.06	5.80	5.61	5.47	5.35	5.26	5.18	5.11
10	.25	1.49	1.60	1.60	1.59	1.59	1.58	1.57	1.56	1.56	1.55	1.55	1.54
	.10	3.29	2.92	2.73	2.61	2.52	2.46	2.41	2.38	2.35	2.32	2.30	2.28
	.05	4.96	4.10	3.71	3.48	3.33	3.22	3.14	3.07	3.02	2.98	2.94	2.91
	.01	10.0	7.56	6.55	5.99	5.64	5.39	5.20	5.06	4.94	4.85	4.77	4.71

Table A.3   CRITICAL VALUES OF F (CONT.)

df for denomi-nator (error)	p	\multicolumn{12}{c}{df for numerator (systematic)}
		1	2	3	4	5	6	7	8	9	10	11	12
11	.25	1.47	1.58	1.58	1.57	1.56	1.55	1.54	1.53	1.53	1.52	1.52	1.51
	.10	3.23	2.86	2.66	2.54	2.45	2.39	2.34	2.30	2.27	2.25	2.23	2.21
	.05	4.84	3.98	3.59	3.36	3.20	3.09	3.01	2.95	2.90	2.85	2.82	2.79
	.01	9.65	7.21	6.22	5.67	5.32	5.07	4.89	4.74	4.63	4.54	4.46	4.40
12	.25	1.46	1.56	1.56	1.55	1.54	1.53	1.52	1.51	1.51	1.50	1.50	1.49
	.10	3.18	2.81	2.61	2.48	2.39	2.33	2.28	2.24	2.21	2.19	2.17	2.15
	.05	4.75	3.89	3.49	3.26	3.11	3.00	2.91	2.85	2.80	2.75	2.72	2.69
	.01	9.33	6.93	5.95	5.41	5.06	4.82	4.64	4.50	4.39	4.30	4.22	4.16
13	.25	1.45	1.55	1.55	1.53	1.52	1.51	1.50	1.49	1.49	1.48	1.47	1.47
	.10	3.14	2.76	2.56	2.43	2.35	2.28	2.23	2.20	2.16	2.14	2.12	2.10
	.05	4.67	3.81	3.41	3.18	3.03	2.92	2.83	2.77	2.71	2.67	2.63	2.60
	.01	9.07	6.70	5.74	5.21	4.86	4.62	4.44	4.30	4.19	4.10	4.02	3.96
14	.25	1.44	1.53	1.53	1.52	1.51	1.50	1.49	1.48	1.47	1.46	1.46	1.45
	.10	3.10	2.73	2.52	2.39	2.31	2.24	2.19	2.15	2.12	2.10	2.08	2.05
	.05	4.60	3.74	3.34	3.11	2.96	2.85	2.76	2.70	2.65	2.60	2.57	2.53
	.01	8.86	6.51	5.56	5.04	4.69	4.46	4.28	4.14	4.03	3.94	3.86	3.80
15	.25	1.43	1.52	1.52	1.51	1.49	1.48	1.47	1.46	1.46	1.45	1.44	1.44
	.10	3.07	2.70	2.49	2.36	2.27	2.21	2.16	2.12	2.09	2.06	2.04	2.02
	.05	4.54	3.68	3.29	3.06	2.90	2.79	2.71	2.64	2.59	2.54	2.51	2.48
	.01	8.68	6.36	5.42	4.89	4.56	4.32	4.14	4.00	3.89	3.80	3.73	3.67
16	.25	1.42	1.51	1.51	1.50	1.48	1.47	1.46	1.45	1.44	1.44	1.44	1.43
	.10	3.05	2.67	2.46	2.33	2.24	2.18	2.13	2.09	2.06	2.03	2.01	1.99
	.05	4.49	3.63	3.24	3.01	2.85	2.74	2.66	2.59	2.54	2.49	2.46	2.42
	.01	8.53	6.23	5.29	4.77	4.44	4.20	4.03	3.89	3.78	3.69	3.62	3.55
17	.25	1.42	1.51	1.50	1.49	1.47	1.46	1.45	1.44	1.43	1.43	1.42	1.41
	.10	3.03	2.64	2.44	2.31	2.22	2.15	2.10	2.06	2.03	2.00	1.98	1.96
	.05	4.45	3.59	3.20	2.96	2.81	2.70	2.61	2.55	2.49	2.45	2.41	2.38
	.01	8.40	6.11	5.18	4.67	4.34	4.10	3.93	3.79	3.68	3.59	3.52	3.46
18	.25	1.41	1.50	1.49	1.48	1.46	1.45	1.44	1.43	1.42	1.42	1.41	1.40
	.10	3.01	2.62	2.42	2.29	2.20	2.13	2.08	2.04	2.00	1.98	1.96	1.93
	.05	4.41	3.55	3.16	2.93	2.77	2.66	2.58	2.51	2.46	2.41	2.37	2.34
	.01	8.29	6.01	5.09	4.58	4.25	4.01	3.84	3.71	3.60	3.51	3.43	3.37
19	.25	1.41	1.49	1.49	1.47	1.46	1.44	1.43	1.42	1.41	1.41	1.40	1.40
	.10	2.99	2.61	2.40	2.27	2.18	2.11	2.06	2.02	1.98	1.96	1.94	1.91
	.05	4.38	3.52	3.13	2.90	2.74	2.63	2.54	2.48	2.42	2.38	2.34	2.31
	.01	8.18	5.93	5.01	4.50	4.17	3.94	3.77	3.63	3.52	3.43	3.36	3.30
20	.25	1.40	1.49	1.48	1.46	1.45	1.44	1.43	1.42	1.41	1.40	1.39	1.39
	.10	2.97	2.59	2.38	2.25	2.16	2.09	2.04	2.00	1.96	1.94	1.92	1.89
	.05	4.35	3.49	3.10	2.87	2.71	2.60	2.51	2.45	2.39	2.35	2.31	2.28
	.01	8.10	5.85	4.94	4.43	4.10	3.87	3.70	3.56	3.46	3.37	3.29	3.23

Table A.3   CRITICAL VALUES OF F (CONT.)

df for denominator (error)	p	1	2	3	4	5	6	7	8	9	10	11	12
						df for numerator (systematic)							
22	.25	1.40	1.48	1.47	1.45	1.44	1.42	1.41	1.40	1.39	1.39	1.38	1.37
	.10	2.95	2.56	2.35	2.22	2.13	2.06	2.01	1.97	1.93	1.90	1.88	1.86
	.05	4.30	3.44	3.05	2.82	2.66	2.55	2.46	2.40	2.34	2.30	2.26	2.23
	.01	7.95	5.72	4.82	4.31	3.99	3.76	3.59	3.45	3.35	3.26	3.18	3.12
24	.25	1.39	1.47	1.46	1.44	1.43	1.41	1.40	1.39	1.38	1.38	1.37	1.36
	.10	2.93	2.54	2.33	2.19	2.10	2.04	1.98	1.94	1.91	1.88	1.85	1.83
	.05	4.26	3.40	3.01	2.78	2.62	2.51	2.42	2.36	2.30	2.25	2.21	2.18
	.01	7.82	5.61	4.72	4.22	3.90	3.67	3.50	3.36	3.26	3.17	3.09	3.03
26	.25	1.38	1.46	1.45	1.44	1.42	1.41	1.39	1.38	1.37	1.37	1.36	1.35
	.10	2.91	2.52	2.31	2.17	2.08	2.01	1.96	1.92	1.88	1.86	1.84	1.81
	.05	4.23	3.37	2.98	2.74	2.59	2.47	2.39	2.32	2.27	2.22	2.18	2.15
	.01	7.72	5.53	4.64	4.14	3.82	3.59	3.42	3.29	3.18	3.09	3.02	2.96
28	.25	1.38	1.46	1.45	1.43	1.41	1.40	1.39	1.38	1.37	1.36	1.35	1.34
	.10	2.89	2.50	2.29	2.16	2.06	2.00	1.94	1.90	1.87	1.84	1.81	1.79
	.05	4.20	3.34	2.95	2.71	2.56	2.45	2.36	2.29	2.24	2.19	2.15	2.12
	.01	7.64	5.45	4.57	4.07	3.75	3.53	3.36	3.23	3.12	3.03	2.96	2.90
30	.25	1.38	1.45	1.44	1.42	1.41	1.39	1.38	1.37	1.36	1.35	1.35	1.34
	.10	2.88	2.49	2.28	2.14	2.05	1.98	1.93	1.88	1.85	1.82	1.79	1.77
	.05	4.17	3.32	2.92	2.69	2.53	2.42	2.33	2.27	2.21	2.16	2.13	2.09
	.01	7.56	5.39	4.51	4.02	3.70	3.47	3.30	3.17	3.07	2.98	2.91	2.84
40	.25	1.36	1.44	1.42	1.40	1.39	1.37	1.36	1.35	1.34	1.33	1.32	1.31
	.10	2.84	2.44	2.23	2.09	2.00	1.93	1.87	1.83	1.79	1.76	1.73	1.71
	.05	4.08	3.23	2.84	2.61	2.45	2.34	2.25	2.18	2.12	2.08	2.04	2.00
	.01	7.31	5.18	4.31	3.83	3.51	3.29	3.12	2.99	2.89	2.80	2.73	2.66
60	.25	1.35	1.42	1.41	1.38	1.37	1.35	1.33	1.32	1.31	1.30	1.29	1.29
	.10	2.79	2.39	2.18	2.04	1.95	1.87	1.82	1.77	1.74	1.71	1.68	1.66
	.05	4.00	3.15	2.76	2.53	2.37	2.25	2.17	2.10	2.04	1.99	1.95	1.92
	.01	7.08	4.98	4.13	3.65	3.34	3.12	2.95	2.82	2.72	2.63	2.56	2.50
120	.25	1.34	1.40	1.39	1.37	1.35	1.33	1.31	1.30	1.29	1.28	1.27	1.26
	.10	2.75	2.35	2.13	1.99	1.90	1.82	1.77	1.72	1.68	1.65	1.62	1.60
	.05	3.92	3.07	2.68	2.45	2.29	2.17	2.09	2.02	1.96	1.91	1.87	1.83
	.01	6.85	4.79	3.95	3.48	3.17	2.96	2.79	2.66	2.56	2.47	2.40	2.34
200	.25	1.33	1.39	1.38	1.36	1.34	1.32	1.31	1.29	1.28	1.27	1.26	1.25
	.10	2.73	2.33	2.11	1.97	1.88	1.80	1.75	1.70	1.66	1.63	1.60	1.57
	.05	3.89	3.04	2.65	2.42	2.26	2.14	2.06	1.98	1.93	1.88	1.84	1.80
	.01	6.76	4.71	3.88	3.41	3.11	2.89	2.73	2.60	2.50	2.41	2.34	2.27
∞	.25	1.32	1.39	1.37	1.35	1.33	1.31	1.29	1.28	1.27	1.25	1.24	1.24
	.10	2.71	2.30	2.08	1.94	1.85	1.77	1.72	1.67	1.63	1.60	1.57	1.55
	.05	3.84	3.00	2.60	2.37	2.21	2.10	2.01	1.94	1.88	1.83	1.79	1.75
	.01	6.63	4.61	3.78	3.32	3.02	2.80	2.64	2.51	2.41	2.32	2.25	2.18

Source: Adapted from Table 18 (pp. 157–163) in E.S. Pearson and H.O. Hartley (Eds.), *Biometrika tables for statisticians, Volume 1* (2nd ed.). New York: Cambridge University Press, 1958. Reprinted by permission.

Writing Research Reports **B**

MODEL RESEARCH PAPER

This appendix describes how to write research reports in the social sciences. It is important for you to know about the many conventions regarding organization of research papers and writing style. Such knowledge allows you to communicate clearly, concisely, and with professionalism to both peers in the social sciences and the general public.

The ultimate destination of any research paper you write is a scholarly journal in one of the social sciences. You should adopt this view even if you are merely fulfilling a class assignment. By doing so, you will acquire and practice habits of thinking and writing that will serve you well in both understanding and communicating research findings.

There are many sources of useful information that expand on the topics covered in this appendix. One of the best sources is free. Each journal publishes a style sheet, a summary of its requirements for submitted manuscripts, at least once a year. Style sheets are short outlines of the following information for a specific journal: where to send manuscripts, the kinds of papers the journal publishes, acceptable style for listing references and citing them within the manuscript, number of manuscript copies to be submitted, and other useful information. An indispensable reference for journals published by the American Psychological Association (APA) is the *Publication Manual of the American Psychological Association* (Fourth Edition, 1994). The APA manual is used as a style guide by many social-science journals. Copies are available in many college bookstores, or they may be ordered directly from the APA Book Order Department, P.O. Box 2710, Hyattsville, MD 20784. Many excellent references on writing style for research writing are available. Here are a few of them: Becker (1986), Day (1988), Friedman and Steinberg (1989), Sociology Writing Group (1991), and Sternberg (1988). Two of the best general references for writing and grammar are Shertzer (1986) and Strunk and White (1979).

Before specific topics are covered, three general principles of research writing in the social sciences should be stressed. First, learn to use a word processor. Computer composition allows you to make changes easily and painlessly. Many programs also provide spelling and grammar checking options. If you are serious about writing research reports or anything else, learning to use a word processor is the most important step you can take. Second, write from an outline. Although a detailed outline or format for research reports is presented in this appendix, use of your own outline within certain sections of the report (particularly the Introduction and Discussion sections) can help you organize your thoughts and present them in a clear and coherent fashion. Third, be prepared to revise your manuscript several times before the final product is achieved. Revision is not a sign of poor writing skill. On the contrary, it is the amateur who avoids revision. The serious writer accepts revision as a natural part of good communication. In fact, a good rule of thumb is to seek critical input after the first few drafts. Others will see problems in content and style that you might miss. Their inputs will improve your final draft. Journals in the social sciences routinely require revisions as a matter of course.

ORGANIZATION OF RESEARCH REPORTS

The vast majority of journals in the social sciences follow a standard outline for research reports. The sections in the standard outline are listed in order in Table B.1. Brief comments on each section follow. An expanded version of the outline and a model paper illustrating the expanded outline are presented at the end of this appendix.

Title

The title of the research paper should identify the variables investigated and indicate their theoretical role in the study. Avoid cause-effect wording in the title of a nonexperimental study.

Abstract

The abstract is a brief overview of the methods, results, and conclusions of the study. It should not exceed 120 words. The purpose of an abstract is to summarize

Table B.1   MAJOR SECTIONS AND SUBSECTIONS OF A RESEARCH REPORT

1. Title
2. Abstract
3. Introduction
4. Method
    a. Participants
    b. Apparatus
    c. Procedure
    d. Analysis (Optional)
5. Results
6. Discussion
7. References
8. Appendices
9. Footnotes
10. Tables
11. Figure captions
12. Figures

the study. A good abstract avoids details but provides enough information for readers to decide if they need or desire further details.

Introduction

The introduction should contain a clear statement of the purpose of the study and provide enough background information to allow the reader to understand why the study was done. The variables investigated should be introduced, and a focused review of relevant literature should be provided. "Focused" means that the literature review should concentrate only on prior studies that are directly relevant to the current study. If there is a theoretical background for the current study, it should be clearly explained. The literature review and theoretical rationale should lead to a clear statement of expected results for the current study.

Methods

The methods section should provide enough information about participants, apparatus, and procedures so that a reader could replicate the study.

Participants. This subsection describes the sample of participants and should contain the following information: sample size, response rate (if not 100%; see "How To Obtain a Sample" in Chapter 7), relevant characteristics of participants that might bear on the generality of the results, an indication of the population represented by the sample, and details of the sampling procedure (see "Sampling Procedures" in Chapter 7), including qualifying criteria and controls on sampling.

Apparatus. This subsection describes any stimuli, measuring instruments, or other equipment used in the study. If stimuli were sampled, the sampling procedure should be described. Original tests or surveys should be described, and complete copies should be included in an appendix. The rule of thumb is to include enough detail so that a replication could be carried out.

Procedure. This subsection describes how the study was carried out. It should include the following: what was done to each participant, identification of the basic research method or design, operational definitions of all manipulated or measured variables (if complex, scoring for measured variables may be covered in the optional Analysis subsection), and description of control techniques used in the study.

Analysis. This optional subsection may be included when either scoring procedures or statistical analysis of the data are complex. If so, details of scoring or analysis are described here. Simple scoring procedures can be incorporated into the Procedure subsection, and simple methods of analyses can be integrated into the Results section.

Results

This section describes what was found in the study and usually summarizes the statistical analysis of the data. Descriptive and inferential statistics bearing on the hypotheses of the study are always included here. The value of alpha used for tests of inference should be stated explicitly in this section. Evidence regarding the reliability of original measures should also be included. Sometimes results are summarized in tables or figures (i.e., graphs). The main goal of this section is to present the results in a clear and orderly fashion. Conventions regarding format and style for presenting results are covered in the section on "Format Conventions."

Discussion

This section should contain a clear statement of conclusions and the reasons for reaching them. As discussed in Chapter 8, three conclusions are possible for each null hypothesis: reject, do not reject, or suspend judgment. The latter conclusion requires justification that goes beyond mere reliance on the tests of inference. For a review of the issues to be considered in reaching a "final" conclusion, see the section in Chapter 8 on "Reliability, Hypothesis Testing, and the Third Option."

Other topics may also be included in the Discussion section if appropriate. The theoretical implications of the results should be considered. This is a mandatory topic if a theoretical rationale was presented in the introduction. Other topics often included are practical applications of the results, procedural criticisms of the study, comparison of the results to other findings in the literature, and suggestions for future research.

End Material

Items 7 through 12 in Table B.1 make up the end material of a research manuscript. References for all sources cited anywhere in the manuscript should be listed in alphabetical order by authors' last names. Formats for references are illustrated in the next section. Appendices include things like copies of original surveys or other measuring instruments, complete listing of stimuli used, mathematical derivations, or any other material too detailed for the body of the manuscript but of interest to readers or reviewers. Footnotes expand directly on specific points in the manuscript. Most journal editors prefer that footnotes be kept to a minimum. Tables and figures are ways of summarizing results. A rule of thumb is not to duplicate material placed in tables or figures in the manuscript. Clear titles and labels for tables and figures are essential. Some conventions for abbreviations are presented in the next section. Remember: tables and figures are supposed to make the results easier for the reader to understand. If they do not fulfill that purpose, they should be eliminated.

FORMATTING CONVENTIONS

Certain conventions for typing, headings, references, etc., are commonly followed. To give you a feel for such conventions, APA guidelines are briefly summarized here. Consult style sheets for variations from these guidelines. Your instructor will tell you where deviations from these guidelines are acceptable for class reports.

Typing

Journal manuscripts should be entirely double-spaced with at least 1-inch margins on all four sides of each page. Do NOT hyphenate words at the ends of lines; type lines a little short or long to avoid hyphenation. All pages should be numbered except for figure pages at the end of the manuscript. A manuscript page header consisting of the first two or three words of the manuscript title should appear in the upper right corner of each numbered page with the page number beneath it. Both items should be flush against the right margin. An alternative is to have the page header and page number on the same line, the number flush against the right margin, and the header five spaces to the left of the number. The title, abstract, introduction, and items 7 through 12 in Table B.1 should each be placed on separate manuscript pages.

The title page should include a running head, the title of the paper, and author names and affiliations. The running head is a shortened title of no more than 50 characters typed in upper-case letters. All items on the title page should be centered. Item placement is illustrated in Table B.2.

The abstract page contains the centered heading "Abstract" followed by the abstract with no indentation of the first paragraph. More than one paragraph in an abstract is seldom necessary or desirable.

The introduction begins on the third manuscript page. The first item on the page should be a centered heading consisting of the full manuscript title just as it appears on the title page. No authors or affiliations should appear on this page. The introduction follows the title immediately.

Typing conventions for the remaining items in the standard outline are covered in subsequent sections.

Headings

APA style allows for five different levels of headings. They are illustrated in Table B.3. Most manuscripts require only three levels of headings. In that case, levels 1,

Table B.2   SAMPLE TITLE PAGE OF A RESEARCH MANUSCRIPT

Sick Humor

1

Running Head: PREFERENCE FOR SICK JOKES

The Prediction of Preference for Sick Jokes

Thomas R. Herzog and Beverly A. Bush

Grand Valley State University

3, and 4 should be used. The sample manuscript at the end of this appendix illustrates the proper use and placement of headings.

Tables and Figures

Tables and figures are placed at the end of the manuscript, as indicated in Table B.1. Tables should be numbered consecutively in the order in which they are first mentioned in the manuscript. Each table should be identified by the word "Table" and an arabic numeral (e.g., Table 1, Table 2, etc.). The same rules should be followed for figures.

    Standard format for a table is illustrated in Table B.4. Note that the heading is level 3 and the title is underlined. Standard format for figure captions is illustrated in Table B.5. Figures follow the caption page immediately, with each figure

---

Table B.3   FIVE LEVELS OF MANUSCRIPT HEADINGS

CENTERED UPPERCASE HEADING (LEVEL 5)

Centered Upper- and Lowercase Heading (Level 1)

Centered Underlined Upper- and Lowercase Heading (Level 2)

Upper- and Lowercase Side Heading (Level 3)

    Paragraph heading (level 4). The heading is followed by the first sentence of the paragraph.

Table B.4   SAMPLE MANUSCRIPT TABLE

Table 1

Mean Preference Ratings as a Function of Joke Category

Joke Category	Mean Rating	Standard Deviation
General	2.84	0.52
Death	3.21	0.55
Dead-Baby	2.33	0.48
Handicapped	2.56	0.50

Note. N = 62 in each category.

Table B.5   FORMAT FOR FIGURE-CAPTION PAGE

Figure Captions

Figure 1. Relationship between mean preference and complexity ratings for different categories of jokes.

Figure 2. Mean preference ratings for different joke categories and rater genders.

on a separate page. Figures should be professionally drawn or computer generated, using quality software and printing devices. Each figure should be labeled on the back with the manuscript page header, the figure number, and the word "TOP" placed to indicate how the figure should be oriented on the printed page.

Abbreviations

Abbreviations should be used sparingly. Too many can easily confuse a reader. If you create your own abbreviations, the term to be abbreviated should be spelled out completely on its first appearance and then followed immediately by the abbreviation in parentheses. Here is an example: "The criterion variable was preference for sick humor (PSH). The two predictor variables were sociability (S) and locus of control (L)." Notice that the abbreviations bear some meaningful relationship to the terms or phrases they represent rather than being arbitrary (e.g., X, Y, and Z). Once abbreviations have been established, they may be used subsequently in the manuscript without further explanation.

Many statistical terms have standard abbreviations that may be used without initial explanation. Several such terms are presented in Table B.6. Statistical symbols usually appear in tables and should be used sparingly in the body of the manuscript. When used, statistical symbols are always underlined.

Reporting Statistical Tests

There is a standard format for reporting the results of statistical tests of inference within a manuscript. A summary statement in prose appears first, followed by a summary of the statistical test. The latter includes (in order) the name of the test-

Table B.6   ABBREVIATIONS FOR STATISTICAL TERMS

Abbreviation	Meaning
N	Number of participants in entire sample
n	Number of participants in part of the sample
M	Sample or treatment mean
SD	Sample or treatment standard deviation
x^2	Chi square
r	Product-moment correlation coefficient
SS	Sum of squares
MS	Mean square
F	F ratio in analysis of variance
df	Degrees of freedom
p	probability value
α	Alpha for test of inference

Table B.7 FORMATS FOR REPORTING TESTS OF INFERENCE

Chi Square

"Gender composition of table partners and eating etiquette were significantly related, x^2 (1, $\underline{N}$ = 84) = 5.82, $\underline{p}$ < .05."

Correlation

"There was a significant positive correlation between extroversion and preference for sick humor, $\underline{r}$ (88) = .46, $\underline{p}$ < .01."

Analysis of Variance

"Rated support for the handgun bill was significantly higher when endorsed by the general than when endorsed by the movie star, $\underline{F}$ (1, 102) = 4.28, $\underline{p}$ < .05."

ing statistic, its degrees of freedom (and possibly sample size, too), the computed value of the statistic, and the probability of obtaining the computed value under the null hypothesis. Table B.7 shows examples of how to make such statements for each of the testing statistics covered in this book.

References

Most journals use the author-date format for citing references within a manuscript. It has two forms. If the author's name is part of the narrative, the publication date appears in parentheses immediately after the name: "Griswold (1986) showed that most social scientists cite themselves more than any other authors." If the author's name is not part of the narrative, both name and date appear in parentheses either at an appropriate place within the sentence or at the end of the sentence: "There is evidence that social scientists tend to cite themselves excessively (Griswold, 1986)." If several works are cited at the same point in the text, they should be arranged in alphabetical order by authors' names. Multiple references to the same author should be arranged in order of publication date, starting with the earliest.

The format for the reference list itself varies widely across social-science disciplines. Standard formats for articles and books for three of the social sciences are illustrated in Table B.8. Many more sample formats may be found in Ellis (1994). Of course, the final authority is the style sheet for a specific journal.

WRITING STYLE

You should strive for the best writing style possible. This section provides advice on writing style for research papers. Remember: your writing style influences the reader's impression of you for better or worse. Poorly written manuscripts are usually rejected immediately by journal editors. Poorly written class assignments will usually get you a bad grade. Take the time and trouble to project a positive image of yourself in the way you write.

Table B.8   REFERENCE-LIST FORMATS
FOR ARTICLES AND BOOKS IN THREE SOCIAL SCIENCES

American Psychological Association Journals

Article

Wharton, A.S., & Baron, J.N. (1987). So happy together? The impact of gender segregation on men at work. <u>American Sociological Review, 52,</u> 574–587.

Book

Goffman, E. (1974). <u>Frame analysis.</u> Cambridge, MA: Harvard University Press.

American Sociological Association Journals

Article

Wharton, A.S., and Baron, J.N. 1987. "So happy together? The Impact of Gender Segregation on Men at Work." <u>American Sociological Review,</u> 55:574–587.

Book

Goffman, E. 1974. <u>Frame Analysis.</u> Cambridge, MA: Harvard University Press.

American Anthropological Association Journals

Article

Wharton, Amy S., and James N. Baron
   1987   So happy together? The Impact of Gender Segregation on Men at Work.   American Sociological Review 52:584–587.

Book

Goffman, Erving
   1974   Frame Analysis.   Cambridge, MA: Harvard University Press.

Jargon

Your choice of language should be matched to the intended audience of your paper. Normally, that will mean professionals in the area of your research. You may be tempted to impress such an audience with your command of technical jargon. Try to suppress that temptation. Even for an audience of professionals, it is a good idea to limit jargon only to situations where it is necessary. Your goal should be clear communication, first and foremost, followed by interest maintenance. Neither goal will be well served by jargon overkill. It will do no harm and may do a lot of good if your research paper can be understood and appreciated by a reasonably intelligent layperson.

Sexist Language

Avoid such language. Do not refer to the male gender when both genders are meant. Gender-biased references can usually be avoided by appropriate rephrasing. For example, "The participant rated his preference for each joke" can be changed to, "The participant rated each joke for preference" or, "Participants rated their preferences for each joke." Avoid using "s/he" to solve the gender problem; it is awkward. The APA *Publication Manual* (1994, pp. 46–60) has many examples of how to avoid gender and ethnic bias and stereotyping of all sorts.

Tense

Most sections of a research report should be written in the past tense because they describe events that occurred in the past (what other researchers found or what was done in the study being described). The present tense may be appropriate in the Introduction and Discussion sections when discussing theories and in the Results sections when referring to tables or figures. Occasionally, the future tense may be used to discuss proposed future research. Seldom should tense be switched within a paragraph and never within a sentence.

Number

Consistency of number (singular or plural) should be maintained throughout a research report. Switching from singular to plural or vice versa is poor style. Here is a common error in student papers: "Each participant made their responses in writing." Here is a better version: "Participants made their responses in writing." Generally, it is best to use plural number throughout a research paper because it reads less awkwardly than singular. The singular version of the sentence above is, "Each participant made his/her response in writing." The "his/her" approach is awkward and also raises the question of gender bias in the ordering of the pronouns.

Miscellaneous

Person. Most research reports are written in the third person (he, she, it, they). First-person references (I, we) are becoming more common. The APA manual (p. 29–30) recommends use of the first person when it will improve clarity or readability.

Voice. Active voice is always preferable to passive voice. The reason is simple: passive voice is dull. "A confederate, dressed in rags, asked participants for a handout" is more interesting than "Participants were asked for a handout by a confederate dressed in rags." Maintaining reader interest is often a problem in research reports. Use of active voice wherever possible is one way of dealing with that problem.

Contractions. Avoid contractions. A research report qualifies as formal writing. Contractions are not appropriate in formal writing.

Sentence and Paragraph Length. Another effective device for maintaining reader interest is to vary sentence and paragraph length. However, extremes of length should be avoided, especially for paragraphs. On the other hand, an occasional short pithy sentence can be very effective: "Avoid contractions."

Common Writing Problems in Student Papers

The discussion of writing style concludes with a brief overview of the most common writing problems seen in student research papers. Your instructor will know whether you read this section carefully by noting whether you avoid these problems in your research reports.

Grammar. The two most common grammar problems involve a switch in number from subject to predicate when the words "data" or "sample" are used as subjects. "Data" is plural and requires a plural verb. Thus, "Data was collected" is incorrect; "Data were collected" is correct. The singular of "data" is "datum," a word seldom seen in research reports. "Sample" is a collective noun, and the rules for such nouns are tricky. Suffice it to say that the oft-seen student sentence, "A sample of 87 young adults were asked to fill out a questionnaire" is incorrect if you mean to refer to the sample as a unit. In such a case, "A sample . . . was . . ." is correct. Better yet, avoid the "were/was" dilemma as follows: "A sample of 87 young adults filled out a questionnaire."

Another common problem is a tendency to use incomplete sentences. Phrases followed by a period may be acceptable in popular writing but are inappropriate in scientific writing. "The experimental method" is incorrect; "The study used the experimental method" is better. Check to see if your sentences have an explicit subject and predicate. They should.

Spelling. Here, correctly spelled, are the most commonly misspelled words the author has seen in student research reports: believe, category, dependent, environment, experimenter, independent, judgment, occurrence, perceive, questionnaire, receive, and separate. You will not be rewarded for sloppy spelling. Use a computer spell checker, have a knowledgeable friend read your paper, or consult a dictionary to avoid misspellings.

Punctuation. Students often connect two separate sentences with a comma, as in, "The results were significant, the theory was supported." This is incorrect. Two correct versions are "The results were significant. The theory was supported," or "The results were significant in support of the theory." If you have a long sentence with many commas and semicolons, you should break it up into separate sentences. Separate chunks are easier for the reader to process.

Usage. When you wish to convey the meaning "have an effect on" in one word, the word to use is "affect," NOT "effect." "The shock effected performance" is incorrect; "The shock affected performance" is correct. Avoid using "effect" as a verb; it is too dangerous. Use "affect."

"That" introduces clauses containing information essential to the meaning of the sentence; "which" introduces clauses containing additional nonessential information. Thus, "Response sheets that contained errors were eliminated" is correct, but "Response sheets which contained errors were eliminated" is not. In most cases, you mean to convey essential information, and "that" is the correct word. Where possible, you should avoid either word, as in, "Response sheets containing errors were eliminated."

"While" and "since" should be used only to refer to temporal events and not as substitutes for "although," "whereas," and "but." "While" describes simultaneous events, and "since" refers to the past. Thus, "Nero fiddled while Rome burned," and "Nero has not fiddled since Rome burned" are correct, but, "While Nero fiddled, he did not actually set the fire" is not. The latter sentence should begin with "although."

"Since" is widely and mistakenly used as a synonym for "because." "The data from color-blind participants were discarded since the illusion requires color vision" is incorrect. "Because" should be substituted for "since."

EXPANDED OUTLINE FOR RESEARCH REPORTS

As promised, this appendix concludes with an expanded version of the outline for writing research reports in Table B.1. A model paper written according to the expanded outline immediately follows this appendix. The expanded outline serves a useful instructional purpose. It specifies exactly which topic should be addressed at every point in the paper and thereby forces you to be explicit. If you are having problems with any topic in research methods, they will be exposed quickly when you try to use the outline. Then they can be dealt with.

Research reports conforming to the expanded outline should contain the following sections in the order given and should explicitly cover the points indicated for each section.

Title

The title should identify the important variables in the study (independent and dependent variables; predictor and criterion variables). Example for an experiment: "The Effects of Anxiety and Practice on Learning." Example for a survey: "Self-Esteem Predicted by Sociability and Anxiety."

Abstract

The abstract is a brief (120 words or less) statement of procedure, results (no statistics), and conclusion. Consult any journal in your field for examples, or see the Model Paper following this outline.

Introduction

The introduction sets the stage for the study to be described. It should contain a clear statement of the purpose of the study and all relevant background information to allow the reader to understand why the study was done. Such background information includes pertinent literature review (if appropriate) and the theory or line of reasoning that led to the variables included in the study and the hypotheses tested. If possible, clear statements of hypotheses to be tested or expected results should be included.

Method

Participants.

Sample. Describe the people (or other organisms) in the sample. Note any characteristics that you think are especially pertinent in limiting the generality of the results. Be sure to mention sample size and response rate (if less than 100%).

Population. Identify the population that you feel is represented by the sample.

Sampling procedure. Clearly describe the sampling procedure, that is, exactly how the participants were obtained from the population. Do NOT use the word "random" unless you are sure it is appropriate. If there were any qualifying criteria participants had to meet to be included in the sample, state them clearly here.

Sampling controls. Describe any variables that were controlled in sampling. Such variables are typically personal characteristics such as gender, age, socio-economic status, etc. To be controlled, the values of such variables must be made to appear in the sample with exact proportions specified in advance by the researcher. Special sampling techniques such as stratified random sampling or quota sampling are often used to exert such control. See Chapter 7 for details on these techniques. If you used such a technique, you should explicitly name it. Each personal variable controlled in sampling should be named and the resulting proportions for each of its values should be specified.

Apparatus.

Describe any stimuli or other instruments used in the research. If an original test or survey was used, briefly describe it and then include a complete copy in the Appendix. If stimuli were sampled, describe exactly how that was done. In general, the guideline here is to include enough detail so that the reader could replicate the study.

Procedure.

Overview. Describe what was done to each participant from start to finish. Include enough detail so that the reader could replicate the procedure.

Research method. Name the basic research method and the specific subcategories (if appropriate) that were used. The three basic methods are the observation study, survey research, and the experiment. Observation studies include all nonexperimental research using observation of behavior other than self-report behavior to measure variables. In the terminology of this book, subcategories include casual, field, and systematic. Further specification might include where the study fell along the dimensions of concealment and participation. Survey research includes all nonexperimental research in which self-report measures of variables are used. Subcategories include interviews and questionnaires. Experiments include all studies with at least one manipulated independent variable. Subcategories include the specific experimental designs: independent-treatments (postest-only or pre-post), nonindependent-treatments (explicit-matching or repeated-measures), or factorial (with complete specifications for each factor or independent variable).

Variables. Name each important variable in the study. That is, name all independent and dependent variables, all predictor and criterion variables, all manipulated or measured variables. Generally, these will be the same variables as in the title of the paper.

Manipulation. For experiments only, operationally define each independent variable. That is, specify exactly how each variable was manipulated and what the researcher did to produce its values. Also, state the specific values of each independent variable and, if possible, the unit of measurement represented by those values.

Assignment. For experiments only, describe how participants were assigned to conditions. What you say here should agree with the type of experiment specified in *Research method* above. If any variables were controlled in assigning participants to conditions, name or otherwise describe them and tell how they were controlled.

Procedure controls. Identify any variables that were controlled in the running of the study (procedures, stimuli, environmental conditions), and tell how they were controlled.

Formal hypotheses.
  1. State each null hypothesis in formal terms.
  2. State each alternative hypothesis in formal terms.
   Formal terms means a prose statement of the form: "In the population, variable A and variable B are not (or are) related" or the use of statistical symbols to say the same thing. Be sure to include the phrase "In the population" in prose statements of hypotheses.

Analysis.

Scoring. Operationally define each measured variable. That is, specify exactly how each measured variable was scored, starting from scratch (the raw data), and including all steps on the way to the final score value for each measured variable. If possible, specify the unit of measurement and the range of possible score values for each measured variable.

Measurement controls. If there were any controls built into the scoring procedures, specify them and describe what they controlled.

Reliability assessment. If reliability of measurement was assessed for any measured variables, describe how it was done.

Descriptive statistics. Specify which descriptive statistics were computed to summarize the data from the study.

Inferential statistics. Describe all inferential tests that were performed to test hypotheses.

Results

Reliability of Measurement. Any reliability coefficients for measured variables should be reported as the very first results. The reason is that if reliability is unacceptably low, the rest of the results are likely to be meaningless.

Descriptive Statistics. The results of all descriptive statistics specified in the Analysis section should be reported here in an orderly fashion. These results may include frequency tables (clearly and completely labeled), correlations, means, standard deviations, or any other appropriate descriptive statistics. If tables or figures are used, there MUST also be some text describing them. Follow conventions described earlier in this appendix for formatting and typing of tables and figures.

Inferential Statistics. Results of all inferential tests specified in the Analysis section should be reported here in an orderly fashion. Remember to make clear to the reader the value of alpha used for tests of inference. Each test reported should include a brief prose description, followed by the name of the statistic in symbol form, its degrees of freedom in parentheses, the computed value of the statistic (from the data; NOT the critical value from a statistical table), and its p value under the null hypothesis. Example: "The correlation between category width and religious liberalism was significant, $r(38) = .72, p < .01$." Example: "Learning and anxiety were significantly related, $F(1, 22) = 16.72, p < .01$."

Discussion

Conclusions. State your conclusions clearly. For each null hypothesis, was it accepted or rejected, or did you suspend judgment? You don't have to give reasons here; just state conclusions.

Reasons. Why did you reach each conclusion? Give your reasons here. If you suspended judgment or reached conclusions opposite to those implied by statistical inference tests, provide adequate justification. Review Chapter 8 on considerations involved in reaching "final" conclusions.

Theoretical Implications. What theories are supported or weakened by the results? If you described a theory in the Introduction, you should certainly reevaluate it here. If the results failed to support part of the theory, how should it be modified? If no theory was described earlier, can you now formulate one that would explain the results? Try very hard to come up with a plausible and testable theory. In many ways, this is the most important section of the paper.

Practical Importance. Can you think of any practical applications of the results? If so, describe them. If not, think harder.

Criticisms. What was wrong with the study? Note any variables that should have been controlled but were not. Mention any serious limitations on the generality of the results.

Future Research. Based on your preceding discussion, offer some suggestions for future research on this topic. If you have proposed a testable theory, describe a study that would further test it. If you have made methodological criticisms, describe a study that corrects those criticisms. Provide enough detail to convince the reader that you have thought about the research implications of the results.

References

Follow the styles and formats described earlier in this appendix.

Appendices

Include copies of all original self-report measuring instruments, stimuli (if possible), mathematical derivations, statistical computations (if required by your instructor), and any other supplements you think would help the reader.

Remaining End Material

Items 9 through 12 in Table B.1 go here, if appropriate. Follow style and formatting conventions described earlier.

MODEL RESEARCH PAPER

A model research paper begins on the page following this appendix. The model paper follows the expanded outline presented in the previous section. It also illustrates most of the format and style conventions discussed in this appendix. Your research papers should always be typed and double-spaced, as described earlier. All format and style conventions illustrated in the model paper should be followed in your papers except where your instructor specifies otherwise.

REFERENCES

American Psychological Association. (1994). *Publication manual of the American Psychological Association* (4th ed.). Washington, DC: American Psychological Association.

Becker, H. S. (1986). *Writing for social scientists: How to start and finish your thesis, book, or article.* Chicago: University of Chicago Press.

Day, R. (1988). *How to write and publish a scientific paper* (3rd ed.). Philadelphia: ISI Press.

Ellis, L. (1994). *Research methods in the social sciences.* Madison, WI: Brown & Benchmark.

Friedman, S., & Steinberg, S. (1989). *Writing and thinking in the social sciences.* Englewood Cliffs, NJ: Prentice-Hall.

Shertzer, M. (1986). *The elements of grammar.* New York: Macmillan.

Sociology Writing Group. (1991). *A guide to writing sociology papers* (2nd ed.). New York: St. Martin's Press.

Sternberg, R. J. (1988). *The psychologist's companion: A guide to scientific writing for students and researchers.* Cambridge: Cambridge University Press.

Strunk, W., Jr., & White, E. B. (1979). *The elements of style* (3rd ed.). New York: Macmillan.

Sick Humor
1

Running head: PREFERENCE FOR SICK HUMOR

Preference for Sick Humor Predicted by
Sociability and Locus of Control

Jane Q. Student

Grand Valley State University

Abstract

A sample of 90 volunteers, evenly divided by sex and life-cycle stage, rated 10 sick jokes for preference using a 5-point scale. Participants also completed a questionnaire containing items assessing two predictor variables, sociability and locus of control. Reliability analysis established that all three variables were reliably measured. In addition, preference for sick humor was positively correlated with an external locus of control and with sociability. The two predictors were also positively correlated. It was concluded that both sociability and external locus of control reflect a tendency to seek meaning outside of oneself. Liking for sick humor probably taps a similar orientation in that it may be used as a psychological mechanism for coping with uncontrollable and unpleasant events.

Preference for Sick Humor Predicted by
Sociability and Locus of Control

The purpose of this study was to find out whether
preference for sick humor could be linearly predicted by
sociability and locus of control. Sick humor is that which
makes light of death, disease, deformity, and suffering.
Frickem and Frackem (1986) found that bookworms were
greatly offended by sick jokes, suggesting that it takes an
outgoing person to have any tolerance for this form of
humor. Flotsam (1987) suggested that sick humor may be a
way of coping with life's uncontrollable tragedies. If so,
locus of control should be a relevant predictor. Thus,
there is reason to predict that both sociability and an
external locus of control should be positively correlated
with liking for sick humor.

From a theoretical standpoint, both sociability
and an external locus of control may represent a tendency
to look outside oneself for meaning, the former in a social
or interpersonal sense, the latter in a search for
causality. As noted earlier, preference for sick humor may
reflect a similar orientation. That is, it may be a coping
mechanism, used primarily by people who view life's trials

as caused by uncontrollable external forces. Thus, theory also predicts that both sociability and an external locus of control will be positively correlated with liking for sick humor.

Method

Participants

Sample. The sample consisted of 90 adult volunteers from the west Michigan area. Two persons who qualified for the study refused to participate, yielding a response rate of 90/92.

Population. The population is midwestern adults.

Sampling procedure. Participants were volunteers. The only qualifying variable was that they had to be at least 18 years of age.

Sampling controls. Participant gender was controlled in sampling by including an equal number of each gender. The sampling procedure for gender was quota sampling.

Apparatus

The questionnaire consisted of two parts. The first part contained eight sick jokes to be rated for preference. The jokes used were the eight jokes in Table 1

of Herzog and Bush (1994), arranged in a random order.
The second part of the questionnaire consisted of 18
items, six for each of the two independent variables and
six filler items, arranged in a random order. These items
are presented in the appendix. The code following each
item indicates which variable it measured (S = sociability,
L = locus of control, F = filler) and whether it was a
positive (+) or a negative (-) item (explained below).
The codes did not appear on the questionnaire seen by
the raters.

Procedure

Overview. Each of 15 researchers obtained six
volunteers following the sampling techniques described
earlier. Participants first rated each of the eight sick
jokes for preference using a 5-point scale and then rated
their agreement with each of the remaining items using a
6-point scale. The scales are described below. Responses
were made in writing by circling the appropriate response
code to the left of each item. Afterward, participants were
thanked and offered feedback about the study.

Research method. This was survey research using a
questionnaire approach.

Variables. The dependent variable was preference for sick humor (PSH). The two independent variables were sociability (S) and locus of control (L).

Manipulation. No variables were manipulated.

Assignment. Because this was not an experiment, there was no assignment to conditions.

Procedure controls. Researchers were not permitted to answer questions or explain the questionnaire items. Directions, definitions, and response choices for questionnaire items were held constant.

Formal hypotheses.

1.   The null hypotheses are that in the population,

   a.   the correlation between PSH and S is 0.

   b.   the correlation between PSH and L is 0.

   c.   the correlation between S and L is 0.

2.   The alternative hypotheses are that in the population, each of the above correlations is not 0.

Analysis

Scoring. For the sick humor jokes, preference was defined as "how much you like the joke, for whatever reason." Permissible responses were 1 = not at all, 2 = a

little, 3 = somewhat, 4 = quite a bit, and 5 = a great deal.
Each of the remaining items was rated for agreement.
Permissible responses were SA = strongly agree, A = agree, MA
= mildly agree, MD = mildly disagree, D = disagree, SD =
strongly disagree. The eight jokes in part one of the
questionnaire were the items scored for the dependent
variable. For the two independent variables, the items in
the appendix coded S (for sociability) and L (for locus of
control) were scored. For the independent variables, half
of the relevant items were positively worded (SA means high
on the variable) and half were negatively worded (SA means
low on the variable). The "+" and "–" codes in the appendix
indicate the relevant items. Scoring for positive items was
SD = 1 through SA = 6. For negative items, scoring was
reversed, with SA = 1 through SD = 6.

The PSH score was the sum of the preference
ratings for the eight jokes. Each independent variable was
scored by summing the scores for the six relevant items.
For locus of control, a high score indicates an EXTERNAL
locus of control. For PSH, scores could range from 8 to 40.
For each independent variable, scores could range from 6
to 36.

Measurement controls. For each independent variable, an equal number of positive and negative items were used. This controls for participants who give consistently extreme responses (SA or SD) without paying attention to the actual content of the items. The scoring procedure places such participants in the middle of the possible range of scores where they will distort the results the least.

Reliability assessment. Internal-consistency reliability was assessed for each variable by computing coefficient alpha.

Descriptive statistics. Correlation coefficients were computed for each pair of variables.

Inferential statistics. The correlation between each pair of variables was tested for significance using standard statistical tables.

Results

Reliability of Measurement. The reliability coefficients were .75, .82, and .79 for PSH, S, and L, respectively. Thus, each variable had reasonable reliability of measurement.

Descriptive Statistics. The correlations among the variables were as follows: r(PSH&S) = .46, r(PSH&L) = .41, and r(S&L) = .39.

Inferential Statistics. The correlation between PSH and S was significant, r(88) = .46, p < .05. The correlation between PSH and L was significant, r(88) = .41, p < .05. The correlation between S and L was significant, r(88) = .39, p < .05.

Discussion

Conclusions. Each pair of variables is positively correlated.

Reasons. The conclusions follow from the tests of inference and the fact that the study had no serious flaws.

Theoretical Implications. As noted in the Introduction, both S and L may represent a tendency to look outside oneself for meaning, the former in a social or interpersonal sense, the latter in a search for causality. PSH may reflect a similar orientation in that sick humor may be a coping mechanism, used primarily by people who view life's trials as caused by uncontrollable external forces. Thus, it not surprising that the three variables are positively related. These results support the theory that all three variables represent a tendency to look outside oneself for meaning.

Practical Importance. Given these results, we can better understand why sick humor reliably follows national tragedies like the Challenger disaster. Such understanding may lead to more tolerance for those who use this method of coping with tragedy.

Criticism. Times and settings for administering the questionnaire were not controlled. The study would have been better if they had been held constant.

Future Research. If humor is a general coping mechanism, then people should prefer humor dealing with those areas of life that most concern them. It follows that if sexual anxiety could be validly measured via questionnaire, it should be positively related to preference for sexual humor.

References

Flotsam, F. (1987). <u>Sick coping mechanisms.</u>
Elmsford, NY: Ill Press.

Frickem, J., & Frackem, Z. (1986). Sick humor
causes bookworms to regurgitate lunch. <u>Journal of Bulimia,</u>
<u>14</u>, 22-32.

Herzog, T. R., & Bush, B. A. (1994). The
prediction of preference for sick jokes. <u>Humor:</u>
<u>International Journal of Humor Research, 7,</u> 323-340.

Appendix

Second Part of Questionnaire Used in This Study

Please respond to each item below by circling only ONE of
the six choices.

Choices: SA = strongly agree

A = agree

MA = mildly agree

MD = mildly disagree

D = disagree

SD = strongly disagree

SA A MA MD D SD   1. I never miss a chance to talk to a
stranger. (S+)

SA A MA MD D SD   2. Most of us are the victims of forces we
cannot control. (L+)

SA A MA MD D SD   3. Overpopulation is the most serious
problem facing humanity. (F)

SA A MA MD D SD   4. Some people won't like you no matter
how nice you are. (L+)

SA A MA MD D SD   5. I really enjoy myself at lively
parties. (S+)

SA A MA MD D SD   6. I believe that dangerous chemicals are
being added to our food. (F)

Sick Humor
13

SA A MA MD D SD 7. I tend to be quiet when I am with people. (S-)

SA A MA MD D SD 8. I prefer a shower to a bath. (F)

SA A MA MD D SD 9. People's troubles usually result from their own mistakes. (L-)

SA A MA MD D SD 10. I am opposed to censorship. (F)

SA A MA MD D SD 11. If I want to know something, I would rather look it up in a book than talk to someone about it. (S-)

SA A MA MD D SD 12. The government should adopt strong measures to stop crime. (F)

SA A MA MD D SD 13. What happens to me is because of my own doing. (L-)

SA A MA MD D SD 14. I like cooked carrots better than raw carrots. (F)

SA A MA MD D SD 15. Whatever is going to happen will happen regardless of what I do. (L+)

SA A MA MD D SD 16. I would rather read than meet people. (S-)

SA A MA MD D SD 17. By getting involved, people can control what happens in their society. (L-)

SA A MA MD D SD 18. I would be unhappy if I could not be

around lots of people most of the time.

(S+)

Glossary

This glossary can also be used as a study guide. To do so, cover the left side of each page and read each definition followed by a bracketed number corresponding to the chapter you are studying. Note any definitions for which you are unable to supply the correct term. Later, review those definitions until you have mastered them. Words or phrases in bold type within definitions are themselves also defined in the glossary.

AB design	A **single-subject design** in which the **dependent variable** is measured during a baseline **control** period (A) and then again during a **treatment** period (B) after the experimental treatment has been introduced. [10]
ABA design	A **single-subject design** in which baseline (A) and **treatment** (B) periods are alternated with the object of showing that the expected behavior change can be reversed and reinstated at the experimenter's discretion. Also known as a **"reversal design."** [10]
Absolute control	A form of **control** in which an **extraneous variable** is not allowed to vary and thus always has the same **value.** [10]
Abstract theory	A **theory** in which a phenomenon is explained in terms of concepts defined solely by means of mathematical relationships. Example: the drive-reduction theory of motivated behavior. See **Theory.** [1]
Accretion	The build-up of something over time. Graffiti or garbage could be the basis of accretion measures.[3]
Additively	Describes how **independent variables** combine their effects when there is no **interaction.** It means that the combined effect of the independent variables can be determined by simply adding together their **main effects.** [12]
Advocacy	The taking of a public position by a researcher regarding the interpretation or use of that researcher's results. [14]
Aftereffect measure	Measure derived from the results or products of previous behavior. Includes **trace measures** and **content analysis.** [5]
Alpha	A specific probability value, stated in advance, that serves as a dividing line between what will be considered large and small probabilities for decision-making purposes when doing a test of statistical inference. [4]
Alternate-forms reliability	A **stability** approach to assessing **reliability** in which different but equivalent measures of the same **variable** are used at two different points in time. Also known as "equivalent-forms reliability." [6]

Alternative hypothesis

A **hypothesis** that includes all logical alternatives to the **null hypothesis.** Also known as the "research hypothesis." The most common alternative hypothesis is that two **variables** are related in a **population.** [4]

Analogical theory

A **theory** in which a phenomenon is explained in terms of its similarities to another phenomenon that is well understood. Example: explaining brain functioning in terms of computer processing. See **Theory.** [1]

Analysis of covariance

A statistical technique in which the influence of a measured **extraneous variable** is removed during an analysis of the **relationship** between an **independent variable** and a **dependent variable.** A form of **statistical control** that can be considered a special case of either **multiple regression** or **analysis of variance.** [9,10]

Analysis of variance (ANOVA)

A statistical technique which compares the actual **variability** among the **sample treatment means** in an **experiment** to an estimate of the variability expected from **random error.** The comparison is summarized in an **inferential** testing **statistic** known as the F ratio. [11]

Anonymity

Refers to a situation in which the researcher does not know the identity of the participants in a study. [14]

Applied research

Research aimed primarily at practical applications. [1]

Asymmetrical order effects

Order effects that depend on the order in which **conditions** are presented in a **repeated-measures design.** Such effects cannot be **controlled.** [10]

Authority

An approach to knowledge in which it is handed down by a trusted source and accepted on faith. [1]

Balancing

A form of **control** in which an **extraneous variable** is made to have the same distribution of **values** in all **conditions** of an **experiment** and thus the same average value in all conditions. [10]

Basic research

Research aimed at discovering general principles underlying natural phenomena. [1]

Behavioral measure

Measure derived from ongoing visible-to-the-naked-eye behavior or features of the objects studied. [5]

Behavioral mapping   Observation research aimed at produciing a chart or map summarizing the events or behaviors that occur in specific physical settings. [3]

Between-subjects variable   In a **factorial design,** refers to an **independent variable** with **values** randomly assigned to different participants. [12]

Biased measurement   Source of confounding due to any systematic difference in the way the **dependent variable** is measured across the **conditions** of an **experiment.** [10]

Blinding   A **control** technique in which an **experiment** is run in such a way that the participants and/or experimenters do not know what **conditions** are being administered. [10]

Casual observation   Informal observation aimed at getting ideas for a more serious follow-up study. [3]

Causal relationship   A **relationship** in which one of the **variables** is the **cause** and the other one is the effect. See **Relationship.** [1]

Cause   A word used to describe situations in which a change on one **variable** is believed to produce a change on another variable. The variable producing the change is referred to as the cause. [2]

Cell frequencies   The numbers in the individual cells of a **frequency table.** [2]

Central tendency   Phrase referring to the location of the center of a **frequency distribution.** [11]

Chi-square   Testing statistic for making inferences about the **null hypothesis** of no **relationship** between **variables** for **frequency-table data.** [4]

Closed responses   A **structured** response format for **survey** items in which the respondent must choose among alternatives supplied by the researcher. Also known as "multiple-choice responses." [7]

Cluster sampling   A sampling procedure in which groups of units with something in common are selected at each step. [7]

Coarse data
Data consisiting of a small number of distinct score **values,** whether or not they are **ordered.** [5]

Coding
The process of establishing objective scoring categories for unstructured **data** produced by a research study. [8]

Coefficient alpha
An **internal-consistency** approach to assessing **reliability** based on the average of the **correlations** among all possible pairs of items or trials measuring the same **variable.** [6]

Cohen's kappa
A measure of **inter-observer agreement** that takes into account the level of agreement that would occur by chance. [4]

Comparative rating scale
Rating scale that provides a frame of reference or a standard of comparison for whatever is being rated. [5]

Comparison rule
The **inductive-inference** rule that specifies the conditions to be met for inferring that a **relationship** exists. It says that one must be able to find out what happens to each **variable** as one looks across **values** of the other variable. [15]

Concealment
Term describing a field researcher whose purpose is concealed from those observed. [3]

Conceptual replication
A research study that investigates the same conceptual **variables (constructs)** as an earlier study but using different methods (typically, different **operational definitions).** [13]

Conditions
Values of the **independent variable** in a **simple experiment;** combinations of values of the independent variables in certain **complex experiments.** [2,9,12]

Confidentiality
Refers to a situation in which the researcher knows the identity of research participants but protects that information from public exposure or unauthorized access. [14]

Confirmation bias
The tendency to favor evidence that agrees with one's current position and to discount evidence that disagrees with it. [7]

Confounding variable	An **extraneous variable** that was not properly ruled out as a possible **cause** in a research study. Such a **variable** confounds the causal interpretation of the results. [2,9]
Constant error	Phrase referring to an error that systematically favors certain **values** of a **variable** over other values. [7,10]
Construct	A **variable** that appears as a concept in a **theory.** [2]
Construct validity	An **empirical-validity** approach in which evidence is gathered that bears on the question of whether a measure yields results consistent with theoretical predictions about the **construct** being measured. [6]
Content analysis	A form of analysis in which the content and/or form of some kind of media is categorized. [3]
Content validity	A **judgmental-validity** approach in which a decision is made about how well a measure **samples** the intended **construct.** Such judgments are typically made for multi-item measures. [6]
Control (a)	The research goal of finding out what causes a phenomenon. [1]
Control (b)	The process of holding a **variable** constant either absolutely or on the average. [2,9,10]
Control in sampling	Sampling in such a way that the **values** of a certain **variable** have specified proportions relative to each other in the **sample** and the proportions are determined by the researcher. [7]
Controlled comparison rule	The **inductive-inference** rule that specifies the conditions to be met for inferring that a **causal relationship** exists. It says that one must compare **values** of the presumed causal **variable** that differ only with respect to the presumed **cause.** [15]
Control-series design	An **interrupted-time series design** with the addition of a **control** group. The group experiencing the potential causal event is compared with a similar group that does not experience the potential causal event. [10]
Convergent validity	Subcategory of **construct validity** dealing with the issue of whether evidence gathered from a variety of

studies shows that a measure of a **construct** yields theoretically appropriate results. [6]

Correlation coefficient

A **descriptive statistic** summarizing the type (positive or negative) and degree of linear **relationship** between two finely measured **variables,** symbolized by the letter r. There are several such statistics for different **data** types; the one defined here is the Pearson product-moment version. [6,8]

Counterbalancing

Form of **balancing** in which each possible order of presenting **conditions** is used for an equal number of participants in a **repeated-measures design** to **control** for **symmetrical order effects.** [10]

Covariate

The measured **extraneous variable** which is controlled statistically in an **analysis of covariance.** [10]

Cramer's V

A statistic for describing the strength of **relationship** between two **variables** in a **frequency table.** [4]

Criterion validity

An **empirical-validity** approach in which evidence is gathered showing that a new measure is related to an existing measure, the criterion, which is assumed to be valid. [6]

Curiosity

The motive for research of wanting to find out everything there is to know about a single phenomenon or **variable.** [1]

Curvilinear relationship

A **relationship** in which the **scatterplot** is well described by a function that is more complex than a straight-line function. Also known as a nonlinear relationship. [2]

Data

Plural noun that refers to the information or output generated by a research study. Its singular form is "datum." [2]

Debriefing

The practice of providing participants with a thorough explanation of a research study, including justification for ethically questionable activities like **stress** induction or **deception,** after the study is over and of removing or treating the effects of any harmful procedures. [14]

Deception

The practice of misleading participants regarding the purpose or some other aspect of a research study. [10,14]

Deductive reasoning

An approach in which knowledge is gained by moving from premises to conclusions following the rules of deductive logic. [1]

Degrees of freedom (df)

The number of observations or scores in a **data** set that are free to vary given certain restrictions placed on the data set. df is generally computed as the number of scores in the data set minus the number of restrictions placed on the data set. [4]

Dependent variable

A presumed effect, that is, a **variable** that is thought of theoretically as an effect. In an **experiment,** the dependent variable is measured. [2,9]

Demand characteristics

Any cues in a research study that signal to participants the kind of performance or behavior expected of them by the **theory** being tested. [10]

Description

The research goal of defining the properties of a phenomenon more fully. [1]

Descriptive statistics

Statistics used to summarize the scores in a **sample.** [4]

Deviation score

The difference between a raw score and the **mean** of a **frequency distribution.** [11]

Diagonal error

The error in reasoning that occurs when the information from only the cells in one diagonal of a **frequency table** is used to reach a conclusion about a **relationship.** [15]

Direct measure

Self-report measure based on a physical format consisting of clear stimuli or questions and responses limited to a choice among given alternatives. Also known as an "objective measure." [5]

Discriminant validity

Subcategory of **construct validity** dealing with the issue of whether a measure of a **construct** yields results different from those yielded by measures of other similar constructs. [6]

Double-blind experiment

An **experiment** in which neither participants nor experimenters know what **conditions** are being administered. [10]

Ecological validity

A phrase describing results that are valid in real-world (nonlaboratory) settings. [3,10,13]

Empirical validity	An approach to assessing **validity of measurement** based on the gathering of empirical evidence. [6]
Empirical verification	An approach to knowledge in which a proposition is regarded as true if it agrees with what is observed. This is the most important distinguishing feature of the scientific approach. [1,15]
Environmental sources	Sources of confounding in an **experiment** attributable to the physical or temporal setting of the study; for example, systematic differences across **conditions** in temperature, lighting, time of day or year. [10]
Equal intervals	A property of numbers referring to the fact that the distance between adjacent numbers is the same for any pair of adjacent numbers. Thus, numbers may be used to represent distances between objects. [5]
Erosion	The wearing away of something over time. Unofficial pathways or other indications of wear and tear would qualify as erosion measures. [3]
Error variance	General phrase referring to the **variability** estimated by the denominator of the F ratio in an **analysis of variance** based on experimental **data.** This variability is a byproduct of **random error** only. [11]
Errors of inference	Errors made when the decision based on a test of statistical inference is incorrect. [4]
Ethics committee	An institutional committee charged with determining if **research proposals** conform to accepted ethical guidelines and to applicable laws and regulations. Also known as an "institutional review board." [14]
Event sampling	Choosing events to observe that meet predetermined qualifications. [3]
Exact replication	A research study that attempts to copy exactly the procedures of an earlier study. [13]
Expected frequencies	Frequencies that would appear in a **frequency table** if the **variables** are not related. [4]
Experiment	A research study containing at least one manipulated **variable.** [2,9]

Experimental design	Phrase referring to how participants are assigned to **conditions** or **treatments** in an **experiment.** [9,10]
Experimental realism	Refers to whether a research study has an impact on participants and makes them take the study seriously. [13]
Experimenter bias	Any systematic differences in an experimenter's behavior across **conditions** that may affect the reactions of participants. **Demand characteristics** attributable to the experimenter. [10]
Experimenter effects	Any characteristic of the researcher that might affect the results of a study and thereby limit the generality of the findings. [13]
Explicit-matching design	A **nonindependent-treatments design** in which the experimenter obtains scores on a participant characteristic judged relevant to the **dependent variable** (the **matching** variable), explicitly forms matched blocks of participants on the matching variable, and then randomly assigns each member of every matched block to a different experimental **condition.** [9,10]
Exploitation	Using others for selfish purposes. [14]
Exploration	The research goal of finding out if a phenomenon exists. [1]
External validity	Refers to the **validity** of inferences about the generality of research findings. [9,10,13]
Extraneous variable	A **variable,** other than the **independent variable,** that is judged to be possibly related to the **dependent variable.** In other words, a possible alternative **cause.** [2,9]
Face validity	A **judgmental-validity** approach in which a measure is regarded as valid if it appears (on the face of it) to measure the intended **construct.** [6]
Factorial design	An **experimental design** with more than one **independent variable. Conditions** are defined by combinations of **values,** one from each independent variable. [12]
Fertility	The property of a good **theory** that refers to its potential for producing brand new predictions that guide research into previously unexplored areas. [1]

Field experiment	Any study with a **manipulated independent variable** (that is, an **experiment**) carried out in a nonlaboratory setting. [10]
Field notes	The **data** record from a **field observation.** [3,4]
Field observation	In-depth observation of a social system with the goal of understanding how the system works. [3]
Final conclusion	A conclusion based on all sources of evidence available to a researcher, including both tests of statistical inference and **reliability** evidence. Three outcomes are possible: reject the **null hypothesis,** do NOT reject it, or suspend judgment. [8]
Fine data	**Data** consisting of a large number of distinct score **values** and in which at least near-**interval measurement** has been achieved. [5]
Fraud	Dishonest reporting of **data,** methods, or results. [14]
Frequency distribution	A table in which each possible raw score **value** is listed in rank **order** and paired with its frequency of occurrence in a set of scores. [11]
Frequency polygon	A graphical representation of a **frequency distribution** in which frequencies are plotted on the vertical axis against rank-ordered raw score **values** on the horizontal axis to depict the shape of the distribution. [11]
Frequency table	A table that shows how frequently each value of one **variable** goes with each value of another variable. Also known as a "contingency table." [2]
Generalization	The process of extending results from **samples** to **populations.** See **Inductive inference.** [1,15]
Graphic rating scale	Rating scale that requires the respondent to make a check mark anywhere along a continuous line anchored at either end (sometimes also in the middle) by descriptive adjectives. [5]
Haphazard sampling	Sampling in such a way that individual units are chosen on the basis of convenience. A rough synonym for **nonprobability sampling.** [7]

Higher-order interaction

In a **factorial design,** refers to an **interaction** involving more than two **independent variables.** [12]

History

Source of **confounding** consisting of any other relevant events besides the experimental **treatment** that occur during the interval between measures of the **dependent variable** in a **one-group pre-post design.** [10]

Honest research

A set of research strategies for avoiding deception that includes making participants fully aware of the purpose of a study prior to participation, studying real behavior-change programs, and doing field research in which participants do not know that they are involved in a research study. [14]

Hypothesis

A relatively specific statement or prediction about what might be true in a **population.** [1,4]

Identity

A property of numbers referring to the fact that each number is distinct from all others numbers. Thus, numbers may be used to represent same-different information. [5]

Immersion

The deep engagement of a researcher with a social system that is typical of **field studies.** Immersion implies an extended period of time, a variety of procedures, and flexibility in use of procedures. [3]

Implicit matching

Phrase referring to the automatic **matching** of participants with themselves across experimental **conditions** achieved by **repeated-measures designs.** [9]

Inadequate comparison

Refers to subtle sources of confounding in an **experiment** such that the "control" condition does not provide an adequate comparison to support the causal conclusion sought by the experimenter. [10]

Independent-treatments designs

Experimental designs featuring random assignment to **conditions** without any **matching** of participant characteristics across conditions. [9,10,11]

Independent variable

A presumed **cause,** that is, a variable that is thought of theoretically as a cause. In an **experiment,** the independent variable is manipulated. [2,9]

Indicator

A **variable** that results from an **operational definition.** [2]

Indirect measure	**Self-report measure** based on a physical format consisting of unclear or ambiguous stimuli and unconstrained or open-ended responding. Also known as "subjective measures." [5]
Inductive inference	The process of reasoning from the particular to the general or from **samples** to **populations**. A synonym for **generalization**. [1,15]
Inferential statistics	Statistics used to make **inductive inferences** from **samples** to **populations**. [4]
Informed consent	The ethical principle that participants in a research study must be given an accurate account of potential risks before they agree to take part and that they must be allowed to withdraw from the study at any time without negative consequences. [14]
Instructional manipulation	A **manipulation** in which the **values** of the **independent variable** are produced by presenting written or verbal material to participants. [9]
Instrument decay	Source of historical **confouding** in which a measuring instrument undergoes a systematic change in one of its components during the pre-post interval in a **one-group pre-post design**. [10]
Interaction	In a **factorial design,** refers to a situation in which the **relationship** between any **independent variable** and the **dependent variable** is different at different **values** of other independent variables. More generally, refers to a situation in which the relationship between two variables is different at different values of a third variable. [12]
Internal consistency	An approach to assessing **reliability** based on measuring the same set of objects on the same **variable** at one point in time. This typically means that the measure must consist of multiple items or trials. [6]
Internal validity	Refers to the **validity** of inferences about **cause** based on research findings. In an **experiment,** refers to the absence of **confounding variables**. [9,10]
Interobserver agreement	The degree to which pairs of observers agree on what they see, an indication of reliability of measurement for an observation study. [3]

Interrupted time-series design

A **quasi-experimental** design in which a potential causal event is embedded within a series of measures of the presumed effect. Timing of the causal event is not under the researcher's **control.** [10]

Interval measurement

The **level of measurement** in which the scores not only convey valid information about **identity** and **order** but also have the property of **equal intervals.** [5]

Interview

An orally administered **survey.** [7]

Invasion of privacy

Refers to unauthorized observation of or other access to sensitive or highly personal areas of the lives of research participants. [14]

Item balance

Property of a set of **survey** items used to measure an attitude or opinion in which the set of items contains an equal number of favorable and unfavorable items. [7]

Judgmental validity

An approach to assessing **validity of measurement** based on the informed judgment of the researcher. [6]

Latent content

Phrase referring to aspects of the respondent's behavior other than the respondent's spoken words in an **interview.** Includes such things as speaking style and body language. [8]

Law

A research finding that has been found to apply in a wide variety of situations. [1,13]

Levels of measurement

A classification of measurement procedures according to the kinds of information provided by the scores. Also known as "scales of measurement." [5]

Likert scale

Rating scale consisting of a set of statements selected to be clearly favorable or unfavorable toward the issue or topic studied, with each statement accompanied by the same **step scale** for responding. [5]

Main effect

In a **factorial design,** refers to the **relationship** between any **independent variable** and the **dependent variable,** ignoring other independent variables. [12]

Manifest content

Phrase referring to meaning of the respondent's spoken words in an **interview.** [8]

Manipulation	A procedure in which a researcher both produces the **values** of a **variable** and assigns the values to the objects being studied. Manipulation of an **independent variable** is the defining feature of an **experiment.** [2,9]
Manipulation check	A direct measure of the **independent variable** in an **experiment,** included to provide empirical evidence on the question of whether the **manipulation** was successful. [9]
Marginal error	The error in reasoning that occurs when only the **marginal totals** of a **frequency table** are used to reach a conclusion about a **relationship.** [15]
Marginal totals	The row and column totals in a **frequency table.** [2]
Matching	A form of **balancing** in which participants are assigned to **conditions** in an **experiment** only after having been equated on one or more **stable participant characteristics** judged to be strongly related to the **dependent variable.** [9,10]
Maturation	Refers to a situation in which the historical influence of growing older is **confounded** with the experimental **treatment** in a **one-group pre-post design.** See **History.** [10]
Mean	A measure of **central tendency** corresponding to the arithmetic average of the scores in a **frequency distribution.** [11]
Mean square	A **variance estimate** calculated while doing an **analysis of variance.** [11]
Measurement	Any procedure for determining what **values** objects of interest have on a **variable** of interest. The outcome of such a procedure is often called a "score" or a "measure." [2]
Measurement-manipulation validity	Refers to the **validity** of inferences about what **construct** or constructs are involved in a particular measure or **manipulation.** [9]
Median	A measure of **central tendency** corresponding to the raw score **value** that falls at the 50th percentile in a **frequency distribution.** [11]

Meta-analysis

A set of statistical procedures for combining and evaluating the results of a number of studies investigating the same **relationship.** [13]

Metaphorical theory

A **theory** in which a phenomenon is explained in terms of concepts that are no better understood than the phenomenon itself. Example: explaining abnormal behavior in terms of demonic possession. See **Theory.** [1]

Mode

A measure of **central tendency** corresponding to the raw score **value** with the highest frequency of occurrence in a set of scores. [11]

Multiple-baseline design

A **single-subject design** in which the **treatment** is administered under multiple circumstances with the object of showing that the expected behavior change occurs only when the treatment is administered. [10]

Multiple measurement

Refers to any **confounding** associated with the two **measurements** of the **dependent variable** in a **one-group pre-post design.** [10]

Multiple regression

A **data**-analysis technique for finding the **correlation** between a set of **independent variables** and a single **dependent variable.** The analysis also typically provides **partial correlations** between each independent variable and the dependent variable, with the influence of all other independent variables removed statistically. [8]

Multi-stage sampling

A form of **cluster sampling** in which each stage of sampling focuses on smaller clusters within the clusters selected at the preceding stage of sampling. [7]

Multitrait-multimethod matrix method

A **construct-validity** approach in which at least two different methods of measuring at least two different **constructs** (or traits) are included in the same study. The pattern of results can be used to assess both **convergent** and **discriminant validity.** [6]

Multivariate analysis of variance (MANOVA)

Analysis of variance with more than one set of **dependent-variable** scores. The technique's distinctive feature is a test of the **relationship** between the **independent variable** and the combined sets of dependent-variable scores. [12]

Mundane realism	Refers to whether a research study deals with events similar to those in real life. [13]
Natural experiment	A research study in which preexisting groups that differ on the **independent variable** are compared. Presumably, nature **manipulated** the independent variable. NOT a true **experiment**. Also known as "selection studies." [10]
Negative linear relationship	A **relationship** in which the **scatterplot** is well described by a straight-line function that tilts downward to the right (a negative slope). [2]
Nominal measurement	The **level of measurement** in which the only valid information conveyed by the scores is **identity** information. [5]
Nonadditively	Describes how **independent variables** combine their effects when there is an **interaction.** It means that the combined effect of the independent variables cannot be determined by simply adding together their **main effects.** [12]
Nonequivalent-groups design	A bad **experimental design** featuring at least two **values** of the **independent variable, measurement** of the **dependent variable** only after the experimental **treatment** has been administered, different participants in each **condition,** but nonrandom assignment to conditions. [10]
Nonequivalent-groups pre-post design	A **nonequivalent-groups design** featuring **measurement** of the **dependent variable** both before and after the experimental **treatment** has been administered. Where **random assignment** is not possible, this is considered an in-between design, not a bad design. [10]
Nonindependent-treatments designs	**Experimental designs** featuring **matching** of participants across **conditions** on one or more **stable characteristics** like intelligence. [9,10,11]
Nonprobability sampling	Any **sampling procedure** in which the probability of any unit being chosen is unknown. Also known as "haphazard sampling." [7]
Null hypothesis	An exact **hypothesis** about a **variable** or variables in a **population.** The most common null hypothesis is that two variables are not related in a population. [4]

Observation study
Nonexperimental research in which **data** are obtained by observing ongoing activities or features of the objects studied. [2,3]

Observational measure
Measure derived from observation of ongoing behavior, its aftereffects, or features of the objects studied. [5]

Observed frequencies
Frequencies in a **frequency table** that are based on the actual **data** of a research study. [4]

Omega squared
A measure of **relationship** magnitude based on **analysis of variance.** It corresponds to the proportion of the total **population variance** for the **dependent variable** accounted for by the variation among the experimental **treatments.** [11]

One-group pre-post design
A bad **experimental design** in which all participants are measured on the **dependent variable,** then given the same experimental **treatment,** and then measured again on the dependent variable. [10]

One-shot design
A bad **experimental design** in which all participants are assigned to only one **condition,** the **treatment** is administered, and then the **dependent variable** is measured. [10]

Open responses
An **unstructured** response format for **survey** items in which the respondent may say or write anything. Also known as "free responses." [7]

Operational definition
A detailed description of the procedures or operations used to measure or manipulate a **variable.** [2]

Operational-definitions rule
The **inductive-inference** rule that stresses clear definitions of terms and specifies that a good way to achieve such clarity is to define key words in terms of what one must do determine where they apply and where they do not. [15]

Order
A property of numbers referring to the fact that they may be ordered from smaller to larger. Thus, numbers may be used to represent rank-order information. [5]

Order effects
Source of **confounding** in **repeated-measures designs** consisting of the effects of any **variables,** other than the

independent variable, that change as a result of repeated **measurement** of the **dependent variable** in the different **conditions** of the **experiment.** Includes variables like practice and fatigue that may accumulate over repeated measurements. [10]

Ordinal measurement	The **level of measurement** in which the scores convey valid information only about **identity** and **order.** [5]
Partial correlation	A **correlation** between two **variables** with the influence of a third variable removed statistically. [8]
Participant attrition	Loss of qualified participants from a research study. [10]
Participation (a)	Term describing a field researcher who plays an active part in what is going on in a social system being studied. [3]
Participation (b)	The practice of treating research "subjects" as active collaborators helping the researcher solve a common problem. [14]
Physiological measure	Measure derived from ongoing but nonvisible behavior or features of the objects studied. Usually requires sophisticated measuring devices to make the invisible behavior or features visible. [5]
Pilot study	Small-scale version of a proposed research study run prior to the main event with the intent of catching and correcting any overlooked problems. [9]
Placebo	A **control** technique in which stimuli or other materials used in an **experiment** look identical but actually differ across **conditions** in a way that **manipulates** the **independent variable.** [10]
Planned comparisons	Powerful statistical procedures that should be used instead of **analysis of variance** to evaluate the **statistical significance** of specific prior predictions about the **relationship** between the **independent** and **dependent variables** in an **experiment.** [12]
Population	All possible objects of a certain kind. Also used to refer to the larger set of objects represented by a **sample.** [1,4,7]

Positive linear relationship	A **relationship** in which the **scatterplot** is well described by a straight-line function that tilts upward to the right (a positive slope). [2]
Post-hoc comparisons	Conservative statistical tests that should be performed only after a **statistically significant** F ratio from an **analysis of variance.** Their purpose is to determine if the **mean** score on the **dependent variable** for any subset of **conditions** differs significantly from the mean score on the dependent variable for any other subset of conditions. [12]
Posttest-only design	An **independent-treatments design** in which the **dependent variable** is measured only after the **treatment** has been administered. [9,10]
Power (a)	The property of a good **theory** that refers to its ability to explain correctly a broad range of phenomena or known facts. [1]
Power (b)	Refers generally to the ability of a research study to detect any real **relationship.** Refers specifically to the probability of correctly rejecting the **null hypothesis** when doing a test of inference or, equivalently, 1 − (probability of a **Type II error).** [10]
Prediction	The research goal of finding out what is related to a phenomenon. [1]
Probability sampling	Any **sampling procedure** in which all units in the pool of potential selectees have a known probability of being selected and it is not 0 or 1. [7]
Procedural control	Refers to all **control** techniques in which procedures are used to achieve **absolute control** or **balancing.** [10]
Procedural sources	Sources of confounding in an **experiment** that involve knowledge about the study on the part of participants or experimenter. [10]
Program evaluation research	Research aimed at assessing social programs and interventions before, during, and after they are implemented. [13]
Quasi-experiment	A research study which resembles an **experiment** but in which the **independent variable** is not fully **manipulated** by the researcher. [10]

Questionnaire	A **survey** administered in writing. [7]
Quota sampling	**Stratified haphazard sampling.** [7]
Randomization	The process of making a **variable** vary randomly or in an unpredictable way. [2,9,10]
Random assignment	Any procedure for assigning participants to **conditions** in an **experiment** in which the assigned condition is determined by chance. NOT the same thing as **random sampling!** [9,10]
Random error	Phrase referring to the influence of chance factors on the results of a research study. [4,10]
Random number table	A table of numbers generated in random order, usually by a computer, used for various **randomization** procedures. [7]
Random sampling	Sampling in such a way that all units in the pool of potential selectees have an equal chance of being selected throughout the selection procedure. [7,10]
Range	A measure of **variability** corresponding to the difference between the highest and lowest scores in a **frequency distribution.** [11]
Ratio measurement	The **level of measurement** in which the scores have all of the properties of **interval measurement** plus a **true zero** point. [5]
Reactive	Term describing a measure that is influenced by the awareness of the objects measured that they are being measured. [3]
Reductionistic theory	A **theory** in which a phenomenon is explained in terms of concepts that are simpler than the phenomenon to be explained. Example: explaining behavior in terms of the activity of neurons. See **Theory.** [1]
Relationship	A property of two **variables** in which the **values** of the two variables change together systematically; that is, specific values on one variable tend to be associated with specific values on the other variable. [1,2]
Reliability of measurement	Property of a good measure that refers to how accurate, precise, close to the truth, low in noise or **random error,** observed scores are. [6]

Repeated-measures design	A **nonindependent-treatments design** in which each participant serves in all experimental **conditions.** [9,10]
Research proposal	Written description of proposed methods for a research study, typically circulated to peers and experts for constructive criticism during the planning stages of a study. [9]
Response rate	The percentage of units selected by a sampling procedure that provide usable **data.** [7]
Reversal design	A **single-subject design** in which baseline (A) and **treatment** (B) periods are alternated. See **ABA design.** [10]
Role-playing	An alternative to **deception** in which participants pretend they are in a certain situation and respond as they think they or someone else would. [14]
Sample	Any subset of all possible objects of a certain kind. Also used to refer to the set of objects actually included in a research study. [1,4,7]
Sample bias	**Constant error** produced by a sampling procedure [7]
Sampling error	**Random error** produced by a sampling procedure. [7]
Sampling rule	The **inductive-inference** rule that defines good sampling. It says that a safe **generalization** about a **population** must be based on a **sample** from the population that is both adequate in size and unbiased. [15]
Scatterplot	A pictorial display of the **relationship** between two **variables** in which each axis represents possible scores on one of the variables and a point is placed in the space for each object at the location defined by the object's scores on the two variables. [2]
Self-report measure	Measures based on reports about the objects being studied rather than direct observation by the researcher. [5]
Semantic differential scale	Rating scale that measures the subjective meaning of a concept using a series of 7-point scales anchored at either end by opposing adjective pairs like "good-bad," "strong-weak," etc. [5]
Sensitivity	The ability of research study to detect small but real **relationships** between the **variables** investigated. [10]

Simple haphazard sampling	**Haphazard sampling** with no variables **controlled in sampling.** [7]
Simple random sampling	**Random sampling** with no variables **controlled in sampling.** [7]
Simplicity	The property of a good **theory** that refers to how few theoretical concepts or **relationships** it contains. Also known as elegance or parsimony. [1]
Simulation	An imitation designed to resemble the real thing in all important functional characteristics. [13]
Single-blind experiment	An **experiment** in which only participants do not know what **conditions** are being administered. [10]
Single-cell error	The error in reasoning that occurs when the information from only a single cell of a **frequency table** is used to reach a conclusion about a **relationship.** [15]
Single-row/column error	The error in reasoning that occurs when the information from only a single row or column of a **frequency table** is used to reach a conclusion about a **relationship.** [15]
Single-subject designs	**Experiments** with a **sample** of one participant. [10]
Skewed distribution	A **frequency distribution** that produces a **frequency polygon** with a long tail at one end. [11]
Solomon four-group design	A 2×2 **factorial design** with presence-absence of a pretest as one of the **independent variables.** Used to investigate whether results for the other independent variable generalize across **values** of the pretesting variable. [13]
Split-half reliability	An internal-consistency approach to assessing **reliability** in which the items or trials comprising the measure are split into equal-sized subsets that are scored separately and then correlated with each other. [6]
Stability	An approach to assessing **reliability** based on measuring the same set of objects on the same **variable** at two different points in time. [6]
Stable participant characteristics	Characteristics of participants that remain the same within a person for the duration of a research study. [10]

Staged manipulation	A **manipulation** in which the **values** of the **independent variable** are produced by staging appropriate events. [9]
Standard deviation	A measure of **variability** corresponding to the square root of the **variance.** [11]
Statistical conclusion	A conclusion based only on a test of statistical inference and thus having only two possible outcomes: reject the **null hypothesis** or do NOT reject it. [8]
Statistical-conclusion validity	Refers to the **validity** of inferences based on statistical tests of inference. [9]
Statistical control	**Control** technique in which an **extraneous variable** is measured before the application of the **independent variable** and its influence is later removed during the statistical analysis. See **Analysis of covariance.** [10]
Statistical regression	The tendency of extreme subgroups to spread out toward the center of a distribution on a second **measurement** of the same variable as a result of unreliability in the measuring procedure. A source of **multiple-measurement confounding** in a **one-group pre-post design** when the pretest is used to select an extreme subgroup for further participation. Also known as "regression toward the mean." [10]
Statistically significant	Phrase used to describe a situation in which a test of inference has yielded a p value that is less than **alpha,** resulting in a decision to reject the **null hypothesis.** [4]
Step scale	Rating scale that requires the respondent to choose one of a graded series of response alternatives. [5]
Stratified haphazard sampling	**Stratified sampling** with **haphazard sampling** of sampling units within the **values** of the controlled **variable.** Also known as **"quota sampling."** [7]
Stratified random sampling	**Stratified sampling** with **random sampling** of units within the **values** of the controlled **variable.** [7]
Stratified sampling	A sampling procedure in which a **variable** is **controlled in sampling** in such a way that its distribution in the **sample** matches its distribution in the target **population.** [7]

Stress	In research methods, refers to immediate negative consequences, physical or psychological, of research procedures. [14]
Structural modeling	A class of **data**-analysis techniques that allow a researcher to fit **cause**-effect models to the observed **relationships** among a set of measured **variables** and to compare the fit of competing cause-effect models. Also known as "causal modeling" and "latent variable modeling." [8]
Structured item	A **survey** item in which the exact form of the stimulus and response formats has been predetermined. [7]
Sufficient probable cause	A phrase describing a **relationship** in which a presumed **cause** is reliably but not always followed by a presumed effect. [2]
Sum of squares	The sum of the squared **deviation scores** in a **frequency distribution.** [11]
Survey research	Nonexperimental research in which **data** are obtained by means of self-report.
Symmetrical order effects	**Order effects** that are the same regardless of the order in which **conditions** are presented in a **repeated-measures design.** Such effects can be **controlled.** [10]
Systematic observation	Observation of specific carefully defined **variables** with the goal of determining whether they are related. [3]
Systematic variance	General phrase referring to the **variability** that contributes to the numerator of the F ratio in an **analysis of variance** based on experimental **data.** This variability contains **random error** plus any systematic effects associated with the **independent variable.** [11]
Testability	The property of a good **theory** whereby it makes clear predictions that could be contradicted by research findings. [1]
Test-retest reliability	A **stability** approach to assessing **reliability** in which the same measure is used at two different points in time. [6]
Theory	An explanation of a phenomenon that specifies its important properties and its **relationships** to other phenomena, including **causal relationships.** [1]

Theory by General Principle

Explaining a research finding by showing that it is a special case of a well-established general principle. See **Theory.** [1]

Theory by Intermediate Mechanism

Explaining a **relationship** by proposing a mechanism that serves as a mediating link between the **variables** involved in the relationship. See **Theory.** [1]

Time sampling

Choosing times at which observations will be made in such a way that a **sample** of typical behavior will be obtained. [3]

Time-series design

Quasi-experimental design in which a series of measures of a presumed effect are made over a period of time. [10]

Trace measures

Measures based on the aftereffects of previous events or behaviors. [3]

Treatment

A synonym for **condition.** [2,9,12]

True zero

A property of numbers referring to the fact that as far as the number system is concerned, zero truly means nothing. Thus, the number zero may be used to represents exactly none of the variable being measured. [5]

Two-group pre-post design

An **independent-treatments design** with two **conditions** in which the **dependent variable** is measured both before and after the **treatment** has been administered. [9,10]

Type I error

The **error of inference** in which the researcher rejects the **null hypothesis** when it is correct. Also known as a "false alarm." [4]

Type II error

The error of inference in which the researcher fails to reject the **null hypothesis** when it is incorrect. Also known as a "miss" because typically a real relationship was missed. [4]

Unobtrusive experiment

An **experiment** in which the participants do not know that they are involved in an experiment. [10]

Unobtrusive measurement

A **measurement** procedure that does not itself influence the resulting measures. Also known as "nonreactive measurement." [3]

Unstable participant characteristics   Characteristics of participants that can change from moment to moment within a person. [10]

Unstructured item   A **survey** item in which the exact form of neither stimulus nor response formats has been predetermined. [7]

Validity   Term used generally to refer to the correctness of an inference. [9]

Validity of measurement   Property of a good measure that refers to how well an observed measure gets at the **construct** it was intended to measure or more generally with the question of just what constructs are being measured by a measurement procedure. [6]

Values   The specific properties that objects have when they differ with respect to a **variable.** Example: red, blue, etc. The terms "levels," "amounts," and "scores" are often used as synonyms. [2]

Variability   Phrase referring to how spread out the scores are around the center of a **frequency distribution.** Also known as "dispersion." [11]

Variable   A general name for a quality that can differ from object to object. Example: color. See **Values.** [2]

Variance   A measure of **variability** corresponding to the average of the squared **deviation scores** in a **frequency distribution.** [11]

Variance estimate   A **sum of squares** based on **sample data** divided by its own **degrees of freedom.** Provides an ubiased estimate of the **variance** of raw scores in a **population.** [11]

Weighted haphazard sampling   **Weighted sampling** with **haphazard sampling** of units within the **values** of the controlled **variable.** [7]

Weighted random sampling   **Weighted sampling** with **random sampling** of units within the **values** of the controlled **variable.** [7]

Weighted sampling   A sampling procedure in which a **variable** is **controlled in sampling** in such a way that its distribution in the **sample** systematically differs from its distribution in the target **population.** [7]

Within-subjects variable

In a **factorial design,** refers to an **independent variable** with all of its **values** assigned to every participant. [12]

Yoking

A **control** technique in which the number and timing of participant-generated events are simultaneously duplicated for matched sets of participants in all **conditions** of an **experiment.** [10]

Bibliography

Adler, P. A. (1985). *Wheeling and dealing: An ethnography of an upper-level drug dealing and smug-gling community.* New York: Columbia University Press.

Aiken, L. S., & West, S. G. (1991). *Multiple regression: Testing and interpreting interactions.* Newbury Park, CA: Sage.

Alfred, R. (1976). The Church of Satan. In C. Glock, & R. Bellah (Eds.), *The new religious consciousness* (pp. 180–202). Berkeley, CA: University of California Press.

American Anthropological Association. (1983). *Professional ethics.* Washington, D. C.: American Anthropological Association.

American Psychological Association. (1986). Guidelines for ethical conduct in the care and use of animals. *Journal of the Experimental Analysis of Behavior, 45,* 127–132.

American Psychological Association. (1990). Ethical principles of psychologists. *American Psychologist, 45,* 390–395.

American Psychological Association. (1994). *Publication manual of the American Psychological Association* (4th ed.). Washington, D. C.: American Psychological Association.

American Sociological Association Committee on Professional Ethics. (1989). *Code of ethics.* Washington, D.C.: American Sociological Association.

Anderson, B. F. (1971). *The psychology experiment: An introduction to the scientific method* (2nd ed.). Monterey, CA: Brooks/Cole.

Anderson, B. F. (1980). *The complete thinker.* Englewood Cliffs, NJ: Prentice-Hall.

Armstrong, P. S., & Schulman, M. D. (1990). Financial strain and depression among farm operators: The role of perceived economic hardship and personal control. *Rural Sociology, 55,* 475–493.

Arnoult, M. D. (1976). *Fundamentals of scientific method in psychology* (2nd ed.). Dubuque, IA: William C. Brown.

Aronson, E., Brewer, M., & Carlsmith, J. M. (1985). Experimentation in social psychology. In G. Lindzey, & E. Aronson (Eds.), *Handbook of social psychology* (2nd ed., pp. 441–486). Hillsdale, NJ: Lawrence Erlbaum Associates.

Bakeman, R., & Gottman, J. M. (1989). *Observing interaction: An introduction to sequential analy-sis.* Cambridge: Cambridge University Press.

Banaka, W. (1971). *Training in depth interviewing.* New York: Harper & Row.

Barlow, D. H., & Hersen, M. (1984). *Single case experimental designs: Strategies for studying behavior change* (2nd ed.). New York: Pergamon Press.

Baron, R. A., & Bell, P. A. (1976). Aggression and heat: The influence of ambient temperature, negative affect, and a cooling drink on physical aggression. *Journal of Personality and Social Psychology, 33,* 245–255.

Bausell, R. B. (1986). *A practical guide to conducting empirical research*. New York: Harper & Row.

Beaman, A. (1991). An empirical comparison of meta-analytic and traditional reviews. *Personality and Social Psychology Bulletin, 17*, 252–257.

Beauchamp, T., Faden, R., Wallace, R. J., & Walters, L. (Eds.). (1982). *Ethical issues in social science research*. Baltimore: Johns Hopkins University Press.

Becker, H. S. (1953). Becoming a marijuana user. *American Journal of Sociology, 59*, 235–242.

Becker, H. S. (1986). *Writing for social scientists: How to start and finish your thesis, book, or article*. Chicago: University of Chicago Press.

Belyea, M. J., & Lobao, L. M. (1990). Psychosocial consequences of agricultural transformation: The farm crisis and depression. *Rural Sociology, 55*, 58–75.

Benbow, C. P., & Stanley, J. C. (1983). Sex differences in mathematical reasoning ability: More facts. *Science, 222*, 1029–1031.

Blumer, M. (Ed.). (1982). *Social research ethics*. London: Macmillan.

Bock, R. D. (1975). *Multivariate statistical methods in behavioral research*. New York: McGraw-Hill.

Bordens, K. S., & Abbott, B. B. (1991). *Research designs and methods: A process approach* (2nd ed.). Mountain View, CA: Mayfield.

Browne, J. (1973). *The used car game*. Lexington, MA: D. C. Heath.

Bruning, J. L., & Kintz, B. L. (1977). *Computational handbook of statistics* (2nd ed.). Glenview, IL: Scott Foresman.

Brunswik, E. (1956). *Perception and the representative design of psychological experiments*. Berkeley and Los Angeles: University of California Press.

Brush, S. G. (1989). Prediction and theory evaluation: The case of light bending. *Science, 246*, 1124–1129.

Burton, N. W. (1981). Estimating scorer agreement for nominal categorization systems. *Educational and Psychological Measurement, 41*, 953–962.

Byrne, D., Ervin, C. R., & Lamberth, J. (1970). Continuity between the experimental study of attraction and real-life computer dating. *Journal of Personality and Social Psychology, 16*, 157–165.

Camilli, G., & Hopkins, K. D. (1978). Applicability of chi-square to 2×2 contingency tables with small expected frequencies. *Psychological Bulletin, 85*, 163–167.

Campbell, D., & Fiske, D. (1959). Convergent and discriminant validation by the multitrait-multimethod matrix. *Psychological Bulletin, 54*, 81–105.

Cohen, J. (1960). A coefficient of agreement for nominal scales. *Educational and Psychological Measurement, 20*, 37–46.

Cohen, J. (1990). Things I have learned (so far). *American Psychologist, 45*, 1304–1312.

Cook, T. D., & Campbell, D. T. (1979). *Quasi-experimentation: Design and analysis issues for field settings*. Chicago: Rand McNally.

Cozby, P. C. (1989). *Methods in behavioral research* (4th ed.). Mountain View, CA: Mayfield.

Darley, J. M., & Batson, C. D. (1973). "From Jerusalem to Jericho": A study of situational and dispositional variables in helping behavior. *Journal of Personality and Social Psychology, 27*, 100–108.

Day, R. (1988). *How to write and publish a scientific paper* (3rd ed.). Philadelphia: ISI Press.

Department of Health and Human Services. (1981, January 26). Final regulations amending basic HHS policy for the protection of human research subjects. *Federal Register, 46*(16), 8366–8392.

Ellis, L. (1994). *Research Methods in the Social Sciences*. Madison, WI: Brown & Benchmark.

Estroff, S. E. (1978). Making it crazy: Some paradoxes of psychiatric patienthood in an American community and a research/dissertation process to encounter them. Paper presented at the annual meeting of the American Anthropological Association, Los Angeles, CA.

Ferris, G. R., & King, T. R. (1992). The politics of age discrimination in organizations. *Journal of Business Ethics, 11*, 341–350.

Friedman, S., & Steinberg, S. (1989). *Writing and thinking in the social sciences*. Englewood Cliffs, NJ: Prentice-Hall.

Gans, H. (1962). *Urban villagers*. New York: Free Press.

Glass, G. V., McGaw, B., & Smith, M. L. (1981). *Meta-analysis in social research*. Beverly Hills, CA: Sage.

Gordon, R. L. (1975). *Interviewing: Strategies, techniques, and tactics* (rev. ed.). Homewood, IL: Dorsey Press.

Graziano, A. M., & Raulin, M. L. (1989). *Research methods: A process of inquiry*. New York: Harper & Row.

Guilford, J. P. (1954). *Psychometric methods*. New York: McGraw-Hill.

Haney, C. (1976). The play's the thing: Methodological notes on social simulations. In M. P. Golden (Ed.), *The research experience* (pp. 177–190). Itaska, IL: F. E. Peacock.

Haney, C., Banks, W. C., & Zimbardo, P. G. (1973). Interpersonal dynamics in a simulated prison. *International Journal of Criminology and Penology, 1*, 69–97.

Harris, R. J. (1985). *A primer of multivariate statistics* (2nd ed.). Orlando, FL: Academic Press.

Hartmann, D. P. (Ed.). (1982). *Using observers to study behavior*. San Francisco: Jossey-Bass.

Hays, W. L. (1973). *Statistics for the Social Sciences* (2nd ed.). New York: Holt, Rinehart and Winston.

Hazlett, T. W. (1992). The legislative history of the Sherman Act re-examined. *Economic Inquiry, 30*, 263–276.

Hedges, L. V., & Olkin, I. (1985). *Statistical methods for meta-analysis*. Orlando, FL: Academic Press.

Henle, M., & Hubbell, M. B. (1938). "Egocentricity" in adult conversation. *Journal of Social Psychology, 9*, 227–234.

Hood, T. C., & Back, K. W. (1971). Self-disclosure and the volunteer: A source of bias in laboratory experiments. *Journal of Personality and Social Psychology, 17*, 130–136.

Huberty, C. J., & Morris, J. D. (1989). Multivariate analysis versus multiple univariate analyses. *Psychological Bulletin, 105*, 302–308.

Humphreys, L. (1970). *Tearoom trade: Impersonal sex in public places*. Chicago: Aldine.

Hunter, J. E., & Schmidt, F. L. (1990). *Methods of meta-analysis: Correcting error and bias in research findings*. Newbury Park, CA: Sage.

Ittelson, W. H., Rivlin, L. G., & Proshansky, H. M. (1976). The use of behavioral maps in environmental psychology. In H. M. Proshansky, W. H. Ittelson, & L. G. Rivlin (Eds.), *Environmental psychology* (2nd ed., pp. 340–350). New York: Holt, Rinehart and Winston.

Jaeger, R. (1984). *Sampling in education and the social sciences*. New York: Longman.

Jaroslovsky, R. (1988, July/August). What's on your mind, America? *Psychology Today*, pp. 54–59.

Jorgensen, D. L. (1989). *Participant observation*. Beverly Hills, CA: Sage.

Kachigan, S. K. (1991). *Multivariate statistical analysis: A conceptual introduction*. New York: Radius Press.

Kamin, L. G. (1974). *The science and politics of IQ*. New York: Wiley.

Kaplan, R., & Kaplan, S. (1989). *The experience of nature: A psychological perspective*. New York: Cambridge University Press.

Kaplan, S., & Kaplan, R. (1982). *Cognition and environment: Functioning in an uncertain world*. New York: Praeger. (Ann Arbor, MI: Ulrichs)

Keith-Spiegel, P., & Koocher, G. P. (1985). *Ethics in psychology: Professional standards and cases.* New York: Random House.

Kelman, H. C. (1967). Human use of human subjects: The problem of deception in social psychological experiments. *Psychological Bulletin, 67,* 1–11.

Keppel, G. (1991). *Design and analysis: A researcher's handbook* (3rd ed.). Englewood Cliffs, NJ: Prentice Hall.

Kerlinger, F. N. (1986). *Foundations of behavioral research* (3rd ed.). New York: Holt, Rinehart and Winston.

Kimmel, A. J. (1988). *Ethics and values in applied social research.* Newbury Park, CA: Sage.

Kintz, N. L., Delprato, D. J., Mettee, D. R., Persons, C. E., & Schappe, R. H. (1965). The experimenter effect. *Psychological Bulletin, 63,* 223–232.

Kirkham, G. L. (1976). *Signal zero.* Philadelphia: Lippincott.

Kish, L. (1965). *Survey sampling.* New York: Wiley.

Kuhn, T. S. (1970). *The structure of scientific revolutions* (2nd ed.). Chicago: University of Chicago Press.

Kurosu, S. (1991). Suicide in rural areas: The case of Japan 1960–1980. *Rural Sociology, 56,* 603–618.

Lazarus, R. S. (1966). *Psychological stress and the coping process.* New York: McGraw-Hill.

Liebow, E. (1967). *Talley's corner.* Boston: Little, Brown.

Likert, R. (1932). A technique for the measurement of attitudes. *Archives of Psychology, 140,* 1–55.

Loehlin, J. C. (1987). *Latent variable models: An introduction to factor, path, and structural analysis.* Hillsdale, NJ: Lawrence Erlbaum.

Lofland, J., & Lofland, L. (1984). *Analyzing social settings: A guide to qualitative observation and analysis* (3rd ed.). Belmont, CA: Wadsworth.

Love, A. M., & Deckers, L. H. (1989). Humor appreciation as a function of sexual, aggressive, and sexist content. *Sex Roles, 20,* 649–654.

Lunneborg, C. E. (1994). *Modeling experimental and observational data.* Belmont, CA: Duxbury.

Marlatt, G. A. (1983). The controlled-drinking controversy: A commentary. *American Psychologist, 38,* 1097–1110.

Marshall, E. (1993). Court orders "sharing" of data. *Science, 261,* 284–286.

Micceri, T. (1989). The unicorn, the normal curve, and other improbable creatures. *Psychological Bulletin, 105,* 156–166.

Middlemist, R. D., Knowles, E. S., & Matter, C. F. (1976). Personal space invasion in the lavatory: Suggestive evidence for arousal. *Journal of Personality and Social Psychology, 33,* 541–546.

Milgram, S. (1963). Behavioral study of obedience. *Journal of Abnormal and Social Psychology, 67,* 371–378.

Milgram, S. (1965). Some conditions of obedience and disobedience to authority. *Human Relations, 18,* 57–76.

Monette, D. R., Sullivan, T. J., & DeJong, C. R. (1990). *Applied social research: Tools for the human services* (2nd ed.). Fort Worth, TX: Holt, Rinehart and Winston.

Mundorf, N., Bhatia, A., Zillmann, D., Lester, P., & Robertson, S. (1988). Gender differences in humor appreciation. *Humor: International Journal of Humor Research, 1,* 231–243.

Nisbett, R., & Ross, L. (1980). *Human inference: Strategies and shortcomings of social judgment.* Englewood Cliffs, NJ: Prentice-Hall.

Nisbett, R. E., Fong, G. T., Lehman, D. R., & Cheng, P. W. (1987). Teaching reasoning. *Science, 238,* 625–631.

Nunnally, J. (1967). *Psychometric theory.* New York: McGraw-Hill.

Nunnally, J. (1978). *Psychometric theory* (2nd ed.). New York: McGraw-Hill.

Pedhazur, E. J., & Schmelkin, L. P. (1991). *Measurement, design, and analysis: An integrated approach.* Hillsdale, NJ: Lawrence Erlbaum Associates.

Putt, A. D., & Springer, J. F. (1989). *Policy research: Methods and applications.* Englewood Cliffs, NJ: Prentice-Hall.

Rathje, W. L., & McCarthy, M. (1977). Regularity and variability in contemporary garbage. In S. South (Ed.), *Research strategies in historical archeology.* New York: Academic Press.

Ring, K. (1967). Experimental social psychology: Some sober questions about frivolous values. *Journal of Experimental Social Psychology, 3,* 113–123.

Ring, K., Wallston, K., & Corey, M. (1970). Mode of debriefing as a factor affecting reaction to a Milgram-type obedience experiment: An ethical inquiry. *Representative Research in Social Psychology, 1,* 67–88.

Rosenhan, D. (1973). On being sane in insane places. *Science, 179,* 250–258.

Rosenthal, R. (1984). *Meta-analytic procedures for social research.* Beverly Hills, CA: Sage.

Rosenthal, R., & Rosnow, R. L. (1975). *The volunteer subject.* New York: Wiley.

Rosenthal, R., & Rubin, D. B. (1984). Multiple contrasts and ordered Bonferroni procedures. *Journal of Educational Psychology, 76,* 1028–1034.

Rossi, P., & Freeman, H. (1985). *Evaluation: A systematic approach* (3rd ed.). Beverly Hills, CA: Sage.

Rubin, Z. (1970). Measurement of romantic love. *Journal of Personality and Social Psychology, 16,* 265–273.

Rubin, Z. (1970, December). Jokers wild in the lab. *Psychology Today,* pp. 18,20,22–24.

Rubin, Z. (1973). Designing honest experiments. *American Psychologist, 28,* 445–448.

Schuman, H., & Scott, J. (1987). Problems in the use of survey questions to measure public opinion. *Science, 236,* 957–959.

Sears, D. O. (1986). College sophomores in the laboratory: Influence of a narrow data base on social psychology's view of human nature. *Journal of Personality and Social Psychology, 51,* 515–530.

Shertzer, M. (1986). *The elements of grammar.* New York: Macmillan.

Smith, H.W. (1991). *Strategies of social research* (3rd ed.). Orlando: FL: Holt, Rinehart and Winston.

Smith, S. S., & Richardson, D. (1983). Amelioration of deception and harm in psychological research: The important role of debriefing. *Journal of Personality and Social Psychology, 44,* 1075–1082.

Sociology Writing Group. (1991). *A guide to writing sociology papers* (2nd ed.). New York: St. Martin's Press.

Solomon, R. L. (1949). An extension of control group design. *Psychological Bulletin, 46,* 137–150.

Sommer, B., & Sommer, R. (1991). *A practical guide to behavioral research: Tools and techniques* (3rd ed.). New York: Oxford University Press.

Spradley, J. P., & Mann, B. J. (1975). *The cocktail waitress: Woman's work in a man's world.* New York: Wiley.

Stanovich, K. E. (1992). *How to think straight about psychology* (3rd ed.). New York: Harper-Collins.

Steininger, M., Newell, J. D., & Garcia, L. T. (1984). *Ethical issues in psychology.* Homewood, IL: Dorsey.

Sternberg, R.J. (1988). *The psychologist's companion: A guide to scientific writing for students and researchers.* Cambridge: Cambridge University Press.

Stevens, S. S. (1946). On the theory of scales of measurement. *Science, 103,* 677–680.

Stevenson, H. W., & Allen, S. (1964). Adult performance as a function of sex of experimenter and sex of subject. *Journal of Abnormal and Social Psychology, 68,* 214–216.

Strodtbeck, F. L. (1951). Husband-wife interaction over revealed differences. *American Sociological Review, 16,* 468–473.

Strunk, W., Jr., & White, E. B. (1979). *The elements of style* (3rd ed.). New York: Macmillan.

Sudman, S. (1976). *Applied sampling.* New York: Academic Press.

Sudman, S., & Bradburn, N. M. (1982). *Asking questions: A practical guide to questionnaire design.* San Francisco: Jossey-Bass.

Thorndike, R. M. (1978). *Correlational procedures for research.* New York: Gardner Press.

Torgerson, W. (1958). *Theory and methods of scaling.* New York: Wiley.

Tripodi, T. (1983). *Evaluation research for social workers.* Englewood Cliffs, NJ: Prentice-Hall.

Walster, E., Walster, G. W., Piliavin, J., & Schmidt, L. (1973). "Playing hard to get": Understanding an elusive phenomenon. *Journal of Personality and Social Psychology, 26,* 113–121.

Webb, E. J., Campbell, D. T., Schwartz, R. D., Sechrest, L., & Grove, J. B. (1981). *Nonreactive measures in the social sciences* (2nd ed.). Boston: Houghton Mifflin.

Whyte, W. F., & Whyte, K.K. (1984). *Learning from the field: A guide from experience.* Beverly Hills, CA: Sage.

Wike, E. L. (1985). *Numbers: A primer of data analysis.* Columbus, OH: Charles E. Merrill.

Williamson, J. B., Karp, D. A., Dalphin, J. R., & Gray, P. S. (1982). *The research craft: An introduction to social research methods* (2nd ed.). Boston: Little, Brown.

Winer, B. J. (1971). *Statistical principles in experimental design* (2nd ed.). New York: McGraw-Hill.

Wright, R. A., & Contrada, R. J. (1986). Dating selectivity and interpersonal attraction: Toward a better understanding of the 'elusive phenomenon.' *Journal of Social and Personal Relationships, 3,* 131–148.

Name Index

Subject Index